The Ultimate Power Query Cookbook for Power BI and Excel

Leveraging Power Query for collecting, combining and transforming your data

Dominick Raimato

bpb

www.bpbonline.com

FIRST EDITION 2024

ISBN: 978-93-55517-395

LIMITS OF LIABILITY AND DISCLAIMER OF WARRANTY

Distributors:

BPB PUBLICATIONS
20, Ansari Road, Darya Ganj
New Delhi-110002
Ph: 23254990/23254991

DECCAN AGENCIES
4-3-329, Bank Street,
Hyderabad-500195
Ph: 24756967/24756400

MICRO MEDIA
Shop No. 5, Mahendra Chambers,
150 DN Rd. Next to Capital Cinema,
V.T. (C.S.T.) Station, MUMBAI-400 001
Ph: 22078296/22078297

Published by Manish Jain for BPB Publications, 20 Ansari Road, Darya Ganj, New Delhi-110002 and Printed by him at Manipal Technologies, Manipal

www.bpbonline.com

Dedicated to

To the data community who strive to change humanity for the better.

Please continue to do the work you do for we would be lost without you.

About the Author

Self-identified as a data nerd, **Dominick Raimato** has had a huge passion for identifying insights and building solutions. You never know what kind of data projects he might be working on such as tracking temperature and humidity trends in his house to building a database of property assessments to make sure his house is in line with other properties to avoid overpaying taxes. Passionate about people, Dominick strives to create solutions that not just help achieve business objectives, but also make people's lives better. If he can help someone get home earlier to eat dinner with their family or eliminate time consuming tasks so they can focus on more important things, he is in his element.

Dominick currently lives in Bergen County, NJ where he can be found around the house working on projects or cooking in the kitchen. His specialty dishes include his homemade meat sauce in the winter and pulled pork bar-b-que on his smoker during the summer. He also ventures into New York City frequently to see his wife perform as a flutist with small ensembles, orchestras, and theaters.

About the Reviewer

Divit aspires to transform the landscape of Cloud Computing, AI, and Data Science by guiding a fresh cohort of professionals. As a senior member of IEEE, his objective is to equip individuals worldwide with advanced expertise in analytics, machine learning, and AI within the next five years, thus raising the global benchmark for technical proficiency. In alignment with the insights of influential thinkers, Divit contends that true accomplishment extends beyond personal success, emphasizing the importance of uplifting others and actively contributing to their pursuit of excellence. His overarching mission is to shape a future in the tech realm that is both skilled and inclusive.

Divit, an accomplished IT professional with a career spanning over two decades, is widely recognized as a prominent speaker and thought leader in the realm of emerging technologies. Hosting popular podcasts like "Tech Talk with Divit," "Live Labs with Divit," and "Cloud Bites with Divit," he provides a platform to showcase technological initiatives and leadership. With roles including Oracle TV's correspondent for Cloud World and a recognized expert, Divit presented on Oracle Database technology at Oracle Cloud World FY 2023.

Beyond his podcast endeavors, Divit is deeply passionate about knowledge-sharing, evident in his participation in international conference talks, technical blogs, Whitepapers, and the authorship of multiple books on emerging technologies. His expertise has gained visibility in leading newspapers and technology magazines worldwide. As a highly skilled technologist, Divit holds professional certifications from Microsoft, Oracle, AWS, Databricks, and has earned a post-graduate certificate from Harvard Business School Online.

Acknowledgement

I want to first and foremost express my gratitude and love to my family, friends, colleagues, and customers for your encouragement as I embarked upon this journey. Notably, thank you to my wife, Nicole, for your love and support every step of the way. I could not do any of this without you. I love you so much! Also, I promise to get back to doing the dishes more frequently.

I want to thank everyone at BPB Publications for their support and guidance through this entire process. Having never written a book before, I would be lost without your expertise during every step of the process. Thank you for the patience and collaborative support of all reviewers, experts, and editors through this entire journey.

I would like to thank my leaders at SHI, Matt Mallory and Brandon Sexton, for your investment in my success and supporting activites like this that allow me to grow.

I would like to thank Audrey Blair for helping me find my voice and take the leap as an active contributor to the Power BI community. Without your encouragement, this book would have just been an idea that would have sat idly in my mind.

I would like to thank Kristen Hubler and her aptly timed book *The Impossible Box* as it helped me get what was a dream out of storage and to go for it. Thank you for also helping me through the process and sharing the challenges of the book writing process.

I would like to thank Michael Heath for the challenges we face together. Having the opportunity to push each other to be the best version of ourselves is unique. Thank you for helping raise the bar each week. I look forward to reading your book one day too.

Finally, I would like to thank all of you reading this book! Your encouragement and support mean the world to me! I hope you enjoy reading it as much as I did writing it.

Preface

Data has infiltrated every aspect of our lives. The expectation of querying data and finding meaningful insights is now going beyond traditional business intelligence teams and becoming a required skill for analysts across the entire organization. While there are many tools out there that can be used to query and transform data, Power Query has proven to be a leader in this space.

This book is an all-inclusive guide to querying and transforming data with Power Query. Starting with accessing data from diverse sources, we walk through how data is transformed, cleansed, merged, appended, and manipulated to turn raw data into a meaningful data model to obtain insights.

Throughout this book, you will learn different ways transform your data to support efficient refreshes while preventing your model from experiencing bloat. We will explore best practices and use cases to help you understand how to best apply these concepts in your real-life scenarios.

This book is intended for anyone who is interested in data analytics or needs to manipulate data for their use. While the primary audience is for data analysts and business intelligence developers who build models for reports and insights, anyone who has a need to transform data will find value with the contents of this book. Whether you are a novice or expert, you will find value from the contents of this book.

With this book, you will obtain the knowledge and skills to query and transform your data queries used for data modelling within Microsoft Excel or Power BI. I hope you will not only learn the concepts in the context of this book, but find success in applying them in your work.

Chapter 1: Introduction to Power Query - Starting with the why, we will explore why Power Query is used to transform and manipulate data for analysis. We will then provide an overview of using Power Query both in Excel and Power BI. Next, we will review the interface and the value of using both the GUI interface and Advanced Editor for our transformations. Lastly, we will provide a brief guide on how to use this book to provide the most value with real life applications.

Chapter 2: Connect to File-Based Data Sources - We will walk through the process of connecting to individual files and multiple files in a single query both on a local device and through SharePoint. The goal at the end of this chapter is to enable all users of Power Query to be able to connect to at least one data source that they can use to complete their training without having to leverage additional resources that might cost additional money. We will also discuss the use of the Power BI Enterprise or Personal Gateway as appropriate.

Chapter 3: Connect to Web-Based Data Sources - Starting with simple web connections like SharePoint lists and tables on web pages, we will pull in data that can be manipulated within Power Query. From there, we will go through the steps to pull in data using web APIs using the web connector and OData connector. We will then use the Web Connector to pull data from a SharePoint list to filter the data coming in and optimize the query. Lastly, using all the concepts covered up to this point we will connect to data in Dynamics 365.

Chapter 4: Connect to Database Sources - We will start with the common SQL-based connections (MSSQL, MySQL, PostgreSQL, etc.) to establish a solid foundation for connecting to databases. From there, we will jump into more advanced and nuanced connectors. We will discuss the differences, challenges, and some considerations with different connectors like Snowflake, Google Big Query, ODBC, Dremio, Redshift, and Analysis Services. Lastly, we will connect to Microsoft's Dataverse and Dataflows and bring them into Power Query.

Chapter 5: Connect to Third-Party Data Sources - We will go through the basics on how to connect to common SaaS platforms for deeper analysis. We will discuss some of the challenges associated with connecting to them as well as some potential additional costs that might be associated with them. While these connectors tend to be a little easier to manage, the goal is to provide a little more context with them including some potential gotchas that might come up during the connection process.

Chapter 6: Managing Data Types - We will dive into the use of data types in Power Query. While this topic may seem straight forward, there are a few implications that need to be considered when selecting data types as not are created equal. How and when you use data types can have implications on the data model and can contribute to bloat. In addition, downstream effects can be had upon the model when queries are merged and even relationships in the model. We will end this chapter talking about best practices when using data types to provide the most efficiencies with your model.

Chapter 7: Transforming Columns - We will review the different ways data can be transformed for use. One of the biggest challenges when working with data is making sure that the data is in a format that we can use. Sometimes these transformations are basic like updating the column headers to something that makes sense while other times we are looking to extract substrings from a long line of text. Regardless of your specific needs, we are able to apply this logic easily in Power Query. The goal is to apply your transformations within Power Query so they are automated as you ingest new data into your model when refreshed.

Chapter 8: Cleansing Columns - We will take transformation another step further and go through the process of cleansing your data. While we would like to think our data is clean and ready to use, we often find issues with our data sets. It could be as simple as a few extra rows at the top of an Excel spreadsheet before the actual data is made available. Sometimes we have errors in cells or even blanks that need to be handled. We also get extra columns that might not be necessary to do what we need to do. As a result, we can easily cleanse the data with Power Query to get everything into shape. Just like the chapter before, the goal is complete automation. This will allow us to never perform these tasks again when we bring new data into the data model.

Chapter 9: Creating New Columns - We will go through the process of creating new columns for our query. We will start by briefly reviewing what transformations we saw in Chapter 7 can be turned into new columns while preserving old columns. We will then dive into splitting columns by delimiters. We will then go through the process to manually create new columns starting with the conditional column tool. From there, we will show you how to create one with your own custom formula. Then we will show you how to save time and energy by creating from example columns if you are not comfortable with writing your own formulas. We will then introduce the concept of the Index and Function columns but reserve the details for later chapters. Lastly, we will go over how to streamline your queries by updating the data type for a custom column using the Advanced Editor.

Chapter 10: Combining and Manipulating Queries - We will talk about transforming the table as a whole. Starting with a quick review of aggregations, we will quickly apply them to the Group By function to help streamline the query and reduce the number of rows. We will also learn how perform aggregations on specific columns using the statistics function that can be used in custom columns. From there, we will go through the process of manipulating tables for better use. Frequently, the data we receive is nicely formatted for use in a tool like excel but does not work well for modelling. We will use the Transpose and Pivot tools to get the data into a usable shape for our analysis.

Chapter 11: Using Python, R, and AI - As a result of your analysis of a data model, you might find you have enough data to create a machine learning model or desire to use R or Python for deeper analysis. Once you have a working model, you might want to integrate them into Power Query to perform predictive analytics. In this chapter, we will discuss the integration of AI, R, and Python in a data model with Power Query. The focus of this chapter will not be on the creation of AI models as that is an entire book unto itself but rather how to apply them in Power Query. This is always a top ask in any Power Query training course and it is important to understand how these tools are leveraged as many think they can apply AI with a few clicks.

Chapter 12: Indexing - We will explore how we can leverage the index column to help establish our star schema in our data model. We will start with a quick review of the Star Schema and why it is the model of choice for Power Pivot in Excel and Power BI. We will then go over what keys are in a data model and what kinds we might use. We will dive into creating a primary key on a dimension table using the index column. From there, we will go over how create a foreign key on a fact table using some advanced formulas within a custom column. Lastly, we will discuss the value of creating alternate keys in Power Query to help optimize our models and simplify their use.

Chapter 13: Parameters - We will review why parameters are a valuable tool when it comes to transforming your queries. To me, considered to be one of the most transformational tools in Power Query, parameters are often ignored and rarely are used to their full potential. We will dive into how we can use parameters to simplify our connections and manage multiple queries at once. We will also dive into how they are a critical component in setting up Incremental Refresh for Power BI. Lastly, we will go over how parameters are helpful for template files and with the Power BI service.

Chapter 14: Functions - We will work to demystify functions in Power Query. Functions allow us to apply repeatable transformations or load data quickly with only a few clicks. What is beneficial about them is that we can create the functions and load them into a template for use with minimal overhead. This allows us to quickly deploy them over and over again without having to search for the code we used before. We will go through the process of taking a query and converting it into a function so it can be deployed again. We will also go through the creation of two common use cases I use all the time for functions – converting time zones from UTC to local time and creating a date table.

Chapter 15: Advanced Web Connections - We will go through the process of creating advanced web connections with Power Query. Using endpoint parameters, we will filter our connections to streamline refresh times. We will also investigate the use of dynamic content such as date ranges and dynamic connection strings to ensure sustainability with our queries. We will also go through the process of creating a function to acquire an OAuth2 Token and leverage it with other queries. Lastly, we will discuss some of the common challenges and limitations you might run into when it comes to using web connectors in Power Query.

Chapter 16: Manipulating Supporting Queries - We will go through the process of manipulating supporting queries for connectors that automatically append files together. Applying specifically to the folder and blob connectors, it is important to understand how changes need to be made in these supporting queries to avoid any rework. This allows you to continue automating your queries without requiring any additional manipulation outside of Power Query. By automating this process, this will simplify future additions to your data model.

Code Bundle and Coloured Images

Please follow the link to download the
Code Bundle and the *Coloured Images* of the book:

https://rebrand.ly/2anl7bu

The code bundle for the book is also hosted on GitHub at **https://github.com/bpbpublications/The-Ultimate-Power-Query-Cookbook-for-Power-BI-and-Excel.** In case there's an update to the code, it will be updated on the existing GitHub repository.

We have code bundles from our rich catalogue of books and videos available at **https://github.com/bpbpublications**. Check them out!

Errata

We take immense pride in our work at BPB Publications and follow best practices to ensure the accuracy of our content to provide with an indulging reading experience to our subscribers. Our readers are our mirrors, and we use their inputs to reflect and improve upon human errors, if any, that may have occurred during the publishing processes involved. To let us maintain the quality and help us reach out to any readers who might be having difficulties due to any unforeseen errors, please write to us at :

errata@bpbonline.com

Your support, suggestions and feedbacks are highly appreciated by the BPB Publications' Family.

Piracy

If you come across any illegal copies of our works in any form on the internet, we would be grateful if you would provide us with the location address or website name. Please contact us at **business@bpbonline.com** with a link to the material.

If you are interested in becoming an author

If there is a topic that you have expertise in,. and you are interested in either writing or contributing to a book, please visit **www.bpbonline.com**. We have worked with thousands of developers and tech professionals, just like you, to help them share their insights with the global tech community. You can make a general application, apply for a specific hot topic that we are recruiting an author for, or submit your own idea.

Reviews

Please leave a review. Once you have read and used this book, why not leave a review on the site that you purchased it from? Potential readers can then see and use your unbiased opinion to make purchase decisions. We at BPB can understand what you think about our products, and our authors can see your feedback on their book. Thank you!

For more information about BPB, please visit **www.bpbonline.com**.

Join our book's Discord space

Join the book's Discord Workspace for Latest updates, Offers, Tech happenings around the world, New Release and Sessions with the Authors:

https://discord.bpbonline.com

Table of Contents

CHAPTER 1

Introduction to Power Query

Introduction

This chapter will provide an overview of Power Query. We will cover the basics of why Power Query is a useful tool and what value it provides for data analysis and reporting. Next, you will learn how to leverage Power Query inside of Microsoft Excel or how to prepare your device to use it inside of Microsoft Power BI. We will then provide an overview of the graphical interface for Power Query and cover the basics of leveraging the M Query language inside the advanced editor. Lastly, we will review how best to leverage this book for success with your projects so you can extract the most value when using Power Query.

Structure

In this chapter, we will cover the following topics:

- Why use Power Query?
- What is Power Query?
- Leveraging Power Query with Excel
- Leveraging Power Query with Power BI Desktop
- Overview of the Power Query graphical interface

- Overview of the advanced editor
- Maximizing Power Query

Objectives

By the end of this chapter, you will understand the value and purpose of Power Query for your analysis and reporting projects. You will be able to set up your device to follow along with the topics found within this book and complete the steps outlined. As you expand your knowledge with Power Query, you will also understand the best way to extract the most value from this book.

Why use Power Query?

In 2015 there was a gentleman, Andrew, who worked in finance and performed reporting for the quality department of his company. For years, he had put together reports for department leaders so they could review their monthly budgets and see if they had met their forecast plan. These reports aimed for cost center leaders to see how they performed against their plan. They received these reports a few days after the financial period closed in a Microsoft Excel file so they could review the details of their actuals and adjust their forecasted spend for the remainder of the year. It seemed like a straightforward task that could be completed quickly.

We could not have been more wrong about how difficult this task was to complete. Andrew shared his story about spending three days assembling ten reports so these department leaders could review them. In surveying the cost center leaders, most of them only spent a total of five minutes reviewing these reports. In addition, a few leaders admitted that they never actually opened them. Andrew spent a lot of time and effort on something that was barely touched by his target audience.

After spending time with Andrew, we understood the core of his challenge. He exported data from their accounting system and needed to transpose it into a format that was easy to consume. But every time he exported the data, he had to complete multiple transformations to force the data to fit into the desired template. He performed the same transformations for each cost center he supported, so he repeatedly spent hours putting together each report for a single department.

Andrew's challenge is not unique. If you are reading this chapter, you likely have a challenge that is quite similar. You have reports and analyses that need to be completed, but you spend hours repeating the same steps. You have wasted hours preparing data for use or have felt the frustration of doing the same thing repeatedly and wondered if there was a better way.

Well, if you feel like Andrew, then there is hope! There is a better way with Power Query! Power Query allows us to apply transformations on our data that can be repeated. By spending a little extra time upfront, we can automate our transformations as we add more data to our models. This process can be daunting at first, but given some time and practice, you will find it easy to do with your data.

One of the benefits Andrew found besides reclaiming three days of his work was his ability to become more proactive with his reports. With three days reclaimed, he could spend time performing meaningful analysis and providing insights to department leaders. He had always wanted to do this but struggled to complete it because he did not have the bandwidth to do so. And this was just the beginning for Andrew, as once he could automate the transformations, he could deliver the reports more frequently. This allowed Andrew to enable cost center leaders to become more proactive with their budgets. With reports coming in on a weekly basis, these leaders could determine if they were going to overspend their forecast and correct course before it became a larger problem. Andrew could never deliver their reports weekly because that would have become his full-time job. However, by simplifying his workload with Power Query, he became a better partner with other leaders in the business and transformed how financial reporting is completed.

While Andrew's scenario might not apply specifically to you, there are multiple use cases where Power Query can prove to be useful. Instead of exporting data from a system, you might connect directly to the underlying database to acquire the data instead of performing an export. Or maybe your initial data source only paints part of the picture, and you need to combine it with another source to provide the full context. As we explore together through this book, we will identify these types of scenarios and navigate them with the assistance of Power Query.

Whether you are a seasoned data professional or a beginner, you probably will encounter someone who will say something along these lines about Power Query: "Why would you perform transformations in Power Query? You need to perform your transformations at the data source. No data professional would ever perform their transformations with Power Query!" As a best practice, we want to provide as much transformation upstream as possible. In a perfect world, every person would have access to a data warehouse and a data engineer to provide transformed data upstream from Power Query.

As wonderful as this sounds, that is just not the reality of the world we live in. Many of you reading this book might not have access to perform transformations on your data at the source. You might have received data in the form of a spreadsheet or a comma-separated value file. Maybe you are connecting to an **Application Programming Interface** (**API**) or using a connection to a third-party software service. In that case, all your transformation will take place inside of Power Query.

In the end, Power Query is designed to simplify the transformation of your data so you can focus on the analysis and insight of your data. That is far more valuable than spending time repeating steps to add new data to your model.

What is Power Query?

Now that we understand why Power Query is a valuable tool, let us talk about what it is. Power Query is an extraction, transformation, and loading tool. You sometimes hear it referred to as an ETL tool. Developed by Microsoft, Power Query is designed to allow users to extract, transform, and load data from disparate data sources and combine them into a single data model. Since many people have Microsoft Office installed on their computers, they can start leveraging Power Query today by opening Microsoft Excel. Others have elected to use a more robust visualization tool, such as Microsoft Power BI, to display their data but will leverage Power Query to get data into their model.

The first step with any project using Power Query will be connecting to and extracting data from various sources. You can connect with a diverse set of data sources ranging from files, databases, and web-based APIs. Some third-party software providers have created their own connectors inside of Power BI, such as LinkedIn, SurveyMonkey, and Zendesk. The best part of Power Query is that it allows you to connect to various data sources all at the same time. This enables you to connect data from different sources into a single model. For instance, you could connect your online sales data inside Dynamics with your customer service data found inside Zendesk. While the systems are different, we can bring the data together to find better insights.

Once we have extracted our data, we are able to perform transformations on it. Through a series of steps, we can go through and make changes to the data we have extracted and make the transformations repeatable. When using Power Query, we can refresh the data whenever we want, so we want to re-apply the same transformations each time we add data to our model. This is where most of the effort is put in to optimize our time in the future, as everything we do now will cascade down for future refreshes.

Once we have completed our transformations, it is time to load our data. When using Power BI, we will be using a data model. However, we have some choices when it comes to Excel. We can load the data we transformed into different sheets inside the file. However, we can load our data into the data model found inside PowerPivot. Instead of storing the data inside the cells, we can leverage it from the model instead.

This is where the most exciting part comes in regarding leveraging Power Query. We can manage large volumes of data with no issues. When performing analysis with Excel, we are limited to one million rows of data. However, if your machine is not properly configured, your performance might be severely degraded, resulting in a lower threshold for your row limit. However, Power Query paired with a data model can handle billions of rows with no issues assuming the resources are available to handle that volume.

As we go through this chapter, you will understand how Power Query serves as an ETL tool and simplifies how you prepare your data for use.

Leveraging Power Query with Excel

Microsoft Office serves as the standard when it comes to productivity software for most businesses. As a result, you likely have access to Power Query already with Microsoft Excel. To leverage Power Query, go to the data tab and expand the get data menu. From there, you can select a data source to get you started or just launch the Power Query editor directly from the menu. Refer to the following figure:

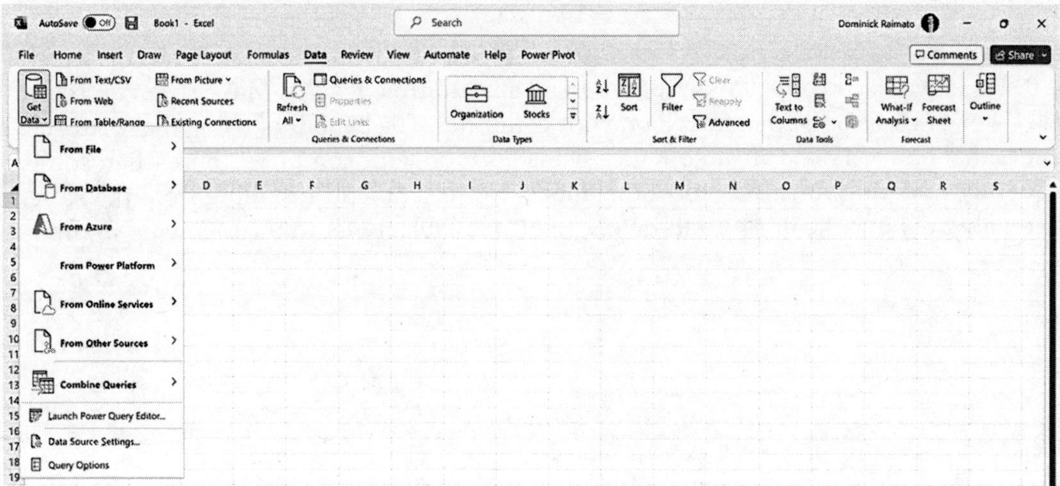

Figure 1.1: Opening Power Query in Excel

If you have a current version of Microsoft Excel already installed on your machine, then you are most likely ready to start using Power Query. Power Query has been available since 2010 but requires an add-in to be installed. In the 2016 edition of Excel, it was integrated with the tool and has been available with every subsequent version. Hopefully, you will be using a newer version of Excel as both the 2010 and 2013 versions are no longer supported, but keep in mind if they are still in use.

Since Power Query is best known for being leveraged with Power BI Desktop, users often ask if there is any advantage to using Microsoft Excel. The short answer is yes, as Excel serves a different purpose than Power BI. For example, a common use case for Power Query in Excel is to cleanse and transform two separate lists into a single table so it can be referenced by a script in PowerShell. You can perform the transformation with Power Query and load it into an Excel spreadsheet, so it is ready to be imported. Always remember that it is important to use the right tool for the right job.

Leveraging Power Query with Power BI Desktop

For many readings, this chapter, Microsoft Power BI Desktop, might be a brand-new tool. Power BI is a data visualization tool that allows for a user-friendly approach to analysis and insight. You can download Power BI Desktop and use it for free for your own visualization and analysis.

The easiest way to install Power BI Desktop is to head over to the Microsoft Store and search for it. When you search for Power BI, you will see multiple results. Make sure you select the Power BI Desktop app to install on your computer. The benefit of using the Microsoft Store is that new versions are automatically installed on your computer. Since Microsoft is frequently updating functions and capabilities, we recommend installing from the store, so you always have the most up-to-date version available. Refer to the following figure:

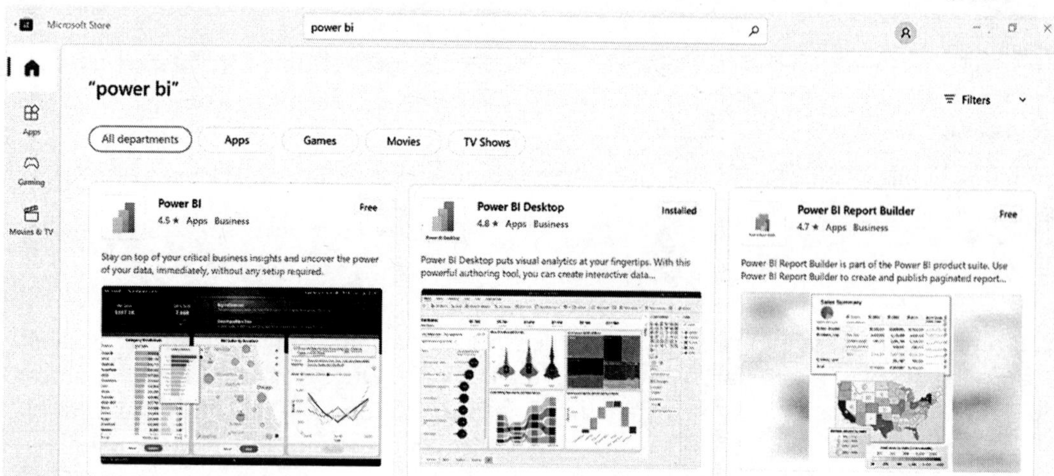

***Figure 1.2:** Install Power BI Desktop for free from the Microsoft Store*

You will note two other applications are available. Power BI Report Builder is useful for designing paginated reports. The Power BI application is designed for you to have easy access to the service in the cloud so you can view content easily from your computer. Since both tools are not using Power Query for editing reports, they will not help you. Feel free to install and explore on your own but make sure you have Power BI Desktop installed before moving forward with *Chapter 2, Connect to File Data Sources*.

If you do not have access to the Microsoft Store, you can easily download Power BI Desktop from the Power BI website. Just navigate to **https://powerbi.microsoft.com/en-us/desktop/** and follow the steps to start your download. The benefit of this approach is that you can control which versions you use and specify which language works best for you.

Once installed, you can open Power Query in a few different ways. The easiest is to get data from the splash screen, select a data source, and click transform to enter the Power Query editor. You can also perform the same action from the home ribbon on the main screen. However, if you want to open Power Query and do not have a data source to connect to, you can simply click on transform data to access the Power Query editor, as shown:

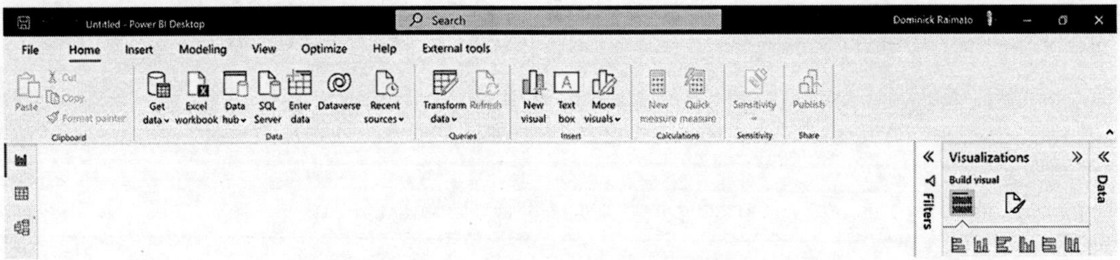

***Figure 1.3:** Opening Power Query inside Power BI*

Unlike Excel, Power Query is available in every version of Power BI. It is important to note that legacy versions of Power Query might be missing newer features discussed in this book. It is recommended that you update Power BI Desktop before continuing your journey to ensure the most recent features are available to you.

Lastly, it is important to note that Power BI Desktop is a valuable tool for performing analysis and visualizing insights. However, the true power is unleashed when content is published into the Power BI service so it can be shared. To leverage the Power BI service, you or your company will need to invest in Power BI licensing to unlock the full potential of the platform.

Overview of the Power Query graphical interface

The Power Query graphical interface is valuable for performing most transformations on your data. In the past, you needed to know the M Query language to get the most out of your transformations. And while that is still true, many of the core transformations are integrated within the graphical interface. That simply means that you can perform most of your transformations with a few clicks of the mouse paired with prompts to guide you. This eliminates the need to memorize every single function available to you and even allows you to generate some code samples.

We will address the specifics in greater detail as we go along in this book. However, it is important to note one key component of the graphical interface called **Applied Steps**. This pane is on the right-hand side of the screen. If it is missing, you can enable it from the view ribbon and select **Query Settings**. This tool allows us to go back to previous transformations we have performed. We can edit past transformations, re-order them, and even delete them. If you ever make a mistake, you can easily roll back your changes with a simple click instead of starting over from scratch. Refer to the following figure:

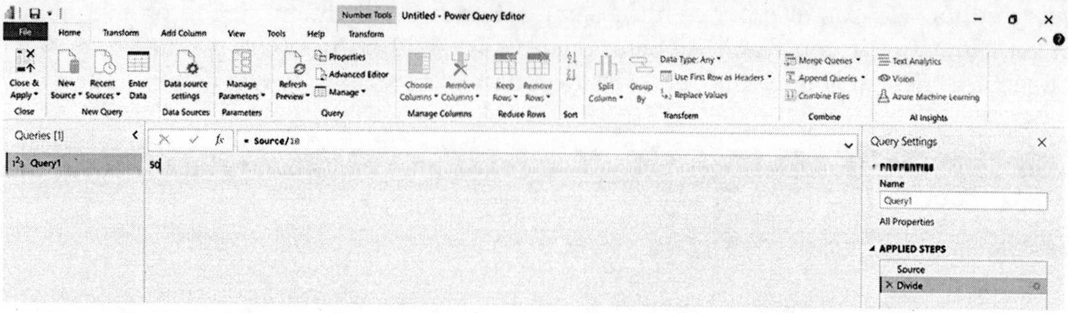

Figure 1.4: Viewing applied steps in the Power Query editor

As you begin your journey with this chapter, it is important to note that while Power Query is available in both Excel and Power BI Desktop, not everything is the same. To start, the interface has variations between them. As an example, adding new data sources to Power Query in Excel takes place on the right side of the home ribbon, while Power Query in Power BI has it on the left, as shown:

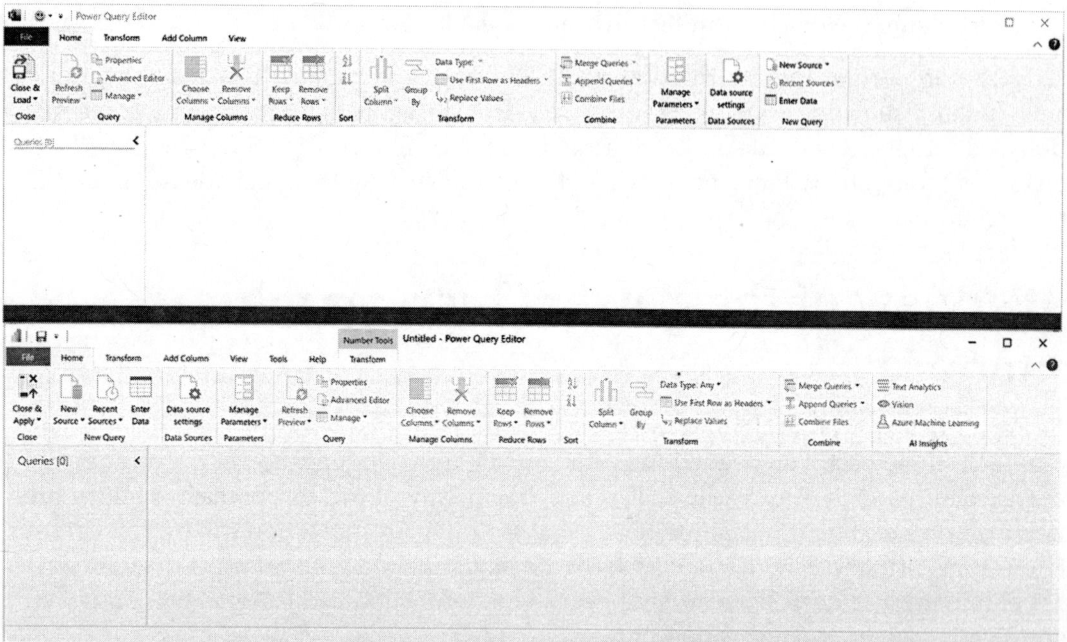

Figure 1.5: Comparison of Power Query in Excel (top) and Power Query in Power BI (bottom)

There are also differences in functionality between the two tools. If you look at the home ribbon for Power Query in Power BI, you will notice the AI Insights section. This allows users to integrate R, Python, and Azure Machine Learning with their data inside Power

Query. However, that functionality is not available in Power Query for Excel. Just the same, there is a structured column section under the transform ribbon in Power Query for Excel that is not available in Power Query for Power BI.

Some of these differences are easier to explain. As an example, Power BI Desktop provides settings that allow integration for R and Python scripts, while Excel does not. At the same time, the structured column function missing in Power BI Desktop does not make much sense as it has no external dependencies.

We call these items out because as you go through this book, you will find that there is not 100% parity between Excel and Power BI. As a result, it is important for you to understand that the screenshots being taken in this book will be primarily from Power Query in Power BI. Therefore, some of the buttons you are looking for might be in a different location than you originally expected. Make sure you look around first to see if something is just in a different location. We also recommend if you have the time and patience, consider trying what you learn in this book in both tools to help broaden your experience with Power Query in both Excel and Power BI. This way, you are prepared regardless of which tool you prefer.

Lastly, make sure when you are reading that you notice any notes that explicitly state functionality that is only available in Excel or Power BI. This will prevent you from searching for functionality that is not present in your preferred application.

Overview of advanced editor

The advanced editor is a must when it comes to Power Query. As you start your journey, you might feel that the advanced editor is not helpful. This is not the case. One of the lessons you will learn is that not everything works as you expect it to when it comes to data. You are going to run into challenges such as query timeouts, custom paths, and even the need to apply special filter rules. While some of this can be accomplished with the graphical interface, you will find yourself working in the advanced editor as you encounter more complex situations.

When using the advanced editor window, we are using the M Query language to modify our transformations. It is a functional-based mashup language designed to enable the transformation and integration of disparate data sources into a single query. Even when performing transformations with the graphical interface, they are translated into M and can be modified using the advanced editor. To get started, go to the home ribbon to launch the **Advanced Editor** screen. Refer to the following figure:

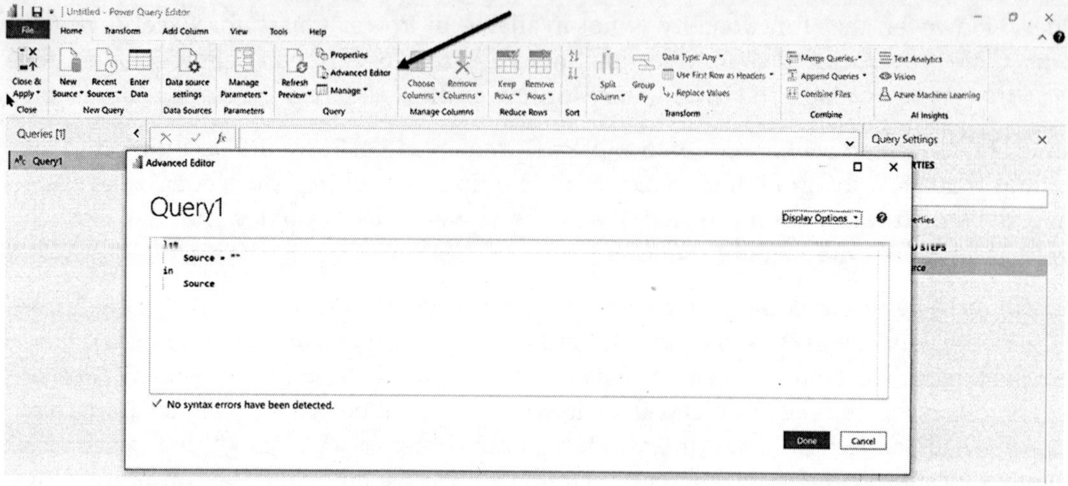

Figure 1.6: Opening the Advanced Editor window in Power Query

With the advanced editor window open, we can now see the core components of our query. Every query has a let expression and an in statement. The **let** expression is where all the transformative steps are applied. Since this is a blank query, there is not much to show at this moment. You will notice that there is only one step titled source that holds a blank value. After the transformation steps have been completed, there is an **in** statement that returns the value for the step identified. Generally, this is the last step in the query.

Let us try building our first custom query from the advanced editor window. After you have opened Power Query, create a new blank query by adding it from the new source menu. From there, open the advanced editor window and enter the following code to return **"Hello World"**:

```
let
  Source = "Hello World"
in
  Source
```

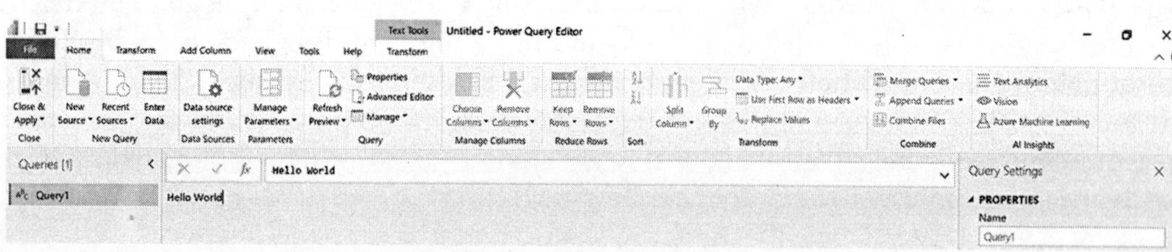

Figure 1.7: Hello World response

We can take this a step further and add some complication to this script by adding an additional step to it like this:

```
let
    Source = "Hello",
    Message = Source & " World"
in
    Message
```

If you are following along in Power Query, you will realize the result was the same for both code snippets. However, the second block was a little different because we applied two steps. In the first step, named **Source**, we simply applied the word hello. We then added a comma at the end of the line, which signified that there would be a second step applied. We named the second step message and concatenated two text strings together with an ampersand (**&**). However, note that the first half of the formula referenced the previous step and then added our text at the end. That is how the M Query language functions by applying transformations a single step at a time and building upon it each step of the way. It is also important to note that while everything we performed was in the **Advanced Editor**, the applied steps pane was updated accordingly. Refer to the following figure:

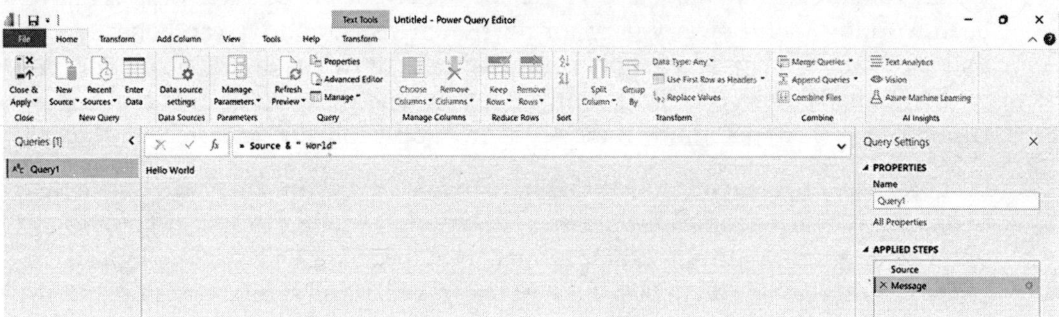

Figure 1.8: Updated Hello World script with two applied steps

For many readers, transformations that will take place within Power Query can be achieved without the use of the advanced editor. However, it is important to note that the ability to make modifications to our code can extend our abilities as we load data into our models. We can leverage the advanced editor to perform multiple transformations at once to simplify how our queries are loaded into our model. An example of this would be filtering a query based on values that might be found between two delimiters. With a small modification to the code, we can extract those values and perform the filtering in a single step which optimizes how our query performs. While not always a requirement, there will be challenges that arise that will require you to use the advanced editor to get the most out of your data.

Naturally, as we go forward in this book, you will learn more about how to manage and update queries using the advanced editor. These are the basics to understand how the language is structured, and you will experience how you can leverage the M Query language in a customized format as you read further along.

Maximizing Power Query

As you embark upon your journey with Power Query, you are going to learn a hard truth that everyone before you had to learn on their own. When working with data, the reality is that each source is akin to a snowflake. They are all unique and provide their own challenges. Some data sources might require no transformation at all, while others will have twenty steps applied. It would be impossible to document every single scenario possible inside of Power Query. However, we have developed a set of guidelines to assist you in getting the most out of this book:

- Treat this cookbook as a guide to preparing the ingredients for your own data models. Because we cannot predict each scenario you are going to encounter, we cannot create the recipes for you. However, these recipes are designed to assist you with specific scenarios you might encounter when working with data. We have taken the time to call out specific use cases and scenarios where these recipes might be helpful.

- Do not think that you must use every recipe in this book to be successful. We have been working with Power Query for nearly ten years, and we can honestly say that some of the recipes have only been used once or twice in our data models. As we mentioned before, each data source is unique and provides its own challenges. Digest use cases to determine if they properly apply to your scenario.

- Best practices are great but sometimes hard to follow. As you will read along in this book, you will learn some best practices that we have found to assist in providing optimized queries. As an example, one best practice will be highlighted in *Chapter 7, Transforming Columns*. It is best to consolidate all similar transformations into a single applied step. While it is ideal to consolidate all data type transformations into a single step, it is not always possible. Always try your best to follow best practices but do not be afraid to bend the rules from time to time.

- Do not shy away from the advanced editor window. Most of your transformations can be performed through a graphical interface. However, to accomplish more complex transformations, you will need the advanced editor at some point to accomplish your transformation goals. Take the time now to get comfortable with how the M Query language operates and how you might be able to simplify your queries with a little customization.

- Remember that if Power Query was easy, everyone would be using it. Data is challenging and often a mess when we receive it. We wish it was not the case, but it is true. When you apply what you have learned, you might find yourself struggling to find the right way to manage a query. As experienced developers, we still find ourselves struggling to get a query under control. The goal of this book is to give you options to make it easier to find the right path for your data models. If what you tried did not work, then use this book to find another path forward.

While it is not an official guideline, do not be afraid to have some fun and celebrate along the way with your learning. If you are like us, sometimes you get so focused on the outcome that you forget that you are doing some amazing work within Power Query. When you accomplish something, take a moment to congratulate yourself and enjoy the moment. Then make sure you document what you learned so you can repeat it again in the future.

Conclusion

In this chapter, we covered the why and the what associated with Power Query. We covered how to use Power Query both in Microsoft Excel and Power BI Desktop. We went through the basics of the graphical interface and some variations you might encounter when using the tool. We also covered the basics around the advanced editor and the M Query language to help provide more context on how to customize our queries. Lastly, we reviewed guidelines to help you be successful when using this book.

In the next chapter, we will be connecting to our first data sources with Power Query so we can start ingesting data for transformation.

CHAPTER 2

Connect to File-Based Data Sources

Introduction

This chapter will walk you through connecting file-based data sources with Power Query. We will walk you through connecting to files of different formats, such as Excel, CSV, and JSON, with the graphical interface and the advanced editor. We will then explore the implications of data refreshes with files and how to work around them by leveraging SharePoint as a storage location.

Structure

In this chapter, we will cover the following topics:

- Understanding file-based connections
- Connecting to tabular files
- Connecting to structured files
- Connecting to folders
- Refreshing file-based connections

Objectives

By the end of this chapter, you will understand how to use Power Query to connect to files directly on your device and through SharePoint. You will learn how to manipulate and manage these file sources so they can be leveraged inside of your data model. You will also learn the implications of connecting directly to file sources and some challenges that might arise as you build your data model. Lastly, you will understand why data connectors are an important part of Power Query even if you are not connecting directly to files on your device.

Understanding file-based connections

Purists in the Power Query arena tend to mock the use of files as a data source. It is understandable, as most people strive for a data model that can refresh with minimal intervention. When file data sources are used, they are often prone to error. If you exported the data from another system, you might have placed an extra filter on the data that was not intended. Copying and pasting data between sheets often leads to challenges. And if you are using Microsoft Excel, the pesky one million row limit can cause a lot of grief with your data model structure. As demonstrated in the following figure, Power Query allows you to connect to a diverse set of file sources to help you simplify the refresh of your data model:

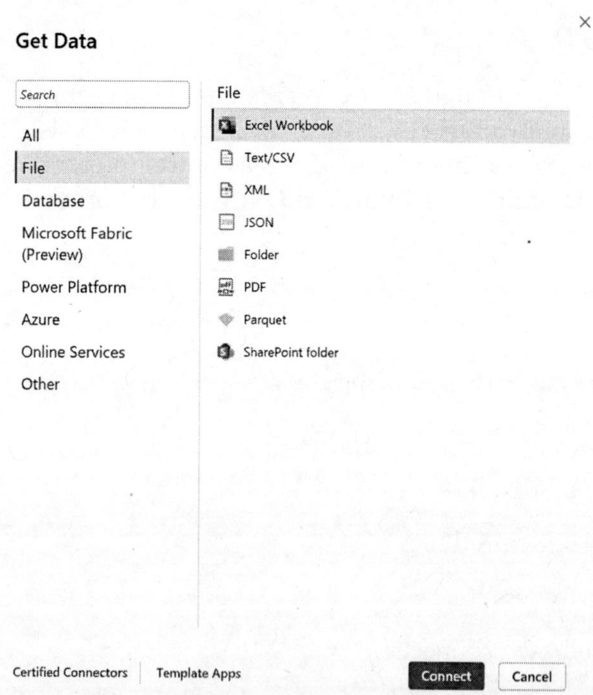

Figure 2.1: List of file-based connections available for Power Query

No question, file data sources can be challenging regarding your data model. However, sometimes you will find yourself in a situation where you must leverage a file data source to complete the job. For example, maybe you are working with third-party software that does not have an API connection to grab the most recent data. Or maybe you do not have database-level access to your accounting system. What happens when a customer or vendor sends you a spreadsheet of data?

These are common scenarios where connecting to files with Power Query is required for your data model. Many will tell you that you need to import this data into a SQL Server or a data warehouse to properly manage it. And while that is nice, it is not often feasible. The people who tell you to import your data into a SQL database do so because they do not understand how Power Query can transform your data from files with a few clicks.

It might not be the best idea to leverage these connectors long-term. No one will agree that it is easier to connect to a file versus a database when you are constantly refreshing the data. But sometimes, it is all you have at your disposal to get something done. In addition, it can provide a great base for a proof-of-concept solution if you need to perform some testing or want to vet a theory you might be researching.

But there is a far more practical use for file connectors and Power Query. In *Chapter 3, Connect to Web-Based Data Sources*, you will learn that you must leverage a file connector and a web connector to manage data returned from web-based endpoints. In *Chapter 4, Connect to Database Sources*, you will learn that you might need file connectors to manage data stored in your data lake. In *Chapter 5, Connect to Third-Party Data Sources*, you will learn that you might need to apply the same principles you learned with web connectors with a connector designed for a specific third-party platform. While you may never intend on connecting to files directly, you will need to understand the connectors as they might play a critical role in your data model.

Lastly, focusing on file sources is important, as not everyone can access the same infrastructure to achieve their goals. You might be a business analyst who has never heard of SQL or does not know what a blob storage container is. Once you have data within your model, you can perform all the transformations this book identifies. Once you understand this chapter, you will be set to learn the true value of Power Query.

Connecting to tabular files

When you think of connecting to files, the mind often races to Microsoft Excel. Regardless of your background, many people have used Excel in the past. The tabular format of spreadsheets allows you to organize your data so you can analyze it quickly. As a result, it is the easiest entry point when it comes to connecting to data within Power Query. To get started, go to the **Get data** menu and select **Excel Workbook**, as shown in the following figure:

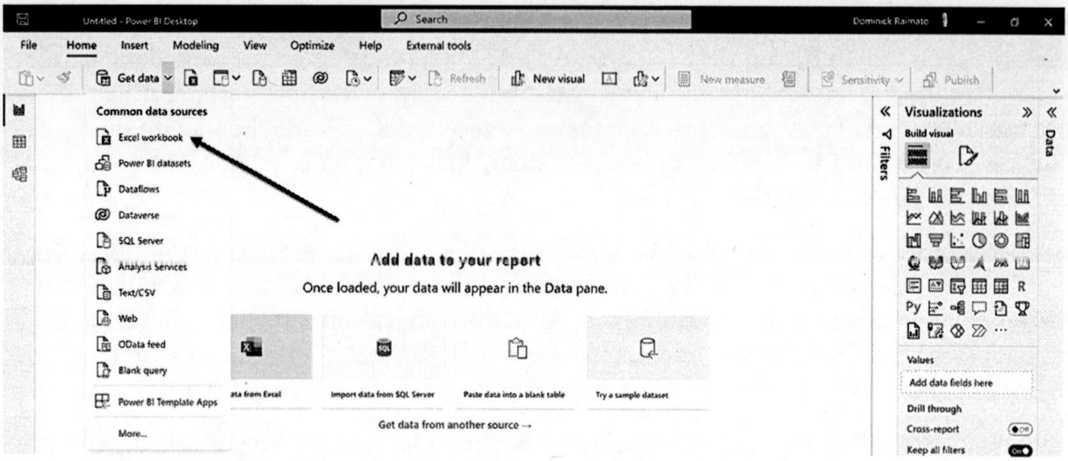

Figure 2.2: Selecting the Excel Workbook connector for Power Query

From there, you will be prompted to select your file. Navigate to where your Excel file is located, select it, and click **Open**. You will then be brought to a new screen like the one in *Figure* 2.3, asking you what you want to import. In this example, you will notice there are two options, but they have different icons. And while the data for both options is technically the same, what they connect to is very different:

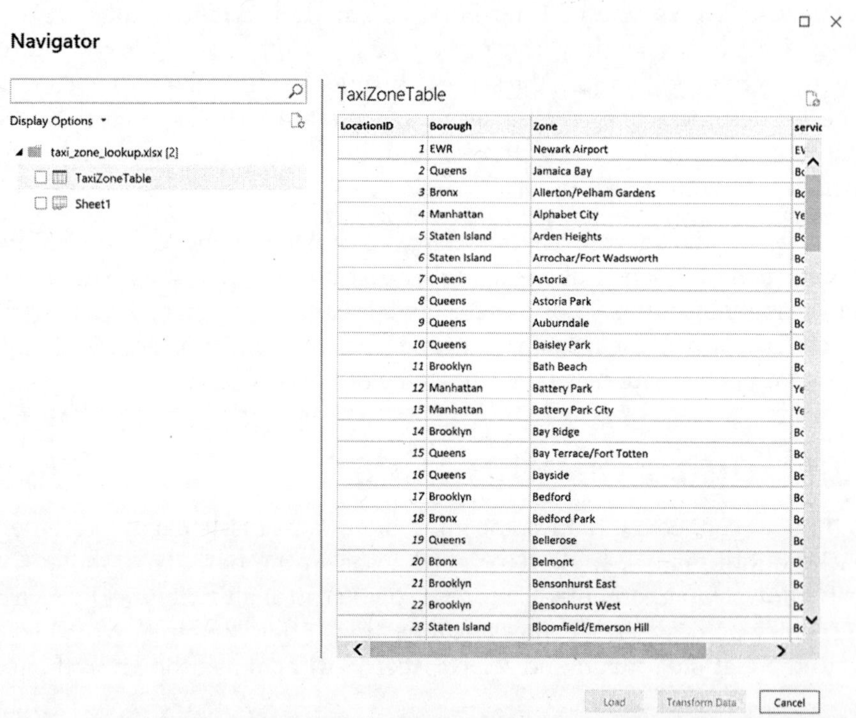

Figure 2.3: Selecting data from an Excel workbook

If you select **Sheet1**, you will bring all the data on a specified spreadsheet. However, selecting **`TaxiZoneTable`** will only bring in the data associated with a table inside Excel. Once you have selected what to bring into your data model, select the check box and click **Transform Data** to open the Power Query Editor. To highlight the difference between these two options, we can select both so you can compare the two:

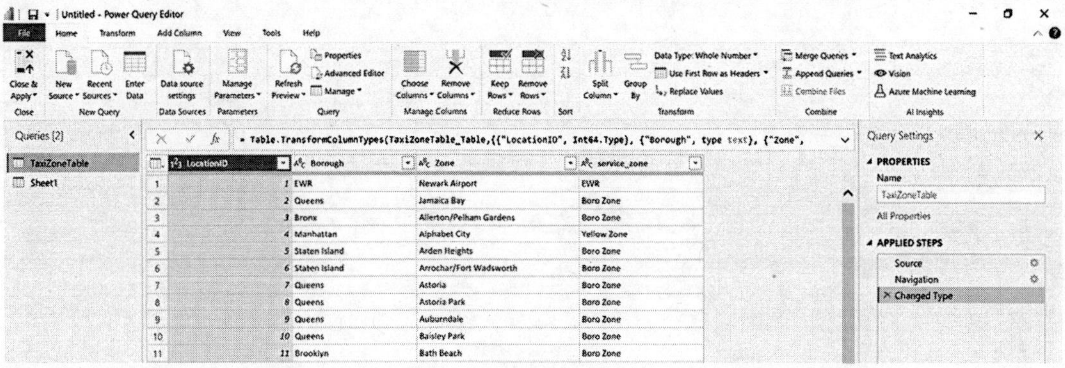

Figure 2.4: *Selecting TaxiZoneTable inside of an Excel workbook*

You will notice that the table we selected from our Excel workbook only brought in four columns, as shown in *Figure 2.4*. However, we did not have the same experience with the sheet itself, as shown in the following figure:

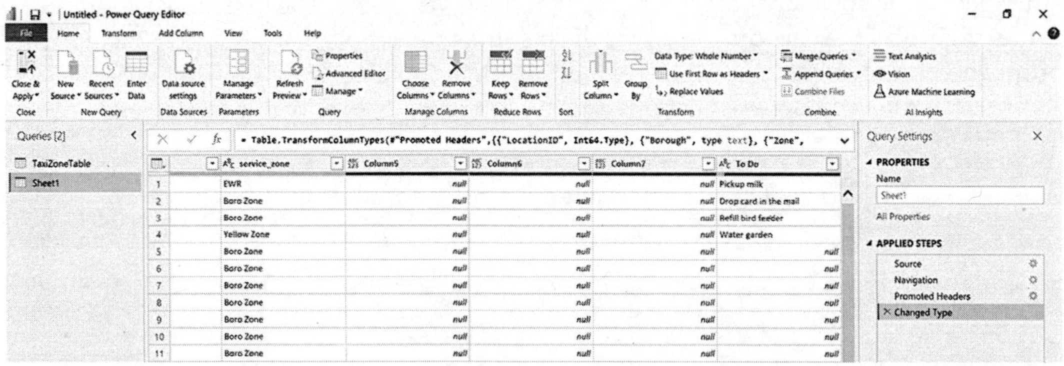

Figure 2.5: *Selecting sheet1 inside of an Excel workbook*

When we brought in the sheet, it included someone's to-do list, which does not apply to our data model. As you will learn in *Chapter 8, Cleansing Data*, we can easily remove these extra columns and move on. But while that is nice, using the table eliminates the extra steps, making our query more efficient. As a best practice, using a table inside of Excel is preferable if it is available over the entire spreadsheet when possible.

When most people think of tabular data, they think of Microsoft Excel. However, **Comma Separated Values (CSV)** files are another common data source that displays data in a tabular format. When data is exported out of a system, it is frequently provided in a CSV format. And while you can open it with Excel, it is subject to the million-row limit, making it unwieldy to manage. However, loading them into Power Query is as easy as Excel files. Since the Power Query editor window is already open, you can go to the **New Source** dropdown and select **Text/CSV**, and select your file, as shown in the following figure:

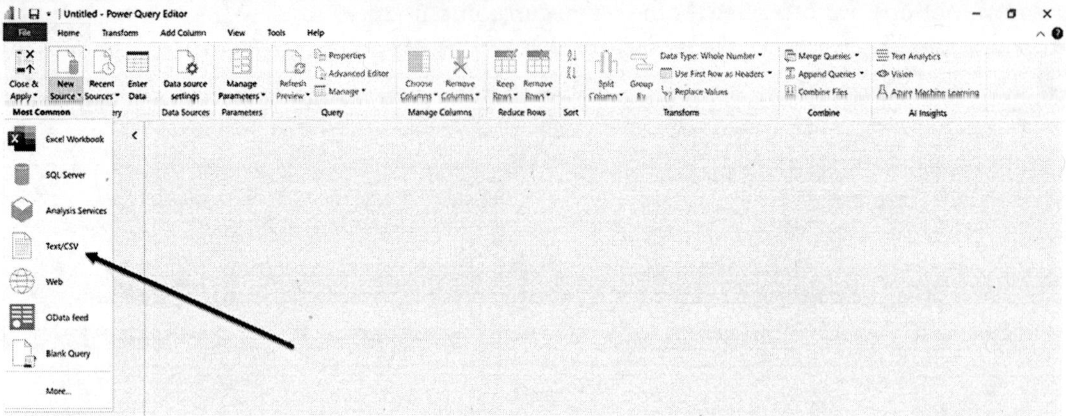

Figure 2.6: Selecting the Text/CSV connector

Once you have selected your file, you will be taken to a window like the one we saw for Excel workbooks. However, in *Figure 2.7*, this one is a little different. It provides a snapshot of the data, but you will notice a few dropdown options at the top. They relate to the specific file structure you are ingesting into Power Query. The first option is around the file origin and the encoding used for the file. In our example, it selected **1252: Western European (Windows)** as the origin. While this file originated from the United States, it was encoded this way, so we must use it to avoid errors. The following figure shows our file of origin encoding:

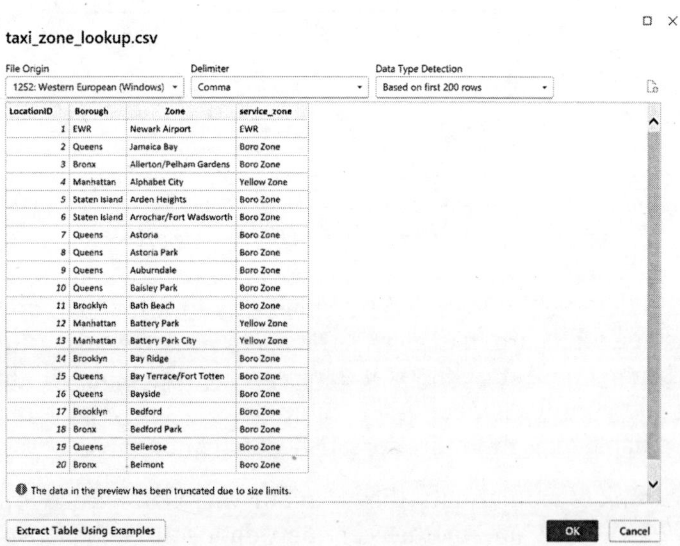

Figure 2.7: Reviewing the data from a CSV file

The second option is focused on the delimiter. The delimiter identifies where your columns are located. It is often assumed that when you are using a CSV file, your delimiter is a comma. However, sometimes you will find different characters, such as colons, semicolons, equal signs, tabs, or even a custom character, such as a vertical bar (|). You might need to select a different delimiter if your data looks wrong.

Lastly, the third option is around detecting the data type of your CSV file. If you want Power Query to attempt to pick the right data type, you can let it decide based on the first two hundred rows of your dataset or the entire dataset. If you prefer more control over your data, you can skip this step and manually assign them when you get the data ingested. Once these options are set, click **OK** and bring your data into the Power Query editor.

Now that you understand how to complete these tasks with the graphical interface, you might wonder how to do so using the advanced editor. Regardless of the file format you are choosing, you will need to start with the same formula:

```
let
  Source = File.Contents("C:\NYC Taxi\taxi_zone_lookup.xlsx")
in
  Source
```

In this code snippet, we have used the **`File.Contents()`** function and specify the path to our file data source. Now that we have identified the file, we need to translate it. Since our code snippet uses an Excel file, we will use **`Excel.Workbook()`** function to perform the translation:

```
let
  Source = File.Contents("C:\NYC Taxi\taxi_zone_lookup.xlsx"),
  Contents = Excel.Workbook(Source, null, true)
in
  Contents
```

The **`Excel.Workbook()`** function provides us with some parameters to simplify how we manipulate our ingested workbooks:

`Excel.Workbook()`	
Parameter	**Description**
`workbook`	Content from an Excel Workbook as binary
`useHeaders`	Indicates if the first row should be used as headers. It can be **`null`** or **`true`**/**`false`**
`delayTypes`	Indicates whether Power Query should attempt to identify column types. It can be **`null`** or **`true`**/**`false`**.

***Table 2.1**: Table of the Excel.Workbook() parameters*

The **`Excel.Workbook()`** function has three parameters. The first parameter is the workbook content which we established in the first step of the query. The next parameter asks about the headers for our file. We will use **`null`** here as we still have another step before we are ready for headers. Lastly, the final parameter, known as delay types, can determine if we want to delay the detection of data types. We will choose true as we are not worried about data types yet. Our code has resulted in listing the available sheets and tables found inside the workbook:

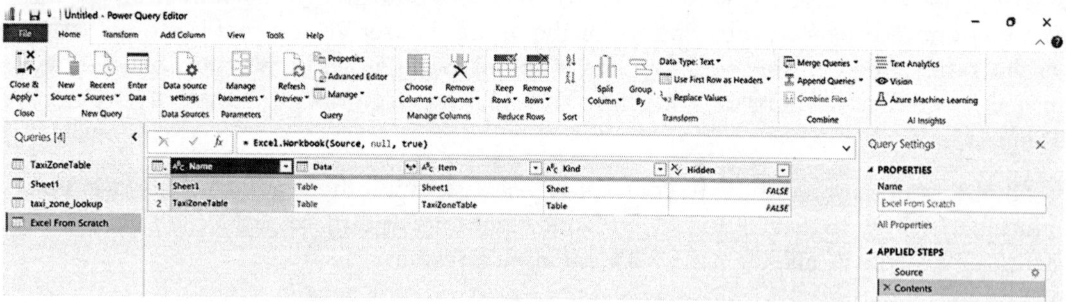

Figure 2.8: Connecting to an Excel workbook with the advanced editor

Now that the connection to the workbook has been established, we can specify what data we want to return. If you note the options available, they are the same as the ones we had with the graphical interface. Since we have a table available, we will use that as our preferred choice when connecting to our Excel workbook. To accomplish this, we will add one more line of code in the advanced editor:

```
let
  Source = File.Contents("C:\NYC Taxi\taxi_zone_lookup.xlsx"),
  Contents = Excel.Workbook(Source, null, true),
  Data = Contents{1}[Data]
in
  Data
```

This might look confusing at first, but it is quite simple. There are three elements to this new line that allow us to extract the data from our table. The first element is the data source. We are using **`Contents`** as our source as we have already performed some transformations on this file. Next, we must specify the row of the data we want to use. Since the **`TaxiZoneTable`** is on the second row, we must specify it with the number one between the curly brackets. You are probably asking why we need to use the number one instead of two, and the answer is simple, table indexes in Power Query always start at zero. Lastly, we must specify the column that contains the content we want. In this case, our field name is data, and it is wrapped in square brackets.

But there is a flaw with this logic. We hard-coded the row number into the query. What happens if the row order changes? Or what if something is deleted? There is a solution to that! Instead of using a numeric value in the curly brackets, we can specify values in columns so it finds the right row for us. So, instead of **{1}**, we can replace that value with specific columns and their expected values as demonstrated below:

```
let
  Source = File.Contents("C:\NYC Taxi\taxi_zone_lookup.xlsx"),
  Contents = Excel.Workbook(Source, null, true),
  Data = Contents{[Item="TaxiZoneTable",Kind="Table"]}[Data]
in
  Data
```

Note that we are now searching for the table name under the **Item** column and the type of item under the **Kind** column. When working with Excel workbooks, it is important that you explicitly state the item name and type, as you can have a spreadsheet and table with the same name. If you wanted to use the spreadsheet instead, you could have **Item** equal **Sheet1** and **Kind** equal sheet to get a similar experience.

To simplify the process, we split each part into its steps. However, if you want to condense everything into a single step, you can easily combine these steps into a single string. You can use the following code so everything shows up as a single step in Power Query:

```
let
  Source = Excel.Workbook(
  File.Contents("C:\NYC Taxi\taxi_zone_lookup.xlsx"),
     null, false){[Item = "TaxiZoneTable", Kind = "Table"]}[Data]
in
  Source
```

To apply the same steps for a CSV file, you will follow a similar format as we saw with the Excel workbook. Instead of using **Excel.Workbook()**, we will use the **Csv.Document()** function to accomplish our goal. The **Csv.Document()** function is a little more complex and requires some knowledge of your source file before using it:

Csv.Document()	
Parameter	**Description**
Source	Content from a CSV document
Columns	The number of columns in a CSV document or a list of column names.
Delimiter	Any number of characters that indicates how rows should be split. The default is ",".

Csv.Document()	
extraValues	Allows you to specify the delimiter, columns, and encoding as the other parameters do. However, this field can also specify **CsvStyle** for how quotes are handled in a document as well as the **quoteStyle**. Each element is listed between square brackets and has a comma between each one. It can only be used if other fields are **null.** Otherwise, this parameter should be **null**.
encoding	Specifies the encoding type based on the source document.

***Table 2.2:** Table of the Csv.Document() parameters*

As you read through the parameters, it becomes clear that we need more intimate knowledge of how our content is structured when we leverage **Csv.Document()**. Because of the variations in CSV documents, we must take the extra time to explicitly specify each element to ensure Power Query understands how to handle CSV content. To achieve the same results as we did with the graphical interface, we would need to add the following code to our advanced editor:

```
let
  Source = Csv.Document(
  File.Contents("C:\NYC Taxi\taxi_zone_lookup.csv"), 4, ",", null, 1252)
in
  Source
```

The result of this code will bring your data into Power Query. Note that in *Figure 2.9*, the column headers appear in the results pane's first row. This is a problem, but we will address this in *Chapter 7, Transforming Columns*.

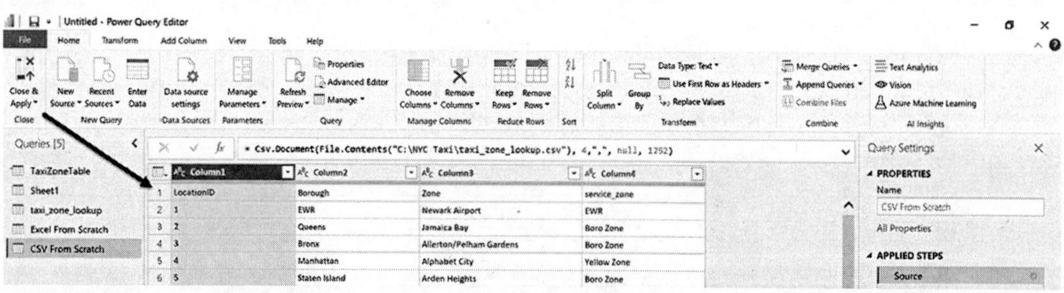

***Figure 2.9:** Column headers showing in the first row of data*

Now that you know the basics of connecting to Excel workbooks and CSV files, we can explore how to leverage structured files.

Connecting to structured files

While the preferred file format for most people is Excel or CSV, many applications provide data in other structured formats. You probably are the benefactor of these files in your daily life but never realize it because the applications you use translate it into a usable format for you to consume. You probably have heard of JSON and XML files, but they are difficult to review every time you open them. With Power BI, we can completely bypass this challenge and use Power Query to ingest these file contents and quickly convert them into a readable format.

Let us start with the JSON format. **JavaScript Object Notation** (**JSON**) is a common data export format that is used with APIs. To get started, we will connect to our JSON file by clicking on the new source dropdown in the Power Query editor, but you will quickly realize that it is not on the list. You will have to click more, bringing up a bigger list of data sources we can use to connect. Select the **JSON file**, click **Connect**, and select your file. For our sake, Power Query takes care of the heavy lifting by adding a few steps, and everything is ready for us with minimal intervention, as shown in the following figure:

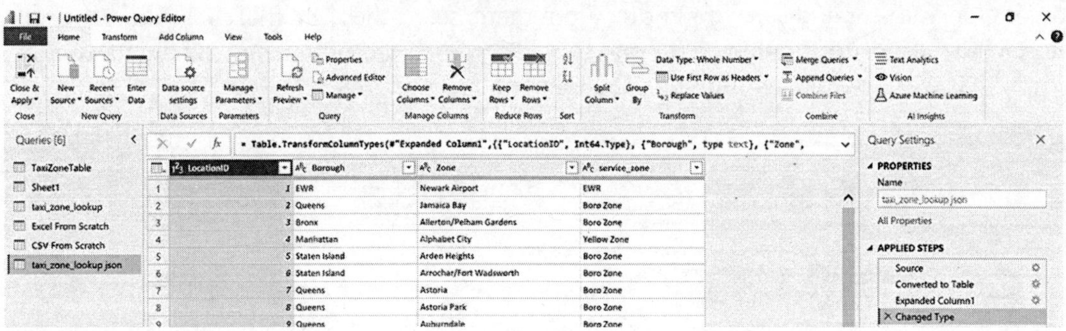

***Figure 2.10**: Sample query using JSON file format*

Like before, we can use the advanced editor to build our connection to a JSON file. We still need to use **`File.Contents()`** to specify our file but will wrap it with **`Json.Document()`** to translate it into a usable format:

```
let
  Source = Json.Document(File.Contents("C:\NYC Taxi\taxi_zone_lookup.
json"))
in
  Source
```

For most situations, we only need the source parameter from the **`Json.Document()`** function:

`Json.Document()`	
Parameter	**Description**
`source`	Content from a JSON file
`encoding`	Specifies the encoding type based on the source document but often is left as null.

***Table 2.3**: Table of the Json.Document() parameters*

As you can see, the **`Json.Document()`** function is much simpler than the Excel and CSV file formats because it was designed to be a straightforward way to share content in a standardized format. However, we are not off the hook yet. There are two more transformations to make this data usable. First, the data returned was in a list format and must be converted into a table. Once converted, the data needs to be expanded to see the records. We will cover these transformations in *Chapter 7, Transforming Data Columns*.

XML Files are imported the same way as JSON files. Like JSON, XML has an easily defined format and is easy to parse. Like before, start by going to the new source dropdown in the Power Query editor and selecting more. From there, select the XML file, click connect, and select your file. Unfortunately, this time the data source did not bring in the data in the format that we expected, as shown in the following figure:

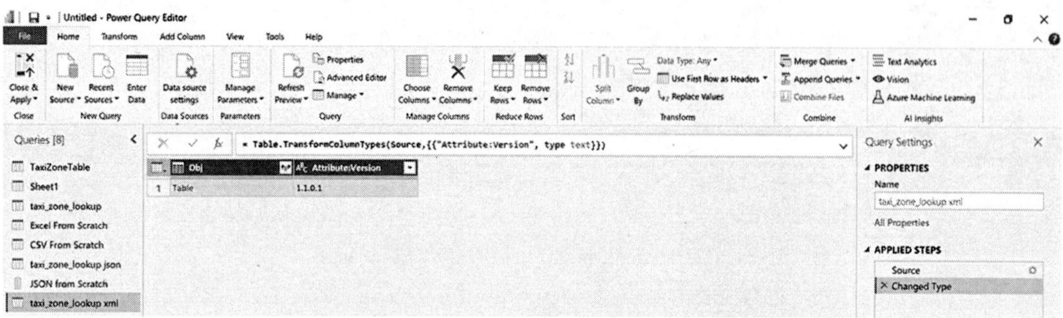

***Figure 2.11**: Sample query using XML file format*

Because of the structure of this XML file, we will need to apply some advanced transformations to get this to work. We will cover these details in *Chapter 7, Transforming Data Columns*.

Like before, we can use the advanced editor to build our connection to an XML file. We still need to use **`File.Contents()`** to specify our file but will wrap it with **`Xml.Document()`** to translate it into a usable format:

```
let
  Source = Xml.Document(File.Contents("C:\NYC Taxi\taxi_zone_lookup.xml"))
in
  Source
```

The **Xml.Document()** function is very similar to the **Json.Document()** function:

Xml.Document()	
Parameter	**Description**
source	Content from an XML file
encoding	Specifies the encoding type based on the source document but often is left as null.

***Table 2.4**: Table of the Xml.Document() parameters*

As you can see, there are a lot of similarities in how both JSON and XML files are handled. While you might find them to be ugly, you will find that both formats are easy to manipulate in Power Query.

The final format we want to cover in this section is a parquet file. A parquet file is a column-based storage file optimized and compressed for faster processing. You will likely not receive raw parquet files for manipulating with Power Query, but you will encounter them depending on your environment. To use a parquet file, select more from the new source. From there, select the parquet file connector, click connect, and provide a URL to your file location. We also can connect to a parquet file using the **Parquet.Document()** function:

```
let
  Source = Parquet.Document(File.Contents("c:\NYC Taxi\taxi_zone_lookup.
parquet"))
in
  Source
```

Of all the file-based functions, the **Parquet.Document()** function is the simplest:

Parquet.Document()	
Parameter	**Description**
source	Content from a parquet file

***Table 2.5**: Table of the Parquet.Document() parameters*

As simple as JSON and XML files, parquet files are just as easy to manage in Power Query. But you might be asking yourself a valid question at this point. You might be thinking that you can easily copy and paste data into a single file with your Excel files. How will you do this with JSON, XML, and parquet files? And for that matter, it may be annoying to copy and paste that data. Fear not Power Query has a connector that eliminates that challenge.

Connecting to folders

The number one complaint people make about Power Query is the frustration of managing data inside a file. People spend hours exporting, copying, and pasting data into a single

Excel spreadsheet to add it to their data model. It is time-intensive and prone to errors. Sure, you might be able to re-export the same data repeatedly, just filtering it to include larger amounts, but what if there are limits? What if you can only export one thousand records at a time? What if you can only export the past thirty days of records?

This is where the folder connector comes in to save the day. It is the best-kept secret in all of Power Query. Many Microsoft employees do not even know it exists. The folder connector serves a specific purpose but delivers exponential efficiencies when adding new data to your model. When you have several files that use the same structure, you can place them into a single folder. From there, the folder connector transforms and combines the files into a single query. No copy and paste. No need to append multiple files. It is a sustainable solution that does not require you to update your queries just to add new data. To get started with the folder connector, you must have a folder with files ready. Ideally, they should all have the same format. An easy way to try this on your own might be with the exports of your bank or credit card statements. Here is an example of a folder we have in place that contains files with the same structure:

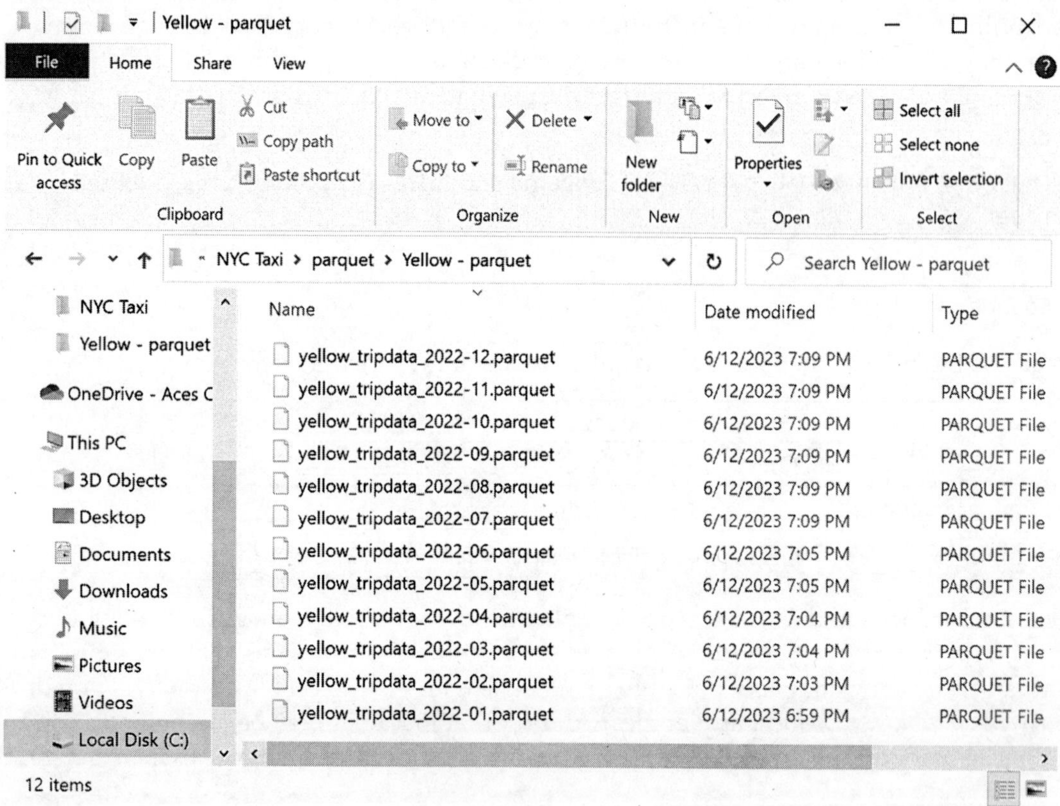

Figure 2.12: Sample folder of data

We will go to the new source dropdown from the Power Query editor and click **More**. From there, select the folder connector, browse to the path where my folder is located, and click **OK**. You will then see a list of files contained in the folder. Click **Combine & Transform Data** to load the data into Power Query, as shown in *Figure 2.13*:

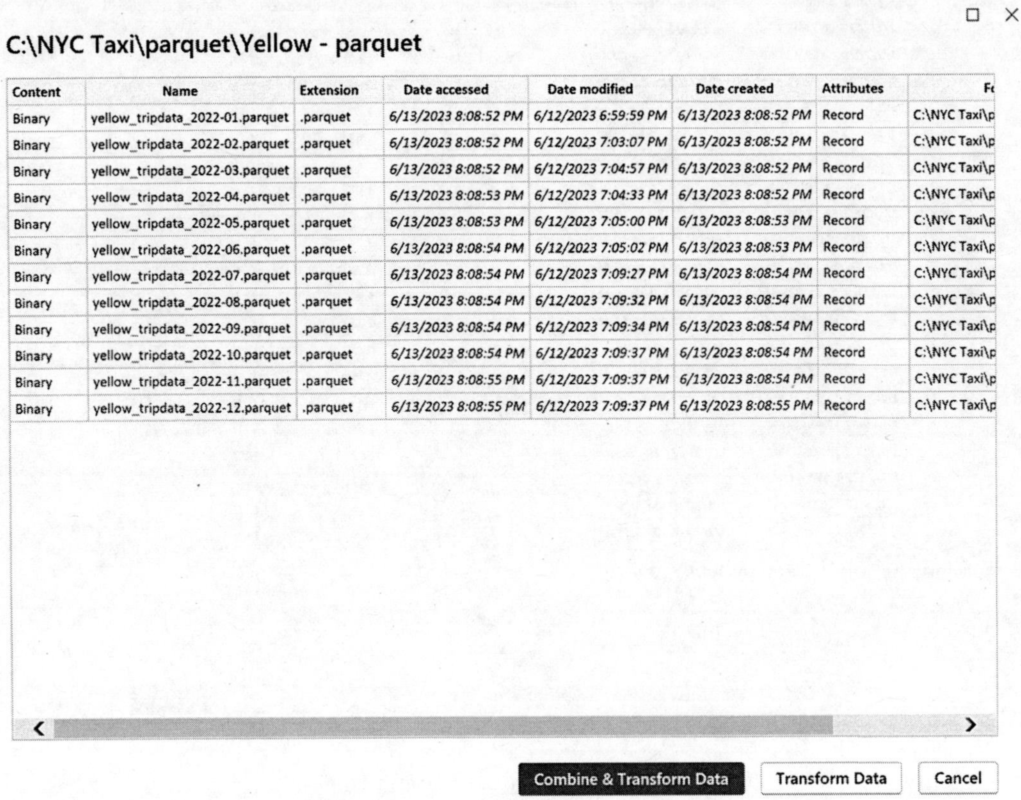

Content	Name	Extension	Date accessed	Date modified	Date created	Attributes	F
Binary	yellow_tripdata_2022-01.parquet	.parquet	6/13/2023 8:08:52 PM	6/12/2023 6:59:59 PM	6/13/2023 8:08:52 PM	Record	C:\NYC Taxi\p
Binary	yellow_tripdata_2022-02.parquet	.parquet	6/13/2023 8:08:52 PM	6/12/2023 7:03:07 PM	6/13/2023 8:08:52 PM	Record	C:\NYC Taxi\p
Binary	yellow_tripdata_2022-03.parquet	.parquet	6/13/2023 8:08:52 PM	6/12/2023 7:04:57 PM	6/13/2023 8:08:52 PM	Record	C:\NYC Taxi\p
Binary	yellow_tripdata_2022-04.parquet	.parquet	6/13/2023 8:08:53 PM	6/12/2023 7:04:33 PM	6/13/2023 8:08:52 PM	Record	C:\NYC Taxi\p
Binary	yellow_tripdata_2022-05.parquet	.parquet	6/13/2023 8:08:53 PM	6/12/2023 7:05:00 PM	6/13/2023 8:08:53 PM	Record	C:\NYC Taxi\p
Binary	yellow_tripdata_2022-06.parquet	.parquet	6/13/2023 8:08:54 PM	6/12/2023 7:05:02 PM	6/13/2023 8:08:53 PM	Record	C:\NYC Taxi\p
Binary	yellow_tripdata_2022-07.parquet	.parquet	6/13/2023 8:08:54 PM	6/12/2023 7:09:27 PM	6/13/2023 8:08:54 PM	Record	C:\NYC Taxi\p
Binary	yellow_tripdata_2022-08.parquet	.parquet	6/13/2023 8:08:54 PM	6/12/2023 7:09:32 PM	6/13/2023 8:08:54 PM	Record	C:\NYC Taxi\p
Binary	yellow_tripdata_2022-09.parquet	.parquet	6/13/2023 8:08:54 PM	6/12/2023 7:09:34 PM	6/13/2023 8:08:54 PM	Record	C:\NYC Taxi\p
Binary	yellow_tripdata_2022-10.parquet	.parquet	6/13/2023 8:08:54 PM	6/12/2023 7:09:37 PM	6/13/2023 8:08:54 PM	Record	C:\NYC Taxi\p
Binary	yellow_tripdata_2022-11.parquet	.parquet	6/13/2023 8:08:55 PM	6/12/2023 7:09:37 PM	6/13/2023 8:08:54 PM	Record	C:\NYC Taxi\p
Binary	yellow_tripdata_2022-12.parquet	.parquet	6/13/2023 8:08:55 PM	6/12/2023 7:09:37 PM	6/13/2023 8:08:55 PM	Record	C:\NYC Taxi\p

Figure 2.13: *Loading data contained inside a folder into Power Query*

You will then see a sample of your data. Assuming it looks correct, click **OK** to continue, as shown in *Figure 2.14*:

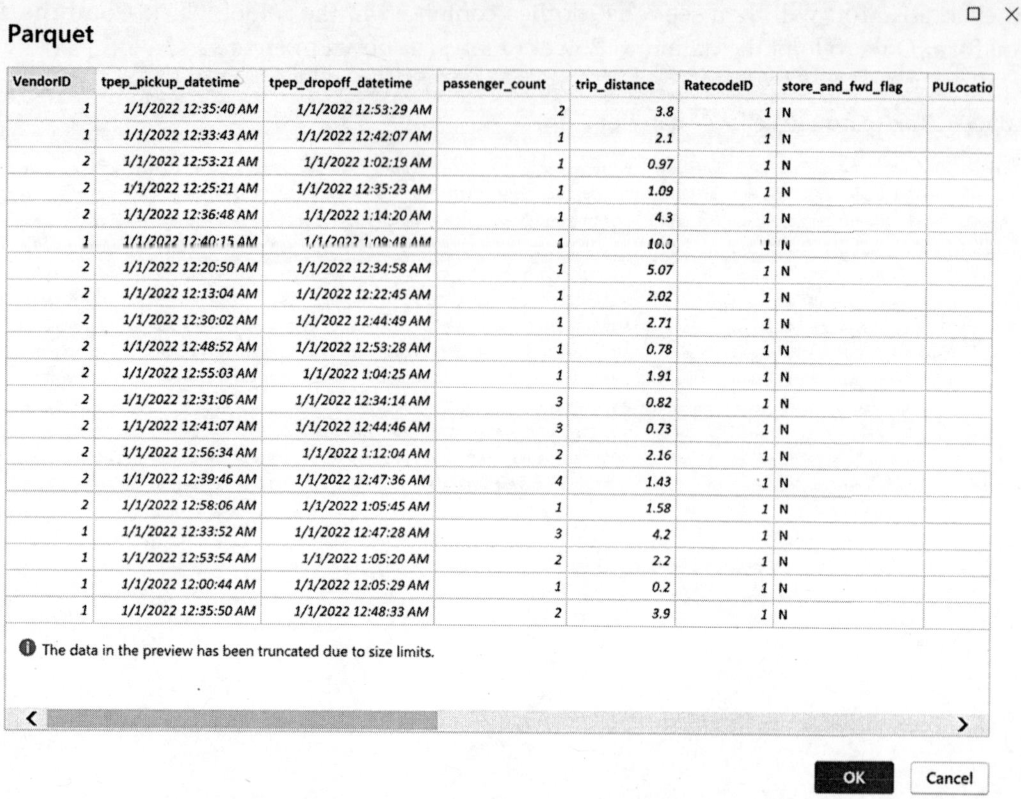

Parquet

VendorID	tpep_pickup_datetime	tpep_dropoff_datetime	passenger_count	trip_distance	RatecodeID	store_and_fwd_flag	PULocatio
1	1/1/2022 12:35:40 AM	1/1/2022 12:53:29 AM	2	3.8	1	N	
1	1/1/2022 12:33:43 AM	1/1/2022 12:42:07 AM	1	2.1	1	N	
2	1/1/2022 12:53:21 AM	1/1/2022 1:02:19 AM	1	0.97	1	N	
2	1/1/2022 12:25:21 AM	1/1/2022 12:35:23 AM	1	1.09	1	N	
2	1/1/2022 12:36:48 AM	1/1/2022 1:14:20 AM	1	4.3	1	N	
1	1/1/2022 12:40:15 AM	1/1/2022 1:09:48 AM	1	10.0	1	N	
2	1/1/2022 12:20:50 AM	1/1/2022 12:34:58 AM	1	5.07	1	N	
2	1/1/2022 12:13:04 AM	1/1/2022 12:22:45 AM	1	2.02	1	N	
2	1/1/2022 12:30:02 AM	1/1/2022 12:44:49 AM	1	2.71	1	N	
2	1/1/2022 12:48:52 AM	1/1/2022 12:53:28 AM	1	0.78	1	N	
2	1/1/2022 12:55:03 AM	1/1/2022 1:04:25 AM	1	1.91	1	N	
2	1/1/2022 12:31:06 AM	1/1/2022 12:34:14 AM	3	0.82	1	N	
2	1/1/2022 12:41:07 AM	1/1/2022 12:44:46 AM	3	0.73	1	N	
2	1/1/2022 12:56:34 AM	1/1/2022 1:12:04 AM	2	2.16	1	N	
2	1/1/2022 12:39:46 AM	1/1/2022 12:47:36 AM	4	1.43	1	N	
2	1/1/2022 12:58:06 AM	1/1/2022 1:05:45 AM	1	1.58	1	N	
1	1/1/2022 12:33:52 AM	1/1/2022 12:47:28 AM	3	4.2	1	N	
1	1/1/2022 12:53:54 AM	1/1/2022 1:05:20 AM	2	2.2	1	N	
1	1/1/2022 12:00:44 AM	1/1/2022 12:05:29 AM	1	0.2	1	N	
1	1/1/2022 12:35:50 AM	1/1/2022 12:48:33 AM	2	3.9	1	N	

The data in the preview has been truncated due to size limits.

OK Cancel

Figure 2.14: Sample of data found inside your folder

Once you click **OK**, your data will load into Power Query. Unlike the other sources we have utilized, this connector adds more to our queries window on the left-hand side. You will see our data under **Other Queries**, but there is also a section called **Transform File** from your query name. This is where the magic happens. In this section, a series of helper queries perform the transformation and combine your content into a single query. We will learn more about manipulating these queries in *Chapter 16, Manipulating Supporting Queries*. Until then, we will use files with the same structure to avoid confusion. In the following figure, you can see how the files have unified into a single table in addition to the helper queries on the left side of the screen:

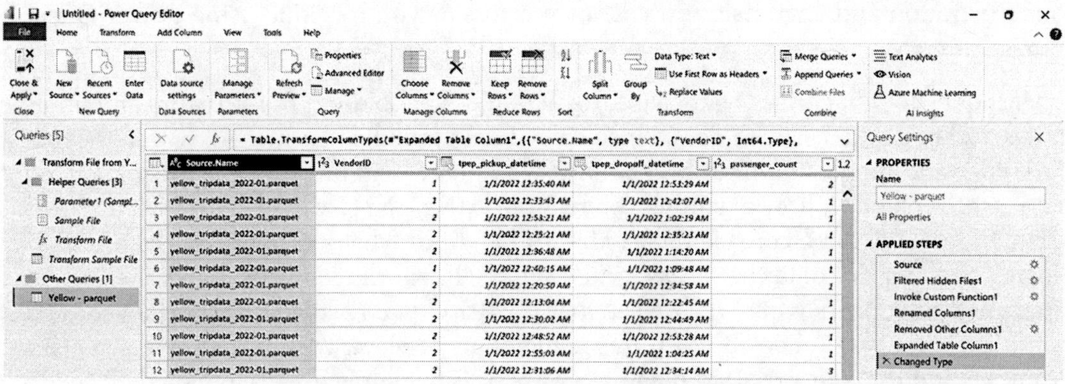

***Figure 2.15**: Combined data loaded into Power Query with the folder connector*

You can go up to the source step on the right-hand side and see what files are included in the current query. If you remember from *Figure 2.12*, the folder we used only had twelve files in it. For the year 2022, there was a file available for each month. If we want to add three new files for the first three months of 2023, we just need to add them and click **Refresh** to add them to the query, as the following figure demonstrates:

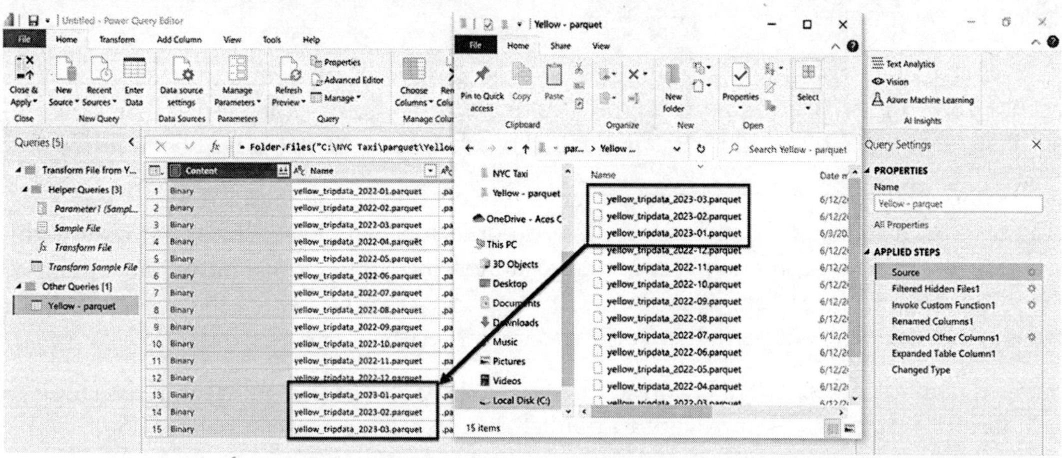

***Figure 2.16**: Adding new data to a folder and having it appear in Power Query*

A common question frequently asked is what file formats can be used with the folder connector. In this example, we used a parquet file. However, you can also use Excel workbook, CSV, JSON, and XML files. You cannot mix and match them, but you are set if they are the same file type.

Another common question that is asked after learning about this connector is if this can all be performed manually inside the advanced editor. Yes, you can use the **`Folder.Files()`** function to connect to your data. The problem is that the effort to combine and transform the data is so significant that it is best to just use the graphical interface. This will reduce your frustration and chances of downstream errors as you continue using Power Query in the future.

The last question that arises when working with files in a folder is the structure and limits of files within a folder. The folder connector will only pull the files present within the root of a folder and there is no limit to the number of files it will process. It is recommended that your file names follow a naming convention so they can be easily identified. In *Figure 2.12,* all files have three core elements. First, it identifies what kind of taxi is in use. This allows us to identify data that is associated with yellow or green taxis. Next, the type of data is identified. In *Figure 2.12,* we see that it is trip data. Lastly, we have the year and month the data was collected. With this convention in place, we can selectively replace files if we find that our exported data has errors or is incomplete. This avoids the need to re-export the entire data set, which will save us time if these scenarios ever arise.

Refreshing file-based connections

Before we continue, we must discuss some of the implications when using a file-based connection in Power Query. As mentioned above, solid use cases for leveraging the file connector to bring data into Power Query exist. However, there are some potential challenges you might run into as you move forward.

The first challenge you might encounter is the speed of your refresh might be very slow. Because 100% of the processing is happening on your device, this process can be slow if you have large amounts of data. It is not a deal breaker, but patience might be required.

The second challenge you might encounter is the location of the data source. If you are using Microsoft Excel and sharing the file with other users, you will find that they will receive errors with their refresh because they cannot find your source files. This happens when you do not place them in a centralized location. If you leverage files on your PC, others might not have access to them and will receive errors.

The third challenge you might encounter is the inability to refresh your data in the cloud. If you are using Power BI and want to publish a data model that can be refreshed, you will need the assistance of a data gateway to facilitate the refresh process. This comes at no additional cost but does require you to maintain a device that is always on when the refresh needs to take place. The result is additional management and configuration to ensure the smooth operation of your refresh. While the refresh speed challenge is unavoidable, the location and cloud refresh challenges can be resolved by placing your data in a cloud-based location.

In the next chapter, we will explore how you can connect to your data in Microsoft 365 to simplify your process. We will also explore simplifying our refreshes by leveraging the web connector to eliminate refresh issues with our files.

Conclusion

This chapter covered connecting to an Excel workbook, CSV, JSON, XML, and parquet files with Power Query. We connected to each type using the graphical interface and how to connect to each type with the advanced editor. We also covered combining multiple files of the same format using the folder connector to simplify data management when we refresh our content. Lastly, we reviewed some challenges you might encounter as you leverage file data sources.

In the next chapter, we will explore using web-based data sources with Power Query to connect to data available through Microsoft 365 and APIs.

CHAPTER 3

Connect to Web-Based Data Sources

Introduction

This chapter will walk you through how to connect to web-based data sources with Power Query. Starting with simple connections like SharePoint Lists and tables on websites, you will learn the basics when connecting to web-based data sources. Next, you will learn how to create more advanced connections using the Web and OData connectors to take your queries to the next level. Lastly, you will learn the basics of connecting to data inside Dynamics 365 and the Dataverse.

Structure

In this chapter, we will cover the following topics:

- Connecting to SharePoint lists
- Connecting to website data
- Connecting to web APIs
- Connecting to files in SharePoint
- Connecting to folders in SharePoint
- Connecting to OData sources
- Connecting to Dynamics 365

Objectives

By the end of this chapter, you will understand how to use Power Query to connect to data found on the web and inside SharePoint. You will learn how to connect to these sources using API calls so you can access the most current and up-to-date information available from your sources. In addition, you will learn how to optimize your queries to reduce refresh times. Lastly, you will learn how to use Power Query to connect to your data inside Dynamics 365 so you can create a data model from the Dataverse.

Connecting to SharePoint lists

When it comes to data projects, collecting data can always be a challenge. Excel has frequently been the tool of choice for consolidating lists of information, but in recent years SharePoint Online has become a worthy competitor. After recent reinvestment from Microsoft, SharePoint lists have become a powerful tool for quickly collecting information by providing a mobile-friendly experience on the web and easy integration with Microsoft Power Apps. In lieu of a database, it provides the basic resources required to store information in a tabular format. In *Chapter 2, Connect to File-Based Sources*, we discussed collecting information from Excel workbooks and CSV files. While not always a suitable replacement, sometimes SharePoint Lists can fill that role that connects to Power Query and does so without requiring a data gateway to refresh when you are using SharePoint Online and the Power BI Service.

We will click on the **New Source** dropdown from the Power Query editor window to get started and select **More**. Next, search for **SharePoint** inside the get data window. You will notice that there are two options for lists, **SharePoint List** and **SharePoint Online List**. Most organizations have moved to Microsoft 365, which means the best option is SharePoint Online list. However, if your organization still uses SharePoint on-premises, you can use SharePoint list.

Regardless of where your SharePoint is located, you will be prompted with a box that asks you to enter your site URL for SharePoint. Note that this is not the URL of the list but rather the site's top level. If you are using SharePoint Online, you can use the 2.0 implementation of the connector, which gives you an advanced option. You can choose one of the two options:

- **All**: Retrieve all columns from a SharePoint List.
- **Default**: Retrieve the columns in the **Default View** of a SharePoint List.

If you are using the SharePoint Online List connector, here is what it looks like when you are configuring your query:

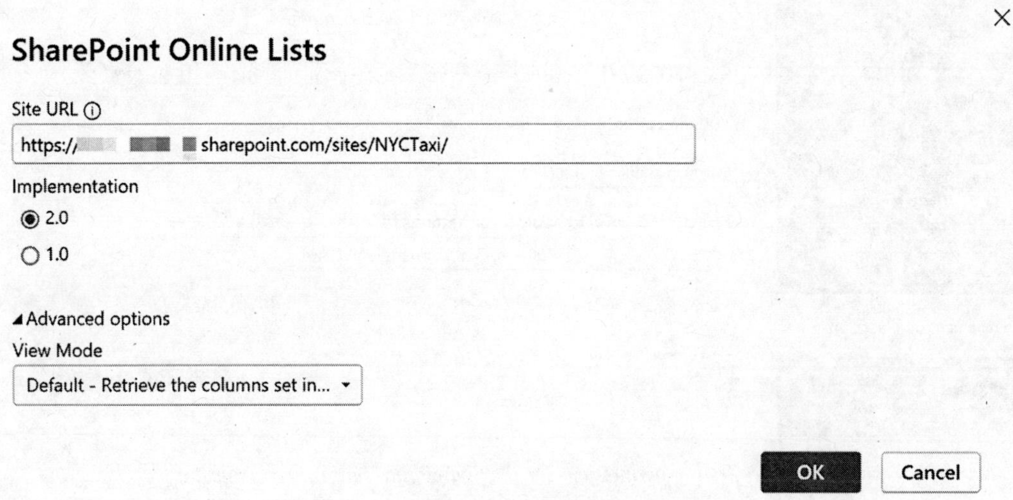

Figure 3.1: *Configuring the SharePoint Online List connector to use the default view mode*

If you have a simple list with no personalized views, we often recommend the default option, as it will help optimize your queries. However, you might also need to use the **All** option if you have columns you need to retrieve that are hidden from the default view. For the sake of this example, we will use the default view mode first, as demonstrated in *Figure 3.1* above.

After we have established the site URL and the view mode, you will be prompted for credentials. We have been presented with three options. The option we need to select for this connection is a Microsoft account, as we are using SharePoint Online. If you are using SharePoint on-premises with the SharePoint list connector, you will need to use your Windows credentials instead and select your current credentials unless you have a service account you can leverage. You can use the anonymous authentication option if your list is shared with no authentication requirements, but this rarely ever happens. With an authentication method selected, you can select the level to which your credentials should be applied. As a best practice, always select the highest-level path, as you can simplify permissions management for the Power BI Service. See the following configuration of the SharePoint Online list permissions:

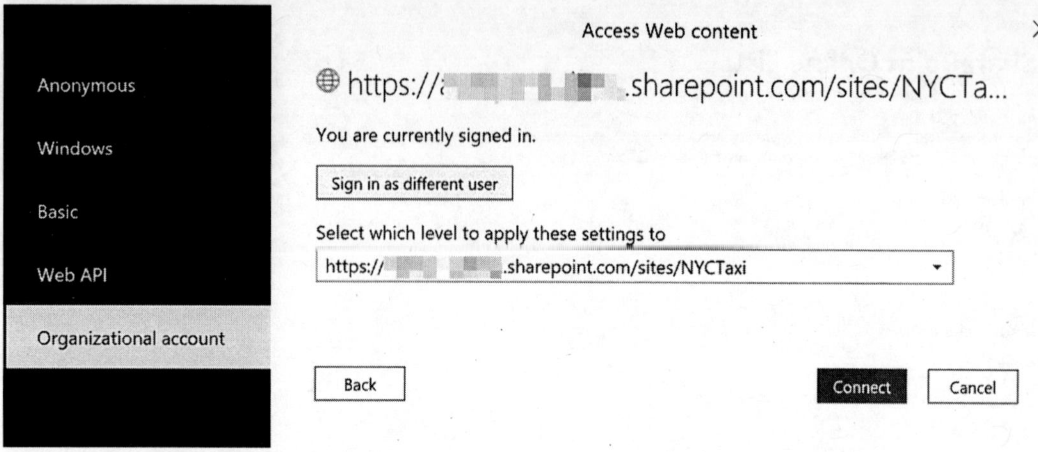

Figure 3.2: Setting permissions for the SharePoint Online List connector

With your authentication set, it is time to select the list on your SharePoint site. Just like the file connectors, we can select a list and preview the data in the navigator pane. Once we have determined which list we want to use, select it with the check box and click **OK**. It is important to note that you do have the ability to pick more than one list at a time if you choose to do so, as shown below:

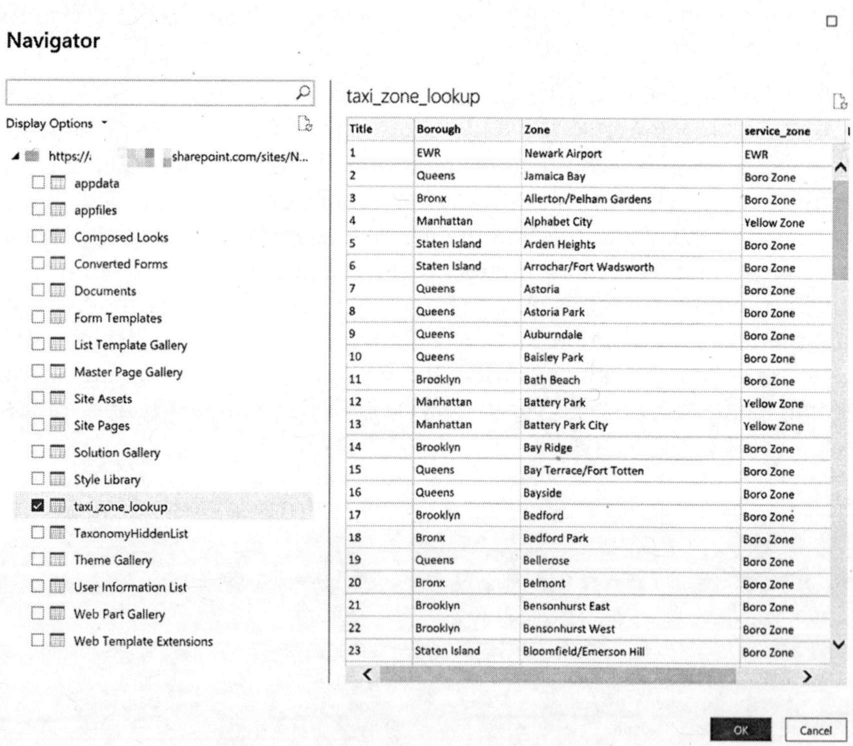

Figure 3.3: Selecting a list from a SharePoint site

After you click **OK**, your list will load into the Power Query editor. In *Figure 3.4*, you will notice that the four columns you selected came in, plus an additional **ID** column. It is merely a coincidence that the taxi zone numbers under the **Title** column match the **ID** column. The **ID** column is reserved by SharePoint and is an index for your list. While you may want to remove it from your list, it is recommended that you keep it as it does not provide much overhead, and it allows you to quickly create a link to a list item when you load your data into your model:

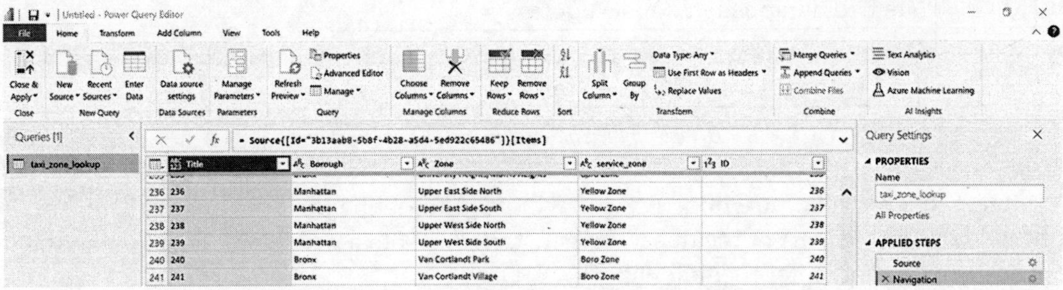

Figure 3.4: SharePoint Online list data using the default view mode

If you are familiar with SharePoint, you know that it tracks who creates and modifies a list item. If you wanted to report when an object was edited and by whom, you might not be able to do it with the default view. If you remember from *Figure 3.1*, we selected the **Default** option, which only brought in the columns we had available in the default view. If you selected all view mode, you would receive all the hidden columns plus any of the columns created by SharePoint to support the list. By bringing in all the columns, this will increase the amount of data being queried. This will result in your refresh slowing down as there is more content included because of the additional columns. Following is a screenshot showing the additional columns that come in with our taxi zone data:

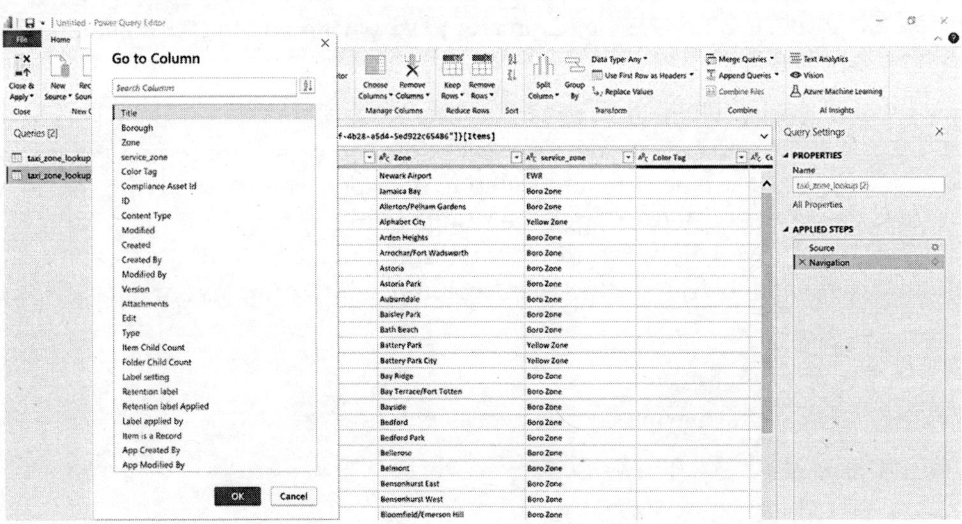

Figure 3.5: SharePoint Online list data using the all-view mode

If you prefer to use the advanced editor to build your query, you can do so using **SharePoint.Tables()** function instead. You will use the same function for SharePoint Online and on-premises applications but must use different parameters to achieve the same goal. Refer to the following table for details:

SharePoint.Tables()	
Parameter	**Description**
`url`	Site URL wrapped in double quotes
`options`	Options wrapped in square brackets to apply options for `ApiVersion`, `Implementation`, and `ViewMode`.

Table 3.1: Table of the SharePoint.Tables() parameters

To connect to a SharePoint Online list, we will need to define the **Implementation** and **ViewMode** options as part of the query. To get started, create a new blank query, open the advanced editor, and enter the following:

```
let
  Source = SharePoint.Tables(
    "https://<tenant>.sharepoint.com/sites/NYCTaxi/",
    [Implementation = "2.0", ViewMode = "Default"]
  )
in
  Source
```

Since we want to specify our view mode, we must specify **Implementation = "2.0"** in our options parameter. We also used the default view option in this example as well. If you want to use all option, just update the parameter to **ViewMode = "All"**, and you will see every column available.

Next, we need to specify which list we want to use. We need to identify the GUID in the Id column that matches our list. We can right-click here and copy it for the next step. Now that we have our list ID, we need to add a step to filter our view down to the source we need. We will create a new step, bring in the results from our first step, and filter it with curly brackets. Lastly, we will return the content from the list by adding a set of square brackets on the end and identifying the **Items** column, which contains our data:

```
let
  Source = SharePoint.Tables(
    "https://<tenant>.sharepoint.com/sites/NYCTaxi/",
    [Implementation = "2.0", ViewMode = "Default"]
  ),
```

```
  ListData = Source{[Id = "3b13aab8-5b8f-4b28-a5d4-5ed922c65486"]}[Items]
in
  ListData
```

If you are using SharePoint on-premises and connecting to a list, simply replace the **`Implementation`** and **`ViewMode`** parameters with **`ApiVersion`** instead:

```
let
  Source = SharePoint.Tables(
    "https://<tenant>.sharepoint.com/sites/NYCTaxi/",
    [ApiVersion = 15]
  ),
  ListData = Source{[Id = "3b13aab8-5b8f-4b28-a5d4-5ed922c65486"]}[Items]
in
  ListData
```

You have the option to select version **`14`**, **`15`**, or **`Auto`** for the **`ApiVersion`** parameter. The default is **`14`**, but non-English SharePoint sites will require version **`15`** to connect. In all reality, unless you run into issues, we recommend using version **`15`** as much as possible.

As you can see, there are only a few nuanced differences between SharePoint Online and SharePoint on-premises when connecting with the list connectors. The biggest hurdle to consider is when using SharePoint on-premises, you will need a data gateway if you wish to refresh your data in the Power BI Service. Otherwise, this solution provides a seamless refreshing experience for all users without having to remap your file location if it moves.

Connecting to website data

It is common for people to find the data they need for a report on a public website. Many find data from government agencies easy, but it sometimes requires a lot of effort to get it into a usable format. In fact, you might remember a time when you spent hours using copy and paste to extract data you found on a website and put it into a spreadsheet just so you could analyze it. Well, you are certainly not alone in this struggle. The good news is Power Query has a way to lift this information off a website with a few simple clicks using the web connector.

You will learn as we continue to go through this chapter that the web connector is very versatile and does a fantastic job at lifting web-based data. However, many do not know how simple it can be to use its core components. To get started, click on the new source drop-down in the Power Query editor and select **Web**. From there, copy and paste the URL from an existing website, put it into the URL field, and click **OK**. Next, you will be prompted for credentials. Since we are starting with a publicly available website, we can leave anonymous selected and click **Connect**. This will open the navigator pane so we can select our data from a website, as shown:

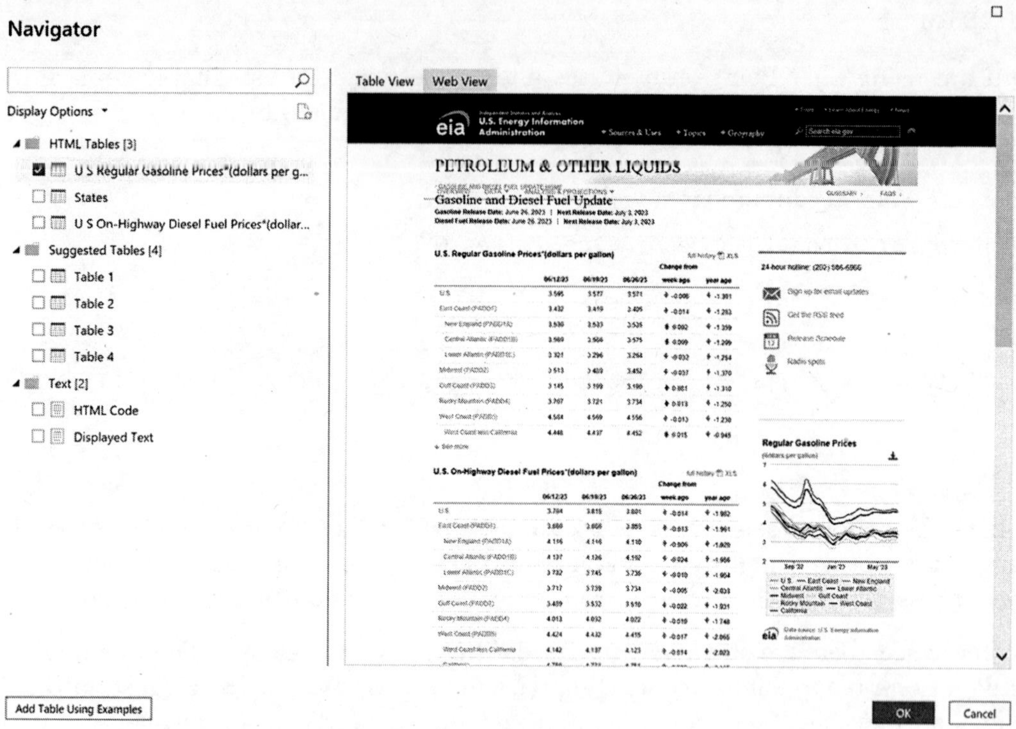

Figure 3.6: Selecting tables with the help of the Web View

Like every other data source, we are now prompted with the ability to select our tables from a website. The web connector allows us to select existing HTML tables on a website but also provides some suggestions. What is convenient is the ability to use the web view to quickly see the website, which can help ensure you pick the right data. Once you have your table selected, just click **OK** to load it to Power Query.

We can use the advanced editor paired with `Web.BrowserContents()` to achieve the same goal. To get started, we will wrap the URL with this new function. The result of this query will be the underlying HTML code for the site:

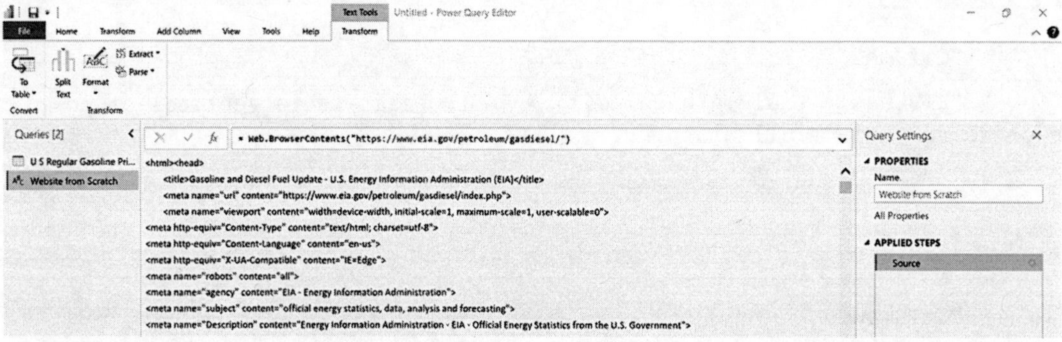

Figure 3.7: *Results from the Web.BrowserContents() function*

While we only needed the URL parameter to complete this connection, there are options available for this function. If required, you can specify the name for an API Key if your site requires it for authentication. You also can specify the conditions to wait for with your query. The connector always waits for the page to load, but you could also wait for a time-out to take place. You can also specify it to wait for a specific CSS selector to exist before starting the query as outlined below:

`Web.BrowserContents()`	
Parameter	**Description**
`url`	Site URL wrapped in double quotes
`options`	Parameters wrapped in square brackets to apply options for `ApiKeyName` and `WaitFor`

Table 3.2: *Table of the Web.BrowserContents() parameters*

Once you have established your connection to the website, you can use the **`Html.Table()`** function to specify your table on the website and extract the data. This tends to be very messy, as demonstrated by the following code sample:

```
let
  Source = Web.BrowserContents("https://www.eia.gov/petroleum/gasdiesel/"),
  TableFromHTML = Html.Table(
    Source,
    {
      {
        "Column1",
        "DIV.basic-table:nth-child(1) > TABLE.basic-table.vertical-divid-
er-after-col-col-4.full-width...."
      },
```

```
      {
        "Column2",
        "DIV.basic-table:nth-child(1) > TABLE.basic-table.vertical-divid-
er-after-col-col-4.full-width...."
      },
      ...
      {
        "Column6",
        "DIV.basic-table:nth-child(1) > TABLE.basic-table.vertical-divid-
er-after-col-col-4.full-width...."
      }
    },
    [
      RowSelector
        = "DIV.basic-table:nth-child(1) > TABLE.basic-table.vertical-divid-
er-after-col-col-4.full-width...."
    ]
  )
in
  TableFromHTML
```

To simplify the excerpt, portions of the code have been truncated. It is important to understand that coding this with the advanced editor tends not to be a common occurrence due to the complexity. However, you might find yourself having to adjust if your data source changes. It is common for websites to be updated or redesigned, so understanding the underlying code is always helpful. The following table breaks down the elements of the **`Html.Table()`** function so you understand how you can manipulate it in the future:

`Html.Table()`	
Parameter	**Description**
`html`	HTML code found on a website
`columnNameSelectorPairs`	Each column is specified as a list contained within curly brackets. The first value is the column name, while the second value is the designated column from the site. Each column is separated by a comma.
`options`	Parameters wrapped in square brackets to apply options for `ApiKeyName` and `WaitFor`

***Table 3.3:** Table of the Html.Table() parameters*

This simple approach makes connecting to website data much easier than before. If the web connector only performed this function alone, it would be a time saver for many. However, the web connector does not stop there, as it allows us to use API endpoints as well.

Connecting to web APIs

Building upon what we learned in the last section, we can extend our use of the web connector to provide more robust connections to API endpoints. Power Query allows us to connect to different APIs with a little configuration of the connector. As a recommendation, most people struggle early on with APIs in Power Query because they have not taken the time to read the documentation and understand how they are intended to operate. It is advisable that you take a few minutes to learn more about your endpoints before attempting any connection with Power Query.

To get started, we are going to use a simple REST API endpoint to connect to the same SharePoint list we used at the beginning of this chapter. This is an endpoint that is available to us through the Microsoft Graph API. For us to successfully connect to our list, we are going to specify the endpoint, determine the correct content type to return, and leverage our organizational account to authenticate the connection. We first need to create a new web connection from the new source dropdown in the Power Query editor. Before entering any information, we will select the advanced radio button to provide us with some additional components for our connection. We will enter our endpoint URL inside the URL parts field. We will also specify a header of **`Content-Type`** and enter **`application/json`** in the field like so:

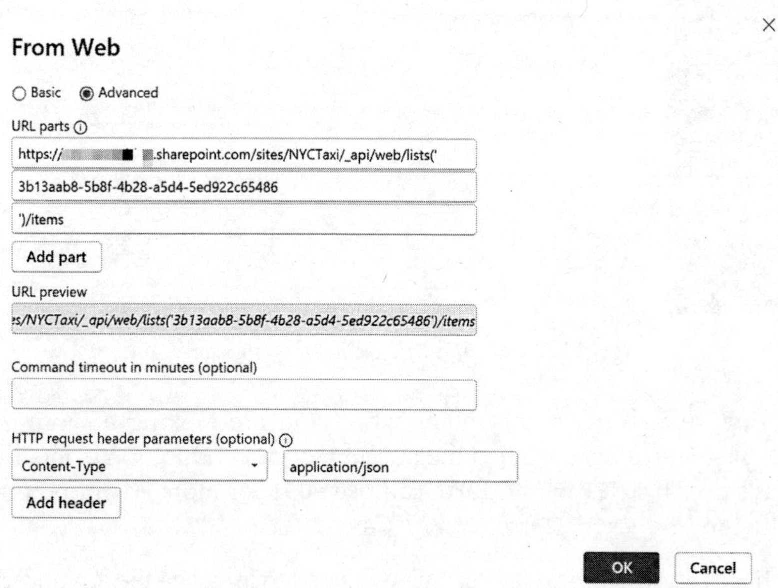

Figure 3.8: *Configuring the web connector for a REST API endpoint*

You will notice a few things about how we entered our data in this window. The first thing is that we split the URL up between three lines. This seems odd but will be easier to explain after we load our data into Power Query. The most important thing to note is how all the URL parts concatenate together in the URL preview field. We have the option to specify a timeout, but it is not required. Lastly, we added our header information in the bottom section. The dropdown allows you to pick from a list of common headers but is by no means an exhaustive list. If your header does not appear in the list, then you can type it in on the left box, followed by entering the appropriate value in the right box. You can add as many headers as required. Once all the components of your connection have been added, you can click **OK**.

Next, we will be prompted for authentication information. There are five authentication methods that appear to us that we can select. Because we are using SharePoint Online, we will use our organizational account from Microsoft to authenticate. However, the other options might still be valid, depending on your API documentation. We often use Anonymous connections when we are passing an API key through the header information found on the previous screen. We use Windows authentication when connecting to an API that is part of an on-premises environment. If you are connecting to a third-party service that has a unique username and password, you will use Basic. Lastly, if you receive an API key for authentication, the web API authentication might be the right choice for you if it is not a part of the URL string or the header. Regardless of your authentication method, click **Connect** after you enter your credentials:

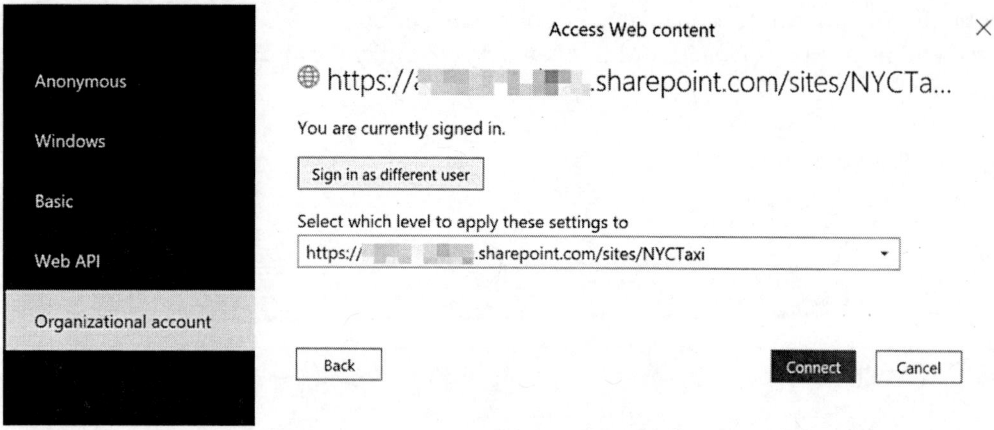

Figure 3.9: *Authentication for the web connector*

It is worth noting something at this point when you are looking at your REST API connection – we never actually specified the method for our endpoint. By default, the web connector always uses the **GET** method. We can use **POST** for more advanced queries, but we will cover that in *Chapter 15, Advanced Web Connections*.

While the graphical interface is nice to use, we will need to leverage the advanced editor to get the most out of this connector. While web connections are useful, they are known to be a little on the slow side. It is important that you optimize your queries as much as possible by filtering out unnecessary columns and rows to speed up your refresh. To accomplish this goal, you will need to use the available parameters within the **`Web.Contents()`** function:

`Web.Contents()`	
Parameter	**Description**
`url`	Site URL wrapped in double quotes
`options`	Parameters wrapped in square brackets to apply options for your query, which include `Query`, `ApiKeyName`, `Headers`, `Timeout`, `ExcludedFromCacheKey`, `ManualStatusHandling`, `RelativePath`, and `Content`

Table 3.4: *Table of the Web.Contents() parameters*

The **`Web.Contents()`** function contains eight options. You will not need every single one each time, but they will be critical for some of your more advanced connections. For example, to achieve the same result as we did above, we will use the following code:

```
let
  Source = Web.Contents(
    "https://<tenant>.sharepoint.com/sites/NYCTaxi/_api/web/lists('"
      & "3b13aab8-5b8f-4b28-a5d4-5ed922c65486"
      & "')/items",
    [Headers = [#"Content=Type" = "application/json"]]
  )
in
  Source
```

In the first parameter, we have specified our URL in three separate parts. Note the ampersands (**&**) concatenating the three parts together. To define our options parameter, we start by setting up a set of square brackets, which will contain all our option values listed in *Table 3.4*. In this case, we only have one set of options to add, which is our header values.

But now we are going to make a change to this code. What if we only wanted to bring back data within the last thirty days? We can apply a filter to our query by manually setting a date, but we want it to be dynamic. We can add a step before our source query and capture the current date and subtract 30 days from it. Once we have that, we can add it to our API endpoint to filter our data like this:

```
let
  FilterDate = DateTime.Date(Date.AddDays(DateTime.LocalNow(), - 30)),
  Source = Web.Contents(
```

```
    "https://<tenant>.sharepoint.com/sites/NYCTaxi/_api/web/lists('"
      & "3b13aab8-5b8f-4b28-a5d4-5ed922c65486"
      & "')/items?$filter=Created ge " & Date.ToText(FilterDate),
    [Headers = [#"Content-Type" = "application/json"]]
  )
in
  Source
```

In short, we have provided a dynamic date filter for our query. If you do this in Power Query, you will not have any issues getting your refresh to work. However, if you are using the Power BI Service, you will never be able to get the refresh to work. The reason is that the connection string keeps changing, and the Power BI Service automatically blocks you from refreshing your data. So how do you resolve this? The answer lies within the **RelativePath** option. This option will allow you to specify the core of your endpoint URL, which will be static, while giving you the ability to create a dynamic query. To make this work, we will simply lift the filter portion of the URL and place it into the options parameter like this:

```
let
  FilterDate = DateTime.Date(Date.AddDays(DateTime.LocalNow(), - 30)),
  Source = Web.Contents(
    "https:// <tenant>.sharepoint.com/sites/NYCTaxi/_api/web/lists('"
      & "3b13aab8-5b8f-4b28-a5d4-5ed922c65486"
      & "')/items",
    [
      RelativePath = "?$filter=Created ge " & Date.ToText(FilterDate),
      Headers = [#"Content-Type" = "application/json"]
    ]
  )
in
  Source
```

This is a subtle change, but by using the **RelativePath** option, we have eliminated any ambiguity with the connection string and made it into a sustainable query. As a best practice, always use the **ReltativePath** option when providing any dynamic data to your connection string. It takes an extra five minutes to configure, but it saves a lifetime of headaches if you decide to publish your content to the Power BI Service.

Some other options that you might find helpful include:

- `Query`: Provides the ability to add query parameters without the need to provide escape characters to avoid errors with your endpoint URLs.
- `ApiKeyName`: If using a key for authentication, you can specify the name of the key with this option. It will pair with the key from the authentication screen.
- `Timeout`: Specifies the duration before the query times out. The default value for this option is 100 seconds.
- `ManualStatusHandling`: This option allows you to provide a list of status codes that you can handle based on the response from the endpoint.
- `Content`: If your endpoint has a message body, the contents of that body go in this option. It will also turn your `GET` method request into a `POST` method request. We will cover this further in *Chapter 15, Advanced Web Connections*.

It is important to note that each web API has its own quirks and challenges. Using these options allows you to manipulate your requests to achieve your goals. As mentioned earlier in this section, it is important that you take the time to read your documentation and understand it. Once you have a clear understanding, plug what you have read into these different options to achieve your goals. If you are running into issues, take your time and verify that your information is correct with a tool like Postman. Power Query does a poor job of surfacing the details of errors from endpoints, and your issue might be something more complex. Lastly, the web connector is designed to work with all diverse types of web-based APIs and is not the REST API we used in this scenario.

Connecting to files in SharePoint

In *Chapter 2, Connect to File-Based Data Sources*, you will remember there was an inherited flaw when it came to refreshing data from file sources. Notably, if you passed your Excel or Power BI Desktop around, the refresh would not work anymore. In addition, if you are using the Power BI Service, you might need to add a data gateway to access your files. These challenges are eliminated when you use the web connector to access files stored in SharePoint.

The easiest way to find the link you need is to open the file in the desktop version of the application. Once you have opened the file, you can go to the file tab, click on info, and select copy path. This will provide you with a pure link to your file. Do not use the copy link function from SharePoint, as it creates a share link that is different than the link we need for this scenario. From there, create a new source with the web connection and paste the link into the window. Once there, delete the `?web=1` that is at the end of the path. This will prevent you from accessing your file. Once in place, click **OK**. If you are prompted for credentials, use your organizational account to sign into SharePoint Online.

The next steps are just the same as what you learned about when you connected to your file in Power Query. Since we are using a Microsoft Excel file, we will follow the steps and best practices for Excel by selecting a table instead of a spreadsheet:

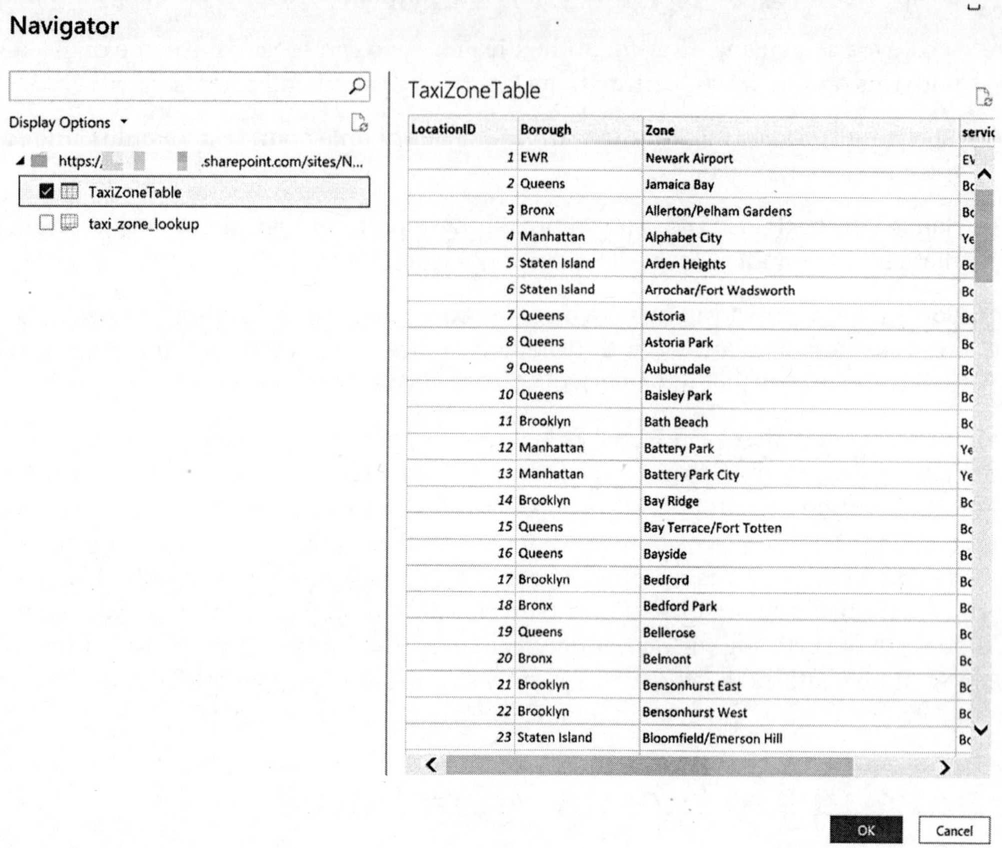

Figure 3.10: *Connecting to a Microsoft Excel file in SharePoint is just like connecting to a file on your device*

It seems like it should be harder than that, but it is quite simple. To make life better, it is just as easy to do the same thing with the advanced editor window. We start by simply calling the file with the **`Web.Contents()`** function and then wrapping that with the **`Excel.Workbook()`** function:

```
let
  Source = Excel.Workbook(
    Web.Contents(
      "https://<tenant>.sharepoint.com/sites/NYCTaxi/Shared%20Documents
/Taxi%20Data/taxi_zone_lookup.xlsx"
    ),
    null,
```

```
    true
  )
in
  Source
```

Once we have our connection set, we just need to identify our entity name and type and bring back the associated data:

```
let
  Source = Excel.Workbook(
    Web.Contents(
      "https://<tenant>.sharepoint.com/sites/NYCTaxi/Shared%20Documents
/Taxi%20Data/taxi_zone_lookup.xlsx"
    ),
    null,
    true
  ),
  ExcelData = Source{[Item = "TaxiZoneTable", Kind = "Table"]}[Data]
in
  ExcelData
```

It is important to provide some guidance on this. First, the user who wants to refresh the query using this file must have access to it. Often people forget to share the source content with the consumer, and it results in errors. Make sure you manage this before sharing your file. Second, we went through these steps with SharePoint, but you can access files from OneDrive and Teams as well. Just follow the same steps to acquire the link, and lastly, this example used an Excel workbook. And while that might be the most common use case, you can perform the same steps with CSV, XML, and JSON files. You will just need to make some adjustments to your query to use the appropriate function to extract the data from the file.

Connecting to folders in SharePoint

The first question that people ask after they have connected to a file in SharePoint is if they can connect to a whole folder. Naturally, that is a great next question. For many, a folder of data is a great solution. An example where this might be useful is if you receive an export on a regular cadence, such as daily, weekly, or monthly through email. If you are just getting new data, you could leverage Power Automate to move the attachment into your folder, so you always have the most current data ready for a refresh. Even better yet, if you are using the Power BI Service, that refresh is automated, which allows you to have fresh data always ready to go without any effort on your part.

Instead of using the Web API to connect to our files, we are going to use a different connector. For this connection, we will use the SharePoint Folder connector to grab documents from our library. To get started, go to **New Sources**, and click more in the **Power Query** editor. From there, search for the **SharePoint Folder** and select it. Next, paste your site URL into the field and click **OK**. Next, you will be asked to enter your credentials. Since we are using SharePoint Online, we will use our Microsoft account and sign in just as we did with the SharePoint List connector. You will then view a screen that shows the files in your shared documents library. Because it is bringing in all documents together regardless of folder structure, click **Transform Data** to continue:

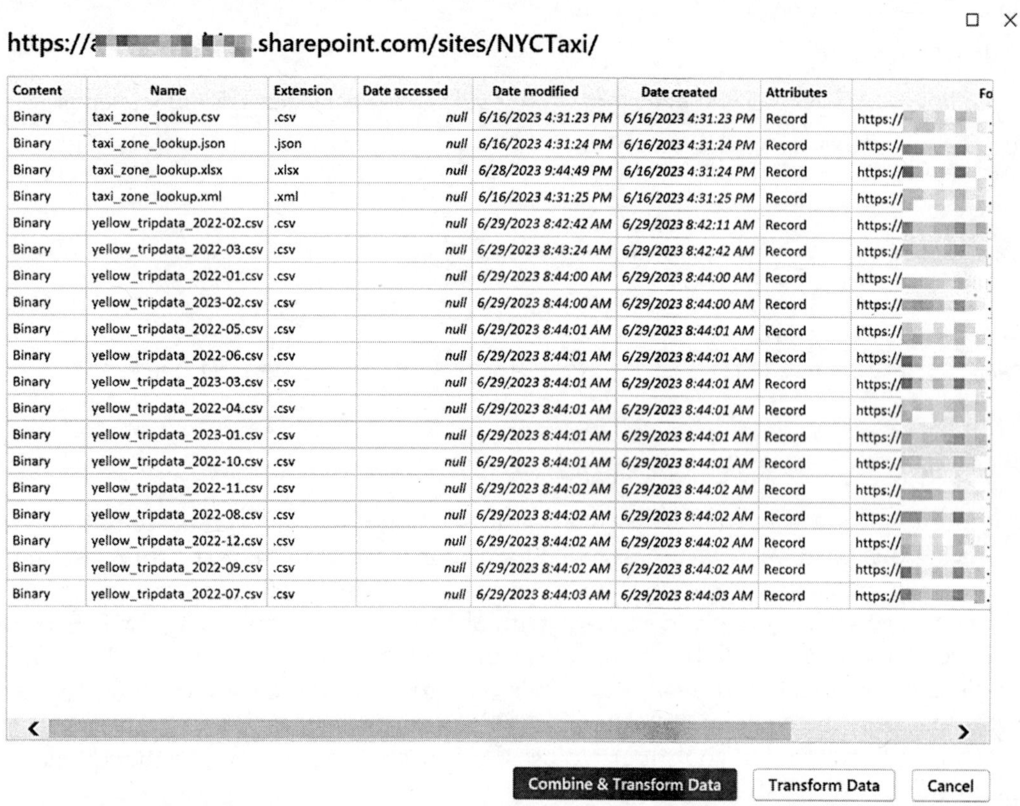

https://[illegible].sharepoint.com/sites/NYCTaxi/

Content	Name	Extension	Date accessed	Date modified	Date created	Attributes	Fo
Binary	taxi_zone_lookup.csv	.csv	null	6/16/2023 4:31:23 PM	6/16/2023 4:31:23 PM	Record	https://
Binary	taxi_zone_lookup.json	.json	null	6/16/2023 4:31:24 PM	6/16/2023 4:31:24 PM	Record	https://
Binary	taxi_zone_lookup.xlsx	.xlsx	null	6/28/2023 9:44:49 PM	6/16/2023 4:31:24 PM	Record	https://
Binary	taxi_zone_lookup.xml	.xml	null	6/16/2023 4:31:25 PM	6/16/2023 4:31:25 PM	Record	https://
Binary	yellow_tripdata_2022-02.csv	.csv	null	6/29/2023 8:42:42 AM	6/29/2023 8:42:11 AM	Record	https://
Binary	yellow_tripdata_2022-03.csv	.csv	null	6/29/2023 8:43:24 AM	6/29/2023 8:42:42 AM	Record	https://
Binary	yellow_tripdata_2022-01.csv	.csv	null	6/29/2023 8:44:00 AM	6/29/2023 8:44:00 AM	Record	https://
Binary	yellow_tripdata_2023-02.csv	.csv	null	6/29/2023 8:44:00 AM	6/29/2023 8:44:00 AM	Record	https://
Binary	yellow_tripdata_2022-05.csv	.csv	null	6/29/2023 8:44:01 AM	6/29/2023 8:44:01 AM	Record	https://
Binary	yellow_tripdata_2022-06.csv	.csv	null	6/29/2023 8:44:01 AM	6/29/2023 8:44:01 AM	Record	https://
Binary	yellow_tripdata_2023-03.csv	.csv	null	6/29/2023 8:44:01 AM	6/29/2023 8:44:01 AM	Record	https://
Binary	yellow_tripdata_2022-04.csv	.csv	null	6/29/2023 8:44:01 AM	6/29/2023 8:44:01 AM	Record	https://
Binary	yellow_tripdata_2023-01.csv	.csv	null	6/29/2023 8:44:01 AM	6/29/2023 8:44:01 AM	Record	https://
Binary	yellow_tripdata_2022-10.csv	.csv	null	6/29/2023 8:44:01 AM	6/29/2023 8:44:01 AM	Record	https://
Binary	yellow_tripdata_2022-11.csv	.csv	null	6/29/2023 8:44:02 AM	6/29/2023 8:44:02 AM	Record	https://
Binary	yellow_tripdata_2022-08.csv	.csv	null	6/29/2023 8:44:02 AM	6/29/2023 8:44:02 AM	Record	https://
Binary	yellow_tripdata_2022-12.csv	.csv	null	6/29/2023 8:44:02 AM	6/29/2023 8:44:02 AM	Record	https://
Binary	yellow_tripdata_2022-09.csv	.csv	null	6/29/2023 8:44:02 AM	6/29/2023 8:44:02 AM	Record	https://
Binary	yellow_tripdata_2022-07.csv	.csv	null	6/29/2023 8:44:03 AM	6/29/2023 8:44:03 AM	Record	https://

Combine & Transform Data | Transform Data | Cancel

***Figure 3.11:** Reviewing files before transformation with the SharePoint Folders connector*

Our next step requires us to filter out the files that do not belong in our query. If you look at *Figure 3.11*, you will notice the first four files do not really belong to what we are doing. To resolve that, we will filter them out. We will discuss filtering at length in *Chapter 8, Cleansing Data*. Until then, we will simply use a filter on the folder path column to clean up our list. Once the list of files is whittled down, we can click on the drill-down button on the upper right-hand corner of the content column to combine our files into a single table. It is hard to see but the arrow in the following image shows you where the drill-down button is located:

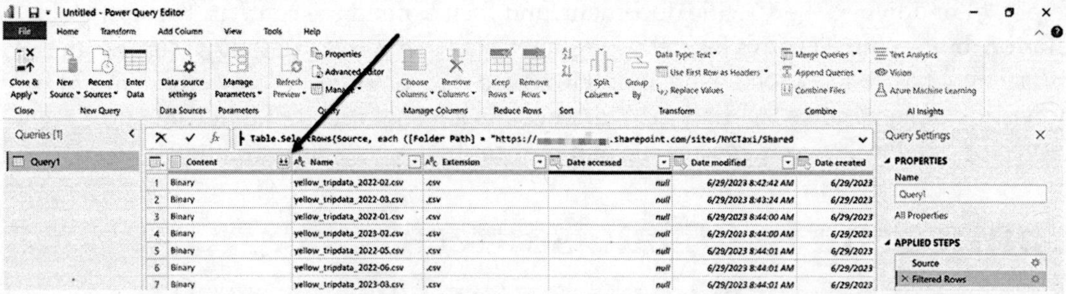

Figure 3.12: Combining content into a single table

This will now create the helper queries we saw back in *Chapter 2, Connect to File-Based Data Sources,* when we used the folder connector.

If you would like to connect to the data source with the advanced editor, the process is simple. We will use the **`SharePoint.Files()`** function to connect to our site as outlined below:

`SharePoint.Files()`	
Parameter	**Description**
`url`	Site URL wrapped in double quotes
`options`	Parameters wrapped in square brackets to apply options. The only current option available is `ApiVersion`. Version 15 is recommended, but version 14 might be required. You can also use `Auto` if you are not sure.

Table 3.5: *Table of the SharePoint.Files() parameters*

Here is the basic code required to access a SharePoint document library:

```
let
  Source = SharePoint.Files(
    "https://<tenant>.sharepoint.com/sites/NYCTaxi/",
    [ApiVersion = 15]
  )
in
  Source
```

Just as we discussed with the folder connector, the code required to combine all the files together into a single query is quite extensive and requires considerable effort. We recommended that you leverage the graphical interface to achieve this result to reduce the time required to implement and the frustration associated with the coding.

After going through these steps, you might be wondering why we did not use this connector to grab an individual file. It is possible to bring in the files inside a document library, filter down to the specific document, and then expand the content. This is a viable solution, but we must always keep the long-term plan in mind. As of today, this document library only has sixteen documents in it. However, if it continues to grow, there might be thousands of documents to bring in all at once. As a result, it is best to leverage the web connector as it targets your specific file and reduces the overall effort to query your data.

Connecting to OData sources

The **Open Data Protocol** (**OData**) connector with Power Query will be reminiscent of using the Web connector we explored earlier in this chapter. In fact, as we go through this section, you might ask yourself why they are even different connectors. It is designed for REST APIs. Because of this, the OData connector will help us with query folding. We will discuss query folding in *Chapter 4, Connect to Database Sources*, in greater detail. However, for now, just understand that it can help us optimize our queries.

In this scenario, we are going to replicate our connection to our SharePoint list but use the OData connector instead. To get started, go to the new source in the Power Query editor and select OData feed. We can expand the advanced options and see that we can split up our URL and preview the entire string in the URL preview window. We have the option to include open-type columns. These columns allow you to use more dynamic content, which allows for more flexibility. We do not need them with SharePoint, so we will leave the box unchecked:

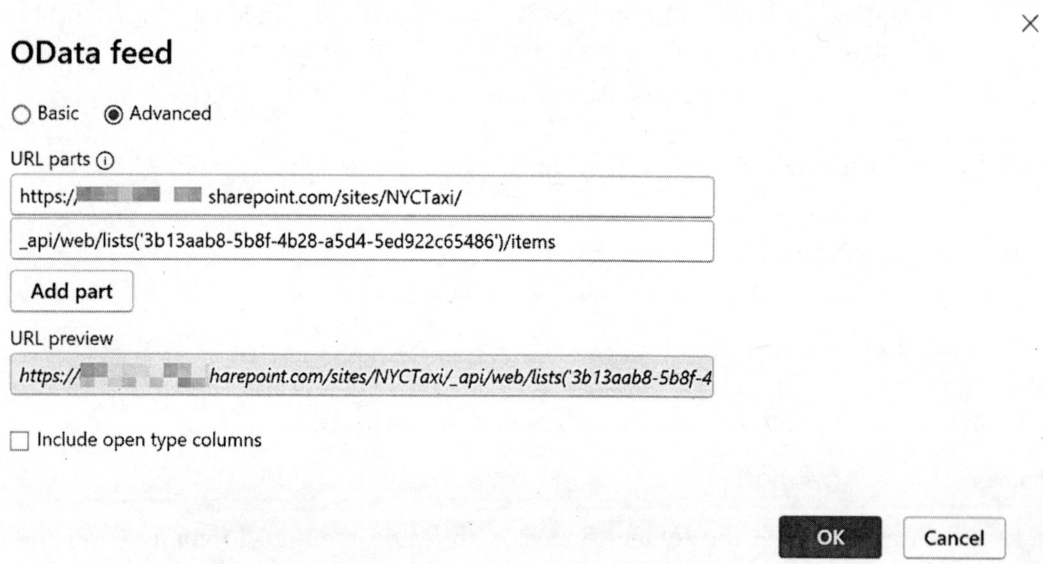

Figure 3.13: Setting up the OData feed connector

After we click **OK**, we will be prompted with a window identical to *Figure 3.8* and will use our organizational account to authenticate since we are using a SharePoint list. We will receive a preview of our data and click **OK** to load it into Power Query. When you look at the data in Power Query, you will notice the extra columns that our query imports at the same time:

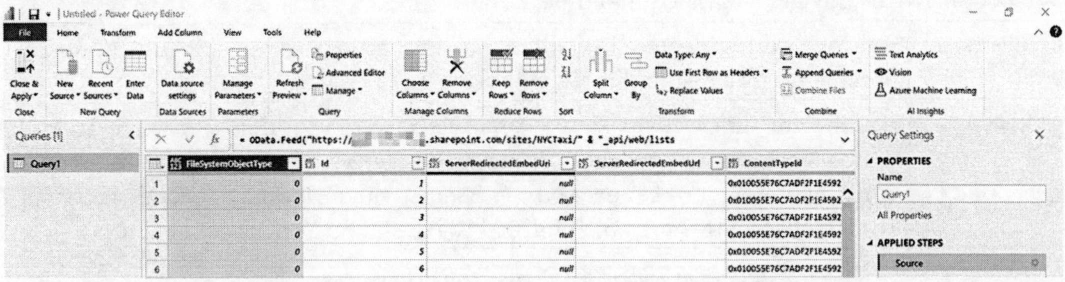

***Figure 3.14:** Data imported with the OData feed connector*

We can clean this up by adding query options to our endpoint URL. OData has five primary types of query options you will find available. They are select, expand, filter, order by, top, and skip. Each query option is activated with a **$** and added to the end of your URL. In our situation, we want to limit the number of fields we need to bring into Power Query. Instead of using the graphical interface, we can easily write this up with the advanced editor:

```
let
  Source = OData.Feed(
    "https://<tenant>.sharepoint.com/sites/NYCTaxi/_api/web/
    lists('3b13aab8-5b8f-4b28-a5d4-5ed922c65486')
    /items?$select=Title,Borough,Zone,service_zone",
    null,
    [Implementation = "2.0"]
  )
in
  Source
```

We simply put in our field names that matched our view, and it eliminated the extra columns and optimized our query. Note that field names are case-sensitive. You will also note that the **`OData.Feed()`** function has a total of three parameters available:

OData.Feed()	
Parameter	**Description**
`serviceUri`	Service URL wrapped in double quotes
`headers`	Set for header values, but often headers are placed inside the options parameter. As a result, this value is set to **`null`**.
`options`	Parameters wrapped in square brackets to apply options for your query which include `Query`, `ApiKeyName`, `Headers`, `Timeout`, `EnableBatch`, `Concurrent`, `ODataVersion`, `FunctionOverloads`, `MoreColumns`, `IncludeMetadataAnnocations`, `OmitValues`, and `Implementation`.

Table 3.6: *Table of the OData.Feed() parameters*

You will note that the **`Implementation`** option was added to our code to specify which version of the OData connector to use. There are only two options, **`2.0`** or **`null`**. As a general guideline, you should always select **`2.0`** unless you run into any errors.

Additional options for the **`OData.Feed()`** that you might find helpful include:

- **`Query`**: Provides the ability to add query parameters without the need to provide escape characters to avoid errors with your endpoint URLs as well as provides dynamic content.
- **`Headers`**: Specified values required to complete the request. Headers are listed inside square brackets, and each one is separated by a comma.
- **`ApiKeyName`**: If using a key for authentication, you can specify the name of the key with this option. It will pair with the key from the authentication screen.
- **`Timeout`**: Specifies the duration before the query times out. The default value for this option is 600 seconds.
- **`EnableBatch`**: A true/false option that enables the generation of a batch request in the event your **`MaxUriLength`** is exceeded.
- **`MaxUriLength`**: Numeric value that defines the max length of a URI sent to the OData service. If exceeded and **`EnableBatch=true`**, then it will send it to a batch endpoint. The default value for this option is **`2048`**.
- **`Concurrent`**: A true/false option that, when set to true, will allow concurrent requests to be made to the service. When set to false, all requests will be managed sequentially. If not specified, the service will determine which option is best.
- **`ODataVersion`**: Numeric value of 3 or 4 that specifies the OData protocol to use with the service. If not specified, all supported versions are queried, and the preferred version will be selected.

- **`FunctionOverloads`**: a true/false option that manages function import overloads and splits them into separate entries in the navigator when set to true. If set to false, they will be listed as a single union in the navigator. When using OData Version 3, the default is false but is true when using OData Version 4.
- **`MoreColumns`**: A true/false option that adds open type columns under a new column titled **More Columns** when set to true. This option is set to false by default.
- **`IncludeAnnotations`**: A list of qualified term names or patterns with the option to use ***** as a wildcard. By default, no annotations are included.
- **`IncludeMetadataAnnotations`**: A list of qualified term names or patterns to include on the metadata requests with the option to use ***** as a wildcard. By default, it includes any annotations noted in the **`IncludeAnnotations`** option.
- **`OmitValues`**: Prevents the OData service from writing out certain values in response. Use **`ODataOmitValues.Null`** to omit null values.

Just like the web connector, there are many features and options to consider. While similar in function and structure, the question arises about whether you should use the web connector or OData connector. The biggest advantage to using the OData connector over the web connector is the ability to leverage query folding. If you can leverage the OData connector, query folding will optimize your query and allow you to potentially use incremental refresh. We will cover query folding in *Chapter 4, Connect to Database Sources*. However, for your knowledge, it is best to use the OData connector whenever possible. Take the time to read your documentation to ensure you understand what is available and map it appropriately to your query. A little work upfront can save you considerable frustration.

Connecting to Dynamics 365

This last connector, Dynamics 365, is a web service that might not apply to every single reader. If you are not familiar with it, Dynamics 365 is Microsoft's enterprise resource planning tool. Not every organization uses Dynamics, but its core data structure has found its way into the entire Microsoft ecosystem. Dynamics 365 runs on a platform called Dataverse. You might have known it by its former name, the Common Data Service. The Dataverse platform is the base of all Power Platform solutions and is even available in a free format within Microsoft Teams. So, while you may not be part of an organization leveraging Dynamics, you might need Dataverse as a data source for other solutions that have been developed in your ecosystem.

To get started, click on the new sources dropdown, and select more in the Power Query editor. We will search for Dynamics to bring back all the available connectors in the get data window. You will notice in *Figure 3.15* that there are options available. There are specialized connectors for Dynamics products, such as Business Central and Customer Insights. If you are leveraging those products, you can leverage those connectors. However, we want to focus on the first two connectors. The **Dynamics 365 Online (Legacy)** connector is a simple OData feed. If you want to use that connector, simply follow the section on OData sources and connect to your data. However, we want to select **Dynamics 365 (Dataverse)** and connect with that instead. Refer to the following figure:

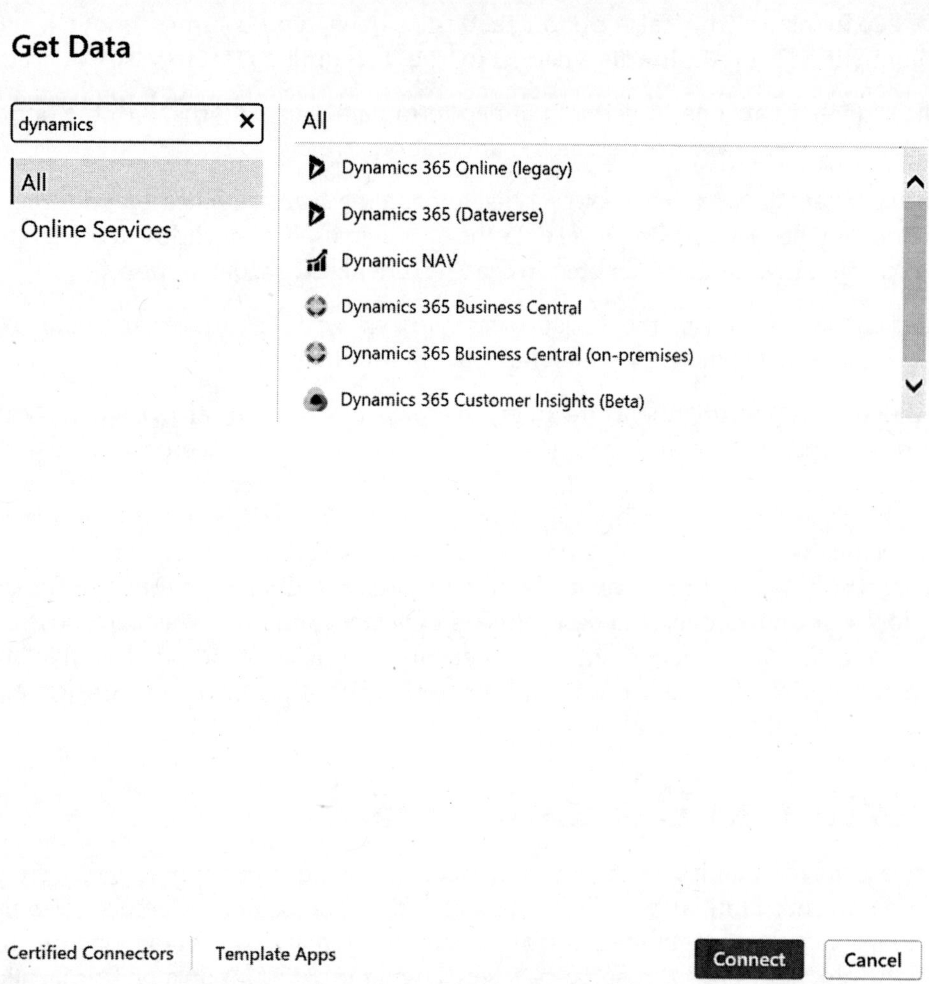

***Figure 3.15:** Finding the right Dynamics 365 Connector*

Once you select your connector, you will need to sign in with your Microsoft account. This is the only option, as Dataverse is a Microsoft-only product. Once you have signed in, you will be able to see all the tables available to you. Navigate to your environment and select the tables you need for your query. If you are having trouble finding it, you can leverage the search at the top of the navigation pane, as shown:

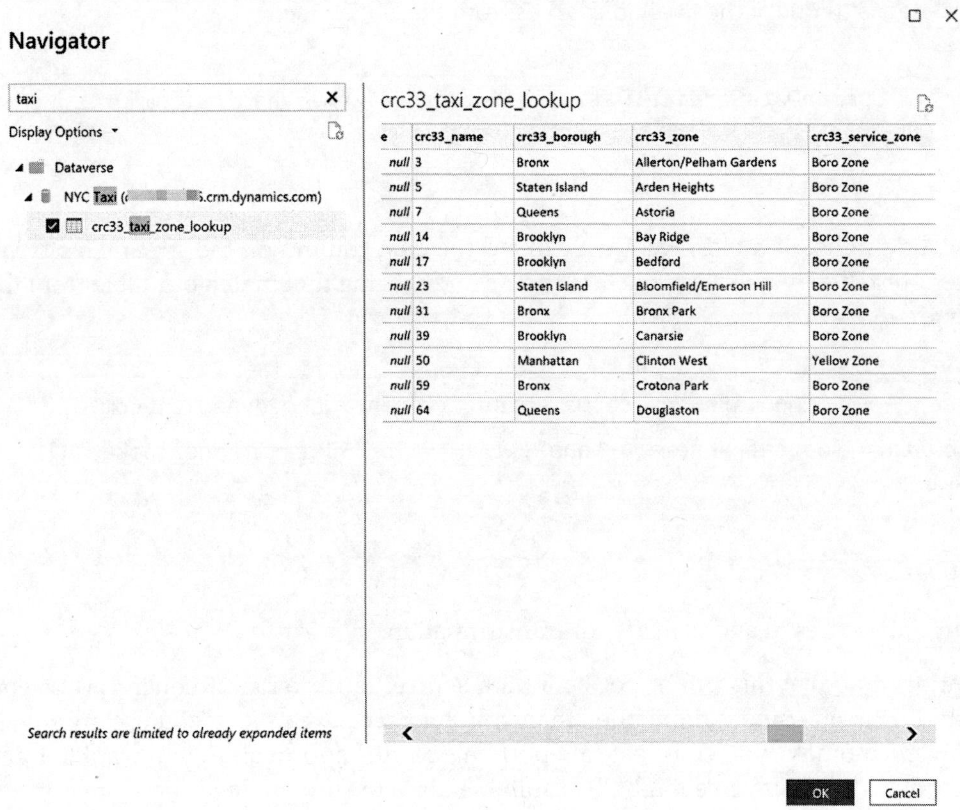

Figure 3.16: *Selecting a table from the Dataverse*

Once you click **OK**, you will be prompted if you want to use **Import or DirectQuery** modes. In *Chapter 4, Connect to Database Sources*, we will dig into this topic deeper, so for now, you can just use **Import**. All your columns should load into Power Query and be ready for transformation.

We will use the **`CommonDataService.Database()`** function to connect to our data stored inside the Dataverse:

`CommonDataService.Database()`	
Parameter	**Description**
`databaseUrl`	URL to your Dataverse environment. This URL can be found by logging into Power Apps and confirming the environment information on the upper right-hand corner of the screen.
`options`	Parameters wrapped in square brackets to apply options. The only current option available is `CreateNavigationProperties`. Only set to false if having performance issues with relationship columns.

Table 3.7: *Table of the CommonDataService.Database() parameters.*

Our first step is to query the available tables from the Dataverse:

```
let
  Source = CommonDataService.Database("<tenant>.crm.dynamics.com")
in
  Source
```

Once we have a list of tables, we must expand the data column on the specific table. We will filter our table by querying the table name and schema that match our table from the Dataverse:

```
let
  Source    = CommonDataService.Database("<tenant>.crm.dynamics.com"),
  TableData = Source{[Schema = "dbo", Item = "crc33_taxi_zone_lookup"]}
[Data]
in
  TableData
```

Now our data comes in and is ready for transformation.

As mentioned above, this might not be a data source you leverage frequently, but you might find yourself using it more often than you think. For example, if you use approvals with Power Automate, you can create a report on past-due approvals. If you want to track historical data, the Dataverse might be a suitable place to store it. Regardless of your use case, Dataverse is becoming more popular as a source of your data and might be useful to you soon. It also has provided a great transition point into our next chapter, which focuses on connecting to database sources.

Conclusion

In this chapter, we covered how to connect to different web-based sources. We started off by connecting to a basic SharePoint list. Next, we used the web connector to extract data from a public website, an API endpoint, and a file hosted in SharePoint. Next, we explored how to grab a folder of data from a SharePoint document library with the SharePoint Folder connector. Next, we explored how to expand functionality with REST APIs using the OData Feed connector. Lastly, we went over the new way to connect to Dynamics 365 and the Dataverse.

In the next chapter, we will explore using database data sources with Power Query so we can connect to larger sets of data through different storage structures.

CHAPTER 4
Connect to Database Sources

Introduction

This chapter will walk you through connecting to database sources with Power Query. We will start this chapter by exploring query folding and query types as they will be critical to understand along with database connections. Next, we will explore how to connect to Microsoft SQL Server to provide a knowledge base when working with databases. From there, we will expand our knowledge to other SQL-based data sources such as Snowflake, Amazon Redshift, and ODBC. Lastly, we will also explore other storage formats such as Azure Blob storage, Azure Data Lake, and Azure Tables.

Structure

The chapter covers the following topics:

- Query folding
- Data connectivity modes
- Connecting to Microsoft SQL server
- Connecting to Azure Synapse Analytics
- Connecting to Azure Cosmos DB

- Connecting to SQL Server Analysis Services
- Connecting to Snowflake
- Connecting to Google BigQuery
- Connecting to Amazon Redshift
- Connecting to ODBC
- Connecting to Dataflows in Power BI
- Connecting to Azure Tables
- Connecting to Azure Blob
- Connecting to Dremio

Objectives

At the end of this chapter, you will understand how to use Power Query to connect to data found inside databases and similar storage containers. You will learn how to configure your connections to balance performance and resources to meet the needs of your consumers. You will also be able to understand how to manage and manipulate database connectors to simplify your connections and optimize their management.

Query folding

Query folding is an important concept critical to the performance of database sources. In a single sentence, query folding is the ability for Power Query to perform transformations on a query but allow it to be performed as a single statement. If you are working with a Microsoft SQL database and want to filter which columns are coming in, your transformations will generate a new SQL statement that will allow your query to be more efficient. Up to this point, we have not discussed any query transformations as our focus has been on data extraction. However, it is important to discuss this topic now because it could change how you choose to structure and ingest data from various databases.

Because of how they are structured, databases are designed to hold substantial amounts of data that can be ingested into Power Query. Because of this, we need to be smart about transforming our data to ensure an efficient refresh. Each transformation we make is a new step inside of Power Query, but if it is not folded, it could be detrimental to our refresh times. If you can keep your query folding intact, you will simply make one request and ingest the millions of rows you are trying to load. However, if you break query folding, you will now have to apply each transformation step on every row loaded into Power Query. This adds time to your refreshes and can even cause issues with your Power BI Premium Capacity if it is in use. In short, you might have issues with your data refreshes if you cannot manipulate the changes within a SQL **SELECT** statement.

As a best practice, it is advisable to transform your data at the server level whenever possible when using a database. This will allow you to have faster refreshes with less demand for resources. It will also allow you to use incremental refresh and hybrid tables, a topic we will cover in *Chapter 13, Parameters*. Naturally, the breaking of query folding might be unavoidable, but a little planning can go a long way when ingesting your data.

Data connectivity modes

Query modes are a critical part of Power Query and how you interact with your data when using Microsoft Power BI. Many users of Power Query ask what the difference is between **Import** and **DirectQuery** modes. Even experienced users of Power Query get confused with this topic. These modes determine how the data will be stored for use within Power BI. Both have their advantages and disadvantages.

Queries using Import mode will do just as it says. Data will be imported into the Power BI model and be right next to the report canvas. This means it is readily available, which provides a quick and seamless experience for report consumers. It also provides a stable dataset to use that will only be refreshed when you tell it to be refreshed. Import mode also allows you to perform any transformation on your query as desired. Since the data is imported into the model, you can do whatever you want to it. However, this could break query folding, so keep that in mind. The key disadvantage to this mode is that it will require you to keep refreshing the data to get the latest data available. If you need up to the second changes in your data source, import mode is not the best choice for your model as it requires you to refresh it. In addition, if your data model gets too large, it will require a premium workspace to accommodate it, which potentially adds licensing costs.

Queries using **DirectQuery** mode will always query your data source for the latest data available. Instead of refreshing, the data is queried when the report is opened. It also keeps your data model down to a smaller size which is helpful when you are trying to avoid additional licensing. The key disadvantage to this mode is that it requires a query every time you use it, resulting in a longer load time. If your queries are not optimized, they will take even longer. You also will run into issues with certain transformations of your data which requires more diligence upstream in the data layer.

After explaining the differences between these modes, most people follow up with a question on which mode they should use. In short, it is really going to depend on several factors that you need to determine for your situation. Things like load time, refresh rates, licensing costs, and transformations all play a role in which option to choose. If your organization has users who hate waiting for a few seconds, you might need to use **Import mode**. However, if you need to have the most up-to-date data in your report, **DirectQuery** might be the right answer. You might even have a use case for both with different reports. Regardless of your choice, it is important to consider these factors to make sure you make the right choice for your report stakeholders and their requirements.

Connecting to Microsoft SQL server

When connecting to database sources, most people are familiar with the **Structured Query Language** (**SQL**) when extracting data. SQL databases use a common language that allows you to jump between various databases. Each version of SQL has its benefits and challenges, but each one connects to Power Query in a similar format. We will use Microsoft SQL Server as our database source to start our journey.

When connecting to Microsoft SQL Server, you will start with the **New Source** dropdown in the Power Query editor and select **SQL Server**. To get started, you only need three pieces of information to get connected. First, you need to specify your **Server,** which can be a server name or IP address. Next, you need to specify your **Database**. This is an optional step, but we strongly recommend you do this if you are using multiple environments for development, testing, and production data. Lastly, the **Data Connectivity Mode** is defaulted on **Import**, but you can change it to **DirectQuery** here if you want. When filled out, it should look like this:

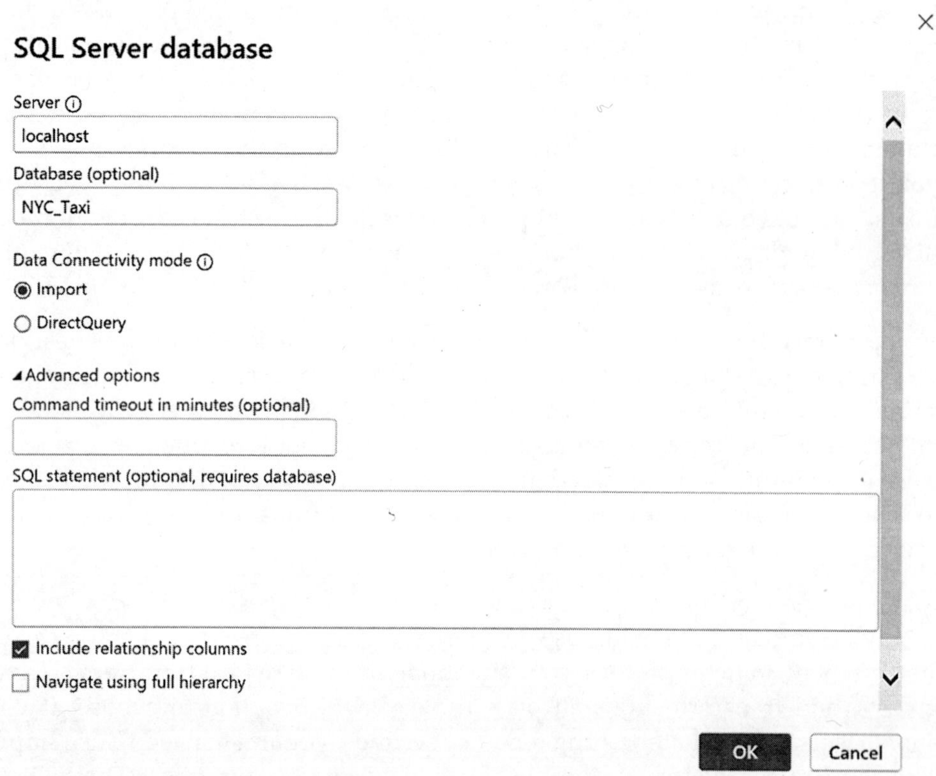

***Figure 4.1:** Setting up a connection to a Microsoft SQL Server*

As shown in *Figure 4.1*, there are advanced options available to you. The first option is to change the timeout of your query. This will override the default of ten minutes. This should be left blank unless you know what you are doing to avoid unnecessary strain on your SQL server. Next, you can provide a SQL statement or query you want the connector to use. As a best practice, we recommend that you do not use SQL statements here but rather create views on your database and query them. This allows for better tracking and documentation. However, if you must use this feature, you are required to specify the database above. Lastly, you have two checkbox options. The first asks you about including relationship columns that are defined in your database. The second asks if you want to group your database objects by schema. Once you have everything set, you can click **OK** to continue.

Next, you will be prompted to provide your authentication information. This will require you to know what authentication method your SQL server is using. If you are using your Microsoft credentials, you will choose your **Windows** or **Microsoft account** options depending on your authentication method. You will pick **Database** if you are using SQL credentials. In our example, we are using Windows credentials to connect to our database:

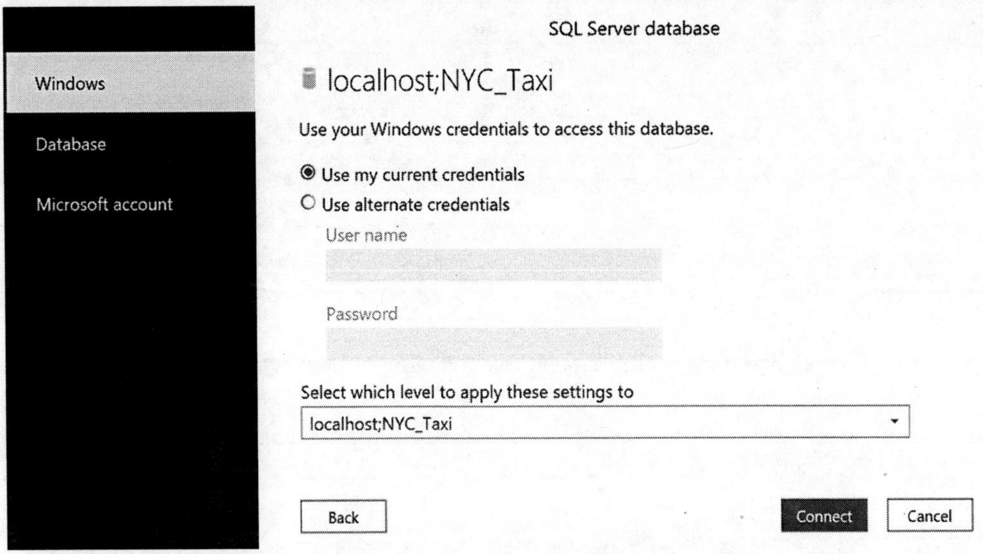

Figure 4.2: *Authenticating to a Microsoft SQL Server*

Once you click connect, you will be prompted with a list of tables and views in your database. You can select multiple objects to load at once and even use the search bar at the top to find them faster. You can tell the difference between a table and view by the icon. As shown in *Figure 4.3*, a table icon has a header row with cells underneath it. However, a view has two tables overlaying each other. You can select your objects, preview the data, and click on **OK** to load as shown below:

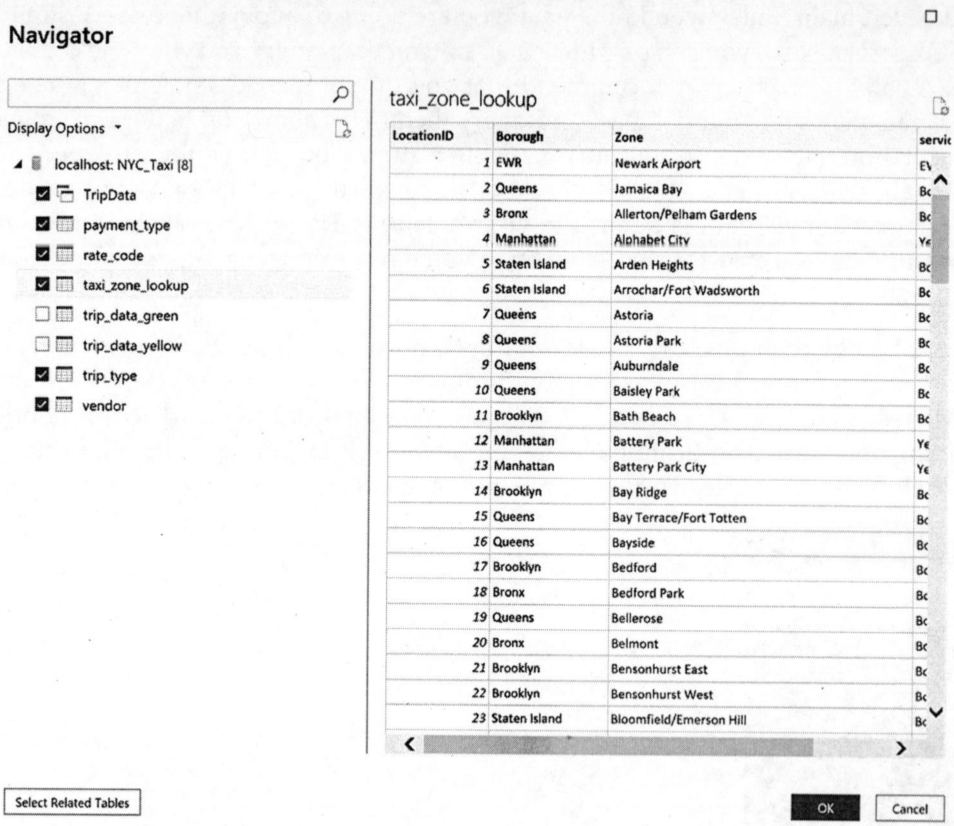

***Figure 4.3:** Selecting and previewing objects from a Microsoft SQL Server*

We can use the advanced editor to connect to our SQL database as well. We will use the **`Sql.Database()`** function to connect to our data source. The parameters for this function are as follows:

`Sql.Database()`	
Parameter	**Description**
`Server`	Server name or IP address
`Database`	Name of database (optional)
`Options`	Options wrapped in square brackets to apply options for `Query`, `CreateNavigationProperties`, `NavigationPropertyNameGenerator`, `MaxDegreeOfParallelism`, `CommandTimeout`, `ConnectionTimeout`, `HierarchicalNavigation`, `MultiSubnetFailover`, `UnsafeTypeConversions`, `ContextInfo`, `OmitSRID`, and `EnableCrossDatabaseFolding`.

***Table 4.1:** Table of the Sql.Database() parameters*

To replicate our connection, we will start with a line of code to bring back the objects on our SQL database:

```
let
  Source = Sql.Database("localhost", "NYC_Taxi")
in
  Source
```

Next, we will need to specify which object we want to return from the list this query returns. Just like we did with Excel workbooks, we need to filter down to the specific table we want and specify the data field to bring back the content we need:

```
let
  Source = Sql.Database("localhost", "NYC_Taxi"),
  TaxiZones = Source{[Schema="dbo", Item="taxi_zone_lookup"]}[Data]
in
  TaxiZones
```

For this request, we did not have to specify any options available to us with the **`Sql.Database()`** function. However, you might need a few of them depending on what your requirements are:

- **`Query`**: A native SQL query used to access data from a database.
- **`CreateNavigationProtperties`**: A true/false option that generates navigation properties on values returned. This option is set to true by default.
- **`NavigationPropertyNameGenerator`**: This option is used to create names for navigation.
- **`MaxDegreeofParallelism`**: Numeric value that sets the **`maxdop`** clause with a query to limit parallelism.
- **`CommandTimeout`**: A numeric duration that limits how long a query is allowed to run on a server before it is canceled. The default is ten minutes.
- **`ConnectionTimeout`**: A numeric duration that limits how long to wait before abandoning a connection to a SQL server. The default is set by the driver used to broker the connection.
- **`HierarchicalNavigation`**: A true/false option to view objects by their schema names. This option is set to false by default.
- **`MultiSubnetFailover`**: A true/false option that sets the **`MultiSubnetFailover`** property on the connection string to the SQL server. This option is set to false by default.

- `UnsafeTypeCoversions`: A true/false option that should only be used if you know what you are doing. If true is selected, Power Query attempts to fold type conversions. This could fail and result in your refresh failing. It is strongly recommended that you do not use this option unless you have a specific use case that has been tested or you are willing to deal with the challenges that might result.
- `ContextInfo`: Binary value that is used for the **`CONTEXT_INFO()`** SQL trigger before your query is run.
- `OmitSRID`: A true/false option that is used to manage **Spatial Reference Identifiers (SRID)**. If set to true, this option omits the SRID when producing well known text from geometric and geographic shapes.
- `EnableCrossDatabaseFolding`: A true/false option for enabling folding across databases. If this option is set to true, it allows query folding across databases that reside on the same server. This option is set to false by default.

At the beginning of this chapter, it was stated that SQL has a standard language. While we have dived deep into Microsoft's version of SQL databases, you might be wondering about other data sources such as Oracle, MySQL, and PostgreSQL. In short, you can use the exact same principles we applied to Microsoft SQL for your other databases. The options for your other SQL databases will vary, but all of them are identified in the list of options detailed above. Following is a list of SQL server types and their associated function:

SQL Data Sources	
SQL Server Sources	**Advanced Editor Function**
Database 2 (Db2)	**`DB2.Database()`**
MySQL	**`MySQL.Database()`**
Oracle	**`Oracle.Database()`**
PostgreSQL	**`PostgreSQL.Database()`**
SAP ASE (formerly Sybase)	**`Sybase.Database()`**
Teradata	**`Teradata.Database()`**

Table 4.2: *Table of SQL server sources and the related advanced editor functions*

But what about Azure SQL databases? How does it fit into the picture? Since Azure is a part of Microsoft, you can apply everything you have done within this section to your Azure databases. While a special connector called Azure SQL Database is available in the New Sources menu, you will quickly realize it is the same SQL Server connector you just used with a new vanity name. The only difference is that you might be asked to use your Microsoft account when you authenticate if your database is set up to use your Azure Active Directory credentials instead of SQL credentials.

Connecting to Azure Synapse Analytics

Azure Synapse Analytics is a powerful service that enables the consolidation of big data and warehousing sources into a single tool. Synapse allows you to bring these tools into a single interface. There are two connectors for Azure Synapse Analytics. The first is **Azure Synapse Analytics SQL** which uses the same process outlined in the Connecting to Microsoft SQL Server in the section before this. The second option, **Azure Synapse Analytics Workspace**, allows you to access workspace content that has been built. To see these options, go to the **New Source** dropdown and select **More**. In the search box, enter synapse to see both connector options as shown here:

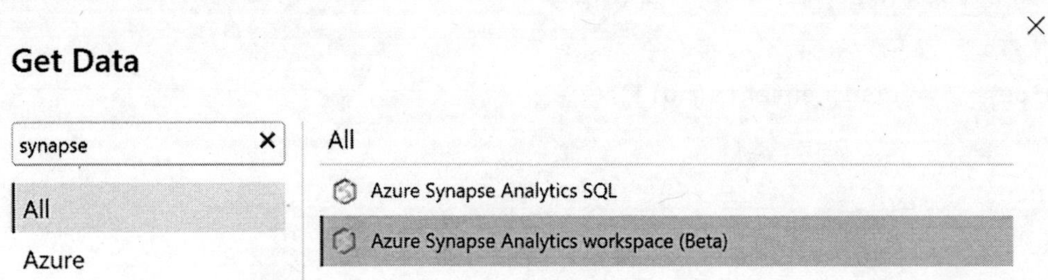

Figure 4.4: *Connector choices for Azure Synapse Analytics*

Since we have already covered connecting to SQL server databases, we will use the workspace connector instead. At this point, you will be prompted for your Microsoft account credentials. This is different as you normally provide them after entering your server information. However, in Azure Synapse Analytics, we do not need to specify these details. Instead, after we authenticate, we will be granted access to the environment and be able to select our tables. Once we connect with our credentials, we will be shown a navigation window that allows us to pick tables out of our workspace that looks like this:

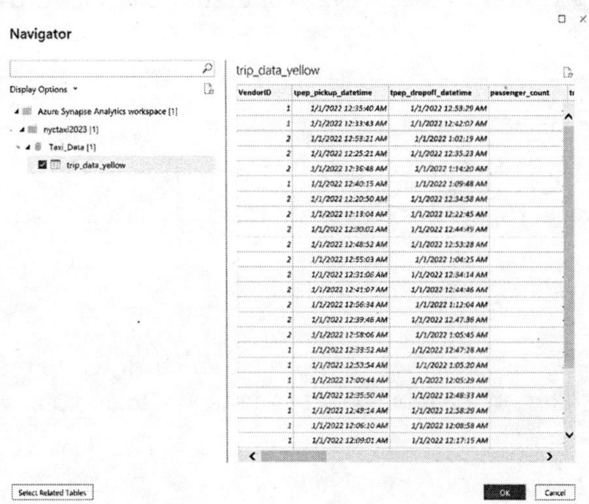

Figure 4.5: *Selecting object from an Azure Synapse Analytics Workspace*

We can connect to Azure Synapse using the advanced editor. To achieve this, we will use the **`Synapse.Contents()`** function to access our environment:

`Synapse.Contents()`	
Parameter	**Description**
`Options`	Microsoft's documentation of the options is not available at the time of publishing. As a result, use `null` for this parameter.

Table 4.3: *Table of the Synapse.Contents() parameters*

There are no details on the options parameter publicly available. To avoid any issues, we will use null as a place holder for this value:

```
let
  Source = Synapse.Contents(null)
in
  Source
```

This query will bring back a list of workspaces that are available to the signed in user. Next, we need to filter the list and expand the data column:

```
let
  Source = Synapse.Contents(null),
  Workspace = Source{[Name="nyctaxi2023"]}[Data]
in
  Workspace
```

Next, we need to identify the database we are connecting to so we can view the available tables:

```
let
  Source = Synapse.Contents(null),
  Workspace = Source{[Name="nyctaxi2023"]}[Data],
  Database = Workspace{[Name="Taxi_Data"]}[Data]
in
  Database
```

Lastly, with our database identified, it is now time to filter down to the table we want to query. We will need to filter on the table name and schema to avoid any name collisions:

```
let
  Source = Synapse.Contents(null),
  Workspace = Source{[Name="nyctaxi2023"]}[Data],
```

```
  Database = Workspace{[Name="Taxi_Data"]}[Data],
  Table = Database{[Name="trip_data_yellow",Schema="dbo"]}[Data]
in
  Table
```

There are quite a few extra steps in this process, but it is important to understand them to ensure you can access the data you are targeting with your query. The better your understanding of Azure Synapse Analytics is structured, the easier it will be to write out your queries. While it might not be as straightforward as using a SQL server connector, it does accomplish the same goal with just a few extra steps in between.

Connecting to Azure Cosmos DB

Azure Cosmos DB is a NoSQL database service offered by Microsoft. While it might not be in use at your organization, there are times when you might need to connect to it. Cosmos DB has two connectors available in Power Query. The newer version is the preferred method, providing the most efficient connection for accessing your data. To get connected, go to the **New Source** dropdown, and click **More**. In the search box, enter **`cosmos`** and select the **Azure Cosmos v2** connector as demonstrated below:

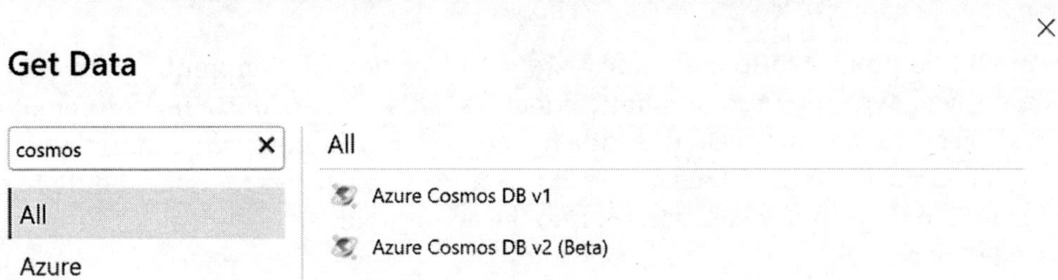

Figure 4.6: *Connector choices for Azure Cosmos DB*

Once you have selected the **v2** connector, you will be prompted for the endpoint for your database. You can find this in the Keys blade of your Cosmos DB resource inside Azure. Next, you have some additional options you can set for your query. The first is the **Number of Retries.** The connector should make if it fails to connect to your endpoint. Next, you can disable the **Enable AVERAGE function Passdown,** which pushes the average aggregation to the server. This is enabled by default. Lastly, you can enable the **`ORDER BY`** clause of the SQL query with the **Enable SORT Passdown for multiple** functions option. Lastly, you should select the data connectivity mode that makes the most sense. Unless this is a small dataset, **DirectQuery** is the recommended option. When finished, your connector screen should look like this:

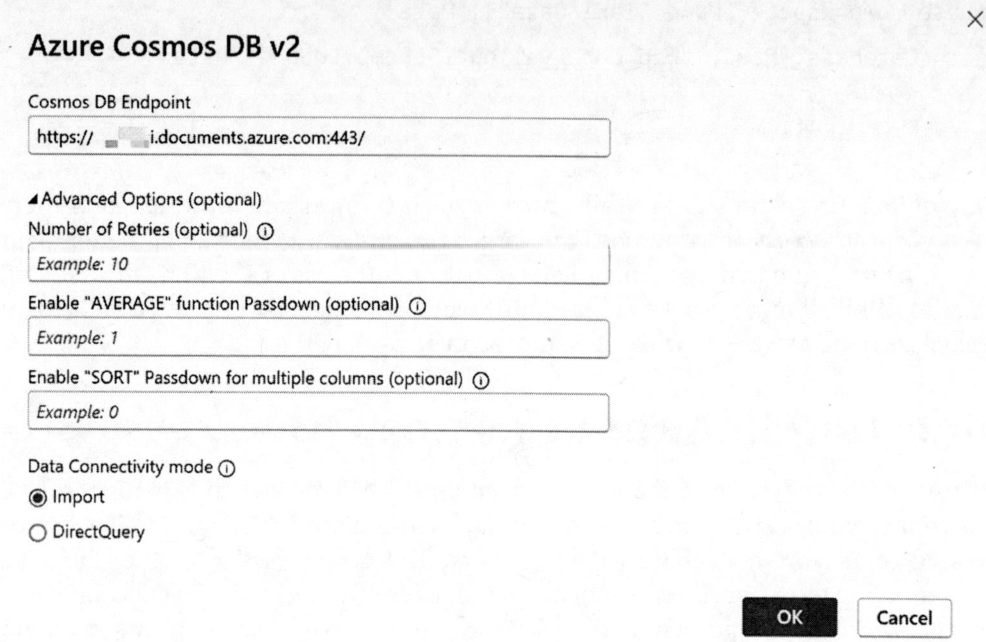

Figure 4.7: *Configuring the Azure Cosmos DB v2 Connector*

Next, you will be prompted to authenticate to your Cosmos DB endpoint. However, up to this point, we have only used account credentials. This connector is a little different as it requires a **Feed Key** to complete the authentication. This also can be found in the key's blade of your Azure Cosmos DB resource in the Azure Portal. It is recommended that you copy your read-only primary key, paste it into the account key field and click **Connect** as demonstrated here:

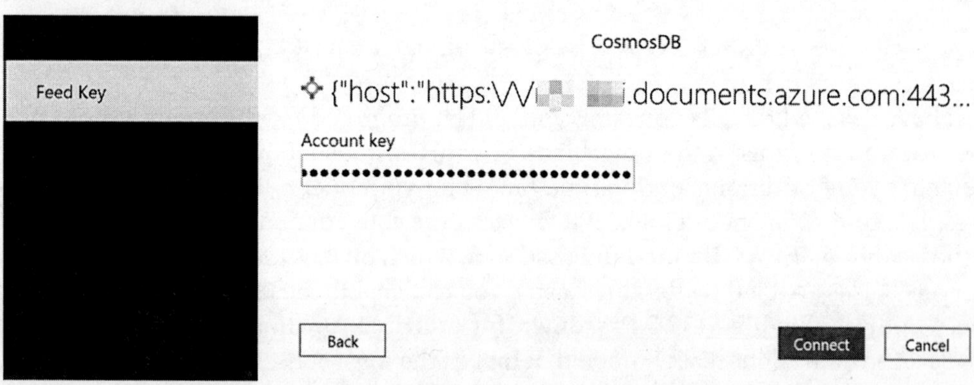

Figure 4.8: *Adding your key information to authenticate with the Azure Cosmos DB v2 connector*

Like other database sources, we next must select the objects we wish to bring into our data model and click **OK,** as shown here:

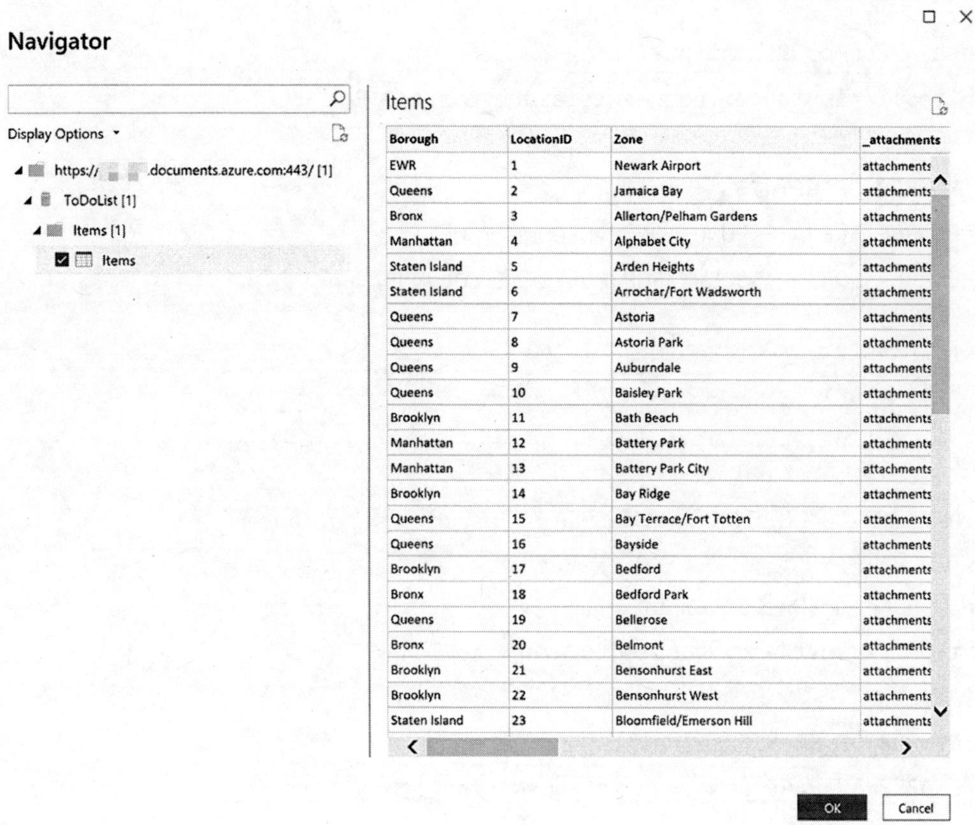

***Figure 4.9:** Selecting objects from Azure Cosmos DB*

We have the option to connect to Azure Cosmos DB using the advanced editor and the **`CosmosDB.Contents()`** function. This function only has two parameters, and unlike some of the other database connectors we have used, the options are the same between the graphical interface and the function itself:

`CosmosDB.Contents()`	
Parameter	**Description**
`Host`	Endpoint URL for your Azure Cosmos DB instance
`Options`	Options wrapped in square brackets to apply options for `NUMBER_OF_RETRIES`, `ENABLE_AVERAGE_FUNCTION_PASSDOWN`, and `ENABLE_SORT_PASSDOWN_FOR_MULTIPLE_COLUMNS`

***Table 4.4:** Table of the CosmosDB.Contents() parameters*

To access our Azure Cosmos DB instance, we must call the URL we used above and declare our options. If we are not going to change them from the defaults, we can just use **`null`** as a placeholder:

```
let
  Source = CosmosDB.Contents(
    "https://<instance>.documents.azure.com:443/",
    [
      NUMBER_OF_RETRIES = null,
      ENABLE_AVERAGE_FUNCTION_PASSDOWN = null,
      ENABLE_SORT_PASSDOWN_FOR_MULTIPLE_COLUMNS = null
    ]
  )
in
  Source
```

Next, we must select the database we want to use from the instance:

```
let
  Source = CosmosDB.Contents(
    "https://<instance>.documents.azure.com:443/",
    [
      NUMBER_OF_RETRIES = null,
      ENABLE_AVERAGE_FUNCTION_PASSDOWN = null,
      ENABLE_SORT_PASSDOWN_FOR_MULTIPLE_COLUMNS = null
    ]
  ),
  Database = Source{[Name = "ToDoList", Kind = "Database"]}[Data]
in
  Database
```

Once we have selected our database, we must select the schema we will use:

```
let
  Source = CosmosDB.Contents(
    "https://<instance>.documents.azure.com:443/",
    [
      NUMBER_OF_RETRIES = null,
      ENABLE_AVERAGE_FUNCTION_PASSDOWN = null,
      ENABLE_SORT_PASSDOWN_FOR_MULTIPLE_COLUMNS = null
    ]
```

```
  ),
  Database = Source{[Name = "ToDoList", Kind = "Database"]}[Data],
  Schema = Database{[Name = "Items", Kind = "Schema"]}[Data]
in
  Schema
```

Lastly, we must specify the table we want to query:

```
let
  Source = CosmosDB.Contents(
    "https://<instance>.documents.azure.com:443/",
    [
     NUMBER_OF_RETRIES = null,
     ENABLE_AVERAGE_FUNCTION_PASSDOWN = null,
     ENABLE_SORT_PASSDOWN_FOR_MULTIPLE_COLUMNS = null
    ]
   ),
  Database = Source{[Name = "ToDoList", Kind = "Database"]}[Data],
  Schema = Database{[Name = "Items", Kind = "Schema"]}[Data],
  Table = Schema{[Name = "Items", Kind = "Table"]}[Data]
in
  Table
```

The new connector Azure Cosmos DB is quite effective and simple to use once you understand how best to leverage it. While you might not be using it today, it is worth considering due to the nature of its quick response times. It is ideal to partner with a data engineer if you are not one yourself to see if Azure Cosmos DB might be a good fit for some of your data projects.

Connecting to SQL Server Analysis Services

SQL Server Analysis Services (**SSAS**) is built upon the same data model that is within Microsoft Excel and Power BI. Think of it as a data model on steroids. When you are connecting to Analysis Services, you are connecting directly to an existing model. As a result, you do not have the ability to make changes to your data model within Power Query, as all those changes must take place at the data layer. However, it is important to review how to perform this connection as it is a common data source and allows for better management of data across your organization.

To connect to SQL Server Analysis Services, simply go to the New Source drop down in the Power Query editor and select Analysis Services. Next, you will specify your server's name or IP address, followed by the database name. You will note instead of an option between **Import** and **DirectQuery** modes, you have a new option called **Connect Live**. This option acts like **DirectQuery** mode except that it provides your user context when you open the file. Because SQL Server Analysis Services has role-based access built into the model, it automatically filters the data based on who is accessing the data. Lastly, you have the option to specify an **MDX or DAX query** to bring back a specific view of the data. When finished, your connector information should look something like this:

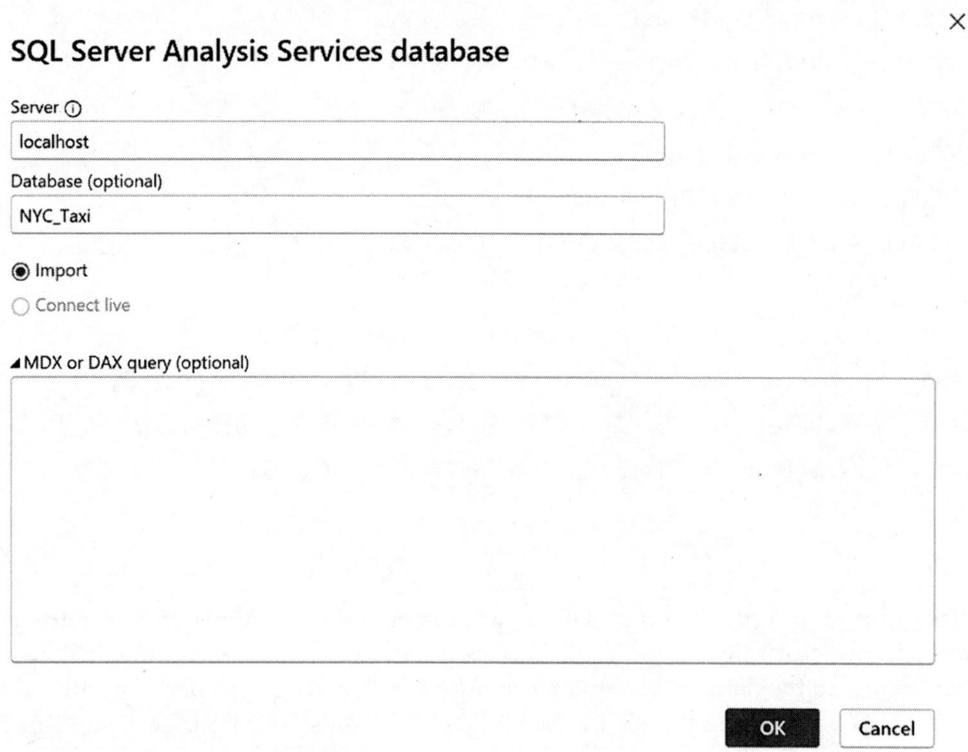

***Figure 4.10:** Connecting to SQL Server Analysis Services*

Next, you will be prompted for credentials. If you are using Connect Live, then you will need to use your Windows or Microsoft account credentials. Once you have authenticated, your data will be loaded into Power BI. From there, you can select your model and the objects you wish to include, as shown below:

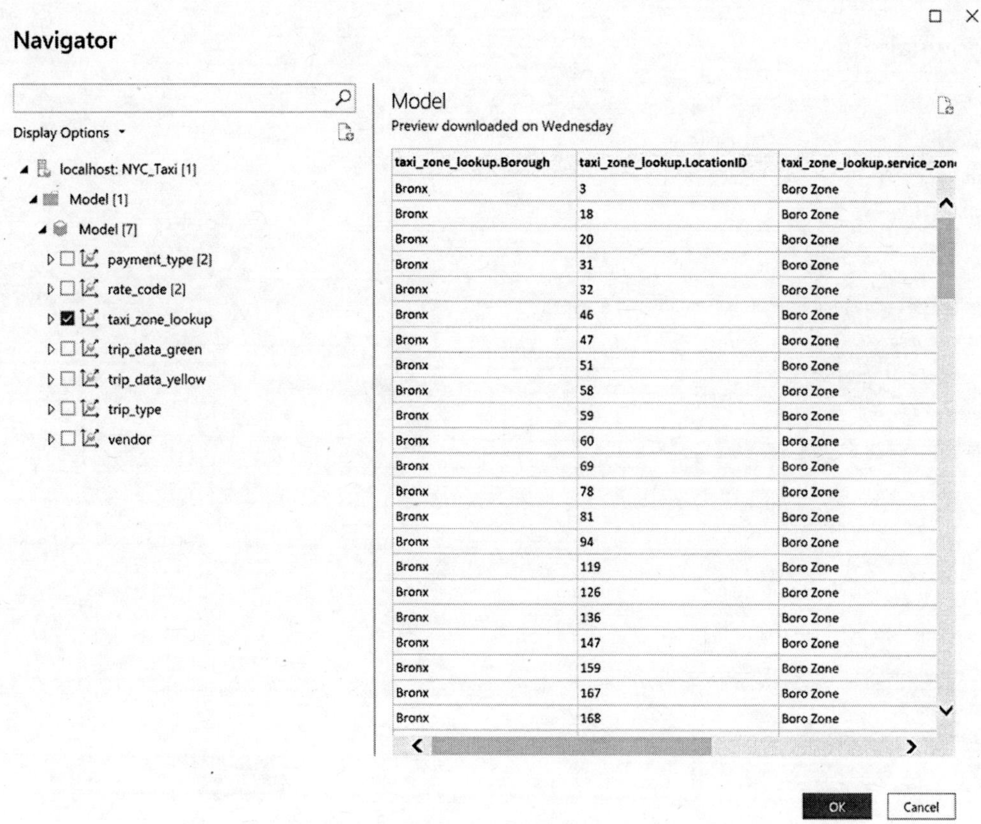

***Figure 4.11:** Selecting model components from SQL Server Analysis Services*

Due of the nature of how SQL Server Analysis Services is designed to work, it does not make sense to connect to the source with the advanced editor. The coding is complex and time consuming. This is counterproductive, especially since this has already been performed in the data layer. While you will not make many changes to your model, it is important to understand how these components operate and how you can integrate them into your local models.

Connecting to Snowflake

Snowflake has become a popular data warehouse solution for many organizations in the last few years. For a long time, the Snowflake connector inside of Power Query was not very robust. However, in 2021, investments were made into the connector to make it a much more powerful connector as it integrated the components Snowflake has developed to make it a popular choice for data warehousing. To connect to a Snowflake database, go to the **New Source** dropdown in the Power Query editor and select **More**. From there, find the **Snowflake** connector and it will bring you a screen that looks like this:

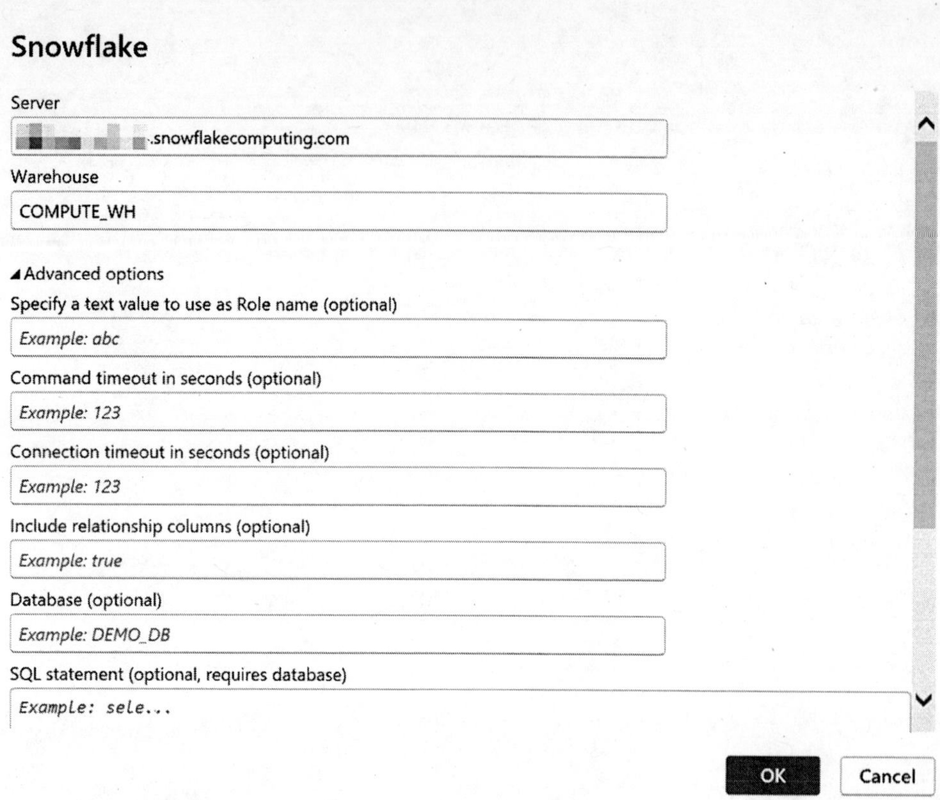

Figure 4.12: *Configuring the Snowflake connector*

When connecting to a Snowflake database, you are required to provide the server's name and warehouse that you are using for your connection. From there, you have advanced options you can use if required. For example, your organization might have assigned you a role. This means you will need to specify that role to have access to the right data. Next, you can specify the command and connection time outs. You also can include relationship columns with your queries as well. Lastly, if you wish to use a specific SQL statement, you can do so at the bottom, but you must specify the database option as well.

After you have completed this, you will be prompted for your credentials. Unless you have a single sign on configured with your Microsoft account, you will use your Snowflake credentials. After authenticating, you will need to navigate through the database and schema to select your object in the database as demonstrated below:

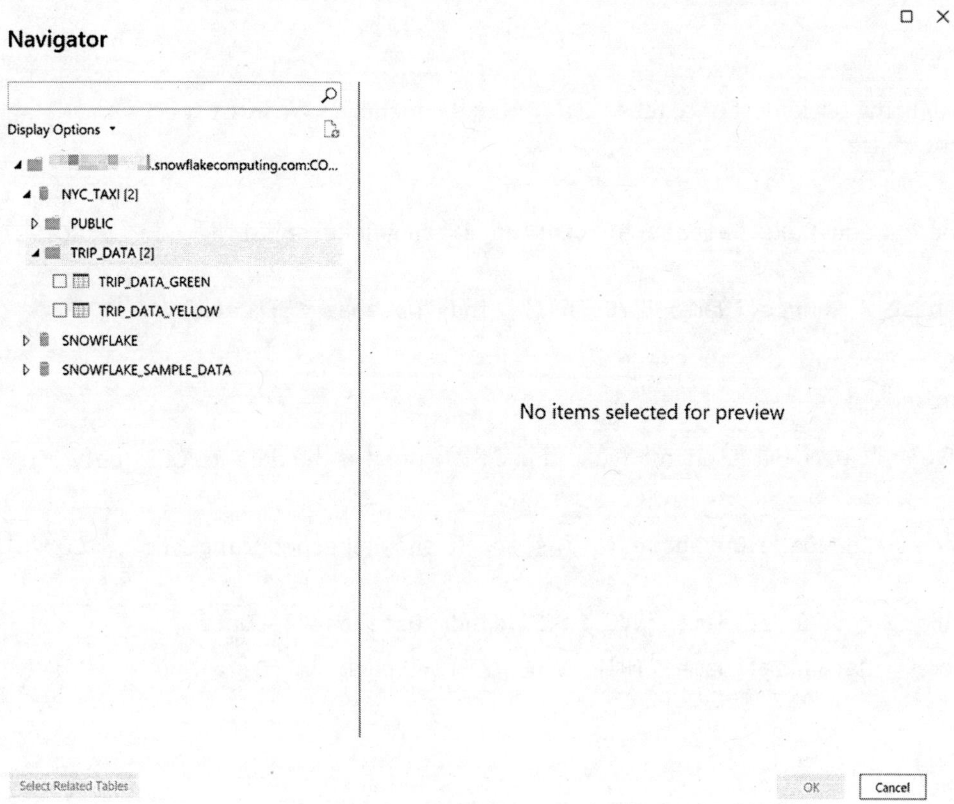

***Figure 4.13:** Selecting objects from Snowflake*

Connecting to Snowflake using the advanced editor is like the other databases sources we have shown. Using the **`Snowflake.Databases()`** function, we can connect to our server:

`Snowflake.Databases()`	
Parameter	**Description**
`Server`	Server URL for your Snowflake instance
`Warehouse`	The specified warehouse used to execute your query
`Options`	Options wrapped in square brackets to apply options for `ConnectionTimeout`, and `CommandTimeout`

***Table 4.5:** Table of the Snowflake.Databases() parameters*

To get started with our connection, we will first use the **`Snowflake.Databases()`** function to connect to our instance:

```
let
  Source = Snowflake.Databases("<instance>.snowflakecomputing.com", "COMPUTE_
WH"),
```

```
in
  Source
```

This will bring back a list of databases found in the instance. We must specify the database we want to use:

```
let
  Source = Snowflake.Databases("<instance>.snowflakecomputing.com", "COMPUTE_
WH"),
  Database = Source{[Name="NYC_TAXI",Kind="Database"]}[Data]
in
  Database
```

Next, we will specify the schema we will use that contains the data for our query:

```
let
  Source = Snowflake.Databases("<instance>.snowflakecomputing.com", "COMPUTE_
WH"),
  Database = Source{[Name="NYC_TAXI",Kind="Database"]}[Data],
  Schema = Database{[Name="TRIP_DATA",Kind="Schema"]}[Data]
in
  Schema
```

Lastly, we must select the object for our query:

```
let
  Source = Snowflake.Databases("<instance>.snowflakecomputing.com", "COMPUTE_
WH"),
  Database = Source{[Name="NYC_TAXI",Kind="Database"]}[Data],
  Schema = Database{[Name="TRIP_DATA",Kind="Schema"]}[Data],
  Table = Schema{[Name="TRIP_DATA_YELLOW",Kind="Table"]}[Data]
in
  Table
```

The updated Snowflake connector provides a few robust features that allow you to quickly get connected to the right data. These changes have allowed Power Query to be a great tool for extracting data while maintaining the security of the data source. If you are part of an organization that stopped using Power Query to access Snowflake data because you could not leverage these facets in the past, it might be worth looking into them again.

Connecting to Google BigQuery

Google BigQuery is a serverless data warehouse designed to manage massive quantities of data in the cloud. Many organizations leverage Google cloud services such as BigQuery, but also leverage the core Microsoft productivity tools such as Excel and Power BI. Connecting to Google BigQuery is quite simple and follows the format of other data sources we have seen in this chapter. To get started, click on the **New Source** dropdown in the Power Query editor and select **More**. If you search for Google BigQuery, you will note that two different connectors are available. These are **Google BigQuery** and **Google BigQuery (Azure AD)**. The primary difference between these connectors is the authentication method. If you select **Azure AD**, you will use your Microsoft account to authenticate. However, if you choose the other connector, you will use your Google account in a web browser to authenticate. Verify your authentication method before selecting your connector, as shown in the following image:

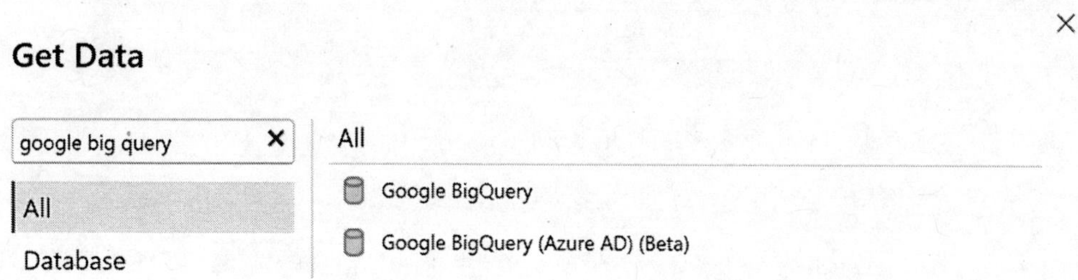

Figure 4.14: *Selecting the right Google BigQuery connector*

Once you have selected the correct connector, you will receive a screen asking for advanced options. Apart from **Billing Project ID**, all these fields are optional to fill out. Billing Project ID will be required if you use the Azure AD connector. Since we are using the non-Azure AD connector, we can leave this blank. We also have additional options we can choose from. For example, we can set the **Use Storage Api** option to false if you prefer to use the REST API over the Storage API. Like other database connectors, you can set the **Connection** and **Command timeout durations** for your queries. You can also specify your SQL statement for your connection, but that will require you to specify your **Project ID**. Once everything is set, you can click **OK** to continue, as shown:

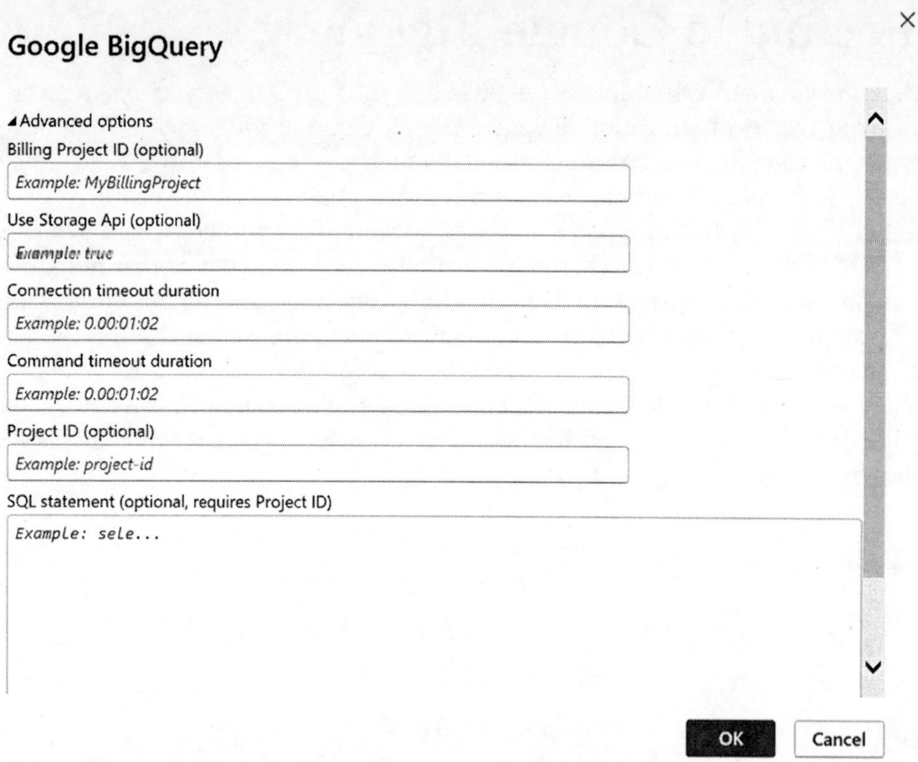

***Figure 4.15:** Configuring the Google BigQuery connector*

Next, you will be prompted to provide your authentication information. Since we are using the non-Azure AD connection, we will be prompted to enter our **Organizational account** credentials for Google. This will open a new webpage and prompt us for credentials. Once you have entered your credentials, the pop-up you see below will close and you can click on **Connect**, as shown in the following figure:

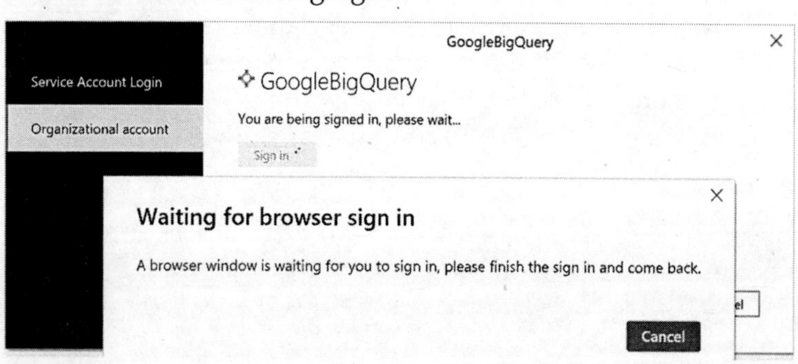

***Figure 4.16:** Authenticating with the Google BigQuery connector*

Once you have completed your authentication, you can navigate the database and schema structure to select the objects you wish to add to Power Query:

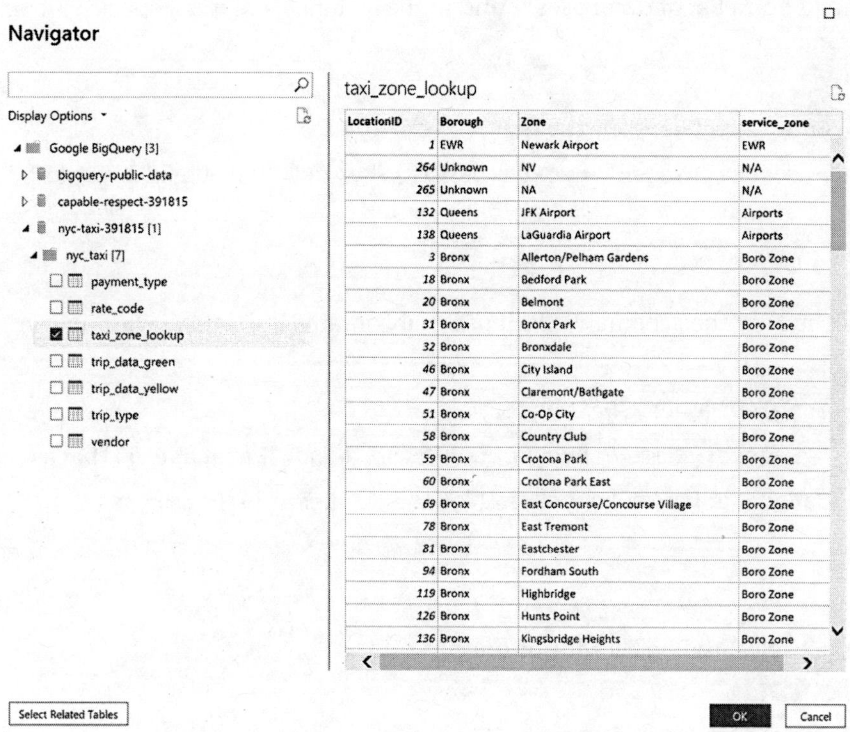

***Figure 4.17:** Selecting objects from Google BigQuery*

Connecting to Google BigQuery using the advanced editor is one of the easiest connections you can make in the advanced editor. Using the **`GoogleBigQuery.Database()`** function, we can connect to our server:

`GoogleBigQuery.Database()`	
Parameter	**Description**
`Options`	Options wrapped in square brackets to apply options for `BillingProject`, `UseStorageApi`, `ConnectionTimeout`, `CommandTimeout`, `Project`, and `SqlStatement`

***Table 4.6:** Table of the GoogleBigQuery.Database() parameters*

To get started with our connection, we will first use the **`GoogleBigQuery.Database()`** function to connect to our instance:

```
let
  Source = GoogleBigQuery.Database(),
in
  Source
```

This will bring back a list of databases found in the instance. We must specify the database we want to use:

```
let
  Source = GoogleBigQuery.Database(),
  Database = Source{[Name=" nyc-taxi-391815",Kind="Database"]}[Data]
in
  Database
```

Next, we will specify the schema we will use that contains the data for our query:

```
let
  Source = GoogleBigQuery.Database(),
  Database = Source{[Name=" nyc-taxi-391815",Kind="Database"]}[Data],
  Schema = Database{[Name=" nyc_taxi",Kind="Schema"]}[Data]
in
  Schema
```

Lastly, we must select the object for our query:

```
let
  Source = GoogleBigQuery.Database(),
  Database = Source{[Name=" nyc-taxi-391815",Kind="Database"]}[Data],
  Schema = Database{[Name=" nyc_taxi",Kind="Schema"]}[Data],
  Table = Schema{[Name="taxi_zone_lookup",Kind="Table"]}[Data]
in
  Table
```

At this point, you are realizing the pattern when connecting to databases. While each platform has their unique connector and options to assist with your queries, the navigation from database to object is the same. While we did not go into detail about the **`GoogleBigQueryAad.Database()`** function, it operates the same way as the **`GoogleBigQuery.Database()`** function. The only difference will be using your Azure AD credentials and specifying the **`BillingProject`** to ensure you connect to the correct resource.

Connecting to Amazon Redshift

Like all cloud platforms, **Amazon Web Services** (**AWS**) also has their own data warehousing solution with Amazon Redshift. Using a columnar architecture for storage, it still performs like many database solutions. To get started, click **More** on the **New Source** dropdown in the Power Query editor. Select the **Amazon Redshift** connector and click on connect.

From there, you will be prompted to provide a link to your server and the database you are connecting to on the server, as shown here:

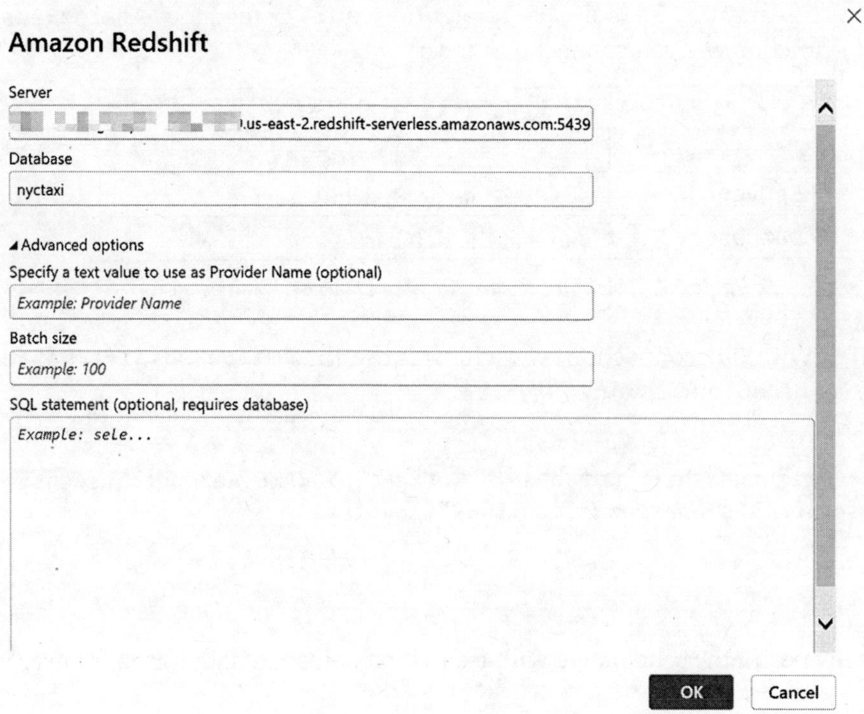

***Figure 4.18:** Configuring the Amazon Redshift connector*

You have three advanced options you can provide with this connector. The first option is the **Provider Name** value that specifies the **Amazon Resource Name** that identifies specific AWS resources. Next, you can specify a **Batch size** to limit the number of rows to retrieve simultaneously. If not changed, the default for this value is one hundred rows per query. Lastly, you can add a **SQL statement** to declare a query for the data you want to ingest with Power Query. Once you click **OK**, you will be prompted for your credentials for either **Amazon Redshift** or your **Microsoft Account**:

***Figure 4.19:** Authenticating to Amazon Redshift*

Once you have completed your authentication, you can navigate the database and schema structure to select the objects you wish to add to Power Query.

Connecting to Amazon Redshift is straightforward. Using the **`AmazonRedshift.Database()`** function, we can connect to our server:

AmazonRedshift.Database()	
Parameter	**Description**
Server	URL to Amazon Redshift server
Database	Name of the database

Table 4.7: Table of the AmazonRedshift.Database() parameters

To get started with our connection, we will first use the **`AmazonRedshift.Database()`** function to connect to our instance:

```
let
  Source = AmazonRedshift.Database("<workgroup>.<AWS Account>.us-east-2.
redshift-serverless.amazonaws.com:5439","nyctaxi")
in
  Source
```

Next, we will specify the schema we will use that contains the data for our query:

```
let
  Source = AmazonRedshift.Database("<workgroup>.<AWS Account>.us-east-2.
redshift-serverless.amazonaws.com:5439","nyctaxi"),
  Schema = Source{[Name="public",Kind="Schema"]}[Data]
in
  Schema
```

Lastly, we must select the object for our query:

```
let
  Source = AmazonRedshift.Database("<workgroup>.<AWS Account>.us-east-2.
redshift-serverless.amazonaws.com:5439","nyctaxi"),
  Schema = Source{[Name="public",Kind="Schema"]}[Data],
  Table = Schema{[Name="taxi_zone_lookup",Kind="Table"]}[Data]
in
  Table
```

One of the challenges that comes with Amazon Redshift is that by design, sometimes you cannot access the server from the public internet. As a result, an ODBC connector is required to broker the connection. You might need to work with your AWS administrator to ensure you have the correct configurations in place to access your Amazon Redshift instance for both Power Query with Microsoft Excel and Power BI, and the on-premises gateway for the Power BI service.

Connecting to ODBC

While **Open Database Connectivity** (**ODBC**) connectors have become outdated, they are still used occasionally with data connectors. For example, Snowflake, Amazon Redshift, and Dremio all have ODBC connectors that you can use. Each platform has its own documentation on how to set up your ODBC settings for your machine. The biggest rule to follow is to make sure you set the right connections up on the right version to match your Excel and Power BI version. If you are using Power BI 64-bit, set up your ODBC 64-bit connector. The same logic holds true for 32-bit instances. To get started, click on the **New Source** dropdown in the Power Query editor and select **More**. You can search for ODBC and select the **ODBC connector**. You will then be prompted to select the specific connector you configured:

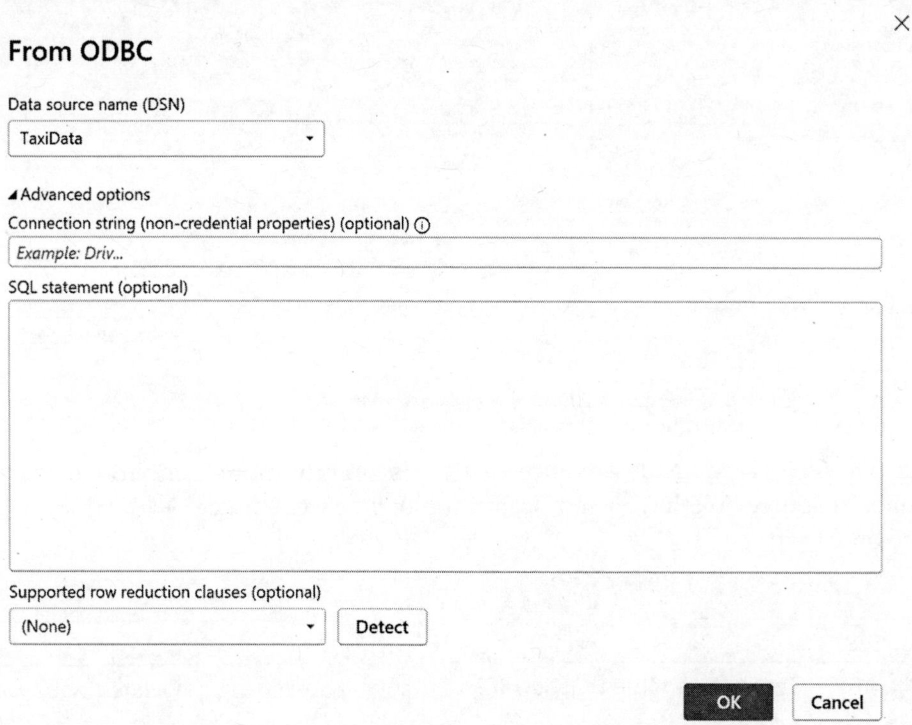

Figure 4.20: *Configuring the ODBC connector*

You have the option to add a connection string for non-credential properties. If your ODBC driver supports it, you can even add an SQL statement. Lastly, you can enable query folding with the **Supported row reduction clauses**, but they cannot be used in combination with an SQL statement. Next, you will navigate through your databases and select the objects you desire to query, as shown:

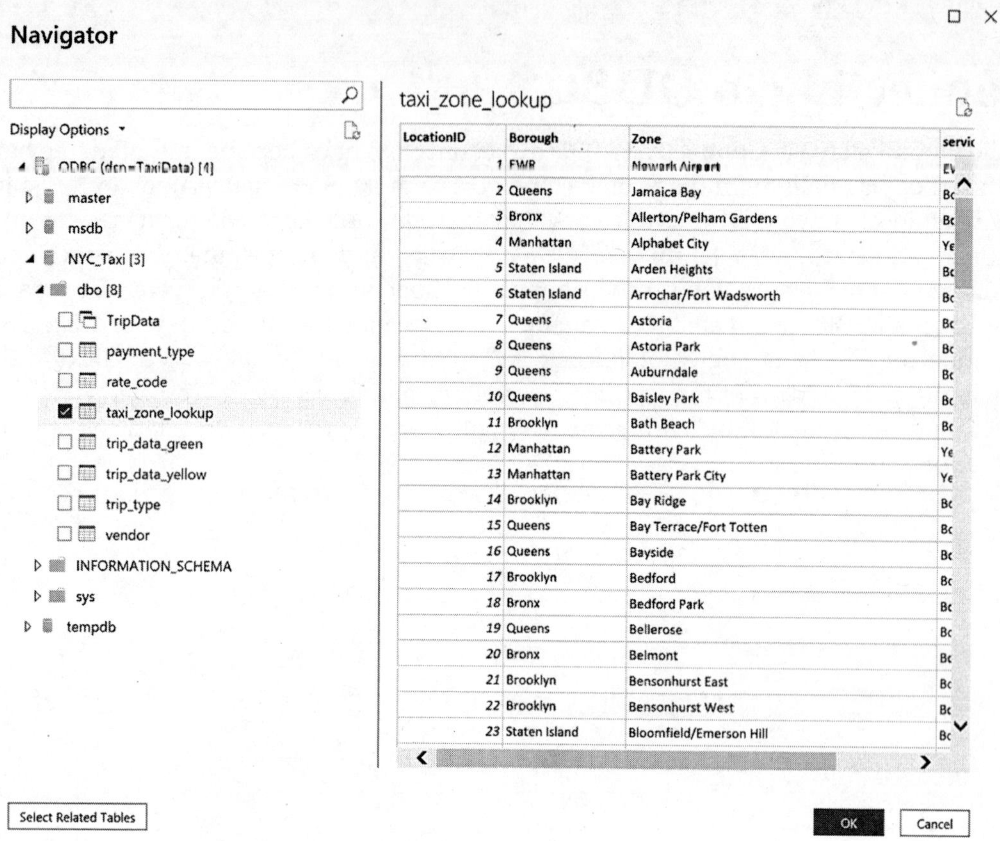

Figure 4.21: *Selecting objects from ODBC*

Connecting to ODBC using the advanced editor is slightly more complicated than the other database sources we have used. Using the **`Odbc.DataSource()`** function, we can connect to our server:

`Odbc.DataSource()`	
Parameter	**Description**
`Connection String`	Text based value that specifies the connection string associated with your ODBC settings
`Options`	Options wrapped in square brackets to apply options for `CreateNavigationProperties`, `HierarchicalNavigation`, `ConnectionTimeout`, `CommandTimeout`, and `SqlCompatibleWindowsAuth`

Table 4.8: *Table of the Odbc.DataSource() parameters*

To get started with our connection, we will first use the **`Odbc.DataSource()`** function to connect to our instance:

```
let
  Source = Odbc.DataSource("dsn=TaxiData", [HierarchicalNavigation=true])
in
  Source
```

You will notice that we used the **`HierarchicalNavigation`** property with this connection. This simplifies the view so we can navigate it easier and bring back a list of databases found on the instance. We must specify the database we want to use:

```
let
  Source = Odbc.DataSource("dsn=TaxiData", [HierarchicalNavigation=true]),
  Database = Source{[Name="NYC_Taxi",Kind="Database"]}[Data]
in
  Database
```

Next, we will specify the schema we will use that contains the data for our query:

```
let
  Source = Odbc.DataSource("dsn=TaxiData", [HierarchicalNavigation=true]),
  Database = Source{[Name="NYC_Taxi",Kind="Database"]}[Data],
  Schema = Database{[Name="dbo",Kind="Schema"]}[Data]
in
  Schema
```

Lastly, we must select the object for our query:

```
let
  Source = Odbc.DataSource("dsn=TaxiData", [HierarchicalNavigation=true]),
  Database = Source{[Name="NYC_Taxi",Kind="Database"]}[Data],
  Schema = Database{[Name="dbo",Kind="Schema"]}[Data],
  Table = Schema{[Name="taxi_zone_lookup",Kind="Table"]}[Data]
in
  Table
```

While the ODBC connector is powerful and flexible enough to handle different database sources, there is a word of caution you must heed. When you share your file, you must have the ODBC settings configured correctly on every machine that receives your file if you wish to refresh your data. In addition, if you plan to use it with the Power BI service, you will need a data gateway in place to perform refreshes and DirectQuery access to your data.

Connecting to Dataflows in Power BI

While not technically a database, Dataflows inside the Power BI service are an excellent location to stage data that might be used frequently. In fact, everything you are learning in this book can be applied to a Dataflow. A common use case for a Dataflow is data that comes from API endpoints. Instead of making the same calls repeatedly, use Dataflows to stage the data in Power BI. From there, you can connect multiple data models to the Dataflow. This helps prevent the throttling of your data source. To get started, click on the **New Source** dropdown in the Power Query editor and click on **More**. From there, search and select the **Dataflows** connector. There is a legacy Power BI Dataflows connector available, but that only brings back data from Power BI. The Dataflows connector brings in data from both Power BI and Power Platform environments, making it much more flexible. Next, you will be prompted to sign in with your organizational account to access your Dataflows. This is the only option as this is a Microsoft cloud-based service. Once you have authenticated, you can navigate to your dataflow and select your objects for your query, as shown in the following figure:

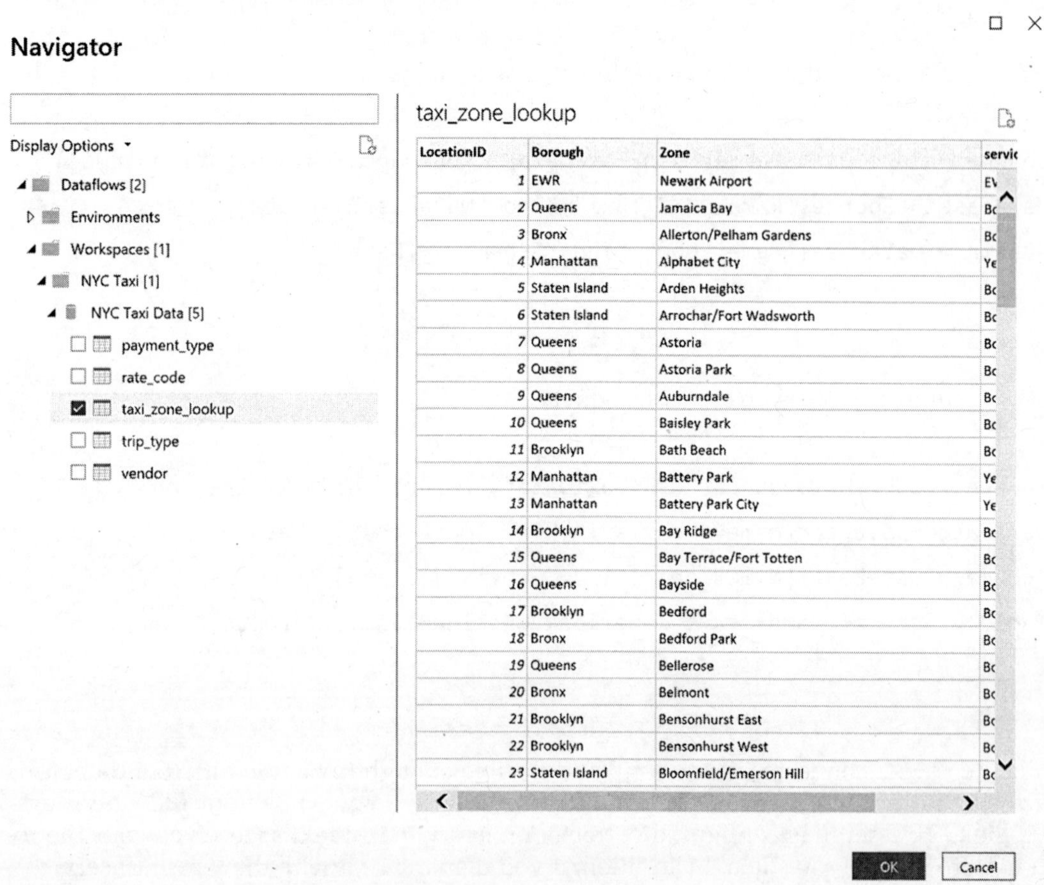

Figure 4.22: Selecting objects from Dataflows

Connecting to Dataflows using the advanced editor is one of the easiest connections we can make. Using the **`PowerPlatform.Dataflows()`** function, we can connect to our server:

`PowerPlatform.Dataflows()`	
Parameter	**Description**
`Options`	Microsoft's documentation of the options is not available at the time of publishing. As a result, use `null` for this parameter.

Table 4.9: *Table of the PowerPlatform.Dataflows() parameters*

To get started with our connection, we will first use the **`PowerPlatform.Dataflows()`** function to connect to our instance:

```
let
    Source = PowerPlatform.Dataflows(null)
in
    Source
```

Next, we need to pick between environments and workspaces to find our Dataflow. Since our Dataflow is in Power BI, we will select workspaces:

```
let
    Source = PowerPlatform.Dataflows(null),
    Workspaces = Source{[Name="Workspaces"]}[Data]
in
    Workspaces
```

Next, we need to select our workspace. You will be tempted to use the **`WorkspaceName`** column to filter this list, but it is not advisable. Because of the self-service nature of the Power Platform, users can easily change these names at a whim. Unlike a database that goes through change control and has limited access, workspace names are frequently updated with no controls in place. As a result, we will filter our list on the **`workspaceId`** column instead:

```
let
    Source = PowerPlatform.Dataflows(null),
    Workspaces = Source{[Name="Workspaces"]}[Data],
    NYC_Taxi_Workspace = Workspaces{[workspaceId="<Workspace GUID>"]}[Data]
in
    NYC_Taxi_Workspace
```

After selecting our workspace, it is time to select the Dataflow. The same principles with workspaces apply here when it comes to names so we should use the **`dataflowId`** column to filter:

```
let
    Source = PowerPlatform.Dataflows(null),
    Workspaces = Source{[Name="Workspaces"]}[Data],
    NYC_Taxi_Workspace = Workspaces{[workspaceId="<Workspace GUID>"]}
[Data],
    Dataflow = NYC_Taxi_Workspace{[dataflowId="<Dataflow GUID>"]}[Data]
in
    Dataflow
```

And finally, we can select our object inside the dataflow. Oddly enough, they do not provide a unique ID for objects inside a dataflow, so we will use the **entityName** column to perform the filtering:

```
let
    Source = PowerPlatform.Dataflows(null),
    Workspaces = Source{[Name="Workspaces"]}[Data],
    NYC_Taxi_Workspace = Workspaces{[workspaceId="<Workspace GUID>"]}
[Data],
    Dataflow = NYC_Taxi_Workspace{[dataflowId="<Dataflow GUID>"]}[Data],
    Table = Dataflow{[entityName="taxi_zone_lookup"]}[Data]
in
    Table
```

This is much easier in the graphical interface. In fact, the Dataflows connector was designed to make data integration with Power BI and Excel much easier. However, digging into how the advanced editor is valuable. One of the neat things about Dataflows is that they are easy to redeploy. So, if you are building a reporting solution that needs to be redeployed with these dataflows, you can quickly make the adjustments you need in the advanced editor and save yourself additional effort when scaling out your reporting solution.

Connecting to Azure Tables

Like Dataflows, Azure Tables provides a schema-less storage solution for data. This solution can be paired with automation and **Internet of Things** (**IoT**) projects to provide quick and structured storage of data that is easily accessed with Power Query. To connect to an Azure Table, go to the **New Source** dropdown in the Power Query editor and select **More**. From there, select the **Azure Table Storage** connector and click **Connect**. From there, you will be prompted for the account name or URL to your table:

Figure 4.23: Configuring the Azure Table Storage connector

Next, you will be prompted to authenticate your connection. However, this time it is a little different. You will be asked to provide an **Account key** that is generated from Azure. You might need to work with an Azure administrator to get this information so you can enter it into the **Account key** field:

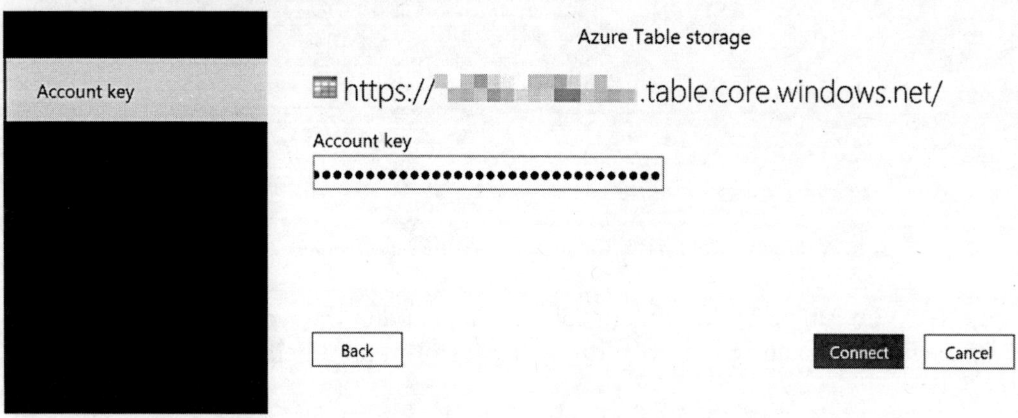

Figure 4.24: *Adding an account key to authenticate with Azure Table Storage*

After you have entered your account key, you will need to select the table you wish to load into Power Query. Unfortunately, the way the data is structured, you will not see it in the preview, as show here:

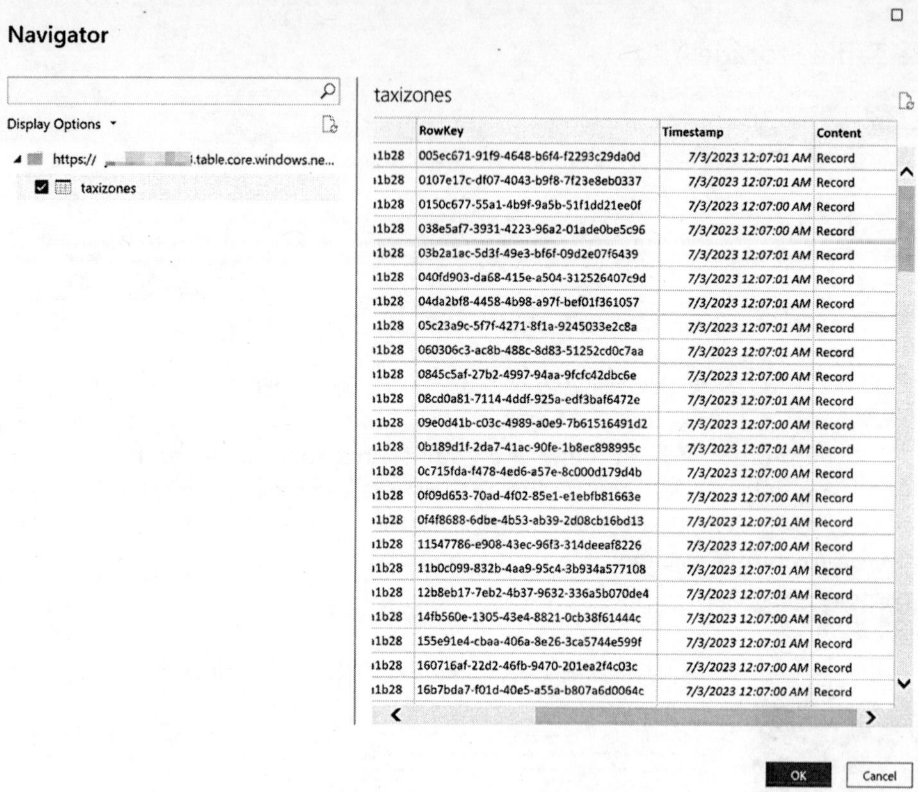

Figure 4.25: Selecting a table from Azure Table Storage

Once ingested, you can go to the content column and expand the records. This will allow you to leverage the data and perform additional transformations before loading them into your model.

Connecting to Azure Table Storage using the advanced editor is very straightforward compared to other connectors. Using the **`AzureStorage.Tables()`** function, we can connect to our server:

`AzureStorage.Tables()`	
Parameter	**Description**
`Account`	Text based value that specifies the account name or link to your storage account
`Options`	Options wrapped in square brackets to apply options for `Timeout`

Table 4.10: Table of the AzureStorage.Tables() parameters

To get started with our connection, we will first use the **`AzureStorage.Tables()`** function to connect to our storage account:

```
let
    Source = AzureStorage.Tables("https://<Account Name>.table.core.win-
dows.net")
in
    Source
```

Once connected to our storage account, we can see a list of tables we can select. We just need to filter the list and retrieve the data:

```
let
    Source = AzureStorage.Tables("https://<Account Name>.table.core.win-
dows.net"),
    Table = Source{[Name="taxizones"]}[Data]
in
    Table
```

This solution works well with smaller datasets that need to be ingested. After a while, the size can become challenging and slow down your refresh. If you find that you data refreshes are taking more than an hour, it might be time to consider other storage solutions for your data.

Connecting to Azure Blob

In the last two sections we started to pull away from traditional databases and started exploring other structured data sources. Azure Blob storage transitions us into data sources that are less structured but still hold our data for us. Azure Blob storage is a cost-effective way to store substantial amounts of data in an easily accessible source for our consumption. While unstructured, Power Query can combine and transform multiple files into a single query just like the folder connector. To connect to a blob, go to the **New Source** dropdown in the Power Query editor and select **More**. From there, select the **Azure Blob Storage** connector. You will be asked to provide the account name or a link to the account:

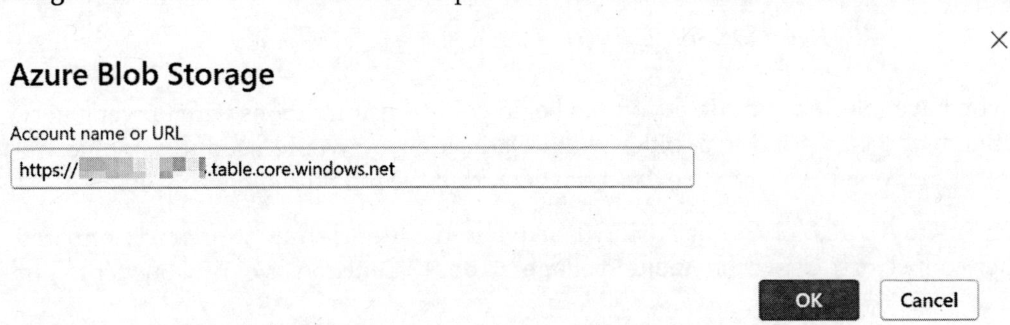

Figure 4.26: *Configuring the Azure Blob Storage connector*

Next, you will be prompted to authenticate. You will be asked to provide either an **Account key** or a **Shared Access Signature (SAS)** token to authenticate. There is also a possibility that your organization has opened the storage container for anonymous access. Consult with your Azure administrator to confirm the proper method for authentication. Once you have authenticated, select the folder or file in your storage container you wish to ingest into Power Query, as shown:

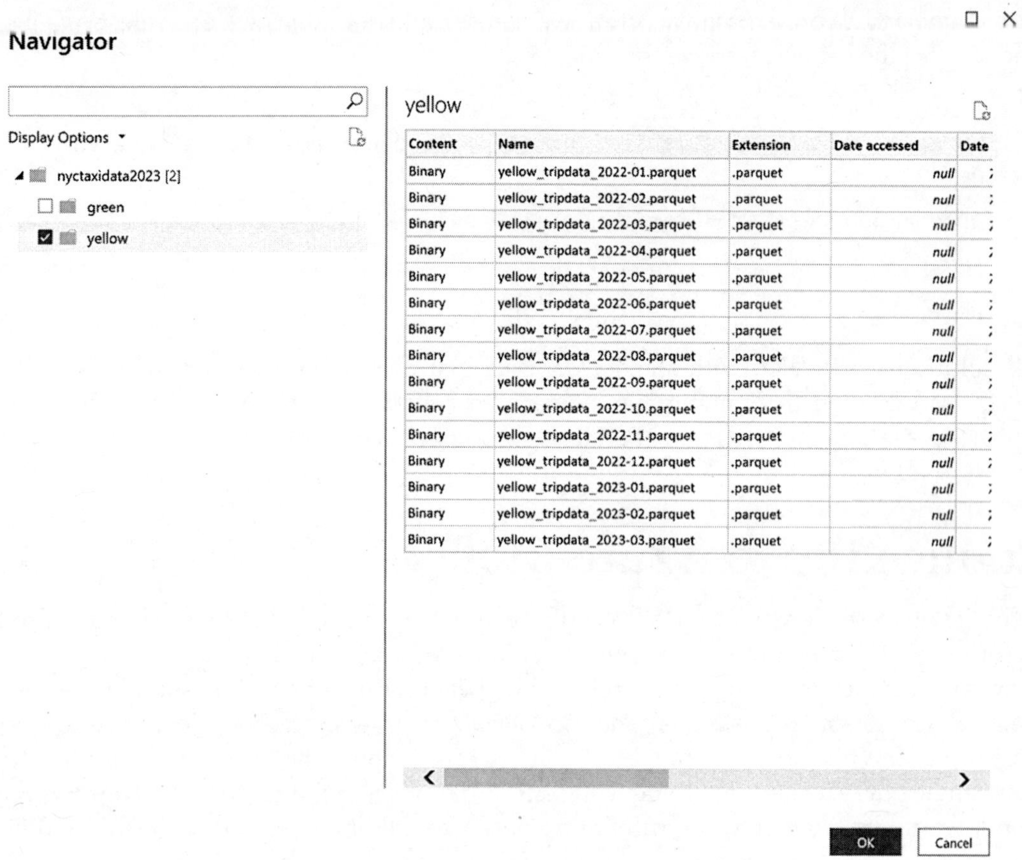

Figure 4.27: *Selecting data from Azure Blob Storage container*

Once you have selected your data, you can begin your transformations with Power Query. Note that if you connected to a folder with data inside, you would need to combine and transform the content column to extract the data from the individual files inside.

Connecting to Azure Blob Storage using the advanced editor is straightforward compared to other connectors. Using the **`AzureStorage.Blobs()`** function, we can connect to our server:

AzureStorage.Blobs()	
Parameter	**Description**
Account	Text based value that specifies the account name or link to your storage account
Options	Options wrapped in square brackets to apply options for BlockSize, RequestSize, and ConcurrentRequests.

Table 4.11: Table of the AzureStorage.Blobs() parameters

To get started with our connection, we will first use the **AzureStorage.Tables()** function to connect to our storage account:

```
let
    Source = AzureStorage.Blobs("<Account Name>")
in
    Source
```

Once connected to our storage account, we can see a list of folders we can select. We just need to filter the list and retrieve the data:

```
let
    Source = AzureStorage.Blobs("<Account Name>"),
    Folder = Source{[Name="yellow"]}[Data]
in
    Folder
```

When using this connector, it is advisable that you restrict the amount of data being extracted. Because of the volume that can be contained within blob containers, the refresh can become long and resource-intensive. If you are using the Power BI service, this can eat into your premium capacity availability, so ensure you are putting in safeguards to manage your refresh effectively.

Lastly, it might be worth considering using the **Azure Data Lake** connector instead of the Azure Blob connector. The connection to the storage container works the same way, except it assumes the data you are accessing is all the same structure and can be combined. This might save you some effort when connecting to a container with static data. Instead of using the **AzureStorage.Blobs()** function, you would use the **AzureStorage.DataLake()** function instead when using the advanced editor.

Connecting to Dremio

Dremio is a Data Lake engine designed to unify diverse data sources while maintaining performance and enabling self-service. Dremio, founded in 2015, recently has new integrations with the Power BI service to help bolster the self-service experience. To leverage Dremio, go to the **New Source** dropdown in the Power Query editor and select **More**. Find the **Dremio Cloud** connector and click Connect. First thing you need to do is specify your server. If you are in the US, your server is **`sql.dremio.cloud`**. If you are in the EU, it is **`sql.eu.dremio.cloud`**. There are additional options available for your query. You can specify your **Project** where your data resides, and the **Engine** used to render that data. The **Tag** and **Queue** options help with routing and selection but are only available with the **Dremio Software** platform. Since we are using the cloud, this does not apply to our scenario. Lastly, we can decide on a **Data Connectivity mode** of **Import** or **Direct Query**:

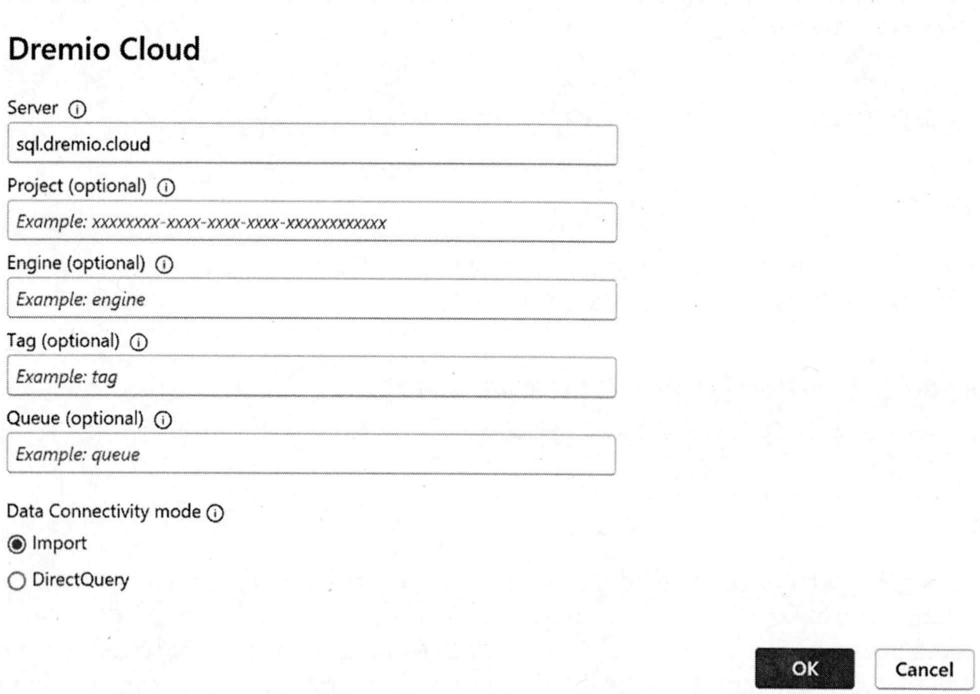

***Figure 4.28:** Configuring the Dremio Cloud connector*

Next, you can select your authentication mode. With Dremio Cloud, you can either use your Microsoft account or you can use a personal access token generated within the cloud service. After authentication, you can navigate through the schema to select the objects for your query.

Connecting to Dremio is straightforward. Using the **`Dremio.DatabaseByServer()`** function, we can connect to our server:

Dremio.DatabaseByServer()	
Parameter	**Description**
`Server`	URL to Dremio cloud server. In the US it is `sql.dremio.cloud`. If the EU, it is `sql.eu.dremio.cloud`.
`Project`	Project ID as assigned by Dremio Cloud

Table 4.12: *Table of the Dremio.DatabaseByServer() parameters*

To get started with our connection, we will first use the **`Dremio.DatabaseByServer()`** function to connect to our instance:

```
let
    Source = DremioCloud.DatabasesByServer("sql.dremio.cloud", null)
in
    Source
```

Next, we will specify the schema we will use that contains the data for our query:

```
let
    Source = DremioCloud.DatabasesByServer("sql.dremio.cloud", null),
    Schema = Source{[Name="Samples.samples.dremio.com",Kind="Schema"]}
[Data]
in
    Schema
```

Lastly, we must select the object for our query:

```
let
    Source = DremioCloud.DatabasesByServer("sql.dremio.cloud", null),
    Schema = Source{[Name="Samples.samples.dremio.com",Kind="Schema"]}
[Data],
    Table = Schema{[Name="NYC-taxi-trips-iceberg",Kind="Table"]}[Data]
in
    Table
```

While this is not as popular of a solution at the time of publication, solutions like these tend to grow quickly over time. So, while you may not need this connector today, you might find yourself needing it in the not-so-distant future.

Conclusion

In this chapter, we covered how to connect to different database sources. We started by connecting SQL server connections regardless of platform. We then explored the use of cloud-based services such as Cosmos DB, Azure Synapse Analytics, Google BigQuery, Amazon Redshift, and Dremio. We also explored how to connect to less structured sources such as Azure Tables, Dataflows, Blob containers and Data Lakes.

In the next chapter, we will explore some common data connectors so **Software as a Service** (**SaaS**) platforms you might encounter for deeper analysis.

Join our book's Discord space

Join the book's Discord Workspace for Latest updates, Offers, Tech happenings around the world, New Release and Sessions with the Authors:

https://discord.bpbonline.com

CHAPTER 5
Connect to Third-Party Data Sources

Introduction

This chapter will walk you through how to connect to third party data sources that have been added into Power Query. We will first talk about how third-party connectors are structured and the considerations around them. Then, we will explore common connectors such as Salesforce, Zendesk, Azure DevOps, Google Analytics, Smart Sheet, and LinkedIn Sales Navigator. We will also explore what you can do if no connector is available within Power Query.

Structure

The chapter covers the following topics:

- Understanding third-party connectors
- Connecting to Salesforce
- Connecting to Zendesk
- Connecting to Azure DevOps
- Connecting to Google Analytics
- Connecting to Smartsheet

- Connecting to LinkedIn Sales Navigator
- Considerations for third-party connectors
- What if there is no connector?

Objectives

At the end of this chapter, you will understand how to use Power Query to connect to data found inside third-party software packages. You will learn how to configure your connections to balance performance and resources to meet the needs of your consumers. You will also take a look at how to manage and manipulate third-party database connectors to meet your organization's needs.

Understanding third-party connectors

Power Query has several third-party connectors available to simplify the process of ingesting data into your models. The concept is simple with these connectors as they are designed to allow you to perform reporting, deeper analysis, or the ability to combine the data with other sources to meet the needs of your solution. The idea is to allow you rapid access to your data with minimal configuration.

For example, the SurveyMonkey connector allows you to connect directly to a survey you have posted within the platform. Now, you can achieve the same goals using their APIs instead, but the connector simplifies the process of connecting and extracting the data. If we used their APIs, we would have to pull back the survey information first. Then, we would pass that information to the questions and the responses to bring back the correct data. Lastly, we would need to design the model behind the data, so it is useful for analysis. Instead, the connector allows us to just pick the survey we want, and it brings back the data in a usable structure with no transformation.

These connectors leverage the functions we have already discussed in the first four chapters of this book. Someone just took the time to create these connectors in Visual Studio so they would be easier to use. If you are using third-party software, take a moment to see if a connector is available because it might save you considerable headaches.

Connecting to Salesforce

Salesforce is a **Customer Relationship Manager** (**CRM**) that helps organizations manage their sales pipelines through a suite of tools. Power Query can connect to Salesforce in two ways. The first way is through the **Salesforce Reports** connector. This allows you to pull data from pre-canned report queries. This is optimal if you are looking to pull a standard report such as open opportunities or won deals. The **Salesforce Objects** connector allows you to access the underlying tables within the platform. While it will require additional effort to implement, you can access all the underlying data to create your own custom reports. To get started, go to the **New Source** dropdown in the Power Query editor and select **More**. When you search for Salesforce, you will see both connectors available, as shown:

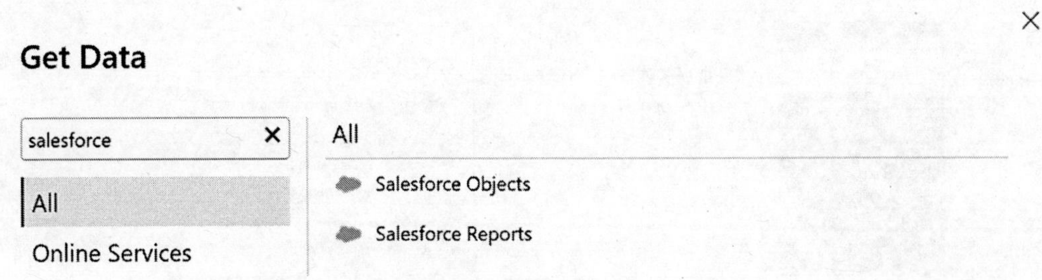

***Figure 5.1:** Options for connecting to Salesforce*

Since the reports require less transformation, we will select **Salesforce Reports** first. You will be brought to a screen that will ask you if you wish to use a **Production** URL or a **Custom** URL. Unless you have a URL for a custom instance, keep production selected and click **OK**. Note that there is a warning for the Salesforce APIs that they only bring back the first two thousand rows for a report. If this is an issue, you will need to use the objects connector instead:

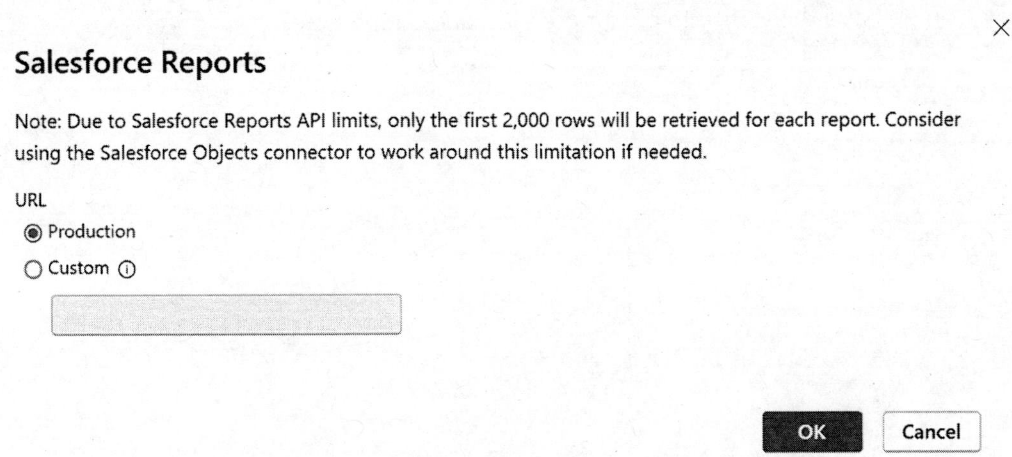

***Figure 5.2:** Configuring the Salesforce Reports connector*

Next, you will be prompted to authenticate to your instance of Salesforce. When you click **Sign In**, a new window will open, asking you to sign in. You can enter your username and password or use one of the single sign-on options listed below. Once you authenticate, you will be asked to allow access to Salesforce via Power Query. Click **Allow** to connect to your instance as shown below:

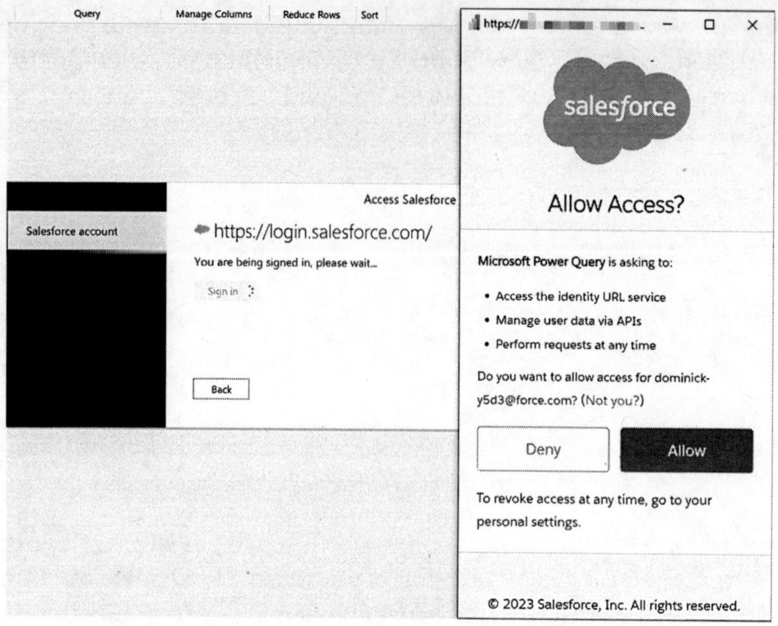

Figure 5.3: Authenticating with the Salesforce Reports connector

After you have authenticated, you can select which reports you wish to bring into Power Query. You do have the ability to pick more than one on this screen:

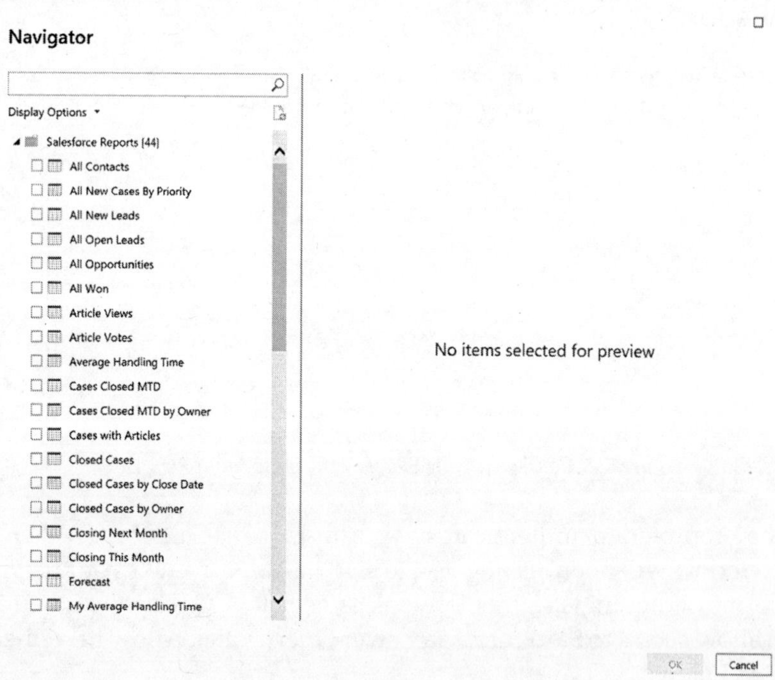

Figure 5.4: Selecting reports from Salesforce

We can use the advanced editor to connect to Salesforce Reports. We will use the **`Salesforce.Reports()`** function to connect to our data source. The parameters for this function are as follows:

`Salesforce.Reports()`	
Parameter	**Description**
`loginUrl`	Login URL for your Salesforce instance. Unless you are using a custom instance, use `https://login.salesforce.com/`
`options`	Options wrapped in square brackets to apply options for `ApiVersion` and `Timeout`.

Table 5.1: *Table of the Salesforce.Reports() parameters*

Once we connect to Salesforce using the **`Salesforce.Reports()`** function, we must filter our results to the report we want to query:

```
let
    Source = Salesforce.Reports("https://login.salesforce.com/"),
    Report = Source{[Name="00OHu00000AOcH5MAL"]}[Data]
in
    Report
```

Resist the urge to use the **Label** field instead of the **Name** field, as labels tend to change. The **Name** field is a unique ID that will ensure future refreshes will be maintained in the event of changes.

If the Salesforce Reports connector does not meet your needs, we can connect to the Salesforce Objects connector instead. Click on the new source dropdown in the Power Query editor and select more. Select **Salesforce Objects** and click on **Connect**. You will be prompted with a similar screen as in *Figure 5.2,* where you are asked to use a production or custom URL. Once again, unless you have a custom instance, just use the production URL. Once you authenticate, you will be brought to the navigation screen to pick which tables you would like to add into your model, as shown:

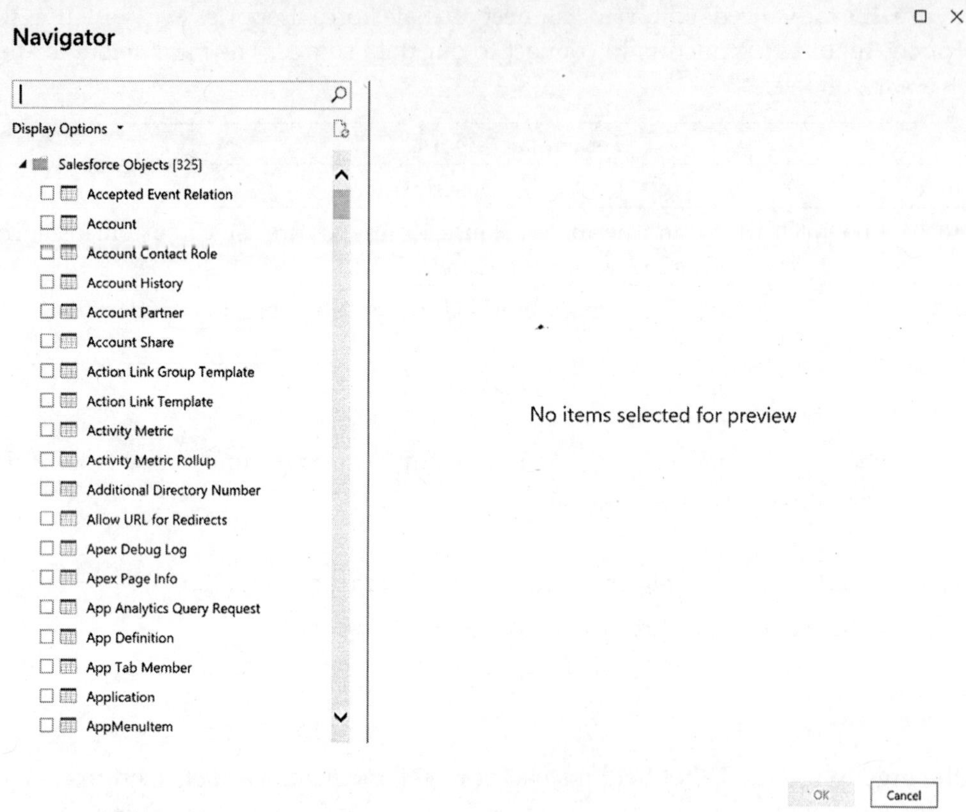

***Figure 5.5:** Selecting tables from Salesforce*

We can use the advanced editor to connect to Salesforce Objects as well. We will use the **`Salesforce.Data()`** function to connect to our data source. The parameters for this function are as follows:

Salesforce.Data()	
Parameter	**Description**
`loginUrl`	Login URL for your Salesforce instance. Unless you are using a custom instance, use `https://login.salesforce.com/`
`options`	Options wrapped in square brackets to apply options for `CreateNavigationProperties`, `ApiVersion` and `Timeout`.

***Table 5.2:** Table of the Salesforce.Data() parameters*

Once we connect to Salesforce using the **`Salesforce.Data()`** function, we must filter our results to the table we want to query:

```
let
    Source = Salesforce.Data("https://login.salesforce.com/"),
```

```
    Table = Source{[Name="Account"]}[Data]
in
    Table
```

You might be asking yourself why it is okay to use a common name with the Salesforce Objects connector. Well, we are using the same field. There is a **`Label`** column that is brought back as well. Salesforce has used a much nicer name for tables as opposed to reports. Regardless, it is always best practice to use the **`Name`** column when filtering this data.

Connecting to Zendesk

Zendesk is a popular web-based customer service and engagement platform organizations use to track interactions with their customers. Organizations like to keep strong tabs on these interactions because they drive customer satisfaction. It is a wealth of knowledge for identifying stale tickets, incident analysis, and overall satisfaction for customers your organization supports. To connect to Zendesk, go to the **New Source** dropdown in the Power Query editor and select **More**. From there, find Zendesk and click on **Connect**. You will be asked to provide the URL to your instance:

Figure 5.6: *Configuring the Zendesk connector*

Next, you will be prompted to provide your credentials. At this point it is important to note that if you did not provide the **`https://`** at the beginning of your URL in the last step, you will receive a warning that your connection is not encrypted. Go back and correct that before signing in. A new window will open for you to enter your credentials. If it is your first time using Zendesk with Power Query, you will be asked to allow Power Query to access your data, as shown:

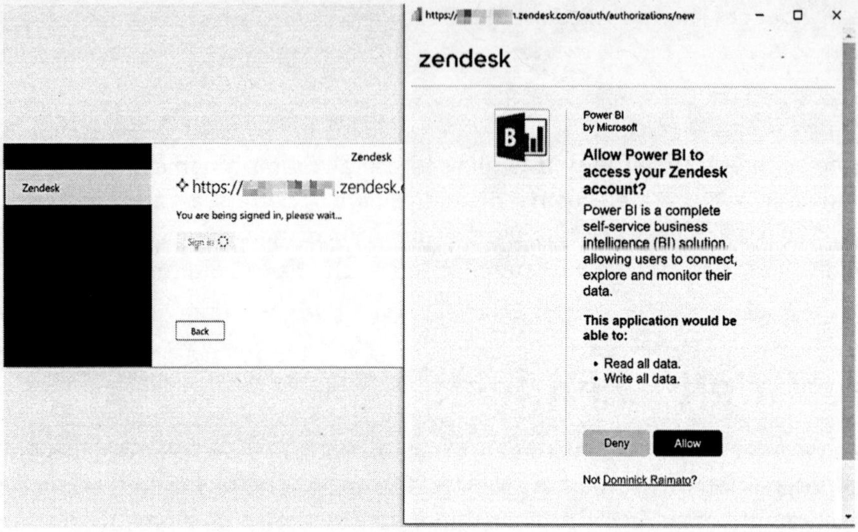

***Figure 5.7:** Authenticating with the Zendesk connector*

Once you have authenticated, you can select the tables you wish to bring from Zendesk into your model:

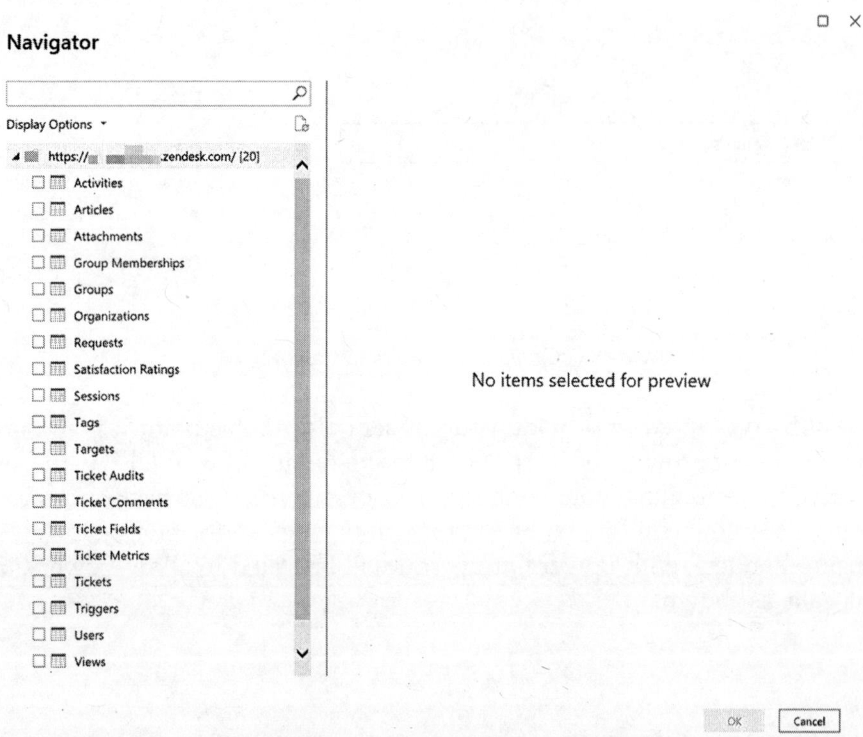

***Figure 5.8:** Selecting tables from Zendesk*

We can use the advanced editor to connect to Zendesk. We will use the **`Zendesk.Tables()`** function to connect to our data source. The parameters for this function are as follows:

`Zendesk.Tables()`	
Parameter	**Description**
`url`	URL to your instance of Zendesk. Must include the `https://` at the beginning to authenticate properly.

***Table 5.3:** Table of the Zendesk.Tables() parameters*

Once we connect to Zendesk using the **`Zendesk.Tables()`** function, we must filter our results to the table we want to query. For Zendesk, it is best to filter on the **`Key`** column:

```
let
    Source = Zendesk.Tables("https://<instance>.zendesk.com"),
    Table = Source{[Key="tickets"]}[Data]
in
    Table
```

It is important to note that there is a limitation with this connector. Unfortunately, the Zendesk connector limits you to one thousand rows of data. You can work around this issue with their API documentation, but it will require the knowledge you will acquire in *Chapter 15, Advanced Web Connections*, to achieve your goal.

Connecting to Azure DevOps

Azure DevOps is a cloud-based collaboration platform designed to blend development tools with services to enable efficient delivery of solutions. Due to its ability to track and manage development projects within Azure DevOps, organizations like to leverage Power Query to perform additional analysis and reporting. We can use Power Query to query data found in the Analytics Views portion of the platform. To get started, click on the **New Source** dropdown in the Power Query editor and click **More**. Next, select **Azure DevOps** and click on **Connect**. To ensure you are querying the right data, you will be asked to identify your organization and team project:

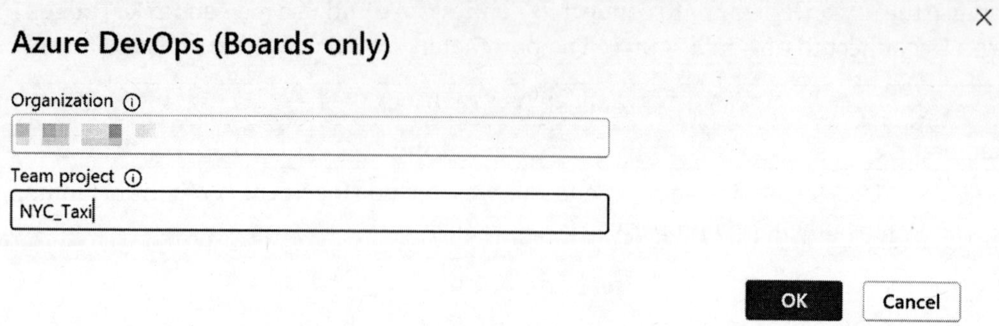

Figure 5.9: Configuring the Azure DevOps connector

Next, you will be prompted for your credentials. Because Azure DevOps is a Microsoft cloud product, you can use your **Organizational Account** to authenticate. However, you can also use a **Personal Access Token** if you prefer:

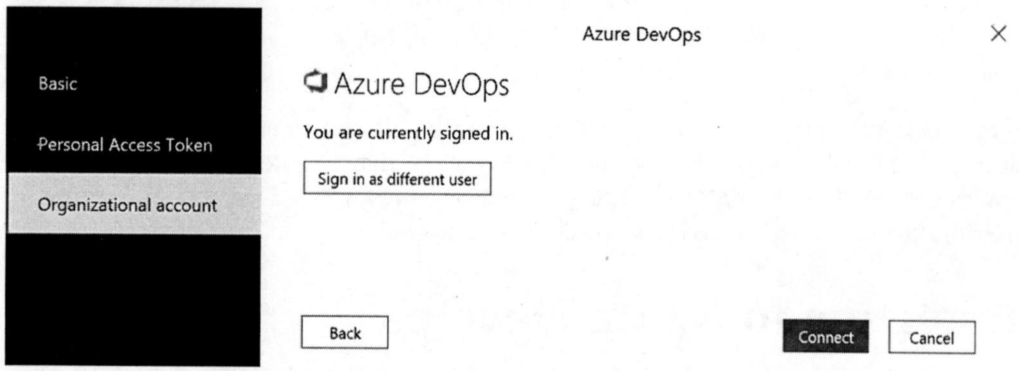

Figure 5.10: Authenticating with the Azure DevOps connector

After you have authenticated, you can select which views you wish to bring into your model, as shown in the following figure:

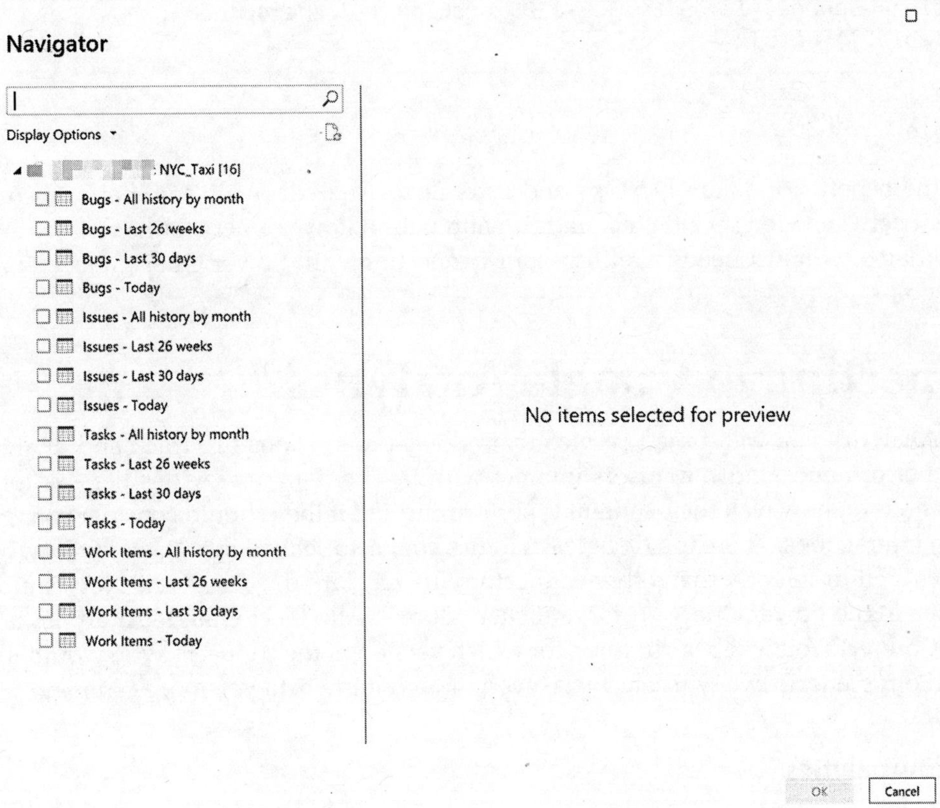

Figure 5.11: *Selecting views from Azure DevOps*

We can use the advanced editor to connect to Azure DevOps. We will use the **`VSTS.AnalyticsViews()`** function to connect to our data source. The parameters for this function are as follows:

`VSTS.AnalyticsViews()`	
Parameter	**Description**
`organization`	Name of your organization. This is the text in the URL of your instance after `https://dev.azure.com/`
`project`	Name of your team project

Table 5.4: *Table of the VSTS.AnalyticsViews() parameters*

Once we connect to Azure DevOps using the **`VSTS.AnalyticsViews()`** function, we must filter our results to the table we want to query. For Azure DevOps, it is best to filter on the **`Id`** column:

```
let
    Source = VSTS.AnalyticsViews("<organization>", "NYC_Taxi"),
```

```
    Table = Source{[Id="9f8f19c8-1309-45c6-bbf1-722bcf464dd0",-
Kind="Table"]}[Data]
in
    Table
```

One of the benefits of Azure DevOps and leveraging Analytics Views is that it ensures alignment between views inside the platform and within Power Query. If the two are ever uncoordinated, you just need to refresh your connection with Power Query, and you are good to go.

Connecting to Google Analytics

Google Analytics is a web-based service that allows organizations to track and analyze website performance and how users interact with it. The data it provides helps inform organizations on how well their content is performing and if they should consider changes based on interactions. There is a Google Analytics connector baked into Power Query, but it behaves a bit differently than other connectors. To get started, click on the **New Source** dropdown in the Power Query editor and click **More**. Next, select **Google Analytics** and click on **Connect**. You will be prompted for which version of the connector you would like to use. In our scenario, we will select **v2.0** even though it is a beta version, as shown:

Figure 5.12: *Configuring the Google Analytics connector*

Next, you will be prompted to authenticate. When you click sign in, a webpage will open and ask for your credentials. If this is your first time signing in, you will be asked to allow access to your data with Power Query. The window will look like the following figure:

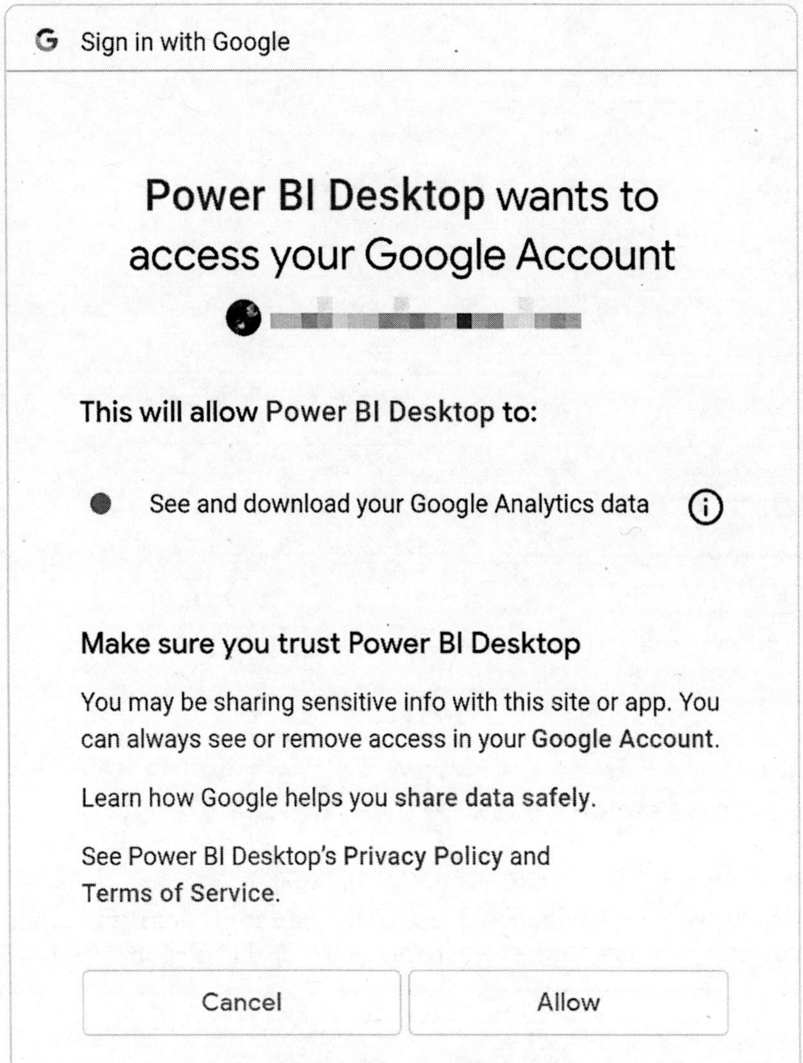

***Figure 5.13:** Authenticating with the Google Analytics connector*

Once you authenticate, you will need to select your objects. However, this is where the Google Analytics connector behaves a little differently. This connector provides two options for you to select. The first is Measure, which provides an aggregation of a particular value. Further down, you can select a **Dimension**, which will group your measure. We will need to select both to have the best experience with our data:

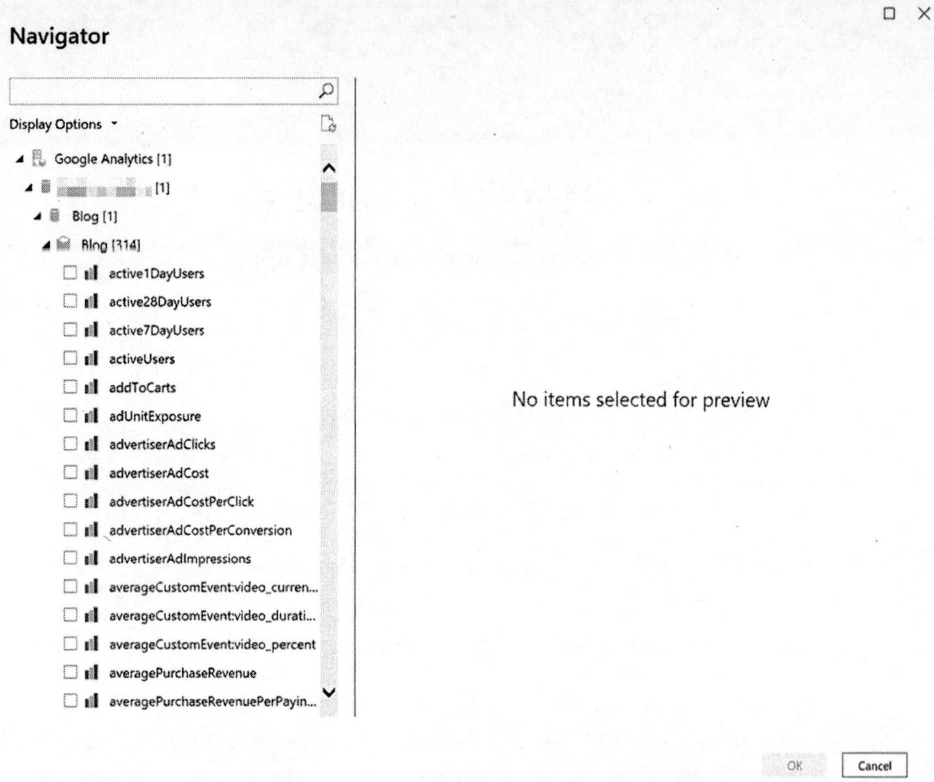

Figure 5.14: *Selecting a measure and cube from Google Analytics*

We can use the advanced editor to connect to Google Analytics. However, we will need to specify more details with our navigation. We will use the **`GoogleAnalytics.Accounts()`** function to connect to our data source. The parameters for this function are as follows:

`GoogleAnalytics.Accounts()`	
Parameter	**Description**
`options`	Specify the implementation for **1.0** or **2.0**. Example: `[implementation = "2.0"]`

Table 5.5: *Table of the GoogleAnalytics.Accounts() parameters*

We will start our connection by using the **`GoogleAnalytics.Accounts()`** function using the v2.0 implementation:

```
let
    Source = GoogleAnalytics.Accounts([Implementation="2.0"])
in
    Source
```

Once we have connected to Google Analytics, we must specify which account we want to view:

```
let
    Source = GoogleAnalytics.Accounts([Implementation="2.0"]),
    Account = Source{[Id="accounts/216837680"]}[Data]
in
    Account
```

After we have selected the account, we must select the property we want to view. We will have to do this twice to get to our cube. Once there, we will need to specify our measure and our cube:

```
let
    Source = GoogleAnalytics.Accounts([Implementation="2.0"]),
    Account = Source{[Id="accounts/216837680"]}[Data],
    Property = Account{[Id="properties/299016560"]}[Data],
    Cube = Property{[Id="properties/299016560"]}[Data],
    Model = Cube.Transform(Cube,
        {
            {Cube.AddAndExpandDimensionColumn, "firstUserSource", {"firstUs-
erSource"}, {"firstUserSource"}},
            {Cube.AddMeasureColumn, "activeUsers", "activeUsers"}
        })
in
    Model
```

Suddenly, that query became far more complex. We will address details around how to use cubes in *Chapter 10, Combining and Manipulating Data*. Until then, it is important to understand that we need a much more intimate knowledge of what is available with Google Analytics when we use the advanced editor. We recommend using the graphical interface to build out your queries but do not be afraid to adjust as you learn about the dimensions that are available.

Connecting to Smartsheet

Smartsheet is a cloud-based project management tool that allows organizations to track the progress of their projects. No organization has ever declined reporting when it comes to projects. Smartsheet makes the integration seamless for easier analysis and reporting. To get started, go to the **New Source** dropdown in the Power Query editor and click on **More**. From there, select **Smartsheet** and click on **Connect**. Smartsheet only has one source, so there is no connector to configure. However, you will need to authenticate using your Smartsheet credentials. If this is your first time using Power Query to connect to Smartsheet, you will need to allow access with your account, as illustrated:

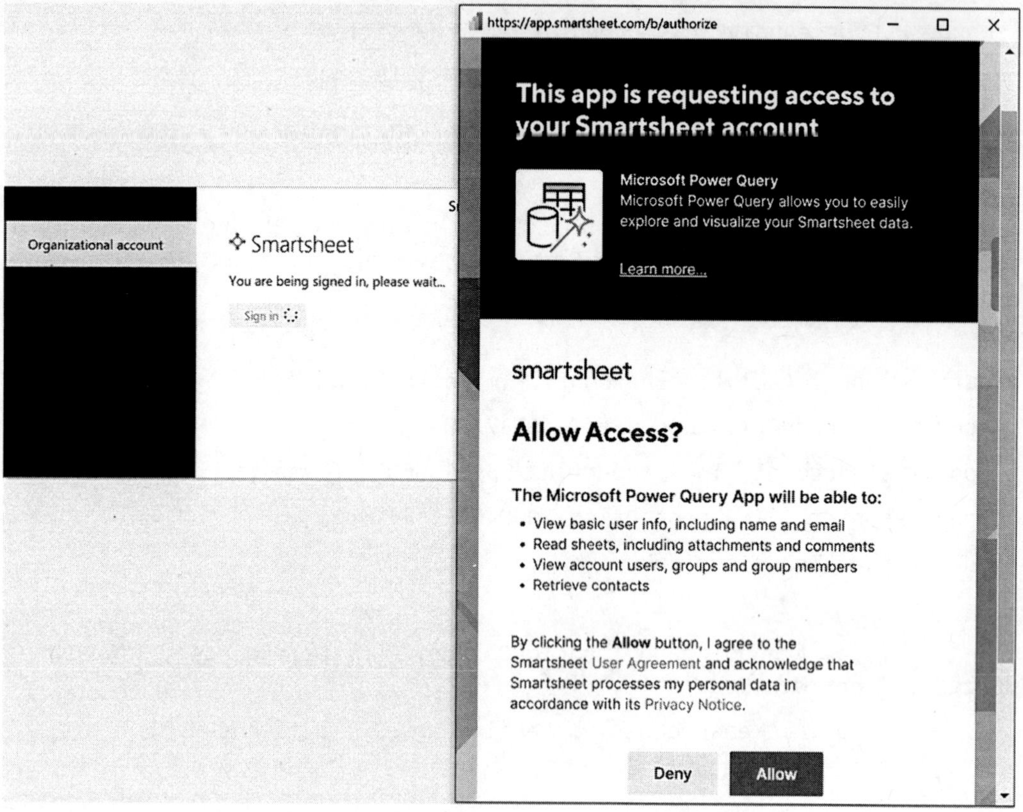

Figure 5.15: *Authenticating with the Smartsheet connector*

Next, you will need to select which objects you wish to return. With Smartsheet, you have three options. In *Figure 5.16*, you will note that there are three different icons available. The icon associated with **1. Task Sheet** is a table of tasks. The icon associated with **2. Task Summary Report,** and **3. Overdue Task Report** are reports that are built into the Smartsheet system. These can be canned or customized for your reporting needs. We will talk about the icon next to **Smartsheet.Query** momentarily. For now, we will select **1. Task Sheet** and click on **OK**:

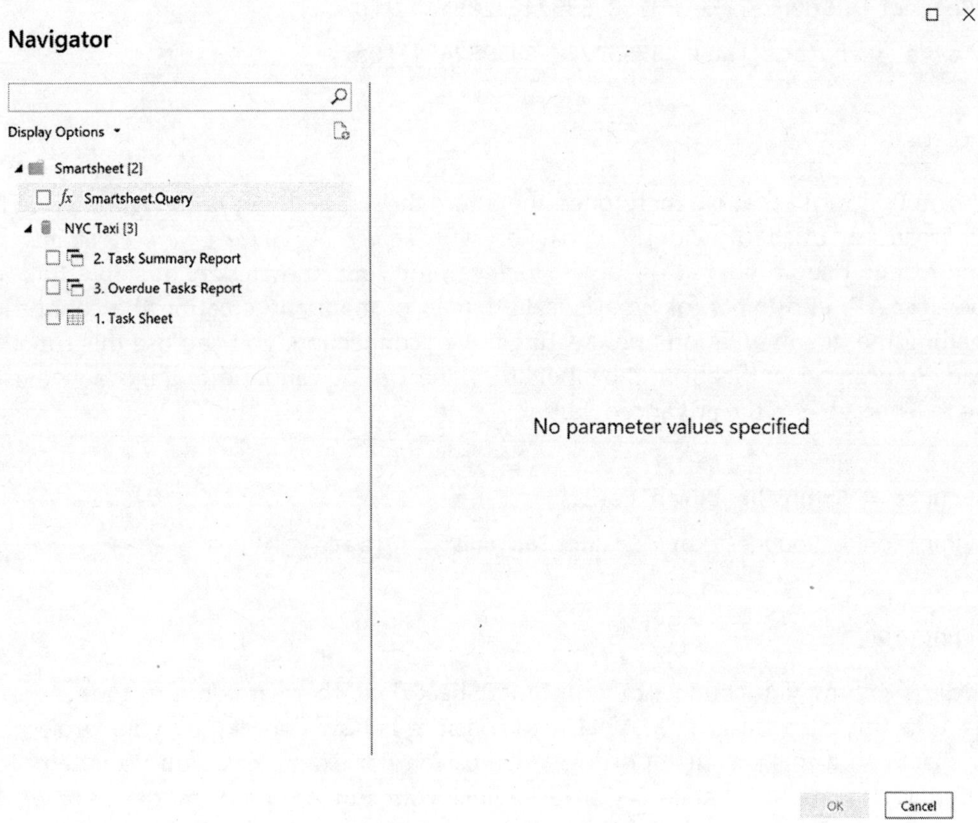

***Figure 5.16:** Selecting objects from Smartsheet*

The hardest part about connecting to Smartsheet with the advanced editor is remembering the name of the function you will use. We will use the **`Smartsheet.Tables()`** function to access our data. There are no parameters to use with this function, so this is the easiest connector you will use within Power Query. Once we connect to Smartsheet, we must filter our response to access the project we want for our query using the **Key** column:

```
let
    Source = Smartsheet.Tables(),
    Project = Source{[Key="1583533740320644"]}[Data]
in
    Project
```

Next, we need to filter the object we want to query. We will use the **Key** column in this context as well:

```
let
    Source = Smartsheet.Tables(),
```

```
    Project = Source{[Key="1583533740320644"]}[Data],
    Tasks = Project{[Key="8755222050459524"]}[Data]
in
    Tasks
```

Now, you will recall that we mentioned the **Smartsheet.Query** object in *Figure 5.16*. This object creates a function inside Power Query. In *Chapter 14, Power Query Functions*, we will perform a deep dive on this topic. However, for your knowledge, this object allows us to select API endpoints for Smartsheet. Instead of manually creating the connection by reading the documentation and creating a web connection, you can use this function instead. You can select this from the navigator pane, or you can modify the code we used above to leverage it in the advanced editor:

```
let
    Source = Smartsheet.Tables(),
    Function = Source{[Key=" function_query"]}[Data]
in
    Function
```

Regardless of how you connect to your Smartsheet data, there are options to meet your needs. One thing that might be of value to consider is how you deploy your projects in Smartsheet could make your reporting much easier. For example, if you use a template repeatedly, you might be able to quickly adjust your Power Query model to meet the needs of your individual project. Minor changes to the Key values will simplify how you deploy reporting for each templatized project you embark upon.

Connecting to LinkedIn Sales Navigator

Our last connector of this chapter, LinkedIn Sales Navigator, is a powerful tool for helping manage leads and contacts within your professional network. Sales organizations always struggle with clear and actionable data. However, pairing Power Query with LinkedIn Sales Navigator, you might be able to take better action with your sales funnel. You can track activities, outcomes, users, and contracts to ensure you are getting the most value out of your investment. To get started, go to the **New Source** dropdown in the Power Query editor and click on **More.** Select **LinkedIn Sales Navigator** and click on **Connect**. To configure the connector, you will be asked to provide the scope for contracts on the platform. You can select specific contracts or return all contracts. You also have an option to filter your contracts by date. In our scenario, we will select **All Contracts**:

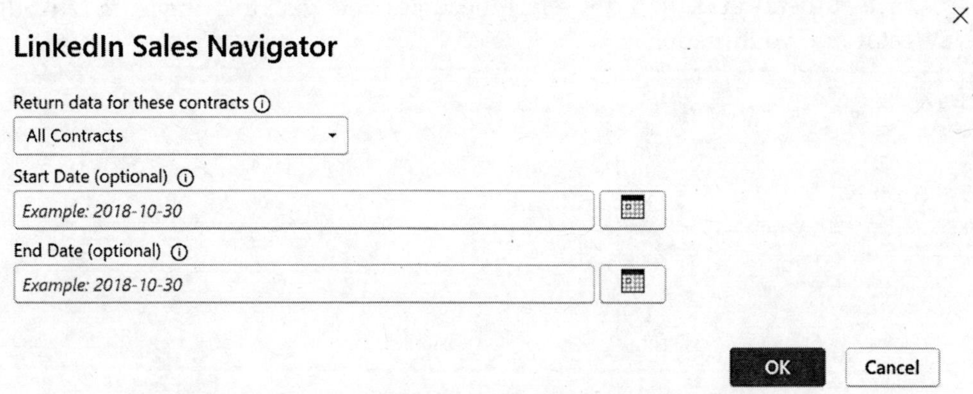

Figure 5.17: Configuring the LinkedIn Sales Navigator connector

Next, you will be prompted to provide your credentials. If it is your first-time using LinkedIn Sales Navigator with Power Query, you will be asked to allow Power Query to access your data:

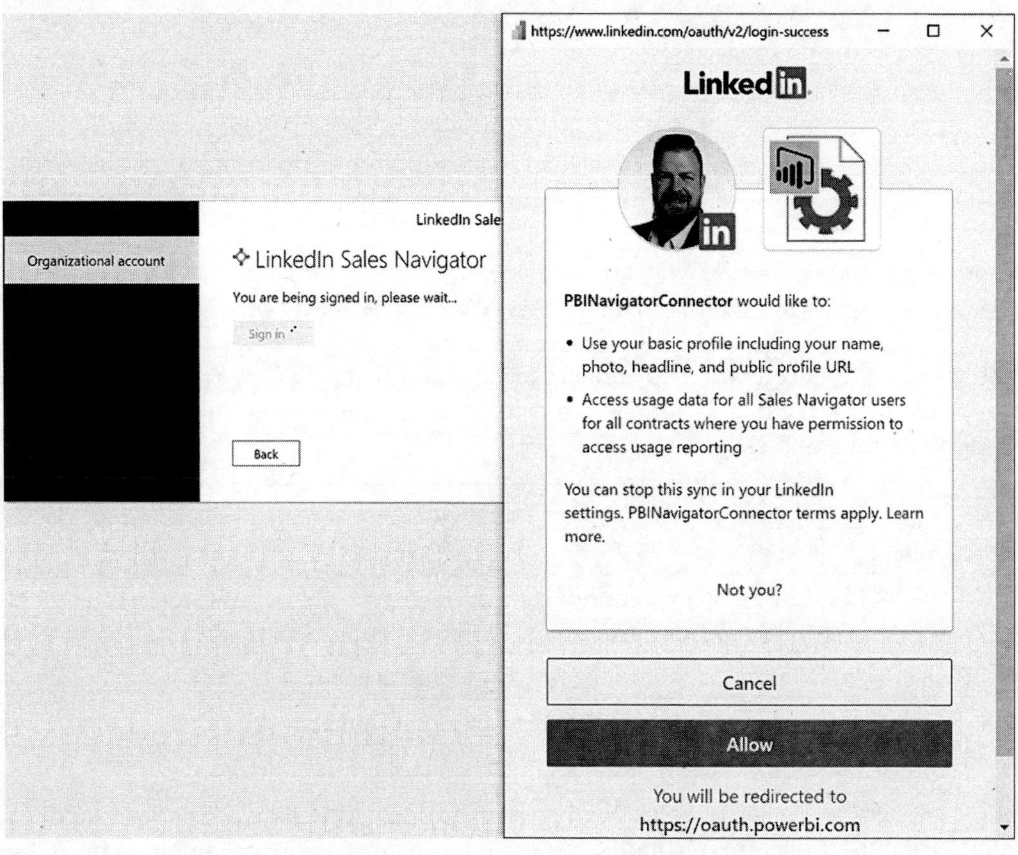

Figure 5.18: Authenticating with the LinkedIn Sales Navigator connector

Once you have authenticated, you can select the tables you wish to bring from LinkedIn Sales Navigator into your model:

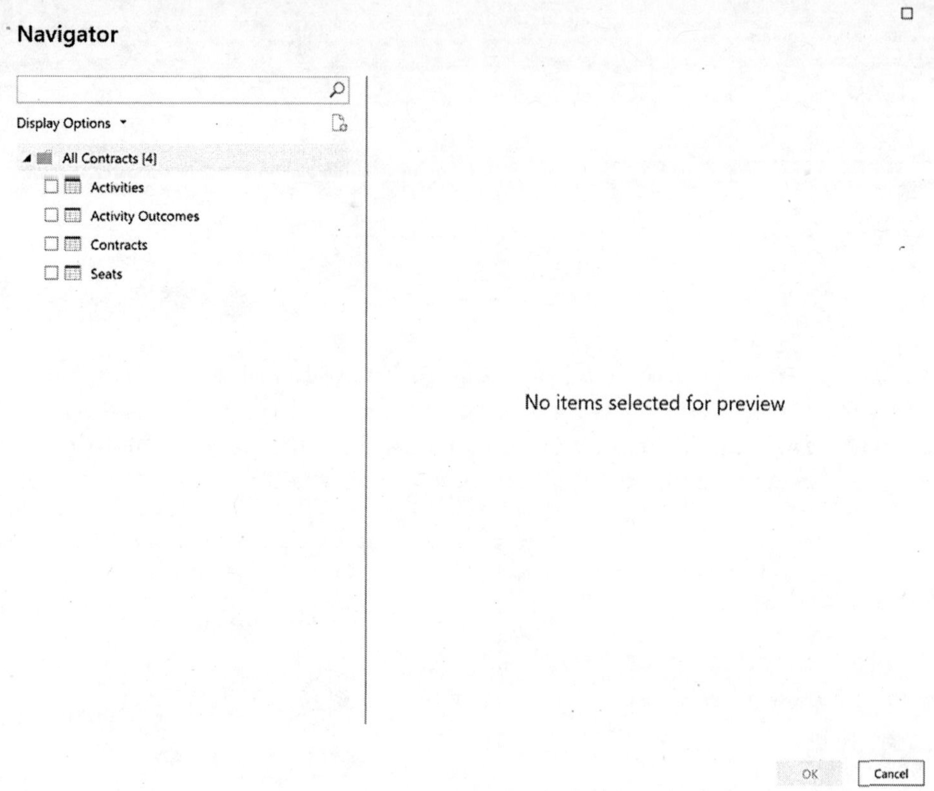

Figure 5.19: *Selecting tables from LinkedIn Sales Navigator*

We can use the advanced editor to connect to LinkedIn Sales Navigator. We will use the **`LinkedIn.SalesNavigator()`** function to connect to our data source. The parameters for this function are as follows:

`LinkedIn.SalesNavigator()`	
Parameter	**Description**
`selectContracts`	Choice on the scope of contracts to ingest. Either **All Contracts** or **Selected Contracts**
`startAt`	Start date filter for contracts. Default is `null`.
`endAt`	End date filter for contracts. Default is `null`.

Table 5.6: *Table of the LinkedIn.SalesNavigator() parameters*

Once we connect to LinkedIn Sales Navigator using the **`LinkedIn.SalesNavigator()`** function, we must filter our results to the table we want to query. For LinkedIn Sales Navigator, it is best to filter on the **`Key`** column:

```
let
    Source = LinkedIn.SalesNavigator("All Contracts", null, null),
    Activity = Source{[Key="exportActivityData"]}[Data]
in
    Activity
```

Keep in mind that your level of licensing for LinkedIn Sales Navigator might impact what resources you are able to leverage from this connector. Because premium features change on the LinkedIn platform on a regular basis, please review the fine print before signing up for a paid subscription to make sure it meets your needs before starting any reporting project with this connector.

Considerations for third party connectors

A consideration you must keep in mind with third-party connectors is the costs that might be associated with using them. It is a little deceiving, but you might find a connector that is available but learn that there is a cost associated with activating it. We have mentioned the SurveyMonkey connector above, but you might have noticed that it is not listed in this chapter. Unfortunately, there is a hefty price tag associated with connecting to data using the SurveyMonkey connector. You will need to balance the cost with the benefits of being able to connect to your data with these connectors. While there is a free tier of SurveyMonkey available to most users, the connector is really reserved for the less casual organizations who are looking to receive considerable results with their surveys.

Not all these connectors will cost additional money. Some might be included with your subscription. Others might have a free tier that throttles after so much use. Others might only bring basic data back and not provide you with the details you desire. This is one of the challenges that comes with our third-party services and one you must keep in mind when you are budgeting. We strongly encourage using these connectors as they simplify your transformations but also caution you when investigating your options because of these hidden costs. Just because you see the connector does not mean it is free. Make sure you research before purchasing any third-party software so you understand the costs associated with connecting directly via Power Query.

In addition, this chapter only covers a small subset of third-party connectors that are available within Power Query. To go through every third-party connector would require an entire book dedicated to the subject. However, there are a few others worth noting. If you are a project manager who leverages Asana or Smartsheet, there are connectors that allow you to connect to your project boards and report on tasks. Technology professionals might consider leveraging the InTune Data Warehouse or Solarwinds Service Desk connectors. If you are creating low/no code apps outside of Power Apps, you should consider the connectors for Quickbase or Zoho Creator. This list of connectors is rapidly changing as new connectors come to market. If you do not see a third-party connector for a platform, consider reaching out to them and inquire about it. Many companies create connectors that can be side loaded into Power Query for your use.

What if there is no connector?

We have looked at only a handful of connectors that are available for third-party software solutions. If you search the list and cannot find anything, do not fret, for there are options for you. Taking what you learned in *Chapter 3, Connect to Web-Based Data Sources*, you will find API documentation available. It will take effort and resources to enable your connection, but you will be able to do everything we have done in this chapter with a little creativity.

If the worst-case scenario arises where you do not have the ability to connect directly to your data, you can leverage what you learned in *Chapter 2, Connect to File-Based Data Sources* to get around these challenges. This might prove to be a more manual process but exporting your data with a few clicks and placing it into a folder might resolve your issue. Sure, it is not a perfect or eloquent solution, but sometimes you must work with what you have.

Keep in mind that if you must resort to manually exporting data, you might be able to set up an automated export that sends your data via email on a regular cadence. With a little help from Power Automate, you can get around this blocker by extracting the file and placing it accordingly. You also might be able to create **Robotic Process Automation (RPA)** with the Power Automate Desktop which also manages the exports for you.

Regardless of your situation, there are always ways around the challenges put forth by third-party software solutions. You are only limited by your creativity. It may not be obvious at first but take everything you will learn on your journey and think about how you can work through these challenges to realize your solutions.

Conclusion

In this chapter, we covered how to connect to different third-party data sources. We took a moment to understand how these connectors function. From there, we explored connectors for Salesforce, Zendesk, Azure DevOps, Google Analytics, Smartsheet, and LinkedIn Sales Navigator. We then discussed considerations for third-party connectors and how to access data in third-party platforms if no connector exists.

In the next chapter, we will finally start transforming our data within Power Query to prepare it for use.

CHAPTER 6

Managing Data Types

Introduction

In this chapter, we will dive into the use of data types in Power Query. While this topic may seem straightforward, there are implications that need to be considered when selecting data types, as they are not created equal. How and when you use data types can have implications on the data model and can contribute to bloat. In addition, downstream effects can be had upon the model when queries are merged and or relationships are created in the model. We will end this chapter by talking about best practices when using data types to provide the most efficiency with your model.

Structure

The chapter covers the following topics:

- Understanding data types in Power BI
- Detecting data types
- Assigning text data types
- Assigning numeric data types
- Assigning date/time data types

- Assigning logical data types
- Updating data types in bulk
- Combining data type transformations
- Understanding efficiencies with data types
- Optimizing data types upstream

Objectives

By the end of this chapter, you will understand how to use Power Query to manipulate data types in your queries. You will learn to configure your data columns for different data types while optimizing your model. You will also learn the implications of these changes and considerations that should be made to optimize your queries. At the end of this chapter, you will be able to set your data types for any column you encounter with ease.

Understanding data types in Power BI

Data types play a critical role in your model design and analytics work. Without data types, Power Query would not know how to transform the data into a usable format. As an example, every address in the United States has a five-digit numeric zip code. However, those who live in the northeast have a zip code that starts with zero. If you use a numeric data type, that preceding zero will be removed, and it becomes a four-digit number. This will cause confusion with reporting and analysis. The zip code `02101` belongs to `Boston`, `MA`, but the zip code `2101` will cause consumers to wonder if it was a mistake and meant to be `21011`, which is `Baltimore`, `MD`.

This example shows why it is important to be able to manipulate data types for queries. We can easily resolve the zip code fiasco by assigning a text data type instead, which will preserve the preceding zero. In addition, it might provide additional flexibility with other countries that use letters in their zip codes. As a result, Power Query allows us to assign the following data types to our columns:

- Text
- Decimal number (float)
- Fixed decimal number (currency)
- Whole number (integer)
- Percentage (float)
- Date / time

- Date
- Time
- Date/time/timezone
- Duration
- Logical (true/false)

Each one of these data types serves a purpose in your model. However, the real value is understanding how to best manage them and put them to use in Power Query. Eventually, you will load your data into your model and leverage it so getting data types correct need to be corrected before you reach the next step. Whether you use a column for a relationship or for reporting, the formatting of the data will matter so we want to make sure the data type is properly assigned before use.

Detecting data types

If you used Power Query in the past, you might remember that you had to assign data types for each query you ingested in Power Query. Over time, connectors that access unstructured data started to assign what it believes to be the right data type based upon an evaluation of the column. Your preference is really a personal choice. However, you can turn this feature on and off as you wish. If you go to the **File** tab in Power Query, you can go to **Options and Settings** and select **Options** to bring up all the behind-the-scenes settings, as shown:

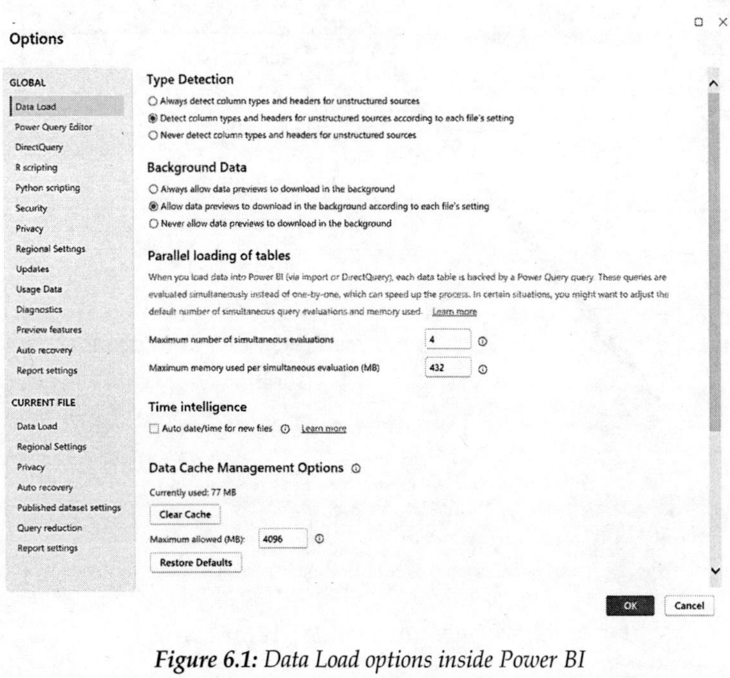

Figure 6.1: Data Load options inside Power BI

Under **Type Detection**, you can see you have three options available. The default option is the one selected in the middle, which detects column types and headers from unstructured data sources based on the settings with the connector. However, you can turn this on to always detect regardless of the connector or never detect. We find that leaving the default works for most people. However, if you prefer to have more control of your column types, we recommend selecting the never detect setting instead.

If you choose to allow Power Query to detect data types, occasionally, there will be an issue with what it predicts. Often, if Power Query is confused, it will default to a generic or text data type to avoid errors. If the data type assigned to your column is incorrect, the remainder of this chapter will help you assign the correct data type for your column. If you encounter any errors with your queries because of your data type change, we will address how to resolve them in *Chapter 7, Transforming Columns* or in *Chapter 8, Cleansing Columns.*

Assigning text data types

The text data type is the simplest one to manage. Text data types are simply strings of character put together. They could be names, descriptions, or a zip code. The purpose of them is to provide context and labels to your data model.

Assigning a text data type in the graphical interface can be managed in three places. The first is on the column header inside the Power Query editor. There is a data type icon that you can click on that provides a dropdown. From there, you can select the **Text** data type to assign it:

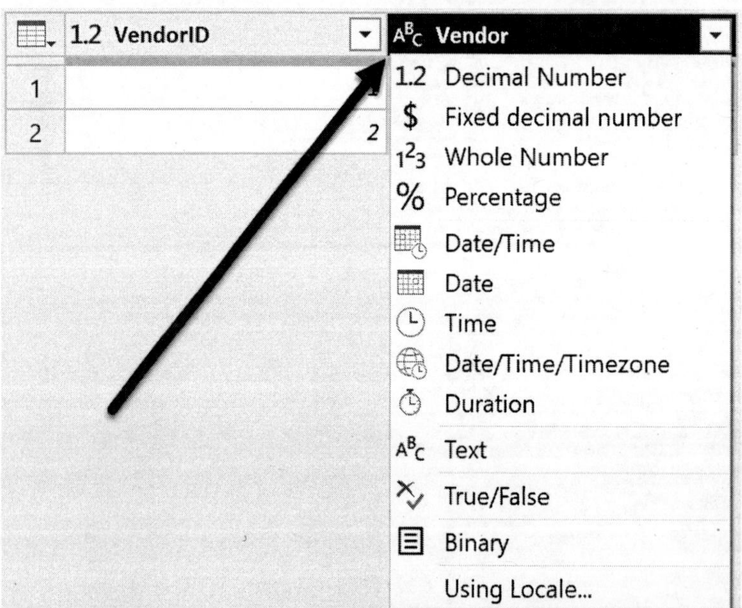

Figure 6.2: *Assigning the text data type to a column*

We also can leverage the data type in the transform ribbon bar in the Power Query editor. Start by selecting the column header. From there, expose the **Transform** ribbon bar. Next, click on the **Data Type** dropdown and select **Text**:

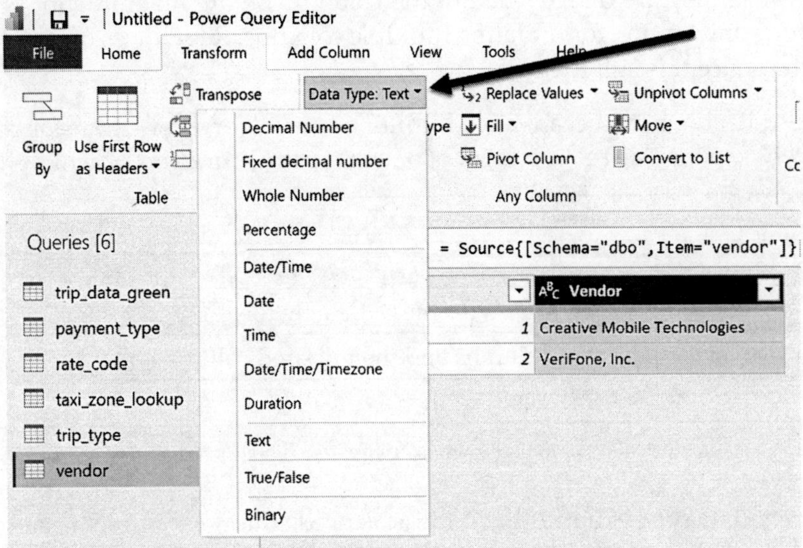

Figure 6.3: Assigning the text data type to a column in the transform ribbon

Lastly, we can change the data type by right-clicking on a column header and selecting **Text** under the **Change Type** sub-menu, as shown:

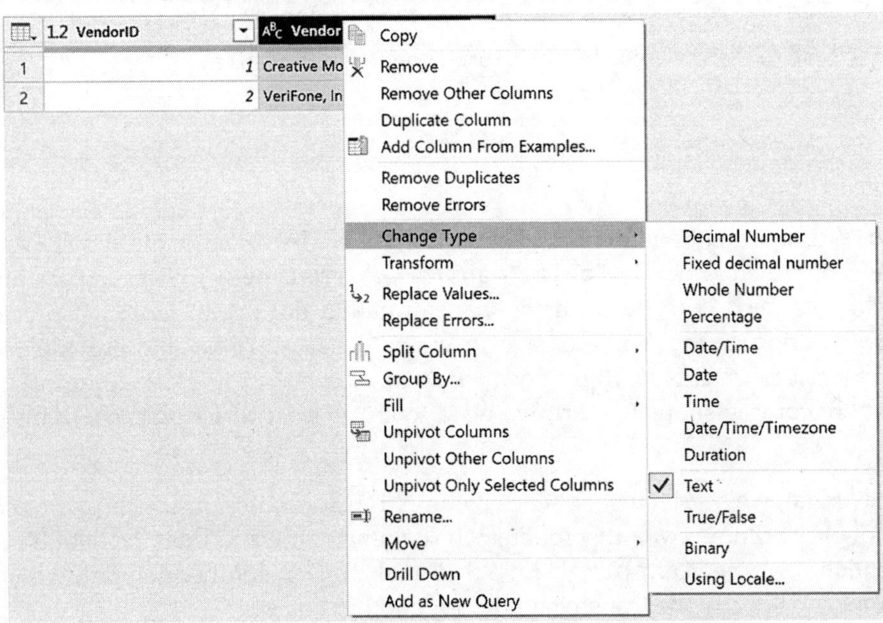

Figure 6.4: Assigning the text data type by right clicking the column header

It is a classic scenario of Microsoft providing multiple ways to accomplish the same thing. As a result, you might be wondering which option is best when updating the data type. The reality of the matter is that all three are perfectly valid. Options one and three are the easiest because they are directly tied to the column you are manipulating. However, option two is our only option for updating multiple columns. Regardless of which method you choose, the concept is still the same.

Changing the data type in the advanced editor is easy. For every transformation we perform, we will use the **`Table.TransformColumnTypes()`** function to achieve our goal:

`Table.TransformColumnTypes()`	
Parameter	**Description**
`Table`	A table in Power Query. Usually the preceding step.
`typeTransformations`	A list of columns and their desired column type.
`Culture`	Specified culture such as `en-US`.

Table 6.1: *Table of the Table.TransformColumnTypes() parameters*

To assign the text data type to a column in the advanced editor, we simply need to call the **`Table.TransformColumnTypes()`** function, identify our table, identify our column, and finally our data type:

```
let
    Source = Sql.Database("localhost", "NYC_Taxi"),
    VendorTable = Source{[Schema="dbo",Item="vendor"]}[Data],
    ChangedType = Table.TransformColumnTypes(VendorTable,{{"Vendor", type
text}})
in
    ChangedType
```

We need to take a moment and break this down a little bit. In our example above, we used the first two parameters inside **`Table.TransformColumnTypes()`**. The first parameter was the table we needed to perform the transformation on. In our case, the preceding step is called **`VendorTable`**. Once we have specified the table, we need to provide a list of columns we want to transform. Right now, we are only transforming one column, but we will have more coming soon. To start, we need to create a set of **`{}`** brackets to initialize the list.

Once we have that, we need to list out each column transformation inside its own set of **`{}`** brackets. For each column, we must identify the column name and then the data type. We used **`{"Vendor", type text}`** to achieve that goal. To add another column, we would add a comma and specify the transformation for another column.

We wanted to start with the text data type first for a couple of reasons. First, it is a common type that we encounter with our data models, but it is also the simplest. There are several ways to represent numbers and dates, so it makes sense for us to start with something easy. However, the other thing to note is that for every other data type moving forward, you will use the same process to update the type if you are leveraging the graphical interface. You will also use the **`Table.TransformColumnTypes()`** to manage any data type changes within the advanced editor. Take a moment and make sure you understand how data type transformations are made with the text data type first because we will continue to reference what we covered in this section over the next few data types.

Assigning numeric data types

We started assigning data types using text because it was the easiest, but if you are using Power Query, you likely care more about the number of data types. Since the primary goal of Power Query is to prepare your data for deeper analysis and reporting, it makes sense that transforming numeric values is a critical step in your process. Power Query allows us to transform our numeric values into whole numbers, decimal numbers, fixed decimal (or currency) numbers, and percentages. Regardless of which type is appropriate for your data, you can easily change it using the graphical interface, as explained in the *Assigning text data types* section of this chapter. However, for this section, we are going to dig into the different data types and address them.

We will start with the whole number data type. You might have heard it referenced as an integer. Simply put, the whole number data type does not have any decimal places. If we use the whole number data type on our column, it will automatically apply rounding logic to find the nearest whole number value. To apply this transformation in the advanced editor, we will use the **`Table.TransformColumnTypes()`** and **`Int64.Type`** to achieve our transformation:

```
let
  Source = Csv.Document(
    File.Contents("C:\NYC Taxi\trip_data_green.csv"),
    [Delimiter = ",", Columns = 20, Encoding = 1252, QuoteStyle = Quote-
Style.None]
  ),
  PromotedHeaders = Table.PromoteHeaders(Source, [PromoteAllScalars =
true]),
  ChangeWholeNumber = Table.TransformColumnTypes(
    PromotedHeaders,
    {{"VendorID", Int64.Type}, {"RatecodeID", Int64.Type}}
  )
```

```
in
  ChangeWholeNumber
```

We are using the same formula for transformation as we did with the text data type. We specify the table we wish to transform and then provide a list of column names and data types. In this example, we updated the **VendorID** and **RatecodeID** columns to use whole number values.

As you tried this code on your own, you might have asked why we used **Int64.Type** and not **Int32.Type** or **Int16.Type**. Simply put, the **Int64.Type** provides the most storage capacity flexibility as its limit is **+/- 9,33,372,036,854,775,807**. If you used **Int16.Type**, it would be limited to **+/- 32,767**. The benefit would be to save your data in a more compressed format. If you have values that you know will not exceed any limits, then it might be worth using a smaller integer format. However, for most people, **Int64.Type** will be the best option.

Next, we have the decimal number format. Decimal numbers will show fractions of the whole number in your column. But there are challenges with how we leverage them. The biggest question when it comes to decimals is the required precision needed for your number. If you use the decimal number type in Power Query, you might lose the precision you need for your analysis. In Power Query, decimal numbers are automatically rounded to two decimal places. This is designed to help manage the column and dictionary size in your model. To apply the decimal type with the advanced editor, we added a new step and assigned the **Decimal.Type** to the column:

```
let
  Source = Csv.Document(
    File.Contents("C:\NYC Taxi\trip_data_green.csv"),
    [Delimiter = ",", Columns = 20, Encoding = 1252, QuoteStyle = Quote-
Style.None]
  ),
  PromotedHeaders = Table.PromoteHeaders(Source, [PromoteAllScalars =
true]),
  ChangeWholeNumber = Table.TransformColumnTypes(
    PromotedHeaders,
    {{"VendorID", Int64.Type}, {"RatecodeID", Int64.Type}}
  ),
  ChangeDecimalNumber = Table.TransformColumnTypes(
    ChangeWholeNumber,
    {{"trip_distance", Decimal.Type}}
  )
```

```
in
  ChangeDecimalNumber
```

For most users of Power Query, this level of precision might be fine. However, you might require precision to four decimal places instead. Unfortunately, because of how Power Query manages this data, we will need to use the text data type instead. This is particularly important to know if you are using latitude or longitude values, as they will need to be represented in text format to get the exact precision you need.

Adjacent to the decimal number type is the fixed decimal number type. While the precision will remain the same as the decimal number, the fixed decimal number type allows you to treat it as currency once you have loaded the model. We just need to use the **Currency.Type** option for our column with the advanced editor:

```
let
  Source = Csv.Document(
    File.Contents("C:\NYC Taxi\trip_data_green.csv"),
    [Delimiter = ",", Columns = 20, Encoding = 1252, QuoteStyle = Quote-
Style.None]
  ),
  PromotedHeaders = Table.PromoteHeaders(Source, [PromoteAllScalars =
true]),
  ChangeWholeNumber = Table.TransformColumnTypes(
    PromotedHeaders,
    {{"VendorID", Int64.Type}, {"RatecodeID", Int64.Type}}
  ),
  ChangeDecimalNumber = Table.TransformColumnTypes(
    ChangeWholeNumber,
    {{"trip_distance", Decimal.Type}}
  ),
  ChangeFixedDecimalNumber = Table.TransformColumnTypes(
    ChangeDecimalNumber,
    {{"fare_amount", Currency.Type}}
  )
in
  ChangeFixedDecimalNumber
```

It is important to note that Power Query will set currency as default to US Dollars. However, once you have loaded it into either Excel or Power BI, you can manage the currency type for display purposes. You can either set a static value or make it dynamic with DAX expressions. Regardless of your choice, you will need to define it there instead of within Power Query.

The last numeric data type we must cover is percentage. The purpose of the percentage type is really to provide a visual representation of a decimal number in a percentage format. Instead of 0.7536, it will read as 75.36%. This accomplishes two goals. The first is making it much more visually appealing to read. The second is to preserve more than two decimal places for precision to allow for a fraction of a percent. We just need to use the **Percentage.Type** option for our column with the advanced editor:

```
let
  Source = Csv.Document(
    File.Contents("C:\NYC Taxi\trip_data_green.csv"),
    [Delimiter = ",", Columns = 20, Encoding = 1252, QuoteStyle = Quote-
Style.None]
  ),
  PromotedHeaders = Table.PromoteHeaders(Source, [PromoteAllScalars =
true]),
  ChangeWholeNumber = Table.TransformColumnTypes(
    PromotedHeaders,
    {{"VendorID", Int64.Type}, {"RatecodeID", Int64.Type}}
  ),
  ChangeDecimalNumber = Table.TransformColumnTypes(
    ChangeWholeNumber,
    {{"trip_distance", Decimal.Type}}
  ),
  ChangeFixedDecimalNumber = Table.TransformColumnTypes(
    ChangeDecimalNumber,
    {{"fare_amount", Currency.Type}}
  ),
  ChangePercentNumber = Table.TransformColumnTypes(
    ChangeFixedDecimalNumber,
    {{"tip_percent", Percentage.Type}}
  )
in
  ChangePercentNumber
```

The bonus with the percentage type is that you do not need to perform any transformations on the value to return it to a percentage value. If you want to take 75.36% of a number, you can just call the value as it performs the decimal conversion.

Regardless of your needs with Power Query, there are numeric data types to meet every occasion. It is important to understand how each one operates before leveraging it to ensure you get the most accurate value for your analysis when building out your queries.

Assigning date/time data types

Following text and numeric values, date and time values are the next most common data type we will encounter within our queries. They also prove to be the trickiest just because of how they can be structured. For a single value, we must consider the date value, time value, time zone, and even formatting of the value. Due to these factors, it is important that you understand how to manipulate them to best optimize your models properly.

When it comes to date and time values, there are five different data types to consider. The default for most queries is **Date/Time**. However, you can select just the **Date** or just the **Time**. You also can select **Date/Time/Timezone** to manage any time offsets you need to consider, and you can use **Duration** to represent time as a duration instead of a moment. As the following figure shows, you have several options, with each having their own implication:

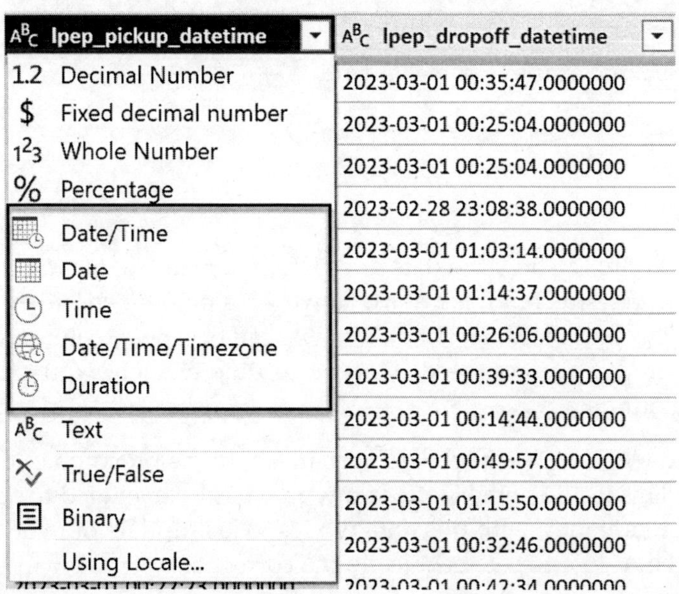

Figure 6.5: The five date and time data types available in Power Query

Just like we showed in the section *Assigning text data types*, you can use the graphical interface to assign any of these types. However, we must dig into each of these data types to understand not just how they are structured, but how you might need to use them in your own models.

We will start with the **Date/Time** data type. This is the default for most queries. In fact, even if your data source only shows the date, it often adds **`12:00:00 AM`** as a time stamp behind the date. The **Date/Time** data type is critical for pinpoint precision of timing, but it is also critical if you leverage incremental refresh and hybrid tables. Without a timestamp, these features do not function properly. We will go into more depth about incremental refresh in *Chapter 13, Parameters*. However, for now, let us focus on setting the correct data type. Just like with the previous sections, we will use **`Table.TransformColumnTypes()`** to set the **Date/Time** data type:

```
let
  Source = Csv.Document(
    File.Contents("C:\NYC Taxi\trip_data_green.csv"),
    [Delimiter = ",", Columns = 20, Encoding = 1252, QuoteStyle = Quote-
Style.None]
  ),
  PromotedHeaders = Table.PromoteHeaders(Source, [PromoteAllScalars =
true]),
  ChangedDateTime = Table.TransformColumnTypes(
    PromotedHeaders,
    {{"lpep_pickup_datetime", type datetime}}
  )
in
  ChangedDateTime
```

This formats our column to show the date and time in a readable format. This might not be the final format we desire, but it is a start. However, a point to consider when it comes to your data models is that the **Date/Time** data type can be a hefty column when it comes to your model's size. If you only need the date or time element, you can extract each individually with your data type.

A common scenario we see is users who do not care about the precision of the time but do need a date value. This is where the **Date** data type is easily leveraged to accomplish this goal. The frequent temptation with this data type is to just update our code by replacing **`datetime`** with **`date`**. While this is technically the correct answer, we will still receive an error. Since our column came in as a text value, Power Query is having trouble in our scenario with extracting the date value. Therefore, we must add a step to convert the **`Date/Time`** column to a **`Date`** only column:

```
let
  Source = Csv.Document(
```

```
    File.Contents("C:\NYC Taxi\trip_data_green.csv"),
    [Delimiter = ",", Columns = 20, Encoding = 1252, QuoteStyle = Quote-
Style.None]
  ),
  PromotedHeaders = Table.PromoteHeaders(Source, [PromoteAllScalars =
true]),
  ChangedDateTime = Table.TransformColumnTypes(
    PromotedHeaders,
    {{"lpep_pickup_datetime", type datetime}}
  ),
  ChangedDateOnly = Table.TransformColumnTypes(
    ChangedDateTime,
    {{"lpep_pickup_datetime", type date}}
  )
in
  ChangedDateOnly
```

The same principle applies if you want to use the **Time** data type. If Power Query cannot identify the time element in the column, you might need to provide a transition step. However, we can combine these two steps into a single step. Instead of providing the transformation and saving it into the **ChangedDateTime** step only to call it in the next step, we can just slip the transformation in to reduce the extra step:

```
let
  Source = Csv.Document(
    File.Contents("C:\NYC Taxi\trip_data_green.csv"),
    [Delimiter = ",", Columns = 20, Encoding = 1252, QuoteStyle = Quote-
Style.None]
  ),
  PromotedHeaders = Table.PromoteHeaders(Source, [PromoteAllScalars =
true]),
  ChangedTimeOnly = Table.TransformColumnTypes(
    Table.TransformColumnTypes(PromotedHeaders, {{"lpep_pickup_datetime",
type datetime}}),
    {{"lpep_pickup_datetime", type time}}
  )
in
  ChangedTimeOnly
```

All we have done is wrapped the **`Table.TransformColumnTypes()`** function that converted the Text column into a Date / Time column with another **`Table.TransformColumnTypes()`** function to convert it to a time column. While this might not optimize your query, it does condense the number of steps that are required.

As wonderful as the last three data types have been, there is always a challenge when managing time. We must always consider time zones and even daylight savings time. To manage this, Power Query has a **Date/Time/Timezone** data type that adds an offset for **Universal Coordinated Time** (**UTC**). When applied, it will add a duration at the end of the column that will show how much the offset is from UTC. Since our data is from New York, NY, the assigned time zone would be Eastern Standard time, so each time stamp would receive an offset of **`-05:00`** to compensate. To leverage this data type, we can use this code to provide the offset we need:

```
let
  Source = Csv.Document(
    File.Contents("C:\NYC Taxi\trip_data_green.csv"),
    [Delimiter = ",", Columns = 20, Encoding = 1252, QuoteStyle = Quote-
Style.None]
  ),
  PromotedHeaders = Table.PromoteHeaders(Source, [PromoteAllScalars =
true]),
  ChangedDateTimeZone = Table.TransformColumnTypes(
    PromotedHeaders,
    {{"lpep_pickup_datetime", type datetimezone}}
  )
in
  ChangedDateTimeZone
```

While this is nice, sometimes you need to do more transformation. We will discuss in *Chapter 14, Power Query Functions,* how to truly manipulate time zones with data. For now, it is important to understand how the data type is structured for future use.

The last data type we will discuss in this section is **`Duration`**. Instead of showing a specific time, **`Duration`** shows us the time that has passed. This is a common data type for sources that measure **Service Level Agreements** (**SLAs**) where it is important to understand how long time has passed before action was taken. The format of duration is **`2.13:27:56,`** which looks confusing but is quite simple. The number before the period is the duration in days. After the decimal, the duration is in hours, minutes, and seconds. This means for our example the total duration is two days, thirteen hours, twenty-seven minutes, and fifty-six seconds. While it is not often used in data models, it does serve a purpose and makes reading time durations much easier than using a decimal number. To leverage the duration data type, we just need to use this snippet of code:

```
let
  Source = Csv.Document(
    File.Contents("C:\NYC Taxi\trip_data_green.csv"),
    [Delimiter = ",", Columns = 20, Encoding = 1252, QuoteStyle = Quote-
Style.None]
  ),
  PromotedHeaders = Table.PromoteHeaders(Source, [PromoteAllScalars =
true]),
  ChangedDuration = Table.TransformColumnTypes(PromotedHeaders, {{"TripDu-
ration", type duration}})
in
  ChangedDuration
```

At this point, you are realizing how complicated managing date and time data types can become. There are several options to consider, and picking the right one is critical. In addition, we have not discussed adding new columns that strip pieces of a date and/or time out of a column. However, we have a couple of things you should consider when you are transforming your columns to make your life easier:

- Do you really need both the date and time values in your column?
- What is the originating time zone for your data?
- Do you need to consider consumers from other time zones?

Taking a moment to identify the answers to these questions can really help optimize your data model size and usability.

At the beginning of this section, we discussed that formatting is another critical component of the date and time data formats. When it comes to these formats, it is important to note that final formatting of them will not take place in Power Query. While we will need to specify whether we want the date only versus date and time in Power Query, how that is shown is managed within Power BI and Excel. You can specify how you want these items formatted. For example, you could format a date in a short format to lead with the month (12/31/2023) or with the day (31/12/2023), or even in a long format (Sunday, December 31, 2023). Regardless of your preferred formatting, this will all take place outside of Power Query.

Lastly, it is always recommended that you leverage date tables in your models whenever possible. In *Figure 6.1*, you will notice that the **Auto Date/Time** option is unchecked under **Time Intelligence**. While it is a great resource for users just starting their journey in Power

BI, it can cause bloat to your model and increase your refresh times. To simplify your refresh, make sure you disable this feature if you use Power Query inside of Power BI to provide the most optimized experience possible.

Assigning logical data types

The final data type we will cover in this chapter is known as a logical data type. This data type is often known also as a Boolean or a **True/False** data type. The power of this data type is great because a column with a true or false value inside can be leveraged easily in calculations. In addition, the way these columns are stored really reduces the space required to represent them if they were a string value or even a `T` or `F`. To leverage the logical data type, we simply need to set the data type with the `Table.TransformColumnTypes()` function:

```
let
  Source = Csv.Document(
    File.Contents("C:\NYC Taxi\trip_data_green.csv"),
    [Delimiter = ",", Columns = 20, Encoding = 1252, QuoteStyle = Quote-
Style.None]
  ),
  PromotedHeaders = Table.PromoteHeaders(Source, [PromoteAllScalars =
true]),
  ChangedLogical = Table.TransformColumnTypes(
    PromotedHeaders,
    {{"store_and_fwd_flag", type logical}}
  )
in
  ChangedLogical
```

Of all the data types, this is the easiest. However, do not skip it and think that it is not important. It may seem trivial when you get your queries loaded, but the time you can save when leveraging it with DAX formulas is considerable. We constantly see formulas that are more complex than they need to be simply because someone did not take a minute to set the right data type for these logical columns. It may seem like a waste of time up front but trust us when we tell you that it makes all the difference.

Updating data types in bulk

At this point, you might be concerned about the effort required to update your data types for every column in your query. If your query only returns fifteen columns, it might take you a bit, but you will eventually get it handled. However, if you are bringing in a dimension table with sixty columns, this could require a lot of effort. As a result, the question always arises if you can handle your updates in bulk.

The short answer is yes, you can update the data type for multiple columns at once. If the columns you wish to update have the same data type, you can assign them all at the same. You will start by selecting the columns you wish to update. You can select sequential columns using *Shift + Click* or non-sequential columns with *Ctrl + Click*. Regardless of your preference, once you have your columns selected, go to the transform ribbon, and select your data type from the dropdown:

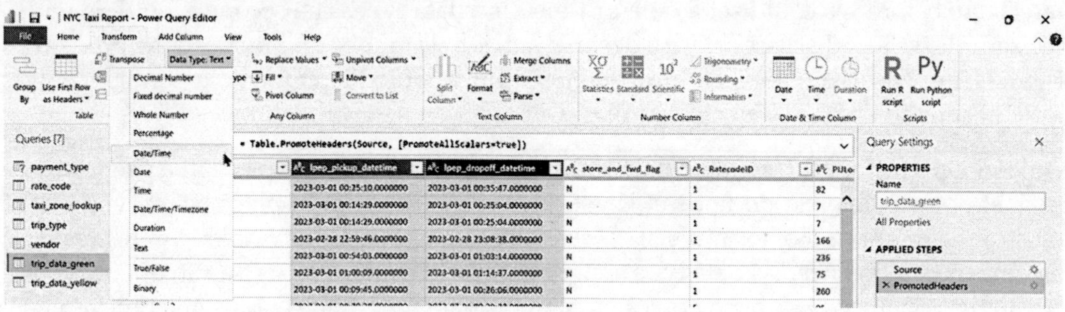

***Figure 6.6:** Assigning the Date/Time data type to multiple columns*

You can repeat this until all data types have been assigned to your columns. While we learned earlier on that there are three different ways to assign data types with the graphical interface, this is the only way you can perform this action for multiple columns. It is also worth noting that there are no shortcuts with the advanced editor. Each column must be individually handled with the M Query language. However, you can use the advanced editor to make updates to data types that were either assigned in error or have changed over time without requiring an additional step.

Combining data type transformations

For most beginners of Power Query, the topic of Data Type is often not considered. Often, we get excited when data is ingested, and the first thing we want to do is get to the analysis as fast as we can. However, this oversight can cause a lot of challenges. For example, if you are using a star schema, the data types for your relationships will need to match after you load your data with Power Query to finalize your model. In *Chapter 10, Combining and Manipulating Queries*, you will learn about how we can append or merge queries together. However, if the data types do not match, there will be issues with the combination.

As a best practice, the first step for your queries should be getting your data types in place before you make any further transformations. This allows you to condense these transformations into a single step early in the query. The benefit of this is that you know exactly where the initial transformations took place. This way, you do not have to spend time looking for a past transformation.

This leads us to another best practice around transforming column types multiple times. It is always best to go back and update the data type for a column in a previous step as opposed to creating a new one. For example, if you have a column come in as text, and you update it to a decimal number. Later, you realize this column really should be a whole number. Instead, it is recommended that you go back to the first step and change the data type to a whole number instead of creating a whole new step.

As with everything, there are exceptions to this rule. The first is with what we experienced in *Assigning Date/Time data types* section. We needed to convert the column from Text to **Date/Time** before we could set a date or time only data type. The second would be with the example we just discussed with a decimal and whole number. If you need the precision of the decimal for calculations in Power Query but want to display whole numbers only, you will need to use two steps to complete this task.

While in a perfect world, all your data transformations would take place in a single step, it is just not possible. So do not fret if you cannot get them all in place before you start your transformations. For example, in *Chapter 9, Creating New Columns*, you might create a custom column that needs a data type assigned. We will explore how you can update your code in the Advanced Editor so you can assign the data type at the exact same time as you perform your calculation. In the end, the goal is to reduce the number of transformations. This ensures your refresh times are not increased because of unnecessary additional steps.

Understanding efficiencies with data types

Your choice of data type can have a considerable impact on your data model size and refresh times. In a star schema model, it is common practice to have a single fact table with multiple dimension tables to provide additional details around the facts. The reason for this approach is the efficiency of the refresh and storage of the query. Just like with SQL server databases, there are implications to our choices with data types, and they should not be taken lightly.

As we discussed in the *Assigning Date/Time data types* section, we can increase the efficiency of the column by using a date only column if we do not care about the time. The same can be said when considering keys between fact and dimension tables. For example, you might be working with data that uses a **Globally Unique Identifier** (**GUID**) that is text-based. If possible, it is always ideal to convert this into an integer value to optimize your data model downstream.

You might also experience a situation where the date value is brought in as a whole number in a `YYYYMMDD` format. This is a common practice and often leaves new users with Power Query at a loss for what to do. They could easily transform the column into a short date format with the skills they learn in this book. However, the use of a date table might serve them best. The question is how they will be using this field in their model. Ideally, the whole number format would provide efficiency with the relationship but might make calculations harder in the future with DAX.

The frustrating part about data types is that there are recommendations that can be made, but because each data model is unique and has its own purpose, you must consider your options before making decisions. It seems trivial, but the choice of data type can have lasting implications on your data model. The key takeaway is the selection of data type should not be taken lightly as it will impact your data model beyond the initial load of data with Power Query.

Optimizing data types upstream

In this chapter, we primarily focused on assigning data types for data sources that do not provide any help with this assignment. However, some data sources will assist you with the assignment of data sources. Data coming from the SQL server will assign the proper data type associated with the underlying table, which can save you the effort of changing data types. If you are, or work closely with, a data engineer and use a SQL-based data source, it is a best practice that data types are properly assigned at the server level.

You might be thinking that there is not much harm in updating these data types in Power Query. There are two primary concerns that come with changing your data type. The first is that **DirectQuery** mode might be disabled for your SQL data source. If you are trying to manage your model size for the Power BI service or want to keep your model file as small as possible, this will likely cause some bloat as your transformation will likely require your query to mode to change to **Import**.

Second, this will likely result in the breaking of query folding. In *Chapter 4, Connect to Database Sources*, we discussed the benefits of query folding. In a perfect world, we would like to maintain this as much as possible to help with the efficiency of our refresh. There are a handful of transformation that will not break folding:

Preserving Query Folding with Data Type	
Data Type from Source	**Allowed Transformations**
Decimal number	Text or date
Whole number	Text, decimal number, or date
Date/Time	Date, date/time/timezone, decimal number, or text
Date	Text or decimal number

Table 6.2: *Allowed data type transformations that preserve query folding using Microsoft SQL Server 2022*

It is very common to see numeric values come in as decimals when they need to be a whole number. Sometimes, the key is a whole number on one table and text on another. If you have someone who can assist you with these challenges, it is recommended that you bring them into the conversation to reap the benefits of having such a robust data source. However, if you must perform these transformations with Power Query, you can do so with the understanding that you might lose additional functionality in the future.

Conclusion

In this chapter, we covered how to manage data types with Power Query. We reviewed the different data types available and how to assign them to different columns with the graphical interface and with the advanced editor. In addition, we discussed best practices around assigning them, such as performing them as the first step before making any additional changes. We also discussed the implications of different data types and considerations you must make when working with SQL-based data sources.

In the next chapter, we will transform existing columns to meet the needs of our data model.

CHAPTER 7
Transforming Columns

Introduction

In this chapter, we will perform our first column transformation with Power Query. We will first focus on properly setting up the column headers and renaming them as required. Next, we will manipulate the format of text values in a column by changing the format, extracting values, and merging them together. We will then apply mathematical functions and extend our date/time transformations. After that, we will move our columns into a position to allow us to pivot and unpivot them as necessary. Lastly, we will address query folding as it applies to transformations and considerations when managing them in Power Query.

Structure

The chapter covers the following topics:

- Why transformations in Power Query?
- Promoting first row as headers
- Renaming columns
- Formatting text in columns
- Extracting values from columns

- Merging columns
- Applying mathematical functions
- Date/Time transformations
- Moving columns in a Query
- Pivot/unpivot columns
- Maintaining query folding in transformations

Objectives

At the end of this chapter, you will understand how to use Power Query to transform your data and prepare it for deeper analysis. This will allow you to create sustainable and reusable transformations to your data to simplify the refresh of your models. You will learn how to perform common transformations that need to take place on your data and apply them with ease within Power Query.

Why transformations in Power Query?

Imagine a world where people send you data, and it is all properly formatted. You would receive an Excel workbook, and all the data is in the correct format and properly structured. You could create a pivot chart and quickly get the answers you are looking for. Or what if you could export data from another platform, and it was ready for use with no transformation? Honestly, the world might be a better place if any part of this was true.

The harsh reality is that data comes to us in a messy format. Quite often, we spend hours trying to prepare our data for use. Sometimes, those transformations only take a few minutes, while others take hours to complete. What is worse is when you need to apply the same transformations again to an updated spreadsheet. This is where Power Query shines and simplifies the process for us. In *Chapter 1, Introduction to Power Query*, we talked about some of the reasons why we want to use this tool. Regardless of how our data comes to us, we will always need to make transformations, and Power Query will assist us in that process.

The first value of using Power Query is the ability to use the graphical interface. While many readers have defaulted to using Excel as their tool of choice for transforming and cleansing data, they have spent many frustrating hours trying to understand how to enable their changes with formulas. If your goal is to become an expert with Excel or Power BI, you will need to learn formulas as you cannot get by without them. However, there is something to be said about simplifying the process for a handful of formulas you may not use as often. Take something as simple as splitting a full name into the first and last name into their own columns. This can be done inside Excel, but you might not remember the exact formula to find the space in the text string that allows it to split properly. With

Power Query, we can easily perform this task with a few clicks and a window that guides us every step of the way.

The second value is the speed at which we can perform the transformations. When you update a formula, Excel must process each cell individually. This can lock up your PC and prevent you from working on anything else. Power Query takes these transformations and applies them through the loading of the data. While it may be resource-intensive, and you may have to wait for the loading of your data to complete, it does not render your device useless.

Lastly, and possibly the most valuable, we can reapply our transformations to updated spreadsheets. If you must export data frequently from a web portal or keep receiving updated spreadsheets, you might need to keep re-applying your formulas repeatedly. Now, you are starting to memorize your formulas and getting better at applying your transformations, but you continue to waste hours doing the same thing repeatedly. With Power Query, our transformations continue to take place every time your data is refreshed, eliminating hours of unnecessary effort.

If you are new to Power Query, the temptation will be strong to transform your source files before loading them. While this might happen occasionally under tight deadlines, you are strongly encouraged to eradicate that behavior and perform your transformations inside of Power Query instead. Like all new things, it will take some time to get used to the different approaches. However, with a little patience, you will find the process of transforming your data much easier in the future with Power Query.

Promoting first row as headers

One of the most common transformations you will encounter when working with file-based data sets is the promotion of headers. When Power Query imports data from a file, it is not always able to determine if the first row of data is a header or not. Instead of assigning the proper column header, it uses a generic name of `Column1`, `Column2`, and so forth as a placeholder while the headers sit in the first row of data. With a single click, we can promote that first row as the column header with a single click of the **Use First Row as Headers** button on the **Transform** tab:

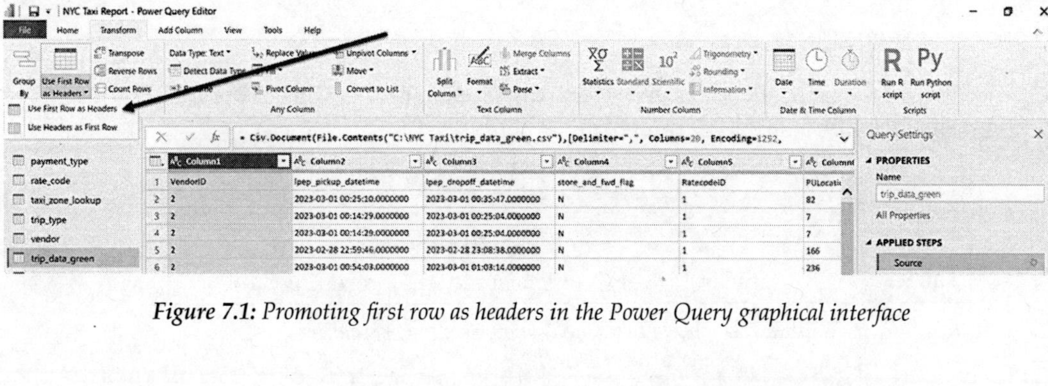

***Figure 7.1:** Promoting first row as headers in the Power Query graphical interface*

Using the dropdown allows us to address a less common issue where you might run into the inverse, where the first row of data was promoted as a header but did not belong there. We can easily reverse this action with the **Use Headers as First Row** option to demote the headers.

We can promote the first row as headers using the advanced editor with the **`Table.PromoteHeaders()`** function. This function takes an existing table and performs the promotion with the following parameters:

`Table.PromoteHeaders()`	
Parameter	**Description**
`Table`	A table in Power Query. Usually the preceding step.
`Options`	Options wrapped in square brackets to enable the `PromoteAllScalars` and Culture options.

Table 7.1: *Table of the Table.PromoteHeaders() parameters*

There are two options available with this query. The first option, **`PromoteAllScalars`**, allows us to promote a header with consideration of the **`Culture`** if set to true. In short, for any values that might require a cultural consideration, such as date or currency, it will look to the **`Culture`** option to properly format the header value. If **`Culture`** is not specified, Power Query will use the default culture locale for the file. To promote our headers and force them to consider using the US formatting of values, we will use the following code:

```
let
  Source = Csv.Document(
    File.Contents("C:\NYC Taxi\trip_data_green.csv"),
    [Delimiter = ",", Columns = 20, Encoding = 1252, QuoteStyle = Quote-
Style.None]
  ),
  PromotedHeaders = Table.PromoteHeaders(Source, [PromoteAllScalars = true,
Culture = "en-US"])
in
  PromotedHeaders
```

The process for using the headers as a first row is easier. The **`Table.DemoteHeaders()`** function only contains a single parameter:

`Table.DemoteHeaders()`	
Parameter	**Description**
`Table`	A table in Power Query. Usually the preceding step.

Table 7.2: *Table of the Table.DemoteHeaders() parameters*

If we must demote the header row to be used in the dataset, we just need to update our code to force the headers into the first row:

```
let
  Source = Csv.Document(
    File.Contents("C:\NYC Taxi\trip_data_green.csv"),
    [Delimiter = ",", Columns = 20, Encoding = 1252, QuoteStyle = Quote-
Style.None]
  ),
  DemotedHeaders = Table.DemoteHeaders(Source)
in
  DemotedHeaders
```

Promoting headers sounds simple enough, but sometimes, there are more complications with the data we ingest. For example, sometimes you query an Excel file that has a few rows at the top that we want to remove because they do not apply to the data we desire. With our old habits, we might go to the file and delete those extra rows. That requires additional effort, and we might not have the ability to edit the source file. However, Power Query allows us to fix this problem by removing rows off the top, as shown:

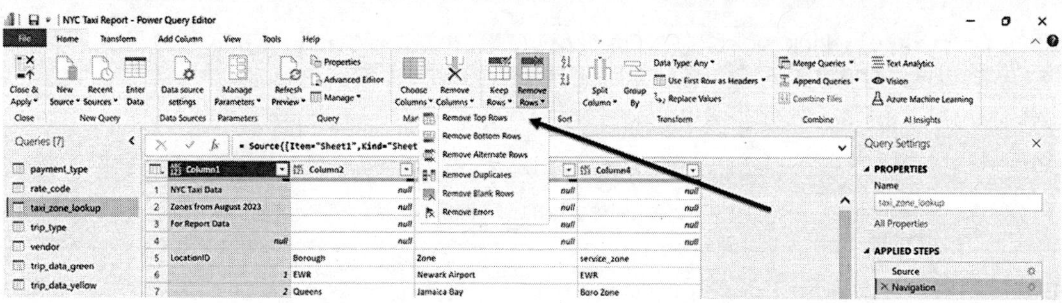

Figure 7.2: Removing top rows from a query

As you can see in *Figure 7.2*, we have four rows on our query at the top that must be removed before we can promote the headers. By clicking on the **Remove Rows** dropdown, we can select **Remove Top Rows** to start this process. You will be prompted with a popup window to enter how many rows you need to remove. In our scenario, we will remove four rows:

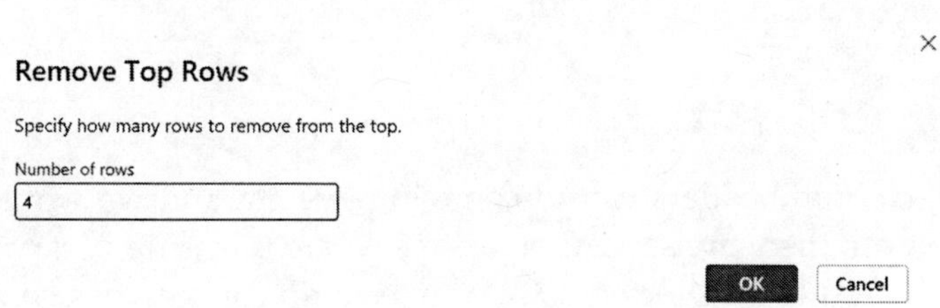

Figure 7.3: Specifying the number of rows to remove from a query

Once we remove our top rows, we can easily apply what we learned about promoting headers as the next step.

To remove rows from a query in the advanced editor, we will use the **`Table.Skip()`** function. This function is simple and allows us to quickly remove the rows undesired in our query:

`Table.Skip()`	
Parameter	**Description**
`Table`	A table in Power Query. Usually the preceding step.
`CountOrCondition`	Specify how many rows to remove. If not specified, only the first row is removed. If a numeric value, it will specify to remove that number of rows. Lastly, you can specify a condition for a column such as `[Zone] <> null` to remove rows until the `Zone` column is no longer empty.

Table 7.3: *Table of the Table.Skip() parameters*

Putting it all together, we will use the following code to remove the first four rows of our data and promote the first row as headers:

```
let
  Source = Excel.Workbook(File.Contents("C:\NYC Taxi\taxi_zone_lookup.
xlsx"), null, true),
  ZoneList = Source{[Item="Sheet1",Kind="Sheet"]}[Data],
  RemoveRows = Table.Skip(ZoneList,4),
  PromotedHeaders = Table.PromoteHeaders(RemoveRows, [PromoteAllSca-
lars=true, Culture="en-US"])
in
  PromotedHeaders
```

When you start to think about it, it is easy to waste so much time fixing column names and removing unnecessary rows from a data set. You might find yourself doing this multiple times a day when exporting data from other systems. Taking a few minutes to update your column names in this way will easily allow you to reduce your effort when utilizing these files.

Renaming columns

In a perfect world, column headers would come in correctly, and we would not need to rename them. However, there are several occasions where this is necessary. For example, the column header needs to be shortened, or a timestamp column was converted to just a date column. Sometimes the column header makes no attempt at telling you what the column values really are in your query. The graphical interface makes renaming your column header easy. You have two options at your disposal. The first option is that you can double-click on the column header, and you can edit the name there. The other option is that you can right-click on the column and select **Rename**, as shown in the following figure:

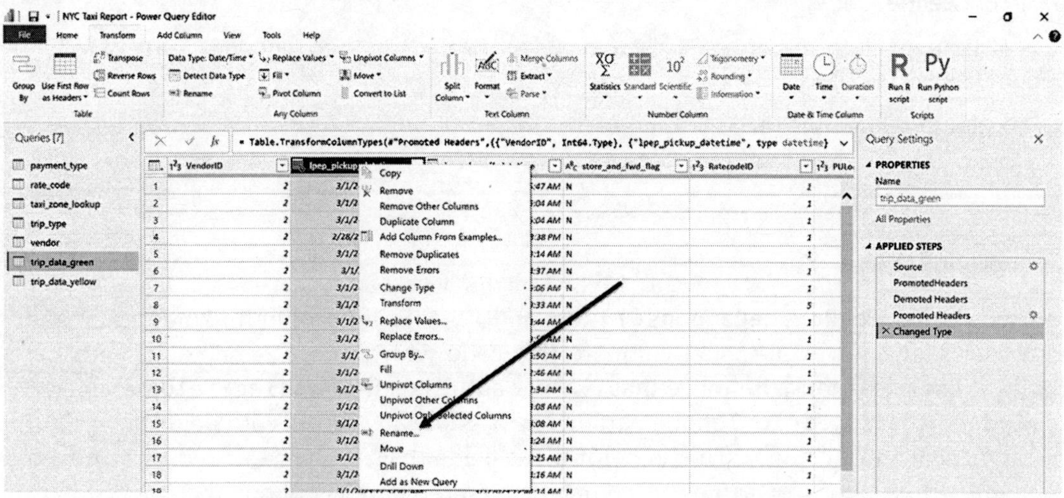

Figure 7.4: Renaming a column header with the graphical interface

The advanced editor allows us to quickly rename columns with the **`Table.RenameColumns()`** function. Even if you choose to use the graphical interface to rename columns, it is important to know about one of the parameters that is available:

`Table.RenameColumns()`	
Parameter	**Description**
`Table`	A table in Power Query. Usually the preceding step.
`Renames`	List of two values that specifies the existing column name and new column name. Multiple columns are separated by a comma.
`MissingField`	Allows you to manage errors with columns that are missing in your query.

Table 7.4: Table of the Table.RenameColumns() parameters

With our current query, the columns that specify our pickup and drop off timestamps are not very friendly. We can easily rename them using this block of code:

```
let
  Source = Csv.Document(
    File.Contents("C:\NYC Taxi\trip_data_green.csv"),
    [Delimiter = ",", Columns = 20, Encoding = 1252, QuoteStyle = Quote-
Style.None]
```

```
  ),
  PromotedHeaders = Table.PromoteHeaders(Source, [PromoteAllScalars =
true]),
  RenamedColumns = Table.RenameColumns(
    PromotedHeaders,
    {{"lpep_pickup_datetime", "PickupDateTime"}, {"lpep_dropoff_datetime",
"DropoffDateTime"}},
    MissingField.Ignore
  )
in
  RenamedColumns
```

We used the **Table.RenameColumns()** function to change our column names and make them friendlier. However, if you compare this code with the code generated with the graphical interface, you will notice that it never addresses the **MissingField** parameter. We used the **MissingField.Ignore** parameter to ignore any errors with fields that might not be present in our query. This is helpful for fields that might be added or removed with different versions of a file. Of course, there are concerns about the downstream implications of your files, but this parameter is handy in the right scenario.

Before we move on from this topic, it is important to address how you rename your column headers. There are best practices around how you name your columns. However, there are also a lot of opinions when it comes to how you name your column headers as well. Regardless of opinions, there are two rules that hold true when it comes to column headers. There should never be a space in a column header, and there should never be a special character. When you are using advanced techniques, particularly with the Power BI service, spaces, and special characters will require you to use substitute characters when you use features like URL filtering.

Next, the question arises about what case to use with your column headers. Should it be all upper case? Or would it be best to use lowercase instead? From an accessibility and inclusion perspective, it is a best practice to use CamelCase for your column headers. This makes your column headers easier to read and allows others who might struggle to identify columns quickly. There are strong opinions in both directions, but CamelCase allows you to create a compact and readable column header that does not use any special characters.

Regardless of which you choose, be consistent to save yourself headaches. You must always remember that case matters with Power Query, and the more consistent you are, the easier it will be for you to avoid typographical errors when writing code in the advanced editor.

Formatting text in columns

A common challenge encountered with text columns is the formatting. We often find text coming in with different case formats which can cause inconsistencies when performing analysis. Remember, the case of your letters counts with Power Query, so we must consider this if we are using a column for further transformations. However, we can cleanse our columns a little more and even add a prefix or suffix to a field.

Starting with the selected case, Power Query allows us to format text in three ways. We can choose to have all the letters as lowercase, uppercase, or we can capitalize each word. To perform this action with the graphical interface, just select the column you wish to transform. Then, expose the **Transform** ribbon and click on the **Format** dropdown to select the desired format:

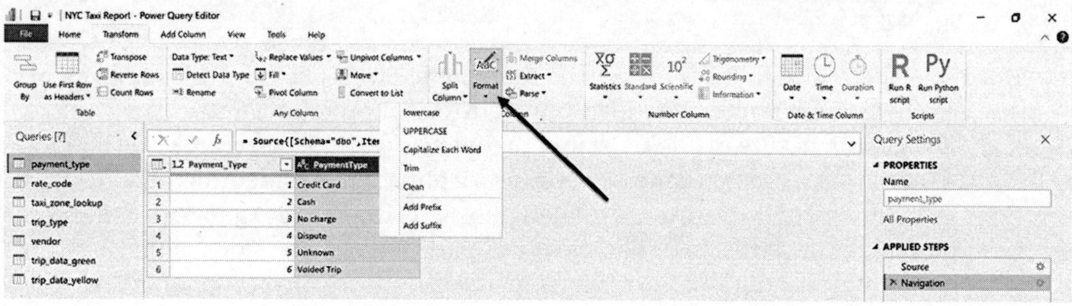

Figure 7.5: Preparing to assign a format to a text column

We can accomplish the same three transformations using the `Table.TransformColumns()` function. It has four parameters that help us achieve the transformations we desire:

`Table.TransformColumns()`	
Parameter	**Description**
`Table`	A table in Power Query. Usually the preceding step.
`TransformOperations`	List of three values to enable the transformation. The first value is the column name, second value is the transformation to be applied, and the third option specifies the data type but is not required. Each transformation can be separated with a comma.
`DefaultTransformation`	Sets a default column type if not specified in `TransformOperations`
`MissingField`	Allows you to manage errors with columns that are missing in your query.

Table 7.5: Table of the Table.TransformColumns() parameters

To put this into context, we want to use the advanced editor to force our text to be all in lowercase. To complete this task, we will use the following code:

```
let
  Source = Sql.Database("localhost", "NYC_Taxi"),
  dbo_payment_type = Source{[Schema = "dbo", Item = "payment_type"]}[Data],
  LowercaseText = Table.TransformColumns(
    dbo_payment_type,
    {{"PaymentType", Text.Lower, type text}},
    null,
    MissingField.Ignore
  )
in
  LowercaseText
```

To perform our transformation, we used the three items in the list to achieve our goal. We identified the column name, identified our transformation to lowercase using **Text.Lower**, and for good measure explicitly stated the type as text. We used a **null** value for the **DefaultTransformation** parameter because we already have identified the desired data type. And for good measure we added the **MissingField.Ignore** to sidestep any errors that might arise for now. The beautiful part of this code block is that we can easily use it for transforming our text into uppercase by using **Text.Upper** instead as our desired transformation. And if you wish to capitalize each word, you can use **Text.Proper** transformation instead.

If you go back to *Figure 7.5*, you will note that there were four other transformations associated with this list. We want to first tackle: trim, and clean. These two formatting options allow us to cleanse our text which makes it usable for our analysis. We want to first look at clean as it is the easiest to understand. Clean allows us to remove **non-printable characters** from a column. This is simply the removal of characters that would not be used in our analysis such as line feeds or other control characters. They get in the way of your analysis, and with a quick click, they are gone. Or, if you use the advanced editor, you can update the code block above to use **Text.Clean** to achieve this transformation.

At first, the trim function does not appear to do much. However, it allows us to quickly remove spaces at the beginning and end of text in a column. Sometimes a space sneaks in at the end or beginning of the text that is found in our columns. This can cause issues with filtering and even measures when you load your data model. When you use the graphical interface, the trim function removes all the spaces before and after your text. However, you might want to keep the spaces at the beginning of the text to aid with formatting. Or you need the spaces at the end for additional transformations. This is where you will need to use the advanced editor to achieve your goal. If you use **Text.Trim**, you will remove all the space before and after your text. However, you can use **Text.TrimStart** to remove preceding spaces or **Text.TrimEnd** to remove trailing spaces from your text. Regardless of your scenario, you can select the trim option that meets the requirements for your solution.

The last two options we have on our format dropdown are adding a prefix or suffix to our text. This will add text to the beginning or end of your existing text. For example, if we wanted to add `PMT:` to the beginning of the payment types, we could go to the **Format** dropdown, select **Prefix**, and enter that text into the window that pops up:

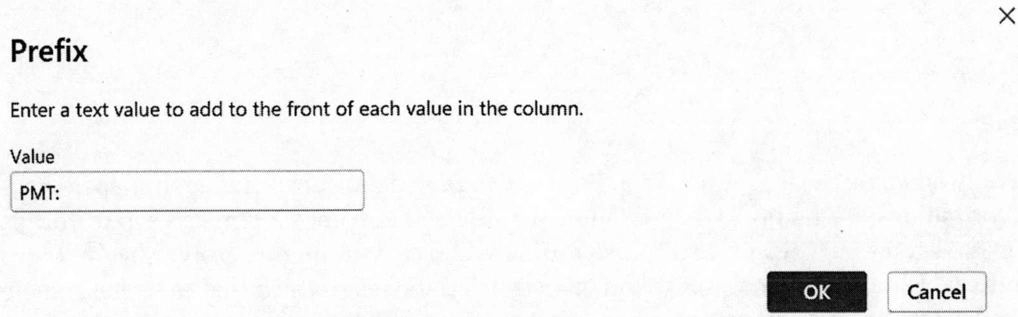

Figure 7.6: Adding a prefix to a column

When adding a prefix to a column, we will still use the **`Table.TransformColumns()`** function to accomplish our task. However, how we apply the transformation will be a little different. Before, we just specified how we wanted our text transformation to occur. Now, we must concatenate our values. To achieve this, we will need to take our prefix, **`PMT:`**, and use the ampersand (**&**) to concatenate it with our existing value. However, since we already identified the column we are using, we will use an underscore as a placeholder for the value. This means our concatenated string code will be **`"PMT: " & _`**. All we need to do is add the word **`each`** before the concatenated code, which applies the transformation to each row in the column. Here is what that looks like in the bigger context of our code:

```
let
  Source = Sql.Database("localhost", "NYC_Taxi"),
  dbo_payment_type = Source{[Schema = "dbo", Item = "payment_type"]}[Data],
  AddPrefix = Table.TransformColumns(
    dbo_payment_type,
    {{"PaymentType", each "PMT: " & _, type text}}
  )
in
  AddPrefix
```

If we need a suffix, we just need to swap our concatenation to use our column value first and connect it to our suffix value. Or, if you would like to get adventurous, you can add a prefix and suffix in one step, as demonstrated in this block of code:

```
let
  Source = Sql.Database("localhost", "NYC_Taxi"),
```

```
  dbo_payment_type = Source{[Schema = "dbo", Item = "payment_type"]}[Data],
  AddPrefixSuffix = Table.TransformColumns(
    dbo_payment_type,
    {{"PaymentType", each "PMT: " & _ & " Payment", type text}}
  )
in
  AddPrefixSuffix
```

It is really amazing what a few clicks or lines of code can do to get your data in shape. These transformations are helpful when dealing with data that comes from surveys or forms. Unless you force survey answers to use multiple choice, you might receive several types of entries. Using the Format tools, you can clean up the text, which makes it presentable and consistent as you perform a deeper analysis of your data.

Extracting values from columns

One of the most common yet frustrating transformations Excel users experience is extracting text from a string. If you are only looking for a set number of characters at the beginning or end of a string, it is easy. However, if you are looking to extract data that is before or after a delimiter, it can become frustrating. It seems so simple, but it often becomes complicated. Especially if you have that delimiter multiple times in a string. Regardless of what you were trying to do, all of it required a formula that caused unnecessary grief. However, Power Query remedies this issue by providing solutions with the graphical interface. We can start by selecting the column we wish to transform, then go to the **Transform** ribbon and expand the **Extract** menu to start the process of extracting portions of text from our column:

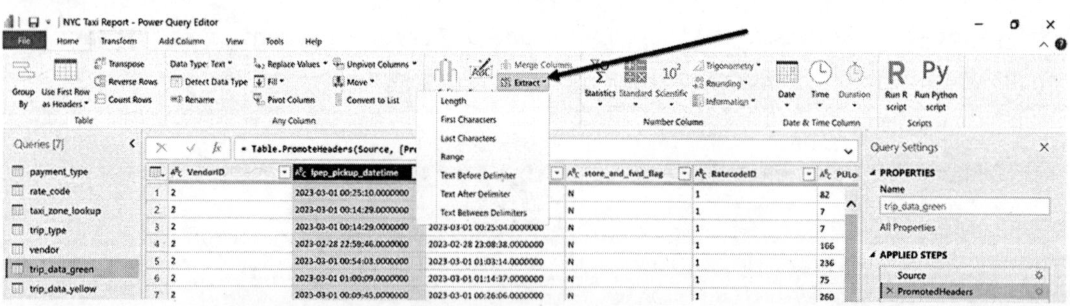

Figure 7.7: Preparing to extract portions of text from a column

To get started, we will pull the first four characters from our column which will serve as the year. When we select the **First Characters** option, we receive a window that asks us to select how many characters to retain from each row of the column:

Figure 7.8: *Specifying how many characters to keep from the beginning of the available text*

To achieve this with the advanced editor, we will continue to use **`Table.TransformColumns()`** to enable our transformation. However, we will add a new function called **`Text.Start()`** to extract the values we need from our string of text:

`Text.Start()`	
Parameter	**Description**
`Text`	Identified string of text
`Count`	Number of characters to retain from the beginning of our string of text

Table 7.6: *Table of the Text.Start() parameters*

If you remember from our last section, *Formatting text in columns,* we needed to use an underscore as a placeholder for our text since we had already identified the column we were transforming. As a result, our code block looks like this:

```
let
  Source = Csv.Document(
    File.Contents("C:\NYC Taxi\trip_data_green.csv"),
    [Delimiter = ",", Columns = 20, Encoding = 1252, QuoteStyle = Quote-
Style.None]
  ),
  PromotedHeaders = Table.PromoteHeaders(Source, [PromoteAllScalars =
true]),
  FirstChar = Table.TransformColumns(
    PromotedHeaders,
    {{"lpep_pickup_datetime", each Text.Start(_, 4), type text}}
  )
in
  FirstChar
```

If we wish to extract the characters at the end of our string of text, we can swap **`Text.Start()`** with **`Text.End()`** to achieve the same result:

`Text.End()`	
Parameter	**Description**
`Text`	Identified string of text
`Count`	Number of characters to retain from the end of our string of text

***Table 7.7:** Table of the Text.End() parameters*

Since we are talking about extracting fixed lengths of data, you might be wondering how we achieve the same in the middle of our string of text. If you are using the graphical interface, you can use the **Range** option. From there, you can specify your starting index and the number of characters you wish to retain. If you can never remember this, the starting index position is the character before the one you wish to extract. We also can use the **`Text.Middle()`** function with the advanced editor to achieve the same result:

`Text.Middle()`	
Parameter	**Description**
`Text`	Identified string of text
`Start`	Beginning position of your index
`Count`	Number of characters to retain from the beginning of the index

***Table 7.8:** Table of the Text.Middle() parameters*

While they take on different function names as their equivalent in Excel, they still perform the same duties. However, the real transformation takes place when you are looking to extract data based on a specific delimiter. In the past, you usually needed to create a complex formula in Excel that finds the character and subtracts it from the length. Instead of having to manage this in a formula, it is as easy as a few clicks. To get started, select the column you wish to transform, go to the **Transform** ribbon, expand the **Extract** menu, and select **Text Before Delimiter**. You will be prompted to the following window:

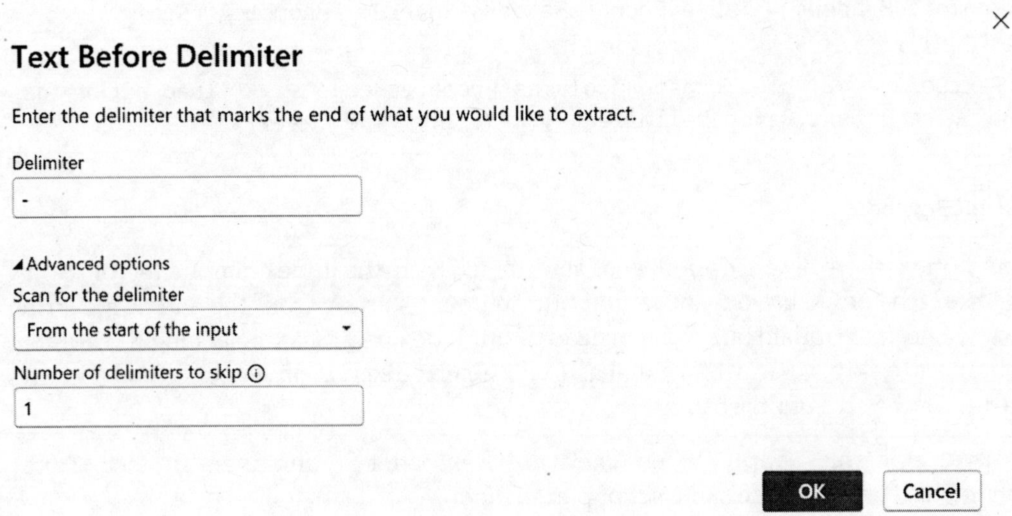

Figure 7.9: *Options for extracting text before a delimiter*

This is where the true ease of Power Query starts to shine. First, we specify what our delimiter will be. But then, we can choose to scan for the delimiter from the beginning or end of the string of text. We also have the option to skip as many delimiters as we need. What does this all mean? This means we do not have to create complex formulas to get around existing delimiters anymore. With this feature in Power Query, we took what used to be a complex query and simplified it to a few clicks.

We can apply this same principle with the **`Text.BeforeDelimiter()`** function inside the advanced editor by configuring these parameters:

`Text.BeforeDelimiter()`	
Parameter	**Description**
`Text`	Identified string of text
`Delimiter`	Identified delimiter value in quotations
`Index`	Number of delimiters to skip. Add `RelativePosition.FromEnd` to work from the end of the string of text.

Table 7.9: *Table of the Text.BeforeDelimiter() parameters*

To replicate what we performed with the graphical interface shown in *Figure 7.9*, we would use this block of code:

```
let

    Source = Csv.Document(File.Contents("C:\NYC Taxi\trip_data_green.
csv"),[Delimiter=",", Columns=20, Encoding=1252, QuoteStyle=QuoteStyle.
None]),
```

```
    PromotedHeaders = Table.PromoteHeaders(Source, [PromoteAllSca-
lars=true]),

    TextBefore = Table.TransformColumns(PromotedHeaders, {{"lpep_pickup_da-
tetime", each Text.BeforeDelimiter(_, "-", 1), type text}})
in

    TextBefore
```

If you notice, there is an option available to us with the Index parameter of **Text.BeforeDelimiter()**. If we want to find our delimiter starting from the end of the string of text, we need to update our code. Instead of our index parameter just being the number of delimiters to skip, we must format it as **{1, RelativePosition.FromEnd}** so it knows to start from the end of the string.

The same principles apply when extracting text after a delimiter. In fact, **Text.AfterDelimiter()** has the same set of parameters:

Text.AfterDelimiter()	
Parameter	**Description**
Text	Identified string of text
Delimiter	Identified delimiter value in quotations
Index	Number of delimiters to skip. Add RelativePosition.FromEnd to work from the end of the string of text.

***Table 7.10:** Table of the Text.AfterDelimiter() parameters*

To change things up, we will grab the text after a delimiter, but we will look from the end of the string of text instead of the beginning. As a result, our code will look like this:

```
let

    Source = Csv.Document(File.Contents("C:\NYC Taxi\trip_data_green.
csv"),[Delimiter=",", Columns=20, Encoding=1252, QuoteStyle=QuoteStyle.
None]),

    PromotedHeaders = Table.PromoteHeaders(Source, [PromoteAllSca-
lars=true]),

    TextAfter = Table.TransformColumns(PromotedHeaders, {{"lpep_pickup_da-
tetime", each Text.AfterDelimiter(_, "-", {1, RelativePosition.FromEnd}),
type text}})
in

    TextAfter
```

What about finding text that sits between two delimiters? What if the delimiters are not the same? Is this even possible? The answer is yes, and it is just as easy. To get started, select the column you wish to transform, expose the Transform ribbon, click on the Extract dropdown, and select **Text Between Delimiters**. From there, you will be prompted to provide information regarding your delimiters:

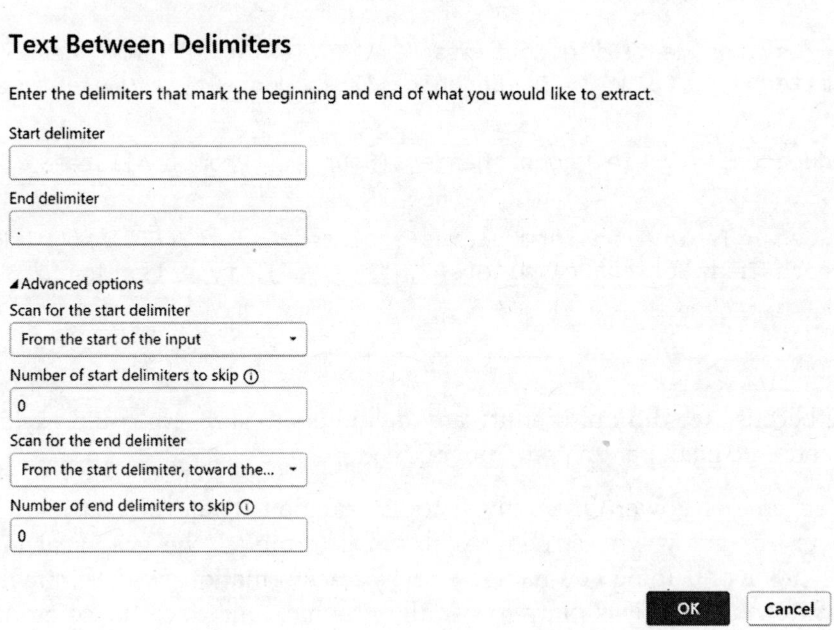

***Figure 7.10:** Preparing to extract text between two delimiters*

You can specify your start and end delimiters here, and they do not have to be the same. From there, you can find your start delimiter from the beginning or end of the string of text and specify the number of delimiters to skip. Then, you can find the end delimiter from the start delimiter or the end of the string of text and specify how many delimiters to skip. It really does not get any more flexible than this when it comes to extracting text with a few clicks of a mouse.

The **`Text.BetweenDelimiters()`** function is a little more complicated as we must handle both start and end delimiter values:

`Text.BetweenDelimiters()`	
Parameter	**Description**
`Text`	Identified string of text
`StartDelimiter`	Identified delimiter value in quotations for the start of your extraction
`EndDelimiter`	Identified delimiter value in quotations for the end of your extraction
`StartIndex`	Number of start delimiters to skip. Add `RelativePosition.FromEnd` to work from the end of the string of text.
`EndIndex`	Number of end delimiters to skip. Add `RelativePosition.FromEnd` to work from the end of the string of text.

***Table 7.11:** Table of the Text.BetweenDelimiters() parameters*

To apply this transformation in context of the advanced editor, we will use this block of code:

```
let
    Source = Csv.Document(File.Contents("C:\NYC Taxi\trip_data_green.
csv"),[Delimiter=",", Columns=20, Encoding=1252, QuoteStyle=QuoteStyle.
None]),
    PromotedHeaders = Table.PromoteHeaders(Source, [PromoteAllSca-
lars=true]),
    TextBetween = Table.TransformColumns(PromotedHeaders, {{"lpep_pickup_
datetime", each Text.BetweenDelimiters(_, " ", "."), type text}})
in
    TextBetween
```

You will note because we did not identify any delimiters to skip, we could exclude the **StartIndex** and **EndIndex** parameters from our code.

In the grand scheme of Power Query, these transformations could be considered quite small. However, for many who struggle with Excel formulas, the graphical interface does an excellent job of helping you navigate tricky transformations with minimal effort. It is important to note that it is okay to use the graphical interface for some of these transformations if you are not comfortable with the code. It is there to help you get started. However, as your skills start to grow, you will find it easier to use the advanced editor so you can create more complex transformations with your queries.

Merging columns

Sometimes we find our data is split between two columns when we really need it in a single column. A notable example might be the combination of a first and last name to create a full name on a dimension table. If your data only comes in with a first name and last name column, you will need to merge the columns together to create a unified field. While you might be considering it to be an extra step, the true benefit of this is that you are able to format the column in a way that best suits the use of your model. For example, you could format it as **FirstName LastName** or **LastName, FirstName**. Regardless of your choices, Power Query enables you to achieve this goal.

The graphical interface makes this process easy to execute. The hardest part is making sure you have selected the columns you wish to merge in the right sequence. When in doubt, start by clicking on a column that does not belong in your merge, then click on the first column you wish to merge. You can then select subsequent columns with a *Shift + click* or *Ctrl + click*. Once you have selected your columns, expose the **Transform** ribbon, and select **Merge columns** to bring them together:

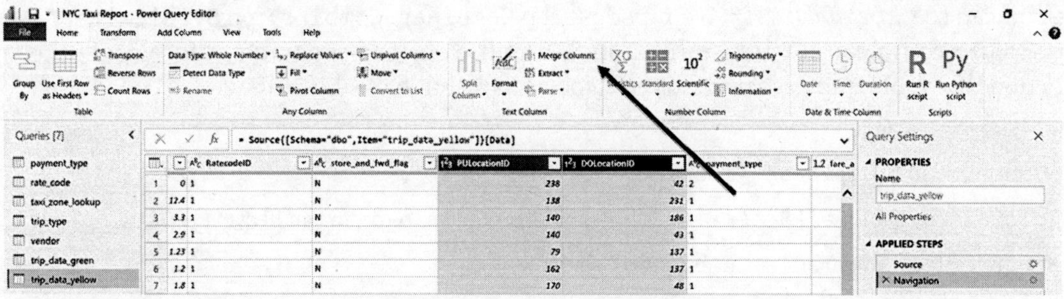

Figure 7.11: Initiating the merge of two columns

You will then be prompted with two questions. First, you can select a separator for the columns. You can choose to have no separator between values, you can choose to have a standard separator such as a colon, semicolon, comma, equals sign, space, or tab, or you can create a custom separator and enter it in the text box as we have. You also can change the merged column name from the default of **Merged**:

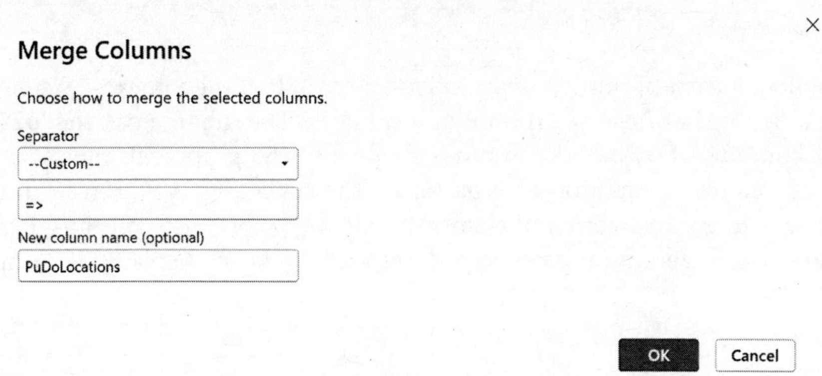

Figure 7.12: Configuring our merged columns

We can perform the merge within the advanced editor in addition to the graphical interface. To perform the merge, we must use the **`Table.CombineColumns()`** function to achieve our goal:

`Table.CombineColumns()`	
Parameter	**Description**
`Table`	A table in Power Query. Usually the preceding step.
`SourceColumns`	List of columns to be combined. Must be ordered in the correct sequence
`Combiner`	Identified separator between columns. Must be used in conjunction with the `Combiner.CombineTextByDelimiter()` function to provide the separation. Separator goes inside the function wrapped in double quotes.
Column	Name of the combined columns

Table 7.12: Table of the Table.CombineColumns() parameters

As you can see from *Table 7.12*, we must use the **Combiner.CombineTextByDelimiter()** function to complete our transformation. We will enter our separator value inside the function in double quotes. The result is a code block that looks like this:

```
let
  Source = Sql.Database("localhost", "NYC_Taxi"),
  TripData = Source{[Schema = "dbo", Item = "trip_data_yellow"]}[Data],
  MergedColumns = Table.CombineColumns(
    TripData,
    {"PULocationID", "DOLocationID"},
    Combiner.CombineTextByDelimiter("=>"),
    "PuDoLocations"
  )
in
  MergedColumns
```

Now this code looks correct, but we will receive an error. If you go back to *Figure 7.11*, it might be hard to see but both selected columns are numeric. The **Table.CombineColumns()** function only combines text-based columns. If you use the graphical interface, Power Query oversees this transformation for you under the covers. However, we can resolve this. Option one is to go upstream and change the data type of these columns. However, we do not have a change data type step and we want to keep this step as compact as possible.

The solution to this problem is simple. For our table parameter, we will update it with a nested **Table.TransformColumnTypes()** function and update these two columns to use a text data type. This will allow us to perform the transformation and merge the columns in a single step:

```
let
  Source = Sql.Database("localhost", "NYC_Taxi"),
  TripData = Source{[Schema = "dbo", Item = "trip_data_yellow"]}[Data],
  MergedColumns = Table.CombineColumns(
    Table.TransformColumnTypes(
      TripData,
      {{"PULocationID", type text}, {"DOLocationID", type text}},
      "en-US"
    ),
    {"PULocationID", "DOLocationID"},
    Combiner.CombineTextByDelimiter("=>"),
```

```
    "PuDoLocations"
  )
in
  MergedColumns
```

It was important to show you how easily what seems like a simple transformation can quickly become a challenge. The more you start to transform your data in Power Query, the more frequently you might run into errors like this one. Data type errors will occur frequently, but getting ahead of these errors by making small adjustments in the advanced editor goes a long way.

Lastly, a common question that occurs with this feature is if it is possible to combine more than two columns at a time. The answer is yes, and while it may not seem obvious on the surface, understanding the advanced editor code confirms it for us. If you go back to *Table 7.12*, the **SourceColumns** function states that it takes a list of columns. If this function only merged two columns, it would have asked for each one as a separate parameter. However, because it is asking for a list in a single parameter, this means we can combine multiple columns at once. Taking a few minutes to understand the underlying functions in the advanced editor often provides hints on how you can force Power Query to do what you desire.

Applying mathematical functions

Mathematical transformations are common in Power Query. Often, we must transform numerical values to provide better meaning. A common transformation of numeric values is converting the temperature between Fahrenheit and Celsius. Maybe you must take the square root of a number to make it usable? Or you just need to perform a basic calculation to correct an error. Regardless of the purpose we can transform our numeric values with Power Query.

To achieve these transformations, we can use the graphical interface and apply them to an entire column. Just like we have in in earlier sections, you can select a column, expose the Transform ribbon, and apply any number of mathematical transformations on your column:

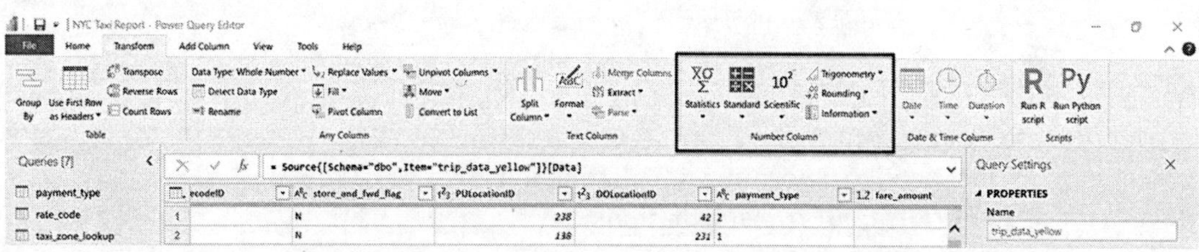

Figure 7.13: *Options for performing mathematical transformations on a column*

While we can use these different tools on an entire column, not every use case will require this. You might need to leverage these functions to perform calculations or return a specific value to assist you with your analysis. For this section, we will focus on how these functions operate and how you might want to use them in your transformations.

If you are looking at *Figure 7.13*, we will start with the **Standard** math functions. In this menu, we start with the standard four functions of add, subtract, multiply, and divide. If you are using the graphical interface, all these buttons do is provide the corresponding operators to your column. For example, if you select add, it will provide a **+** sign and the specified formula to the underlying code to achieve your result. Power Query does not need to do anything special for these operators. In fact, the Percentage and Percent Of functions just facilitate the math to beautify your percentage values in Power Query. However, there are a few special operators that require special functions to achieve the correct result.

The first special operator we encounter is the Integer-Divide. This function returns the integer, or whole number, value of two numbers when divided. We use the **`Number.IntegerDivide()`** function to achieve this result:

`Number.IntegerDivide()`	
Parameter	**Description**
`Number1`	The dividend or numerator
`Number2`	The divisor or denominator

Table 7.13: *Table of the Number.IntegerDivide() parameters*

We also can perform a Modulo division which returns the remainder of a divide operator. We use the **`Number.Mod()`** function to achieve this result:

`Number.Mod()`	
Parameter	**Description**
`Number`	The dividend or numerator
`Divisor`	The divisor or denominator

Table 7.14: *Table of the Number.Mod() parameters*

Now that we understand the basic operators available to us, we can turn to **Scientific** and trigonometry transformations. To apply a transformation on a numeric value using trigonometry, we just need to determine which function is correct. We can use the following table as a guide to perform our transformations:

Trigonometry functions	
Function name	**Power query function**
Sine	`Number.Sin`
Cosine	`Number.Cos`
Tangent	`Number.Tan`
Hyperbolic Sine	`Number.Sinh`
Hyperbolic Cosine	`Number.Cosh`
Hyperbolic Tangent	`Number.Tanh`
Arcsine	`Number.Asin`
Arccosine	`Number.Acos`
Arctangent	`Number.Atan`

Table 7.15: *Table of trigonometric functions and their equivalent in Power Query*

Scientific functions perform the same way in Power Query. We just need to activate the correct function to achieve the desired outcome:

Scientific functions	
Function name	**Power query function**
Absolute Value	`Number.Abs`
Exponent	`Number.Exp`
Factorial	`Number.Factorial`
Logarithm (Base-10)	`Number.Log10`
Logarithm (Natural)	`Number.Ln`
Square Root	`Number.Sqrt`

Table 7.16: *Table of scientific functions and their equivalent in Power Query*

While these functions are simple, there was one that was left out. If you desire to raise a number to a specific power, you must use the **`Number.Power()`** function to achieve this. If you are using the graphical interface, you can easily square or cube a number with a click. However, anything beyond that will require you to perform the transformation in the advanced editor with the **`Number.Power()`** function:

`Number.Power()`	
Parameter	**Description**
`Number`	The base number
`Power`	The exponent of the number

Table 7.17: *Table of the Number.Power() parameters*

Next, we have the option to round our numeric values. The graphical interface gives us three options. The first is round, which rounds the number towards the nearest whole number. However, we also have the option to force numbers to be rounded up or down regardless of distance from the nearest whole number. Regardless of the method you choose, you can select the precision of your rounding to the desired decimal place. We can use the **`Number.Round()`**, **`Number.RoundUp()`**, or **`Number.RoundDown()`** functions the exact same way in the advanced editor because all three have the exact same parameters:

`Number.Round(),Number.RoundUp(), and Number.RoundDown()`	
Parameter	**Description**
`Number`	The number to be rounded
`Digits`	The number of digits the number will be rounded to. Use zero to round to a whole number.

Table 7.18: *Table of the Number.Round(), Number.RoundUp(), and Number.RoundDown() parameters*

Here is the secret about rounding. While the graphical interface gives us these three options, there are two other rounding functions available in the advanced editor. You can use the **`Number.RoundTowardZero()`** or **`Number.RoundAwayFromZero()`** functions to force the rounding relative to zero. You could create a conditional statement if you wanted to and use the first three functions we used, but these two make life easier if your use case requires it.

The **`Statistics`** functions will be the last item we address in this section. We saved this group for last because unlike the other transformations we used, which could be applied to an individual object on a column, these functions apply to an entire column and return a single result. In short, these functions wrap around an entire column name and return a single result.

A common use case might be to perform analysis on trip distances. We want to know a few dimensions such as the total distance traveled, minimum distance, maximum distance, and so on. We can use these statistical functions to quickly understand the details of our dataset and provide a result:

Statistical functions	
Function name	**Power query function**
Sum	`List.Sum(Trips[Distance])`
Minimum	`List.Min(Trips[Distance])`
Maximum	`List.Max(Trips[Distance])`
Median	`List.Median(Trips[Distance])`
Average	`List.Average(Trips[Distance])`
Standard Deviation	`List.StandardDeviation(Trips[Distance])`
Count Values	`List.NonNullCount(Trips[Distance])`
Count Distinct Values	`List.NonNullCount(List.Distinct(Trips[Distance]))`

Table 7.19: *Table of Statistical functions and their equivalent in Power Query*

The statistical functions go a long way in assisting with supporting queries. For example, if you do not have a date table available to you, it is possible to create one that dynamically reacts to the minimum and maximum dates available. This way you never have to worry about your date table not scaling. In *Chapter 15, Advanced Web Connections*, we will use the count values function to handle paging with Web APIs. The practicality of these functions alone does not provide the best value, but if you can learn to harvest their abilities, they will serve you well in the future.

As we mentioned at the beginning of this section, these functions might not be applied to entire columns. However, when we arrive at *Chapter 9, Creating New Columns*, you will be able to apply these functions to create complex calculations inside of Power Query. The trick is understanding how Power Query manages them so you can quickly apply them.

Date/Time transformations

Depending on the requirements for your data model, you may find yourself transforming date and time columns to meet your needs. The question must be focused on what you are trying to accomplish with the outcome of your model. For example, our current query has specific dates and times that customers were picked up for trips. While this granularity is nice, we might be interested in various kinds of information. For example, we might want to understand trip density by day of the week or hour of the day. We also might need to extract these elements to properly adjust for daylight savings time, something we will cover in *Chapter 14, Functions*. Regardless of the purpose, we can leverage these functions to make our lives easier. The graphical interface makes these transformations easy. Between the **Date**, **Time**, and **Duration** menus, we can transform our data into something usable for our analysis:

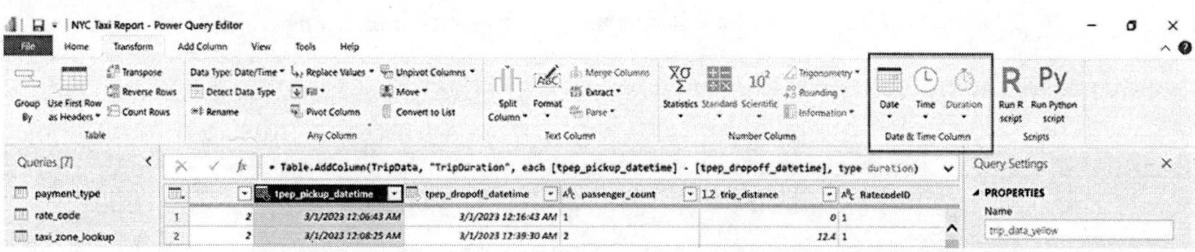

***Figure 7.14:** Options for performing Date/Time transformations on a column*

We will start with our date transformations. These are quite common and helpful for highly aggregated analysis. All date functions follow a common hierarchy:

- Year
- Quarter
- Month
- Week
- Day

This hierarchy allows us to quickly manipulate our columns to aggregate at any of these levels and all are structured in a similar format. To help you understand this structure, we will look at the options available for the year. The graphical interface allows us to extract the year, start of year, and end of year from our column. If we use the **`Table.TransformColumns()`** function, we will achieve the same results. Following is an explanation of how these options are leveraged in the graphical interface and advanced editor in addition to the expected outcome for a timestamp of **`7/28/2023 9:32:25 AM`**:

Year Transformations		
Graphical interface	**Power query function**	**Sample result**
Year	**`Date.Year`**	2023
Start of Year	**`Date.StartOfYear`**	1/1/2023 12:00:00 AM
End of Year	**`Date.EndOfYear`**	1/1/2024 12:00:00 AM

Table 7.20: *Table of transformations by year on a timestamp*

In short, our transformations update the column to either bring back the desired element, year in this case, or bring back the start or end of the period. The same proves true for the transformation of quarter using a timestamp of **`7/28/2023 9:32:25 AM`**:

Quarter transformations		
Graphical interface	**Power query function**	**Sample result**
Quarter	**`Date.QuarterOfYear`**	3
Start of Quarter	**`Date.StartOfQuarter`**	7/1/2023 12:00:00 AM
End of Quarter	**`Date.EndOfQuarter`**	10/1/2023 12:00:00 AM

Table 7.21: *Table of transformations by quarter on a timestamp*

As you can see, the transformation of quarter parallels the transformation of a year. This is because the value used to represent them is numeric. As we transition to month, you will note that there is a change as now we can represent a month with both a number and a name. Here are the transformations we can apply for a month using a timestamp of **`7/28/2023 9:32:25 AM`**:

Month transformations		
Graphical interface	**Power query function**	**Sample result**
Month	**`Date.Month`**	7
Start of Month	**`Date.StartOfMonth`**	7/1/2023 12:00:00 AM
End of Month	**`Date.EndOfMonth`**	8/1/2023 12:00:00 AM
Days in Month	**`Date.DaysInMonth`**	31
Name of Month	**`Date.MonthName`**	July

Table 7.22: *Table of transformations by month on a timestamp*

We received two new options to collect. We can extract the number of days in a month, and we can extract the name of the month. Next, we can extract information about a date in the context of a week. Here are the transformations we can apply for a week using a timestamp of **`7/28/2023 9:32:25 AM`**:

Week transformations		
Graphical interface	**Power query function**	**Sample result**
Week of Year	**`Date.WeekOfYear`**	30
Week of Month	**`Date.WeekOfMonth`**	5
Start of Week	**`Date.StartOfWeek`**	7/23/2023 12:00:00 AM
End of Week	**`Date.EndOfWeek`**	7/30/2023 12:00:00 AM

Table 7.23: *Table of transformations by week on a timestamp*

If you have not figured it out already, Power Query uses the Gregorian Calendar for the start and end of the week. If you choose, you can adjust this by stating which day of the week is the start of your week. For example, if your week starts on a Monday, you can add **`Day.Monday`** as the second parameter. This will force all your transformations to use Monday as the start of your week instead of Sunday.

The last part of our date hierarchy is the day. Here are the transformations we can apply for a day using a timestamp of **`7/28/2023 9:32:25 AM`**:

Day transformations		
Graphical interface	**Power query function**	**Sample result**
Day	**`Date.Day`**	28
Day of Week	**`Date.DayOfWeek`**	5
Day of Year	**`Date.DayOfYear`**	209
Start of Day	**`Date.StartOfDay`**	7/28/2023 12:00:00 AM
End of Day	**`Date.EndOfDay`**	7/29/2023 12:00:00 AM
Name of Day	**`Date.DayOfWeekName`**	Friday

Table 7.24: *Table of transformations by day on a timestamp*

Just like we could with the week transformations, **`Date.DayOfWeek()`** allows us to set a different day as the start of our week.

At this point, we have been able to extract every single element of a date for us to view. However, there are three remaining transformations that are worth noting. The first one is the age transformation. If you activate this feature, it provides a duration from your timestamp to the current date and time using the **`DateTime.LocalNow()`** function. It simply takes the current date and time and subtracts the value in your column. Since it does not use any formal functions, here is what it looks like in the advanced editor:

```
let
  Source = Sql.Database("localhost", "NYC_Taxi"),
  TripData = Source{[Schema = "dbo", Item = "trip_data_yellow"]}[Data],
  Age = Table.TransformColumns(
    TripData,
    {{"tpep_pickup_datetime", each DateTime.LocalNow() - _, type duration}}
  )
in
  Age
```

The last two functions bring back the earliest and latest timestamps available. However, if you remember from the *Applying mathematical functions,* section of this chapter, this is simply using the statistical functions of **`List.Min()`** and **`List.Max()`** to bring back the earliest and latest date, respectively, on a column.

Date transformations can become quite complicated. However, time transformations are much simpler. In short, there are far fewer options available, making them easier to navigate. Here are the transformations we can apply for the time using a timestamp of **`7/28/2023 9:32:25 AM`**:

Time transformations		
Graphical interface	**Power query function**	**Sample result**
Hour	**`Time.Hour`**	9
Start of Hour	**`Time.StartOfHour`**	7/28/2023 9:00:00 AM
End of Hour	**`Time.EndOfHour`**	7/29/2023 10:00:00 AM
Minute	**`Time.Minute`**	32
Second	**`Time.Second`**	25

Table 7.25: *Table of transformations by time on a timestamp*

Time transformations are much easier to manage and navigate as they are less complicated. It is worth noting that hours are represented in 24-Hour notation. Meaning that 12:00 AM is hour 0 through 11:00 PM which is hour 23. This avoids complications and challenges when trending data when you load your query into your model.

The last transformation topic to cover in this section is focused on **`Duration`**. You might never need these transformations, but they provide a lot of value in simplifying analysis. If you remember from *Chapter 6, Managing Data Types,* the duration value has a specific format. The transformations on these can transform what is hard to read into something easier to analyze. Here are the transformations we can apply for the duration of **`8.06:22:11.6664905`**:

Duration transformations		
Graphical interface	**Power query function**	**Sample result**
Days	**`Duration.Days`**	8
Hours	**`Duration.Hours`**	6
Minutes	**`Duration.Minutes`**	22
Seconds	**`Duration.Seconds`**	11.6665
Total Years	**`Duration.TotalYears / 365`**	0.2264
Total Days	**`Duration.TotalDays`**	8.2654
Total Hours	**`Duration.TotalHours`**	198.3699
Total Minutes	**`Duration.TotalMinutes`**	119021944
Total Seconds	**`Duration.TotalSeconds`**	714131.6665

Table 7.26: *Table of transformations by duration*

If you specify a particular element of the duration such as days or hours, it only returns that portion. However, if you use the total, it adds up the entire time and applies a fraction of the period to make it easier to perform mathematical functions on it.

Once again, just like in *Chapter 6, Assigning Data Types*, date and time values is proving to be a challenge due to their complexity. But there is one problem that we did not address. If your organization uses a different date to start the fiscal year or falls into a 4-4-5 or 4-5-4 calendar, you will not find the satisfaction you desire with Power Query. This is why date tables are important. A well-structured date table can help you avoid these challenges and accelerate your analysis. In short, these transformations are helpful, but might be better served in a calculation or in the construction of a date table instead.

Moving columns in a query

Sometimes when we extract data, the columns are not in the correct order for our use. If we are using a SQL-based data source, we can often ask a data engineer to create a view or table to organize our data in a logical sense. However, we do not have that ability when working with files or web-based sources. With Power Query, we can easily re-arrange the order of our columns with a quick drag and drop of our columns in the graphical interface. To accomplish this task, just click on the header of a column and drag it to the correct position in your query. This allows you full control of where you are moving your columns.

However, you might just need to move a column a position to the left or right. Or maybe you want to move it all the way to the beginning or end. You can right-click on a column and under the **Move** submenu, you can move the column accordingly:

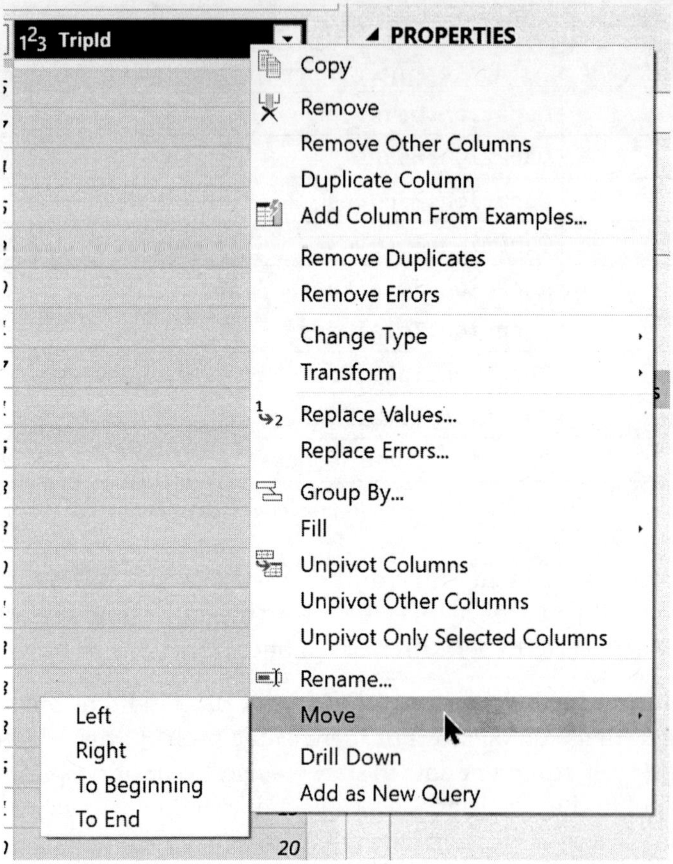

Figure 7.15: *Moving columns to the beginning or end of a table*

Regardless of your methodology for moving your columns in the graphical interface, Power Query uses the **`Table.ReorderColumns()`** function to set the order in the advanced editor:

`Table.ReorderColumns()`	
Parameter	**Description**
`Table`	A table in Power Query. Usually the preceding step.
`ColumnOrder`	List of column names in the order they are to be displayed on the table in Power Query
`MissingField`	Allows you to manage errors with columns that are missing in your query.

Table 7.27: *Table of the Table.ReorderColumns() parameters*

While the drag and drop method works well for tables that only have five to ten columns, the advanced editor code can speed up the process. This will allow you to quickly implement your change while setting the order as you expect:

```
let
  Source = Sql.Database("localhost", "NYC_Taxi"),
  TripData = Source{[Schema = "dbo", Item = "trip_data_yellow"]}[Data],
  ReorderColumns = Table.ReorderColumns(
    TripData,
    {
      "TripId",
      "Airport_fee",
      "congestion_surcharge",
      "total_amount",
      "improvement_surcharge",
      "tolls_amount",
      "tip_amount",
      "mta_tax",
      "extra",
      "fare_amount"
    }
  )
in
  ReorderColumns
```

Naturally, people view this to organize columns and make them easier to view. However, this functionality serves a particularly important purpose. If we ever want to pivot or unpivot our columns, we need to get them in the right order before we do anything. So, while there is an element of beautification of our table, there is a technical purpose behind our movement.

Pivot/unpivot columns

With our columns in the right position, we are ready to start pivoting and unpivoting our columns. If you are familiar with Excel and PivotTables, you have already been pivoting your data. In short, pivoting your data is simply taking unique values held within a single column and converting them into their column. Unpivoting reverses that process and makes columns unique values in a single column.

A common challenge you might experience with your transactional data is the splitting of line-item details into multiple columns. With our sample query, you can see that the total amount of a taxicab ride is split into multiple categories. As you can see, each fare has the potential to be assessed as **`Airport_fee`**, **`congestion_surcharge`**, **`improvement_surcharge`**, tolls, tip, and MTA tax on top of the base fare:

	TripId	Airport_fee	congestion_surcharge	improvement_surcharge	tolls_amount
1	1	0	0	1	0
2	2	1.25	2.5	1	0
3	3	0	2.5	1	0
4	4	0	2.5	1	0
5	5	0	2.5	1	0
6	6	0	2.5	1	0
7	7	0	2.5	1	0
8	8	0	2.5	1	0
9	9	0	2.5	1	0
10	10	0	2.5	1	0
11	11	0	0	1	0
12	12	0	2.5	1	0
13	13	0	2.5	1	0
14	14	0	2.5	1	0

Figure 7.16: Example of how fare data is structured in multiple columns

To make things worse, our query does not have a total charge amount. Now, we can easily get around this issue by creating a custom column and totaling up all these fields. However, if you need to be able to quickly extract elements of a fare, you might find yourself making individual calculations for each column with DAX in your data model. It will work, but what if you could create one measure to perform the total calculation and then apply filters for the line items you need?

To achieve this, we will simply unpivot our columns to the column headers to become individual lines on our table. However, we need a unique identifier to maintain continuity with our trips. That is where our **`TripId`** column will assist us. To get started, we will highlight our unique identifier column, expose the **Transform** ribbon, and under the **Unpivot Columns** menu we will select **Unpivot Other Columns**. You will notice that our data has changed considerably:

	TripId	Attribute	Value
1	1	Airport_fee	0
2	1	congestion_surcharge	0
3	1	improvement_surcharge	1
4	1	tolls_amount	0
5	1	tip_amount	0
6	1	mta_tax	0.5
7	1	extra	1
8	1	fare_amount	8.6
9	2	Airport_fee	1.25
10	2	congestion_surcharge	2.5
11	2	improvement_surcharge	1
12	2	tolls_amount	0
13	2	tip_amount	12.54
14	2	mta_tax	0.5
15	2	extra	6
16	2	fare_amount	52.7
17	3	Airport_fee	0
18	3	congestion_surcharge	2.5
19	3	improvement_surcharge	1
20	3	tolls_amount	0

Figure 7.17: Our taxi fare unpivoted

As you will notice, our data has been simply put into three columns. The first column is our **TripId**. Next, we have each of our former column headers in the **Attribute** column. Lastly, we have the values that were found inside each of our former columns next to their attribute. We now have a sleek and thin table that is easier to manage.

We can use the advanced editor to achieve our pivots in two ways. We have the option to use **Table.Unpivot()** and **Table.UnpivotOtherColumns()** to achieve our desired outcome. It is a matter of personal preference and ease. We will investigate both to see how they function. First up is **Table.Unpivot()**:

Table.Unpivot()	
Parameter	**Description**
Table	A table in Power Query. Usually the preceding step.
PivotColumns	List of column names to be unpivoted and placed into the attribute column.
AttributeColumn	Name of our attribute column
ValueColumn	Name of our value column

Table 7.28: *Table of the Table.Unpivot() parameters*

When using the **Table.Unpivot()** function, we need to specify which columns need to be unpivoted into the attribute column. To achieve the results in *Figure 7.17*, we would use the **Table.Unpivot()** function like this:

```
let
  Source = Sql.Database("localhost", "NYC_Taxi"),
  TripData = Source{[Schema = "dbo", Item = "trip_data_yellow"]}[Data],
  UnpivotData = Table.Unpivot(
    TripData,
    {
      "fare_amount",
      "extra",
      "mta_tax",
      "tip_amount",
      "tolls_amount",
      "improvement_surcharge",
      "congestion_surcharge",
      "Airport_fee"
    },
    "Attribute",
```

```
    "Value"
  )
in
  UnpivotData
```

This method works, but it requires considerable effort to add in all the columns that need to be unpivoted to the attribute column. It gets the job done, but it might be more efficient if we use **`Table.UnpivotOtherColumns()`** instead:

`Table.UnpivotOtherColumns()`	
Parameter	**Description**
`Table`	A table in Power Query. Usually the preceding step.
`PivotColumns`	List of column names to that will not be pivoted.
`AttributeColumn`	Name of our attribute column
`ValueColumn`	Name of our value column

Table 7.29: *Table of the Table.UnpivotOtherColumns() parameters*

When using the **`Table.UnpivotOtherColumns()`** function, we need to specify which columns will not be unpivoted into the attribute column. To achieve the results in *Figure 7.17*, we would use the **`Table.UnpivotOtherColumns()`** functions like this:

```
let
  Source = Sql.Database("localhost", "NYC_Taxi"),
  TripData = Source{[Schema = "dbo", Item = "trip_data_yellow"]}[Data],
  UnpivotData = Table.UnpivotOtherColumns(TripData, {"TripId"}, "Attri-
bute", "Value")
in
  UnpivotData
```

Instead of having to type out the name of all these columns, this method appears to be a better option. So, the obvious answer is to use **`Table.UnpivotOtherColumns()`** every time, right? In short, the answer is not to base which function to use on this scenario alone. In this scenario, we only had one unique column. However, you might run into a situation where you have multiple unique columns and only three or four columns to pivot. In that case, **`Table.Unpivot()`** might be easier to type.

There is no fixed answer here. The reality of this choice is you must select what works best. For some readers, you will pick one that meets your needs most of the time and stick with it regardless of your scenario. Others might change between the two.

Since we have unpivoted our columns, how do we pivot them back? If our query brought our data in as it is shown in *Figure 7.17*, we can easily pivot it back. Simply select both the attribute and value columns, expose the **Transform** ribbon, and click **Pivot Column**. You will be prompted to provide information before you continue:

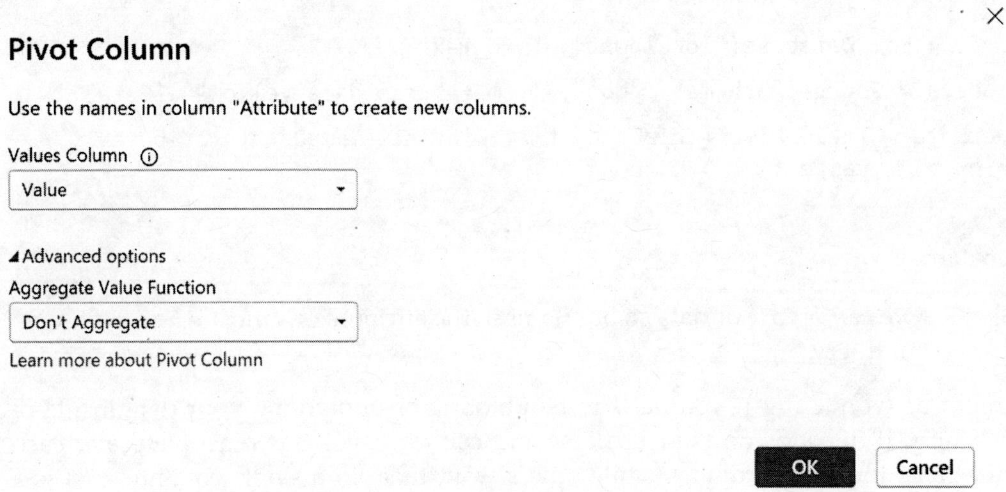

***Figure 7.18:** Preparing to pivot your column*

To pivot your column, you must provide the column where the values will come from. We will use the **Values Column** as it has the data inside of it that we need. However, there is a step that many miss because it is hidden under advanced options. Power Query automatically applies a count aggregation on your column by default. While they are trying to be helpful, our situation does not call for an aggregation. Since we have the values we need in our fields, we can simply change the aggregation to **Don't Aggregate,** which will transpose the values into their new columns.

The **`Table.Pivot()`** function enables us to perform the same action inside the advanced editor. While it seems like a simple transformation, the underlying function requires a little diligence:

`Table.Pivot()`	
Parameter	**Description**
`Table`	A table in Power Query. Usually the preceding step.
`PivotColumns`	List of column names to be pivoted that are contained within the Attribute column
`AttributeColumn`	Name of our attribute column
`ValueColumn`	Name of our value column

***Table 7.30:** Table of the Table.Pivot() parameters*

When we unpivoted our columns, we needed to specify which columns were being moved into the attribute column. The same is true when we go to pivot our data. However, we have the benefit of our new column names being in our existing attribute column. We can simply leverage **List.Distinct()** to assemble the list for us as demonstrated here:

```
let
  Source = Sql.Database("localhost", "NYC_Taxi"),
  TripData = Source{[Schema = "dbo", Item = "trip_data_yellow"]}[Data],
  PivotData = Table.Pivot(TripData, List.Distinct(TripData[Attribute]),
"Attribute", "Value")
in
  PivotData
```

Just like that we can pivot our data so our items in the attribute column are now their own columns in our query.

You might be wondering if you need to be pivoting or unpivoting your data inside of Power Query. It depends on your use case and comfort level. Some people prefer each attribute to be their own column while others want them in a single column. That is a decision that is left up to you as the owner of the data model. Regardless of your choice, you are equipped with the knowledge to achieve this goal within Power Query.

Maintaining query folding in transformations

After all that we have reviewed, now it is time to take a moment and talk about query folding. Some of the transformations we discussed today maintain folding and help with your refresh rates. Others are not as cut and dry.

If you have a strong command of Transact SQL, then you know which of these transformations can be performed in a SQL query. However, sometimes the challenges are not as obvious as they seem. For example, take merging two columns together. If the two columns are text-based, you can do so and maintain your folding. However, if you need to change your data type, this might break your folding.

If you are using a SQL-based data source, take a few moments after you complete a transformation to confirm that your query folding has been maintained. Yes, this can be a bit of a hassle, but it is better to find out while you are developing the model instead of when you go to deploy the model. If you are working with a development or test database that has a fraction of the data available, this is even more important. Your query performance depends on your ability to maintain folding and will be critical whether you are refreshing the entire query or using an incremental refresh for your model.

Conclusion

In this chapter, we covered how to transform your data within Power Query. We started with the basics of promoting column headers and changing their names. After that, we manipulated text in columns by formatting it, extracting it, and merging it into a single column. We also went into detail on how to transform numeric data with mathematical functions and how to perform transformations on date/time data. We then went through the steps to re-arrange our columns and then pivot and unpivot them to meet the needs of our data model. Lastly, we touched again on query folding and how it is important to continually verify if your folding is intact.

In the next chapter, we will explore how to clean up our columns even further to assist with the preparation of our data model.

CHAPTER 8
Cleansing Columns

Introduction

In this chapter, we will start to filter and further transform our data for use. We will first explore the column profile tools to help us understand the quality of our data. From there, we will explore ways to filter, replace, fill cells, and remove duplicate values within a column. Next, we will remove columns that are not required within our data model. Lastly, we will explore considerations when it comes to cleansing columns within Power Query.

Structure

The chapter covers the following topics:

- Column profile tools
- Filtering data
- Replace values in a column
- Replace errors in a column
- Using fill up/down
- Remove duplicate values

- Remove extra columns
- Remove top/bottom rows
- Considerations with cleansing columns

Objectives

By the end of this chapter, you will be able to understand how to use Power Query to filter and replace data that does not meet the quality standards for your model. This will allow you to provide a clean data model free of errors while managing potential issues that might arise with future refreshes from your sources.

Column profile tools

As you continue your transformation journey, you will realize there comes a time when you might need to cleanse your data. While transforming column data is nice, we often run into situations where there are errors that come in from our data sources. For example, you might have a distance column that uses text. Or maybe there are some characters in your source that cannot be read by Power Query. You might even find that your source data is not an accurate representation of your model, and it requires you to reconsider your source.

The column profile tools help us get started with our review and simplifies the process of quickly analyzing our data. These tools are integrated inside the graphical interface to assist with the process of understanding our data. These tools do not perform any cleansing transformations. They are designed to provide a quick view of the data to help you act on your data. Therefore, you will not use the advanced editor with these tools.

The first tool that is available to you is the column quality indicator that sits right below your column header. You might not have noticed this before because if your data is properly cleansed, this indicator almost looks like it is a stylized line for your column header. Here is what the column profile indicator looks like on an active data set:

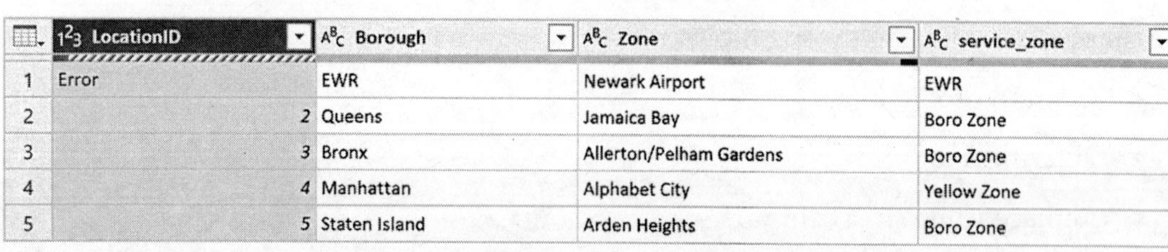

	LocationID	Borough	Zone	service_zone
1	Error	EWR	Newark Airport	EWR
2	2	Queens	Jamaica Bay	Boro Zone
3	3	Bronx	Allerton/Pelham Gardens	Boro Zone
4	4	Manhattan	Alphabet City	Yellow Zone
5	5	Staten Island	Arden Heights	Boro Zone

Figure 8.1: Column profile indicator for our taxi zone lookup query

For our **Borough**, **Zone**, and **Service_Zone** columns, we do not have any errors. The result is a solid teal line. However, we notice that **LocationID** is different. Instead, we see some red and an error on the first line of our query. This indicates that there are errors in this column. The benefit is that while there are errors, it appears that, based on the sample size, there are only a few to correct. We can dig deeper and learn more about the errors with some of the data preview tools under the **View** ribbon in the Power Query editor. If we select the **Column quality** option, it provides us with a little more context to our situation, as shown:

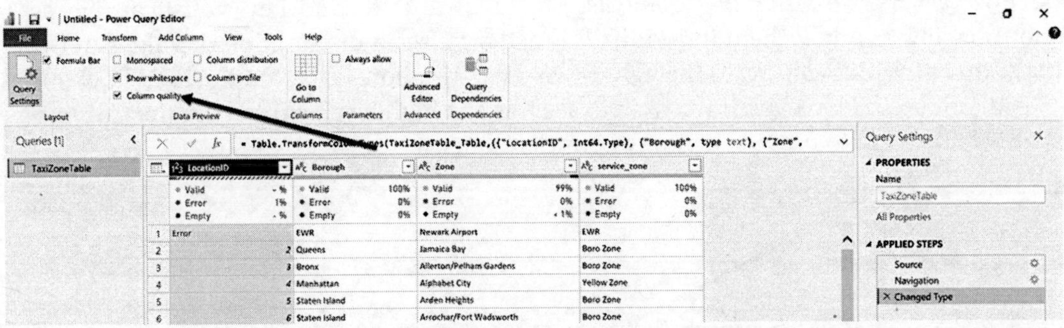

Figure 8.2: Enabling column quality in the Power Query editor

As demonstrated in *Figure 8.2*, the column quality option provides us with a breakdown of the column values found within a query. It provides a percentage of values that are returning with errors in a column. For our **`LocationID`** column, only one percent of our values are returning with errors which does not seem too bad. This view also provides details on potential missing values in a column. Situations may vary, but if your data model requires specific columns to always have a value, this view quickly identifies any issues. Our **`Zone`** column, while showing no errors, has a few cells that are missing values. While we have percentages, we still do not understand the overall impact. We can use the **Column profile** option to expand our view of the data:

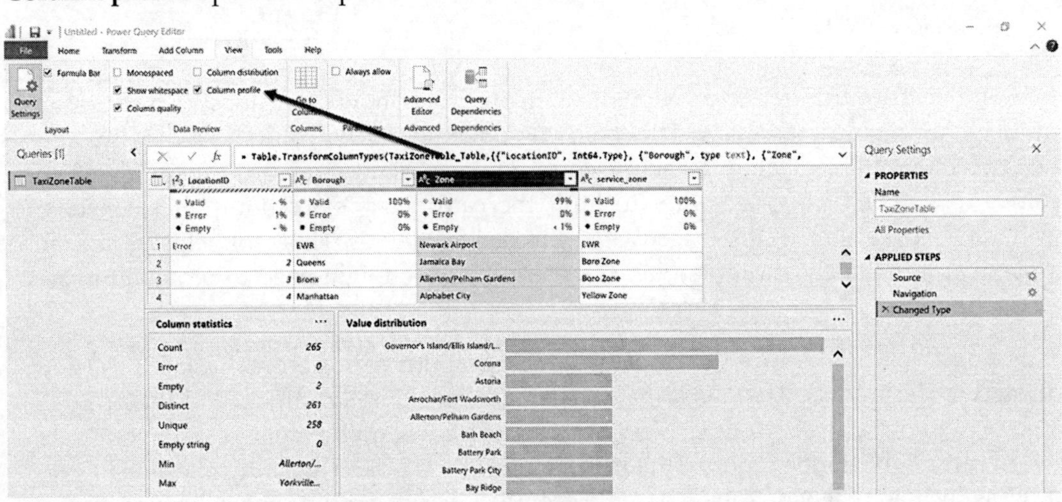

Figure 8.3: Viewing the profile for the Zone column in our query

The column profile option provides context to our data. In performing our analysis of the **Zone** column, we can learn a few key facts about our data. For example, we know that there are two hundred sixty-five rows of data, but two are empty. We have no errors to resolve in this column. In addition to those values under column statistics, we can see the different measures we would find with our statistical transformations that we learned about in *Chapter 7, Transforming Columns.* This allows us to find key statistical figures without having to apply them individually. Lastly, we see a distribution of values in the column that provides context to the values we see. This allows us to understand how our data is distributed. However, if we wish to see this at a high level, we can use the **Column distribution** option to provide a view of our distribution:

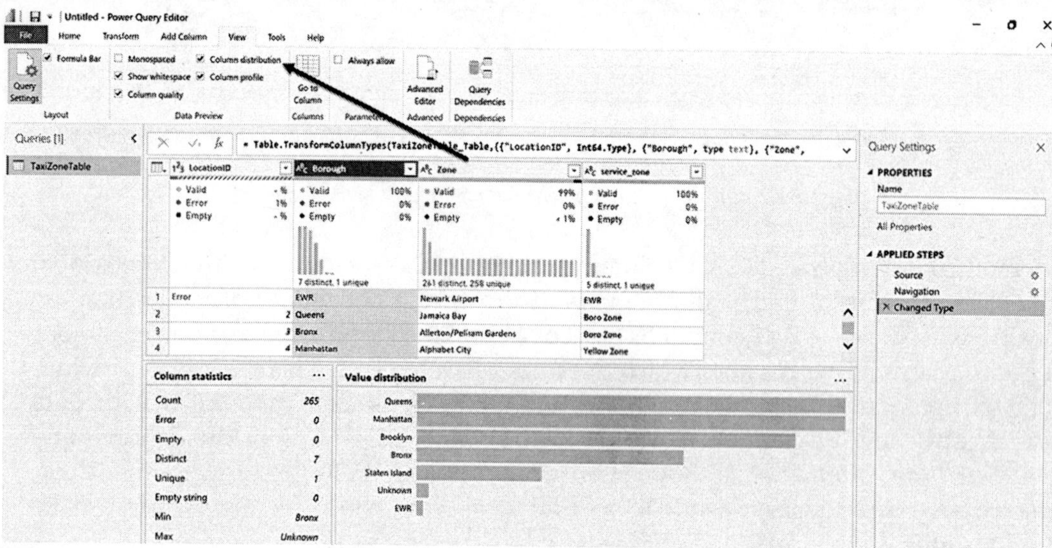

Figure 8.4: *Enabling the column distribution option inside the Power Query editor*

The column distribution option provides us with context on how our values are distributed without requiring deep analysis. This helps us understand the column cardinality and the distribution of these values to help inform how we might structure a column. When it comes to Power Query, we want to limit the cardinality of columns that consume considerable space such as text-based values in our fact tables. This tool helps us see the complexity immediately and potentially signals where we might need to provide further investigation.

At this point, you will notice that a considerable amount of screen real estate has been dedicated to these tools. There is a reason they are considered options, and they can be turned on and off when required. These tools are ideal when you are ingesting your data early on but might not be required later in your journey. You might turn these views on and off as they are needed. You also might feel they do not provide the value you desire when trying to understand your data. In the end, you must decide which of these tools, if any, should be in use when transforming your data with Power Query.

Now that we have these tools at our disposal and we have identified errors, we must take the next step. If you click into a cell that has been classified with an error, this helps us know how to go about resolving our potential issues. In our case, the error can easily be resolved by resolving the data type in Power Query from whole number to text:

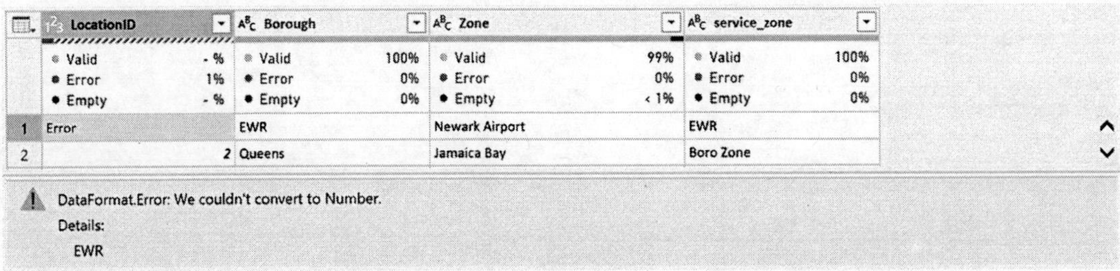

Figure 8.5: *Identifying our column error by selecting the cell value*

However, this might not be the way to resolve errors going forward. In that case, we must use different methods to cleanse our data. Using our column profile tools, we can quickly identify our potential issues and work to cleanse them from our data model in Power Query.

Filtering data

One of the first concepts people learn in Excel is how to filter their data. The tabular format provides a simple approach for us to shrink our query to the rows we need to provide the most value. Ideally, we would filter our data before it arrives in the Power Query editor. However, not every data source provides us with an opportunity to achieve this. If that is not an option, we can leverage the filtering tools available to us with Power Query to achieve our results.

The graphical interface lends itself to providing multiple options when it comes to filtering our data. To the right of our column header, we have a dropdown that provides us with an option on how to filter our data:

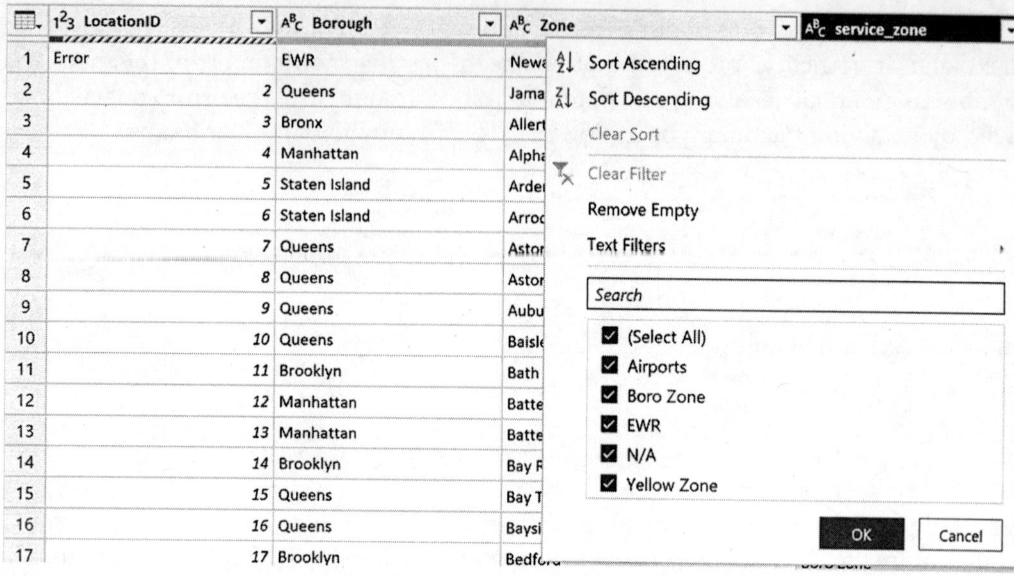

Figure 8.6: Filtering values options on a column

The easiest option for many is to simply unselect the values in the dropdown menu that do not apply. For example, we do not want to see any rows of data with **`N/A`** as the service zone. We can simply uncheck that item. In addition, we only want to see **`Yellow Zone`** records, so we could uncheck **(Select All)** and then check **`Yellow Zone`**.

This method works well, but you are locked into specific values. And while our list is short, it might be harder to manage if it was larger. For example, we want to return only rows that contain the word **Zone**. We could select the two values available, but what if they added additional zones to our data set? Our solution is hardcoded to use those two values. Instead, we can use the **text filters** option to provide better directions on how to filter our data:

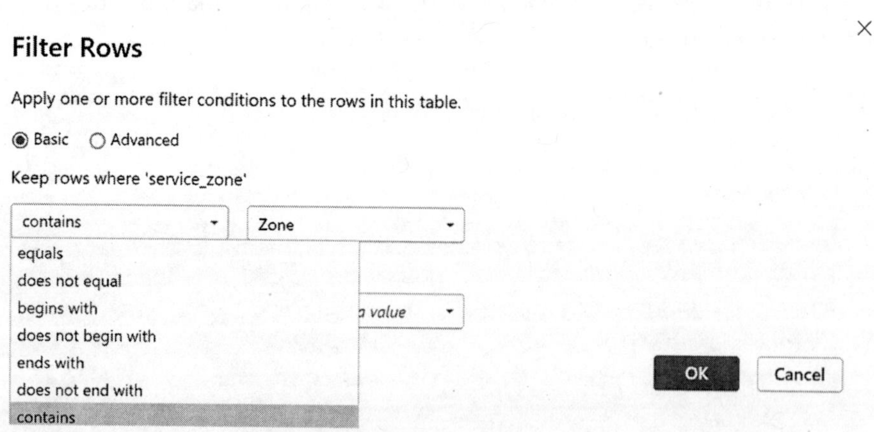

Figure 8.7: Applying text filters to a column

With text filters, we can provide better instructions on how we want our data filtered. In our example, we want to return any row that **contains** the word **Zone** inside. We could also use the **ends with** option instead and achieve the same result with our current query. With text, we can filter on a specific string of text, whether that text is available at the beginning or end of a string, or if it is contained within a string. This provides flexibility with our filter context and enables us to provide the right level of precision necessary. In addition, you can add a second statement. If both statements must be true, you can use **And** option to link them together. If only one statement must be true, you can use the **Or** option.

We have similar rules available for number filters and date / time filters. For number filters, we can apply greater than, greater than or equal to, less than, less than or equal to, and between filters. Date / time filters work similarly except that greater than is called after and less than is called before. In addition, there are relative date / time filters that allow you to filter in the last number of years, months, weeks, days, hours, minutes, or seconds. There are also prebuilt filters to select rows that are in the current, next, or previous year, month, week, day, hour, minute, or second.

The next option we can use to filter a column is the **remove empty** option. This option removes rows that have empty cells in a column. However, there is something sneaky happening in the background with this option. Empty cells often are represented as **`null`**. However, sometimes we end up with data that finds its way into the cell. The cell shows as blank, but it is not represented with a **`null`** value. We can use this option to force both scenarios out of our models with a single click. In addition, if you want to apply this logic to mitigate issues in the future but do not have blank values available, your only easy option is to apply this filter to prevent blank values from coming into your mode.

The last option we have is hidden in a different location. Sometimes we want to remove any errors in our query. Now, this is not a common practice and should be reserved for use only when there are no options around resolving an error, as this is a very indiscriminate approach to filtering. However, if the situation arises, you can right-click on a column header and select **Remove Errors** to filter any cells that contain errors:

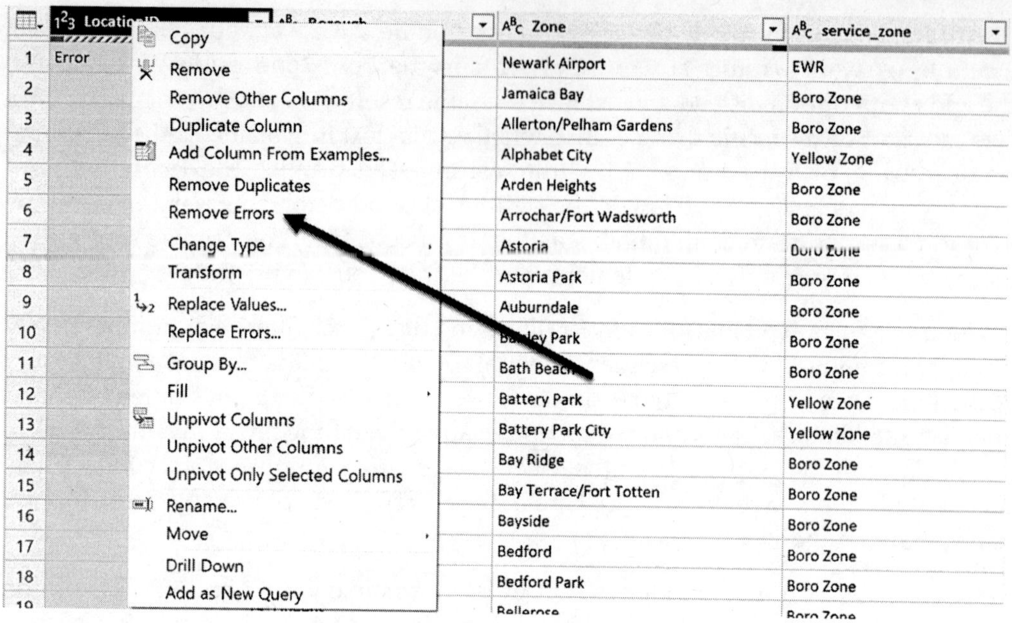

Figure 8.8: Removing errors from a column

With a single click, your errors are removed and are no longer an issue within your model. Instead of writing a complex rule, this simplifies the process and provides the handling of errors.

Now, the graphical interface provides us with many tools to help with our filtering. However, you will find as you continue your journey that you might need to leverage the advanced editor to get the most out of your filtering. For example, our text, number, and date/time filters only allow us to make two filter statements when we might have more. Another challenge is that case counts with text, so we might need to provide a transformation to manage text in both upper and lowercase format. Sometimes, we can use the graphical interface to get us started, but we will, at a point, need to use the advanced editor to achieve our desired outcome.

The advanced editor uses the **`Table.SelectRows()`** function to apply our filters. There are only two parameters for this function, but it can be tricky to use because of one item required for your condition parameter:

`Table.SelectRows()`	
Parameter	**Description**
`Table`	A table in Power Query. Usually the preceding step.
`Condition`	Conditional statement for the filter context. Must start with `each` to apply to every row in the query.

Table 8.1: *Table of the Table.SelectRows() parameters*

The condition parameter must always start with **each** to prevent issues with your filter. If you are new to using the advanced editor, it is an easy item to miss. Using the **Table.SelectRows()** function, we can filter our data set to only show the **Yellow Zone** service zones in our query:

```
let
  Source = Excel.Workbook(File.Contents("C:\NYC Taxi\taxi_zone_lookup_er-
rors.xlsx"), null, true),
  TaxiZoneTable_Table = Source{[Item = "TaxiZoneTable", Kind = "Table"]}
[Data],
  ChangedType = Table.TransformColumnTypes(
    TaxiZoneTable_Table,
    {
      {"LocationID", Int64.Type},
      {"Borough", type text},
      {"Zone", type text},
      {"service_zone", type text}
    }
  ),
  FilteredRows = Table.SelectRows(ChangedType, each ([service_zone] = "Yel-
low Zone"))
in
  FilteredRows
```

As you can see from the preceding example, we set a filter for the **Service_Zone** to be applied as a condition for each row in the query. If we want to add another condition to our query, we could use **or** to require one to be true or **and** for both to be true. Using **and**/**or** allows you to expand your conditional statements. You can chain multiple statements together as you need until your data is adequately filtered:

```
let
  Source = Excel.Workbook(File.Contents("C:\NYC Taxi\taxi_zone_lookup_er-
rors.xlsx"), null, true),
  TaxiZoneTable_Table = Source{[Item = "TaxiZoneTable", Kind = "Table"]}
[Data],
  ChangedType = Table.TransformColumnTypes(
    TaxiZoneTable_Table,
    {
      {"LocationID", Int64.Type},
```

```
        {"Borough", type text},
        {"Zone", type text},
        {"service_zone", type text}
      }
    ),
    FilteredRows = Table.SelectRows(
      ChangedType,
      each ([service_zone] = "Yellow Zone") or ([service_zone] = "Boro Zone")
    )
in
    FilteredRows
```

We also can use the text, number, and date/time filters in the advanced editor. We could achieve the same outcome by adjusting our code to verify a row contains the word **Zone**:

```
let
    Source = Excel.Workbook(File.Contents("C:\NYC Taxi\taxi_zone_lookup_er-
rors.xlsx"), null, true),
    TaxiZoneTable_Table = Source{[Item = "TaxiZoneTable", Kind = "Table"]}
[Data],
    ChangedType = Table.TransformColumnTypes(
      TaxiZoneTable_Table,
      {
        {"LocationID", Int64.Type},
        {"Borough", type text},
        {"Zone", type text},
        {"service_zone", type text}
      }
    ),
    FilteredRows = Table.SelectRows(ChangedType, each Text.Contains([service_
zone], "Zone"))
in
    FilteredRows
```

When using **Table.SelectRows()**, you can filter your text data by leveraging different conditions to meet the condition. Each function has two parameters. The first is the column you are looking to check and the second is the value you are looking for. This applies to any of these functions:

Text filters	
Condition type	**Power query function**
Equals	`[Column] = "Value"`
Not equals	`[Column] <> "Value"`
Begins with	`Text.StartsWith([Column], "Value")`
Does not begin with	`not Text.StartsWith([Column], "Value")`
Ends with	`Text.EndsWith([Column], "Value")`
Does not end with	`not Text.EndsWith([Column], "Value")`
Contains	`Text.Contains([Column], "Value")`
Does not contain	`not Text.Contains([Column], "Value")`

Table 8.2: *List of conditions for text filters*

For numeric filters, we just use the standard operators that you learned in your mathematics courses:

Number filters	
Condition type	**Power query function**
Equals	`[Column] = N`
Does not equal	`[Column] <> N`
Greater than	`[Column] > N`
Greater than or equal to	`[Column] >= N`
Greater than	`[Column] < N`
Greater than or equal to	`[Column] <= N`
Between	`[Column] >= N1 and [Column] <= N2`

Table 8.3: *List of conditions for numeric filters*

For date / time filters, we have several conditions available to us:

Date/time filters	
Condition type	**Power query function**
Equals	`[Column] = #date(YYYY, MM, DD)`
Is before	`[Column] < #date(YYYY, MM, DD)`
Is after	`[Column] > #date(YYYY, MM, DD)`
Between	`[Column] > #date(YYYY, MM, DD) and [Column] < #date(YYYY, MM, DD)`
This year	`Date.IsInThisYear([Column])`
Next year	`Date.IsInNextYear([Column])`
Previous year	`Date.IsInPreviousYear([Column])`
This quarter	`Date.IsInThisQuarter([Column])`
Next quarter	`Date.IsInNextQuarter([Column])`
Previous quarter	`Date.IsInPreviousQuarter([Column])`
This month	`Date.IsInThisMonth([Column])`
Next month	`Date.IsInNextMonth([Column])`
Previous month	`Date.IsInPreviousMonth([Column])`
This day	`Date.IsInThisDay([Column])`
Next day	`Date.IsInNextDay([Column])`
Previous day	`Date.IsInPreviousDay([Column])`
This hour	`DateTime.IsInThisHour([Column])`
Next hour	`DateTime.IsInNextHour([Column])`
Previous hour	`DateTime.IsInPreviousHour([Column])`
This minute	`DateTime.IsInThisMinute([Column])`
Next minute	`DateTime.IsInNextMinute([Column])`
Previous minute	`DateTime.IsInPreviousMinute([Column])`
This second	`DateTime.IsInThisSecond([Column])`
Next second	`DateTime.IsInNextSecond([Column])`
Previous second	`DateTime.IsInPreviousYear([Column])`

Table 8.4: *List of conditions for date/time filters*

For relative date filtering, we must specify the unit of time we would like to use and then the duration:

Relative date/time filters	
Condition type	**Power query function**
Previous N years	`Date.IsInPreviousNYears([Column], N)`
Next N years	`Date.IsInNextNYears([Column], N)`
Previous N quarters	`Date.IsInPreviousNQuarters([Column], N)`
Next N quarters	`Date.IsInNextNQuarters([Column], N)`
Previous N months	`Date.IsInPreviousNMonths([Column], N)`
Next N months	`Date.IsInNextNMonths([Column], N)`
Previous N weeks	`Date.IsInPreviousNWeeks([Column], N)`
Next N weeks	`Date.IsInNextNWeeks([Column], N)`
Previous N days	`Date.IsInPreviousNDays([Column], N)`
Next N days	`Date.IsInNextNDays([Column], N)`
Previous N hours	`DateTime.IsInPreviousNHours([Column], N)`
Next N hours	`DateTime.IsInNextNHours([Column], N)`
Previous N minutes	`DateTime.IsInPreviousNMinutes([Column], N)`
Next N minutes	`DateTime.IsInNextNMinutes([Column], N)`
Previous N seconds	`DateTime.IsInPreviousNSeconds([Column], N)`
Next N seconds	`DateTime.IsInNextNSeconds([Column], N)`

***Table 8.5:** List of relative date/time filters*

When you pause for a moment and look at all these potential conditions, you start to realize there are several options to select from already. How could there be any more options available? What is great about the advanced editor is that we can take our transformations from *Chapter 7, Transforming Columns* and apply them to our filters. For example, if you wanted to filter dates for the month of **`July`**, you could use **`Date.Month([Column]) = 7`** to achieve that outcome.

But things get more interesting when we want to use transformations to prevent issues with our filters. Backing up for a moment, we wanted to filter our service zones to rows that had the word **`Zone`**. However, we run into an issue if our filter is not using the right case for each of the letters. Because of case sensitivity, a cell that has the value of **`zone`** would not be included because of the missing capital **`Z`**. We can take what we have previously learned about text formatting and apply it to our filter to ensure all future cells are properly accounted for even if there is a typographical error:

```
let
```

```
  Source = Excel.Workbook(File.Contents("C:\NYC Taxi\taxi_zone_lookup_er-
rors.xlsx"), null, true),
  TaxiZoneTable_Table = Source{[Item = "TaxiZoneTable", Kind = "Table"]}
[Data],
  ChangedType = Table.TransformColumnTypes(
    TaxiZoneTable_Table,
    {
      {"LocationID", Int64.Type},
      {"Borough", type text},
      {"Zone", type text},
      {"service_zone", type text}
    }
  ),
  FilteredRows = Table.SelectRows(
    ChangedType,
    each Text.Contains(Text.Lower([service_zone]), "zone")
  )
in
  FilteredRows
```

By adding **`Text.Lower()`** to our code, we will force the values in the column to use lowercase characters, thus always ensuring our condition will always return the correct match.

The conditions for filtering your data can be quite complex, but Power Query rises to the challenge and has about every possible combination available for you to cleanse your data. Hopefully, you are starting to see how we continue to build upon previous knowledge to help simplify our queries while squeezing everything we can out of them. Taking a few moments with the advanced editor allows you to step up your transformations which prevents you from taking additional steps in your journey.

Replace values in column

While filtering might be the most common way to deal with bad data, sometimes we can simply clean up a value for a row in a column. Often, we find rows of data that might be blank, or the item in the cell might not be our desired end state. We can simply replace our values with a more desirable value with a simple applied step.

If we reference *Figure 8.3*, you will remember that the **Zone** column in our example has two empty values. Since we might use this field in our model for display purposes, we will want to tag it, so it is clear and easy to understand. Instead of having a blank value, we can use **Unknown** as a placeholder to prevent confusion. To perform this transformation, right-click on the column header and select **Replace Values** to get started:

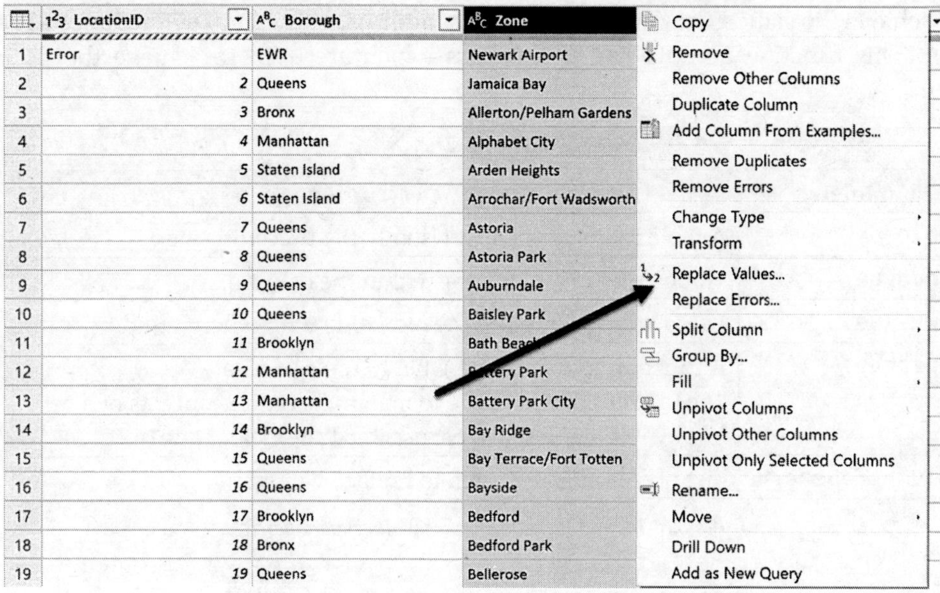

Figure 8.9: *Initiating the process to replace values*

A new window will appear where we can specify the **Value To Find** and the new value that we will use to replace it. You also have additional options such as the match must occur for the entire contents of a cell instead of a portion of a cell. You also can replace using a special character if appropriate:

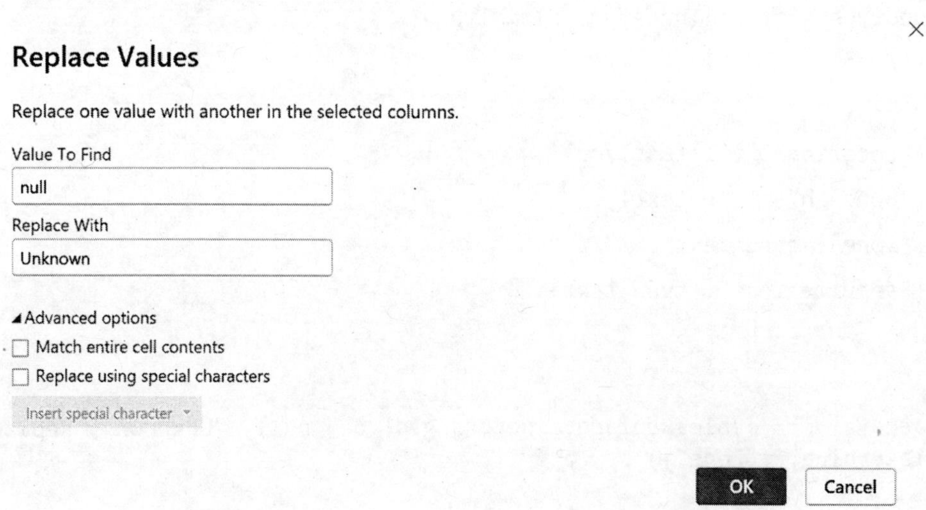

Figure 8:10: *Identifying the value to find and the replacement value*

It is not well documented, but if you use the word **null** for either the value to find or replace with, Power Query interprets it as an empty cell. If you do not specify anything, it will leave the cell appearing blank but not officially empty.

We can achieve the same goal with the advanced editor using the **Table.ReplaceValue()** function. This function accepts five parameters which are used to achieve the desired outcome:

Table.ReplaceValue()	
Parameter	**Description**
Table	A table in Power Query. Usually the preceding step.
OldValue	Value you are looking for within the column.
NewValue	Value you will replace the old value with when found.
Replacer	A function to determine what to replace. Use ReplacerReplaceValue to match the entire contents of a cell. If only replacing portions, use Replacer.ReplaceText.
ColumnsToSearch	List of columns to search to replace values.

Table 8.6: *Table of the Table.ReplaceValue() parameters*

To replace the blank cells in our **Zone** column, we can use the following code:

```
let
  Source = Excel.Workbook(File.Contents("C:\NYC Taxi\taxi_zone_lookup_er-
rors.xlsx"), null, true),
  TaxiZoneTable_Table = Source{[Item = "TaxiZoneTable", Kind = "Table"]}
[Data],
  ChangedType = Table.TransformColumnTypes(
    TaxiZoneTable_Table,
    {
      {"LocationID", Int64.Type},
      {"Borough", type text},
      {"Zone", type text},
      {"service_zone", type text}
    }
  ),
  ReplacedValue = Table.ReplaceValue(ChangedType, null, "Unknown", Replac-
er.ReplaceValue, {"Zone"})
in
  ReplacedValue
```

This code allows us to replace those **`null`** values with **`Unknown`** with a simple line of code. Now, if you recall from *Figure 8.10* that we did not specify for the value to find to match the cell perfectly. At this point you might be wondering why the use of **`Replacer.ReplaceValue`** to match the entire cell. The reason is that we are looking for an empty cell, and for that to work, you must match it perfectly. The graphical interface manages that for you seamlessly, so you are unaware. However, if you choose to write the code with the advanced editor, this is something you need to understand to avoid errors.

This is a simple cleansing transformation that can simplify your overall transformation. The wonderful thing about this transformation is that it allows you to disposition items instead of suppressing them. Blank cells are a part of the transformation process, but with a label they are much easier to understand in context.

Replace errors in a column

We can replace errors in our columns just like we did with values. However, it is important to be careful about this form of indiscriminate replacement. When dealing with errors, it is always recommended that you take the time to research the cause and resolve it either upstream at the data layer or with transformations in Power Query. However, sometimes that cannot be done. We can use this function to disposition these errors so we can continue with our analysis. Right-click on the column header and select **Replace Errors** to get started:

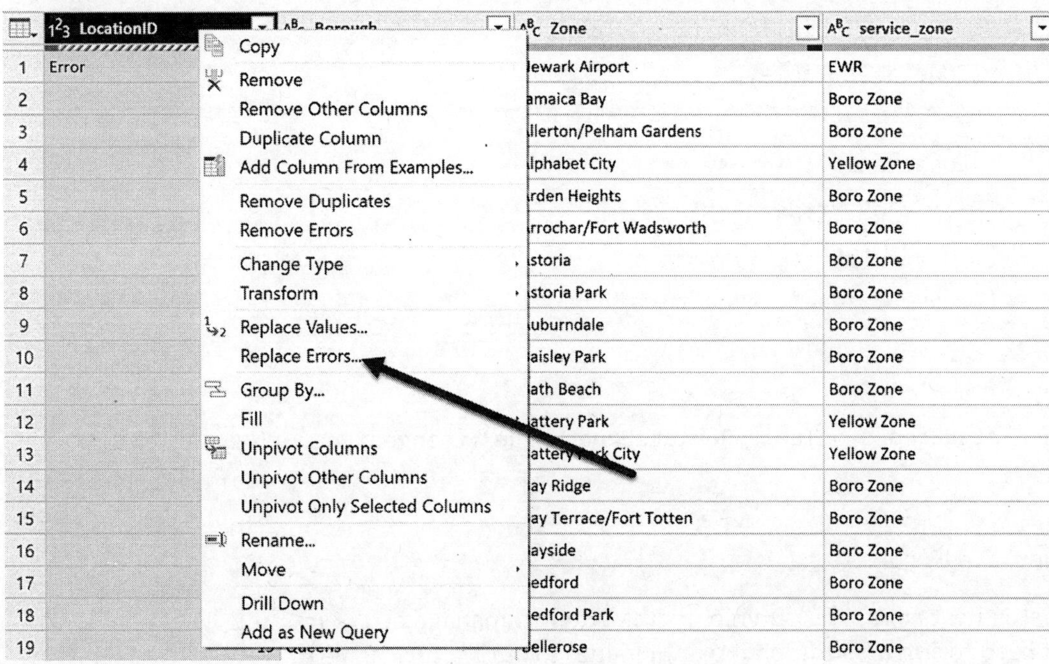

***Figure 8.11:** Initiating the process to replace errors*

Just like when replacing values, you will be prompted to provide a value for the replacement. However, in this context, you will only need to provide that value. Cells with errors are easily identifiable by Power Query, so no additional input is needed. It is important to note that you must select a value that fits within the data type of the column. In our example with **LocationID**, we will need to use a whole number, or we will still have an error.

Replacing errors with the advanced editor is just as simple and streamlined. We accomplish it using the **Table.ReplaceErrorValues()** function to achieve the desired result.

Table.ReplaceErrorValues()	
Parameter	**Description**
Table	A table in Power Query. Usually the preceding step.
ErrorReplacement	List of columns and the replacement value for an error in a pair.

Table 8.7: *Table of the Table.ReplaceErrorValues() parameters*

To replace the errors in our **LocationID** column, we will use the following code:

```
let
  Source = Excel.Workbook(File.Contents("C:\NYC Taxi\taxi_zone_lookup_er-
rors.xlsx"), null, true),
  TaxiZoneTable_Table = Source{[Item = "TaxiZoneTable", Kind = "Table"]}
[Data],
  ChangedType = Table.TransformColumnTypes(
    TaxiZoneTable_Table,
    {
      {"LocationID", Int64.Type},
      {"Borough", type text},
      {"Zone", type text},
      {"service_zone", type text}
    }
  ),
  ReplacedErrors = Table.ReplaceErrorValues(ChangedType, {{"LocationID",
0}})
in
  ReplacedErrors
```

What is neat about this function is that we can manage errors in multiple columns. We just need to add an additional pair of values to our list to achieve the result. This comes in handy when you must disposition errors across multiple columns in a query. Remember, the goal here is to disposition errors. While you may be able to resolve errors with your current query, this might not be a sustainable solution in the long term to make sure you are doing your diligence to resolve errors as soon as possible.

Using fill up/down

A common scenario that occurs with Excel files is situations where people have created a merged cell to group items together. While this is nice from a visual perspective inside Excel, it causes grief with Power Query. The result is we have rows of empty cells which does nothing to help our data model. But Power Query has already anticipated this challenge and has an easy solution. We could use replace values, but that does not work in our situation because we have multiple replacement values. Instead, we will select our column, expose the **Transform** ribbon, and click on the **Fill** drop-down, as shown:

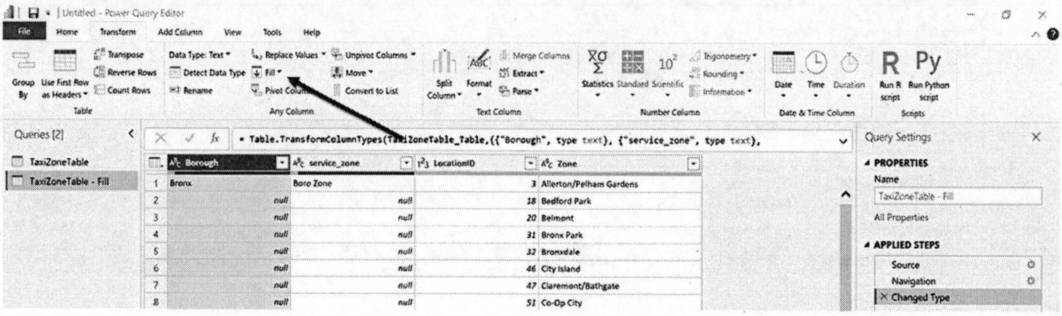

***Figure 8.12:** Selecting the fill drop down on the transform ribbon*

We have two options with our fill direction. If we select down, Power Query will take a value and fill in each empty cell below it until it comes across a cell that is not empty. From there, it will take that new value and repeat this process until it comes to the last row in the query. If you select up instead, it performs the same transformation but in reverse from the last row of the query to the top. This feature also can be initiated by right-clicking on the column header, exposing the **Fill** submenu, and selecting the fill direction you wish to use.

The advanced editor allows us to use the **`Table.FillDown()`** and **`Table.FillUp()`** functions to fill in empty cells and receive our desired result:

`Table.FillDown() and Table.FillUp()`	
Parameter	**Description**
`Table`	A table in Power Query. Usually the preceding step.
`Columns`	List of columns to fill in the specified direction.

***Table 8.8:** Table of the Table.FillDown() and Table.FillUp() parameters*

Both the **`Table.FillDown()`** and **`Table.FillUp()`** functions have the same parameters. The sole difference between them is the direction of the fill. One benefit to using the advanced editor for this transformation is that we can apply the fill on multiple columns at once, assuming that they both are heading the same direction. We can apply our fill on both the **Borough** and **service_zone** columns with this code:

```
let
  Source = Excel.Workbook(File.Contents("C:\NYC Taxi\taxi_zone_lookup_fill.
xlsx"), null, true),
  TaxiZoneTable_Table = Source{[Item = "TaxiZoneTable", Kind = "Table"]}
[Data],
  ChangedType = Table.TransformColumnTypes(
    TaxiZoneTable_Table,
    {
      {"Borough", type text},
      {"service_zone", type text},
      {"LocationID", Int64.Type},
      {"Zone", type text}
    }
  ),
  FilledRows = Table.FillDown(ChangedType, {"Borough", "service_zone"})
in
  FilledRows
```

This function is not one that sees frequent use. However, there are times when it is critical to your data cleansing. It is important to note that if you need to use the **fill** function, you should apply it as soon as possible in your transformation. The most common mistake people make with this function is performing another transformation ahead of this that causes issues like filtering rows or changing the sort order. This can cause your data to become inaccurate, so take the time to make sure everything is in the proper place before using the fill function.

Remove duplicate values

It is common for values to appear in a column more than once. Sometimes, we must remove the duplicate values to make our query more concise. Power Query allows us to remove these duplicate items within the graphical interface. Right-click on the column header and select **Remove Duplicates** to get started, as shown in the following figure:

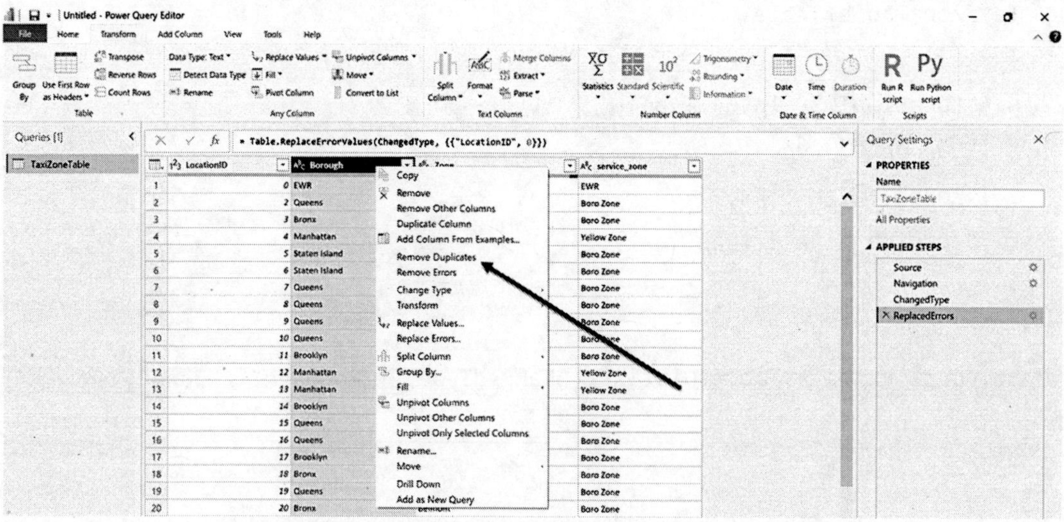

Figure 8.13: Initiating the process to remove duplicate values from a column

Once activated, Power Query will filter the query to the unique values found within the selected column. But there might be a problem with this approach. In our example, we have shrunk our list down too far. If our goal was to find a list of boroughs, then this solution would work. A little-known trick is that this function can be applied to more than one column. Instead of looking for a distinct list of values in a single column, it looks for a distinct set of values between multiple columns.

This process is easier to see in action using the **`Table.Distinct()`** function in the advanced editor. This function has two parameters which help us achieve the desired outcome:

`Table.Distinct()`	
Parameter	**Description**
`Table`	A table in Power Query. Usually the preceding step.
`EquationCriteria`	List of columns to search for distinct values.

Table 8.9: Table of the Table.Distinct() parameters

In this scenario, we want to make sure there are no duplicate values between the **`Borough`** and **`Zone`** columns. We can use this block of code to achieve that result:

```
let
  Source = Excel.Workbook(File.Contents("C:\NYC Taxi\taxi_zone_lookup_er-
rors.xlsx"), null, true),
  TaxiZoneTable_Table = Source{[Item = "TaxiZoneTable", Kind = "Table"]}
[Data],
  ChangedType = Table.TransformColumnTypes(
```

```
      TaxiZoneTable_Table,
      {
        {"LocationID", Int64.Type},
        {"Borough", type text},
        {"Zone", type text},
        {"service_zone", type text}
      }
    ),
    RemoveDuplicates = Table.Distinct(ChangedType, {"Borough", "Zone"})
in
    RemoveDuplicates
```

Note that we listed both columns in the second parameter. This enables us to filter our query and return only distinct results of the combined columns.

This is another feature that must be used with caution. Because of the indiscriminate nature of this function, there is a potential for issues with your data model. This function is best served for filtering down a list for another transformation or for the creation of a dimension table from an existing fact table. It is strongly recommended that you validate the data you are using after performing this transformation to ensure no downstream issues will result from this function.

Remove extra columns

A common challenge you might experience when querying data is the addition of extra columns that might not belong. Sometimes these columns are full of meaningless data while other times they are blank cells that came in as part of a spreadsheet. Regardless of the situation, Power Query allows us to clean up these columns with only a few clicks.

Removing columns in the graphical interface can be managed in two ways. The first way is where we select which columns we wish to remove. The easiest way to delete a column is to select a column and use the delete key to remove it. The second way to do it is to right click on a column header and click on **Remove**. The third way to achieve our goal is to select a column and go to the **Remove Columns** dropdown in the home ribbon and select **Remove Columns**, as shown here:

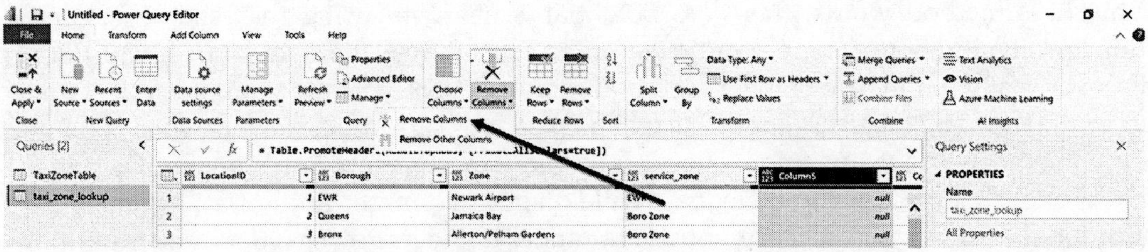

Figure 8.14: Removing columns inside the Power Query editor

Once selected, the selected columns will be removed from the query. You can select multiple columns using *Shift + click* or *Ctrl + click* to remove multiple columns at once.

You can use the **`Table.RemoveColumns()`** function inside the advanced editor to remove these extra columns:

`Table.RemoveColumns()`	
Parameter	**Description**
`Table`	A table in Power Query. Usually the preceding step.
`Columns`	List of columns to remove from the query.
`MissingField`	Allows you to manage errors with columns that are missing in your query.

Table 8.10: Table of the Table.RemoveColumns() parameters

A benefit from using the advanced editor is the ability to manage errors with the **`MissingField`** parameter. We can remove our extra columns using the following block of code:

```
let
  Source = Excel.Workbook(File.Contents("C:\NYC Taxi\taxi_zone_lookup.
xlsx"), null, true),
  Sheet1_Sheet = Source{[Item = "Sheet1", Kind = "Sheet"]}[Data],
  RemoveTopRows = Table.Skip(Sheet1_Sheet, 4),
  PromoteHeaders = Table.PromoteHeaders(RemoveTopRows, [PromoteAllScalars =
true]),
  RemoveColumns = Table.RemoveColumns(
    PromoteHeaders,
    {"Column5", "Column6", "To Do List"},
    MissingField.Ignore
  )
in
  RemoveColumns
```

While this method works, there are potential issues with using the remove columns function. In situations where you do not have control over the data source, you might discover that columns are being added and removed from your original query. If we are using the **`MissingField.Ignore`**, this will help us avoid any refresh errors when columns are removed without our knowledge. However, it is common to have columns added into a query without our knowledge. While one or two might not impact your refresh, additional columns could cause your data model to bloat. Power Query has a solution for that. If you go back to *Figure 8.14*, you will notice that there is a second option in the dropdown called **Remove Other Columns**. This function allows us to select the columns we wish to keep and remove the other columns.

When using the advanced editor, there is a little confusion with this function. While we are removing other columns, we are really selecting the columns we wish to keep. Therefore, the function we will use is **`Table.SelectColumns()`** to keep the columns we need:

`Table.SelectColumns()`	
Parameter	**Description**
`Table`	A table in Power Query. Usually the preceding step.
`Columns`	List of columns to keep from the query.
`MissingField`	Allows you to manage errors with columns that are missing in your query.

Table 8.11: *Table of the Table.SelectColumns() parameters*

To achieve the same result as above, we will use **`Table.SelectColumns()`** in our block of code to keep our required columns:

```
let
  Source = Excel.Workbook(File.Contents("C:\NYC Taxi\taxi_zone_lookup.
xlsx"), null, true),
  Sheet1_Sheet = Source{[Item = "Sheet1", Kind = "Sheet"]}[Data],
  RemoveTopRows = Table.Skip(Sheet1_Sheet, 4),
  PromoteHeaders = Table.PromoteHeaders(RemoveTopRows, [PromoteAllScalars =
true]),
  SelectColumns = Table.SelectColumns(
    PromoteHeaders,
    {"LocationID", "Borough", "Zone", "service_zone"}
  )
in
  SelectColumns
```

With the options to remove columns or remove other columns, the question that arises is which option is the best to choose. The reality of the matter is whichever one is easiest to use. If you have a query with thirty columns and you need to remove two of them, removing columns might be the easiest. But if you have the same thirty columns and only need two, removing other columns is easier. The only exception to the rule might be if the column you are removing is a system-generated column from a data source. For example, SharePoint has several supporting columns that are loaded with a query. They can sometimes cause refresh errors because of how they are ingested. Therefore, while it might be more difficult to execute, removing other columns would be a more stable solution.

Remove top/bottom rows

If you read *Chapter 7, Transforming Data,* then you should remember that we introduced the topic of removing the top rows of a query to clean up our transformation. In our scenario, we had four rows at the top of our spreadsheet that arrived with our query. While we could have opened our Excel files and deleted them manually, we used the **Remove Top Rows** function on the home ribbon so we could line up our headers in row one and then promote them. We even used `Table.Skip()` in the advanced editor to achieve our desired outcome.

Unfortunately, this only tells a small portion of the story when it comes to managing rows of data. It is common when working with Excel to have additional rows at the bottom of your query. Maybe someone put a total or notes after the last row of data. Regardless of the reason, we can leverage Power Query to clean this scenario up:

	LocationID	Borough	Zone	service_zone
261	261	Manhattan	World Trade Center	Yellow Zone
262	262	Manhattan	Yorkville East	Yellow Zone
263	263	Manhattan	Yorkville West	Yellow Zone
264	264	Unknown	NV	N/A
265	265	Unknown	NA	N/A
266	null	null	null	null
267	null	null	null	null
268	null	null	null	null
269	Total Zones	265	null	null

Figure 8.15: *Extra rows at the bottom of the query*

With the graphical interface, we can follow the identical steps we did before just selecting **Remove Bottom Rows** and entering the number of rows we need to remove. If we want to use the advanced editor, we can use `Table.RemoveLastN()` to achieve the same result:

`Table.RemoveLastN()`	
Parameter	**Description**
`Table`	A table in Power Query. Usually the preceding step.
`CountOrCondition`	Count of rows to remove or a condition that must be met to stop removal.

Table 8.12: *Table of the Table.RemoveLastN() parameters*

We can leverage **`Table.RemoveLastN()`** and remove the last four rows of data in our query using this code to strip the last four rows from our model:

```
let
  Source = Excel.Workbook(File.Contents("C:\NYC Taxi\taxi_zone_lookup.
xlsx"), null, true),
  Sheet1_Sheet = Source{[Item = "Sheet1", Kind = "Sheet"]}[Data],
  RemoveTopRows = Table.Skip(Sheet1_Sheet, 4),
  PromoteHeaders = Table.PromoteHeaders(RemoveTopRows, [PromoteAllScalars =
true]),
  SelectColumns = Table.SelectColumns(
    PromoteHeaders,
    {"LocationID", "Borough", "Zone", "service_zone"}
  ),
  RemoveBottomRows = Table.RemoveLastN(SelectColumns, 4)
in
  RemoveBottomRows
```

Two other scenarios might not be as common and are not as straightforward. The first scenario is where we have rows with no data present. These rows provide no value and were for a visual purpose. We can remove these rows from the graphical interface by selecting **Remove Blank Rows** in the **Remove Rows** dropdown in the graphical interface. This function will scan the entire row, and if no data is present, it will be removed from the query. While this can be done with the advanced editor, the code required is far more complicated than the graphical interface. Therefore, it is recommended that you use this feature as is in the graphical interface.

Another common scenario we encounter with our queries is a situation where there are total rows in the middle of our query. This commonly occurs with file-based sources, and the removal of these rows is critical. In the **Remove Rows** dropdown, you can select **Remove Alternate Rows,** which prompts you for additional information, as illustrated below:

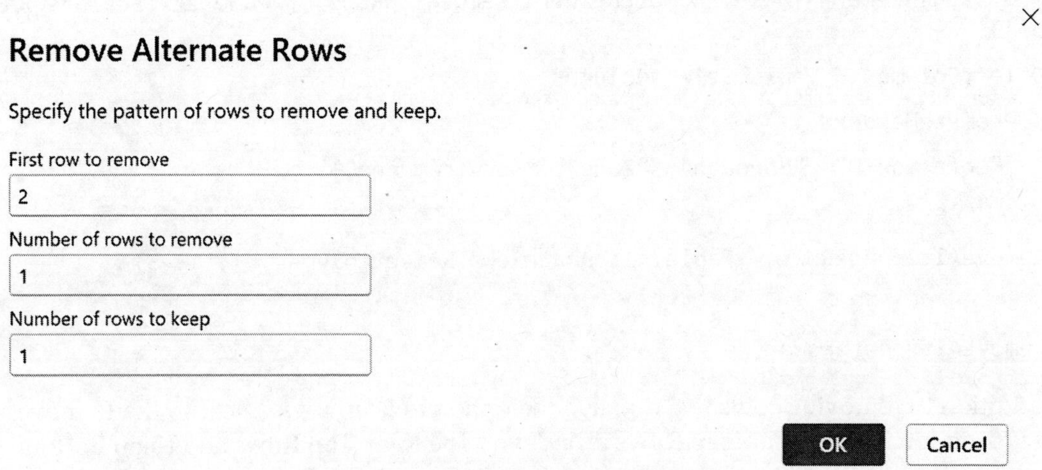

Figure 8.16: Removing alternate rows from a query

We are prompted for three pieces of information. The first question is asking which row is first to be removed. Next, we specify how many rows will be removed, followed by how many rows to keep. In *Figure 8.16*, we will be removing every other row, starting with the second row. Essentially, it removes all even numbered rows.

Using the advanced editor, we can use **`Table.AlternateRows()`** to achieve the same outcome. While the parameter names are not the most obvious, they align with the prompts in the graphical interface:

`Table.AlternateRows()`	
Parameter	**Description**
`Table`	A table in Power Query. Usually the preceding step.
`Offset`	Number of rows to keep before starting.
`Skip`	Number of rows to remove at each occurrence.
`Take`	Number of rows to keep at each occurrence.

Table 8.13: Table of the Table.AlternateRows() parameters

Instead of removing every other row, we will use a scenario where we have groups of five rows followed by a total row. We will keep our **`Skip`** parameter set to one while adjusting our **`Take`** parameter to five:

```
let
  Source = Excel.Workbook(File.Contents("C:\NYC Taxi\taxi_zone_lookup.
xlsx"), null, true),
  Sheet1_Sheet = Source{[Item = "Sheet1", Kind = "Sheet"]}[Data],
  RemoveTopRows = Table.Skip(Sheet1_Sheet, 4),
```

```
  PromoteHeaders = Table.PromoteHeaders(RemoveTopRows, [PromoteAllScalars =
true]),
  SelectColumns = Table.SelectColumns(
    PromoteHeaders,
    {"LocationID", "Borough", "Zone", "service_zone"}
  ),
  RemoveAlternateRows = Table.AlternateRows(SelectColumns, 1, 1, 5)
in
  RemoveAlternateRows
```

In addition to removing rows, we do have the option to keep rows. Next to the Remove Rows dropdown, there is a **Keep Rows** dropdown. The **Keep Top Rows** and **Keep Bottom Rows** functions act just like their counterparts in Remove Rows. Both options prompt you for the number of rows to keep from a query. In fact, while the functions are different, the parameters are the exact same:

`Table.FirstN() and Table.LastN()`	
Parameter	**Description**
`Table`	A table in Power Query. Usually the preceding step.
`CountOrCondition`	Count of rows to keep or a condition that must be met to stop retention.

Table 8.14: *Table of the Table.FirstN() and Table.LastN() parameters*

But there is one more function available to us under Keep Rows. We can use **Keep Range of Rows** to retain rows in the middle of our query. We will be prompted to provide the first row we wish to retain, followed by the number of rows that should be kept, as shown:

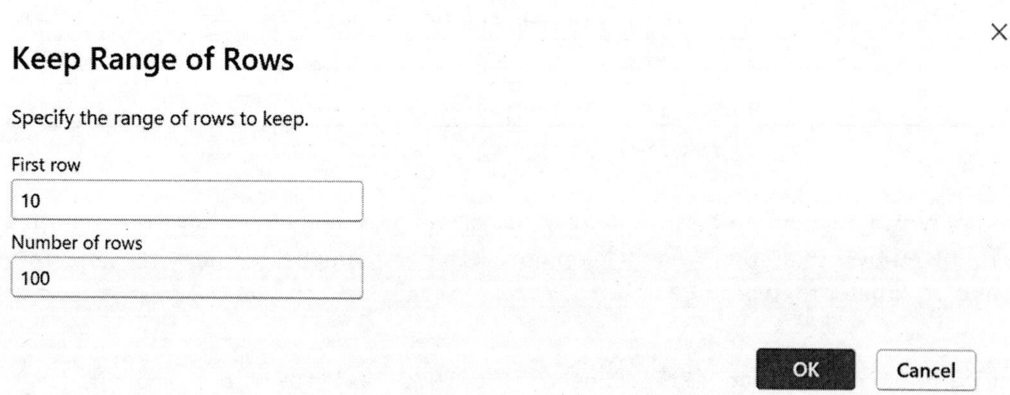

Figure 8.17: *Keeping a range of rows from a query*

We can use **`Table.Range()`** in the advanced editor to achieve the same outcome. Initially, the parameter names do not make sense, but they align with the graphical interface:

`Table.Range()`	
Parameter	**Description**
`Table`	A table in Power Query. Usually the preceding step.
`Offset`	Number of rows to skip before retaining rows.
`Count`	Number of rows to keep.

Table 8.15: *Table of the Table.Range() parameters*

We can see the **`Table.Range()`** function in this block of code to match the outcome from *Figure 8.17* above:

```
let
  Source = Excel.Workbook(File.Contents("C:\NYC Taxi\taxi_zone_lookup.
xlsx"), null, true),
  Sheet1_Sheet = Source{[Item = "Sheet1", Kind = "Sheet"]}[Data],
  RemoveTopRows = Table.Skip(Sheet1_Sheet, 4),
  PromoteHeaders = Table.PromoteHeaders(RemoveTopRows, [PromoteAllScalars =
true]),
  SelectColumns = Table.SelectColumns(
    PromoteHeaders,
    {"LocationID", "Borough", "Zone", "service_zone"}
  ),
  KeepRange = Table.Range(SelectColumns, 9, 100)
in
  KeepRange
```

Now you might be wondering why go through all this effort to keep or remove rows of data with these functions. With everything covered earlier in this chapter, the same outcome could be applied without these functions. To a degree, these functions help speed up the transformation process. In addition, some of these functions will find their way back to us in *Chapter 14, Functions,* as we look to expand our use of the M Query language. While they might not be part of your daily development, these functions will be useful soon when paired with the right scenario.

Considerations with cleansing columns

Some readers might be wondering why the cleansing of data was not being managed in the data layer. Ideally, we would be able to perform all cleansing activities upstream, but the realities of life sometimes force us to use Power Query to perform these transformations. As we discussed in *Chapter 7, Transforming Columns*, we must consider query folding when using database sources. In addition, some of your transformations might break your DirectQuery mode. Like everything else, take your time and pay attention to make sure your model is transforming your data as efficiently as possible.

Conclusion

In this chapter, we covered how to cleanse your data within Power Query. We started with reviewing column profiles to help identify potential problems with our data. From there, we filtered our data from our query. Next, we replaced values and errors that might occur in a column. Then we went through the process of filling in empty cells with the fill function. Lastly, we went through the process of removing duplicate values, unwanted columns, and unwanted rows in a query.

In the next chapter, we will expand upon our knowledge of transformations to create new columns in our queries.

Join our book's Discord space

Join the book's Discord Workspace for Latest updates, Offers, Tech happenings around the world, New Release and Sessions with the Authors:

https://discord.bpbonline.com

CHAPTER 9
Creating New Columns

Introduction

In this chapter, we will create new columns within our queries. We will first explore the appropriate time to create new columns and when to use Power Query to achieve this. Next, we will review our transformations from *Chapter 7, Transforming Columns* and learn how they can be applied. Then we will navigate through options for creating new columns, such as splitting, duplicating, conditional, custom, and columns from examples. We will introduce advanced columns that you might use, followed by changing data types while creating columns. Lastly, we will discuss caution when it comes to creating new columns in Power Query.

Structure

The chapter covers the following topics:

- When to create columns
- Creating columns in Power Query
- Transformations as new columns
- Splitting columns

- Duplicating columns
- Creating conditional columns
- Creating custom columns
- Creating columns from example
- Introduction to advanced columns
- Changing data types
- Cautions with creating columns

Objectives

By the end of this chapter, you will understand how to use Power Query to create new columns for your data model. This will allow you to provide additional context and value to your queries while eliminating additional transformations from your data sources.

When to create columns

It is common for people to create their own columns in a query. Frequently, there are use cases where it makes sense to create new columns based on the needs of your data model. A fitting example of this would be when you have two columns that hold first and last names separately, but you need them together in a specific format for visualization purposes. You also might need to create a complex calculation to simplify your analysis. Other times, you just might need a flag on your rows of data to indicate something specific.

When creating new columns in your query, it is important to consider what purpose it will provide. As you create columns for your query, it will expand the size and footprint. If you needed to create a date table from scratch inside of Power Query, you might find yourself in a situation where you are adding columns that might not provide any value to your query. A notable example is if you are adding details of the week number or day of the week. If your analysis is not going that deep, it might not be of value to add these columns to your date table.

While the idea of creating a column is helpful, it is important to consider the necessity of a column before adding it to your model. It is easy to become overzealous and add columns that never will be used. In the past, the goal has been for users to bring every bit of data they could in and then filter it down. While that method was easier for many analysts, that is no longer the standard as our queries continue to grow. It is better to be prescriptive and only add the columns necessary to complete our objectives which helps manage the size and usability of the model as it continues to scale.

Creating columns in Power Query

The process of creating columns in Power Query can be as simple or complex as you desire. Many who start their column creation journey think they must know all the different formulas and calculations to be successful. However, sometimes simplicity is key, and with the help of applied steps, you can achieve your desired outcome. In short, do not think that when you create a column everything must be done in a single step for you to be successful. In fact, the truth is quite the opposite.

If you are just starting your journey with Power Query, you might find the opportunity to use multiple steps to achieve your goals can help you understand how to structure your formulas better. Do not take this as a sign of failure, but rather an opportunity to gain experience. Once you understand the steps you applied, you could go back and create your own formula leveraging the logic you applied in multiple steps and attempt to complete the process in a single step.

As we explore this chapter, you will realize how simple the transformation process can be with the assistance of the graphical interface and a little artificial intelligence inside our queries.

Transformations as new columns

Unbelievably, you have learned several ways to create new columns already. In *Chapter 7, Transforming Columns,* we went through the diverse ways you could modify an existing column using different transformations. The problem with this approach is that it replaces the existing data in the new transformed format.

A splendid example where you might want to add a column instead of replacing one is with a timestamp column. You may need to keep the original timestamp column for deeper analysis but want to be able to extract the date at the end of the month for cleaner reporting. If we transform the timestamp column to show the end of the month, we will lose the detail. However, if we create a new column, we can retain both.

If you expose the **Add Column** ribbon in Power Query, you will note that it looks like the **Transform** ribbon. In fact, it almost looks identical if you look at the transformations from text, from number, and from date and time, as shown:

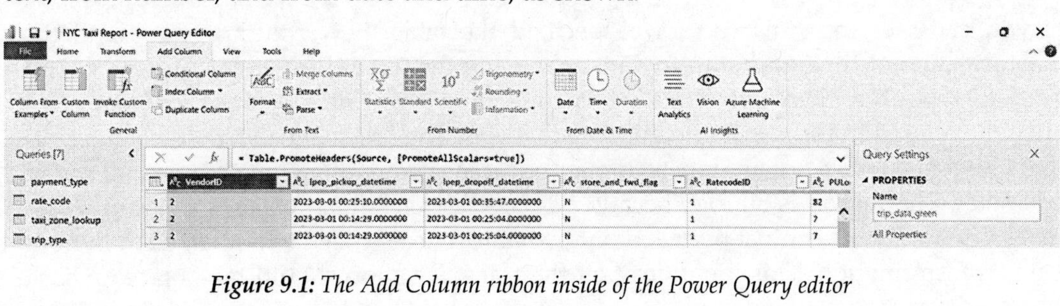

***Figure 9.1:** The Add Column ribbon inside of the Power Query editor*

This means that everything we learned in *Chapter 7, Transforming Queries*, applies to this chapter when it comes to creating columns. As mentioned earlier, this is a simple first step to enable our transformations with the graphical interface.

While the graphical interface makes everything seem identical, the code underneath the covers is different. The advanced editor uses the **`Table.AddColumn()`** function to create the new column:

`Table.AddColumn()`	
Parameter	**Description**
`Table`	A table in Power Query. Usually the preceding step.
`NewColumnName`	Name of the new column you are adding to the query.
`ColumnGenerator`	The value being transformed and placed into rows of the new column.
`ColumnType`	Data type specified for the new column

Table 9.1: *Table of the Table.AddColumn() parameters*

To see this transformation in action, we will extract the date that is contained within the **`lpep_pickup_datetime`** column of our query. The result is a code block that looks like this:

```
let
  Source = Sql.Database("localhost", "NYC_Taxi"),
  GreenTripData = Source{[Schema = "dbo", Item = "trip_data_green"]}[Data],
  PickupDate = Table.AddColumn(
    GreenTripData,
    "PickupDate",
    each DateTime.Date([lpep_pickup_datetime]),
    type date
  )
in
  PickupDate
```

As you can see from this code, we specified the table, new column name, and the transformation of the timestamp to date only using the **`DateTime.Date()`** function, and the data type. But there are some differences from the **`Table.TransformColumns()`** function we used in *Chapter 7, Transforming Columns*. The first is the fact that we must use a column name instead of an underscore for our transformation in the **`ColumnGenerator`** parameter. The reason is simple, because we are referencing an existing column as we create a new column, it must be called out by name. We also need to add an **`each`** in front of our transformation. This identifies that the transformation should take place on each row. Without this, you will receive an error. This is a common mistake that can easily be resolved.

Now, while the graphical interface manages many of these transformations for you, it does not customize your exact result. For example, if you extract the date from a timestamp column, the default name of the column is `Date`. Instead of adding a new step to update the column name, you can jump into the advanced editor and make this change. You can also update data types quickly without having to insert additional steps as well. While the process of creating some of these transformation columns might be easier with the graphical interface, you can simplify your steps and code by performing small adjustments as you go along with the advanced editor. By doing so, you will make your code more concise and easier to follow when you come back to amend it in the future.

Splitting columns

Splitting columns is a common transformation that is used on text-based data. Some common scenarios include the splitting of a full name, splitting of address components, or software versions. Regardless of your solution requirements, this can easily be performed within Power Query.

The option for splitting columns can be confusing. While we are technically adding columns to our query, the option is not available inside the **Add Columns** ribbon with the Power Query editor. Instead, it is available inside both the **Home** and **Transform** ribbons. Most users leverage this function under the **Home** ribbon because it makes more logical sense, but both ribbons achieve the same goal. Regardless of where you choose to invoke the **Split Columns** function, the options are the same, as shown:

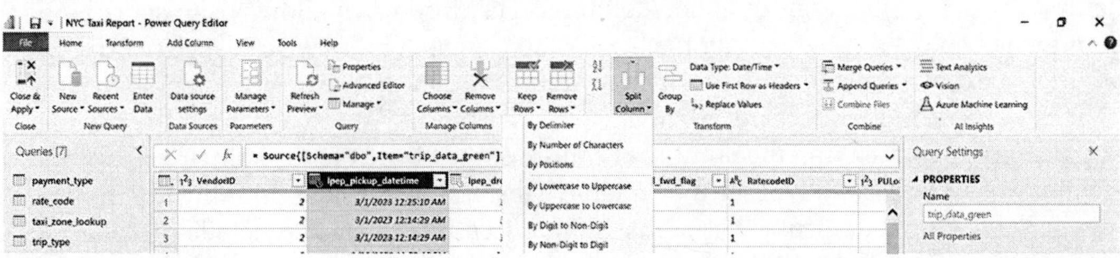

***Figure 9.2:** Options for splitting your selected column*

When splitting your columns, you have seven options from which you can choose. For most transformations, the option to **Split Column by Delimiter** will be the most common. When selected, you will receive a detailed prompt window asking you to provide information about your transformation, as shown in the following figure:

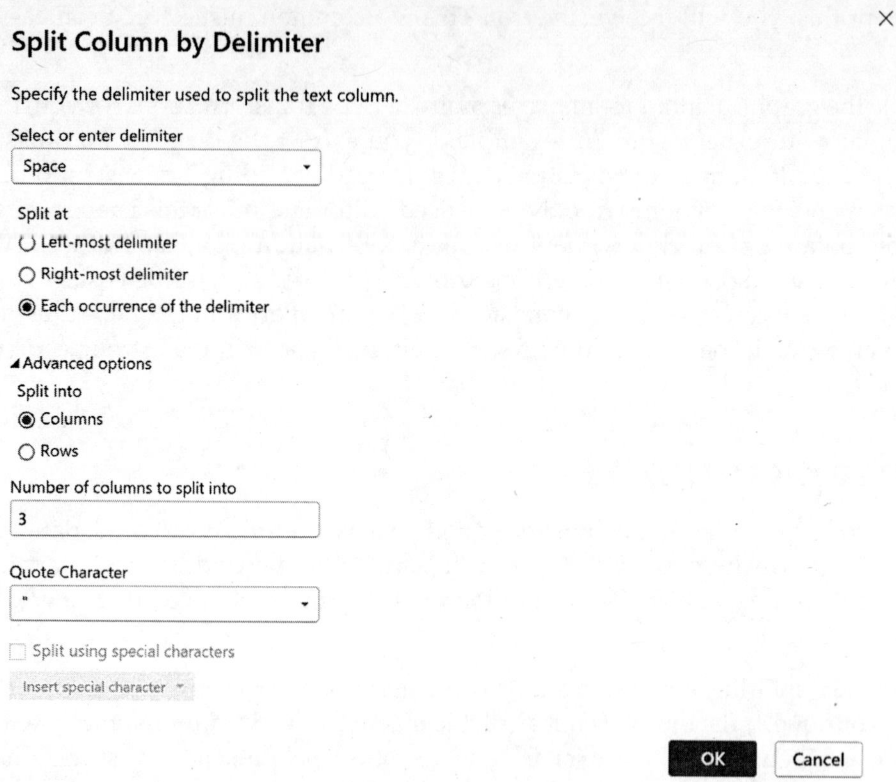

Figure 9.3: Options for splitting a column by delimiter

The first thing we must identify is the delimiter. The dropdown allows us to specify our delimiter as a colon, semicolon, comma, space, tab, equals sign, or we can specify our own delimiter. Next, we must identify the split location. We can choose to split only on the left, or **Right-most delimiter** occurrence, or at each occurrence. We can also limit the number of occurrences by specifying the number of columns resulting from the split. If you expand the advanced options, you will see that you have the option to split a column into multiple rows instead. We will discuss that scenario in a little bit. Using the details provided in *Figure 9.3*, the result of our split columns looks like this:

	VendorID	lpep_pickup_datetime.1	lpep_pickup_datetime.2	lpep_pickup_datetime.3	lpep_dropoff_datetime
1	2	3/1/2023	12:25:10 PM	AM	3/1/2023 12:35:47
2	2	3/1/2023	12:14:29 PM	AM	3/1/2023 12:25:04
3	2	3/1/2023	12:14:29 PM	AM	3/1/2023 12:25:04
4	2	2/28/2023	10:59:46 AM	PM	2/28/2023 11:08:38
5	2	3/1/2023	12:54:03 PM	AM	3/1/2023 1:03:14
6	2	3/1/2023	1:00:09 AM	AM	3/1/2023 1:14:37
7	2	3/1/2023	12:09:45 PM	AM	3/1/2023 12:26:06
8	2	3/1/2023	12:39:30 PM	AM	3/1/2023 12:39:33
9	2	3/1/2023	12:03:07 PM	AM	3/1/2023 12:14:44
10	2	3/1/2023	12:42:56 PM	AM	3/1/2023 12:49:57
11	2	3/1/2023	1:13:10 AM	AM	3/1/2023 1:15:50
12	2	3/1/2023	12:28:03 PM	AM	3/1/2023 12:32:46

Figure 9.4: Result of split columns by delimiter

As demonstrated in *Figure 9.4*, our original timestamp column was split into three columns. On the surface, this seems like a simple transformation, but there is a lot going on under the covers with the advanced editor. Using the **`Table.SplitColumn()`** function allows us to start our process of achieving our desired outcome:

`Table.SplitColumn()`	
Parameter	**Description**
`Table`	A table in Power Query. Usually, the preceding step.
`SourceColumn`	Name of the column that is to be split.
`Splitter`	Function assigned to determine the type of split, such as delimiter or the number of characters.
`ColumnNamesOrNumber`	List of new column names or the number of columns for the data to be split into.
`Default`	Default value to enter if the split does not provide data for a specified column.

Table 9.2: *Table of the Table.SplitColumn() parameters*

To achieve the same result as we saw in *Figure 9.4*, we need to structure our code block to take the **`lpep_pickup_datetime`** column and split it based on the space. To achieve this, we will need to use a block of code that looks like this:

```
let
  Source = Sql.Database("localhost", "NYC_Taxi"),
  GreenTripData = Source{[Schema = "dbo", Item = "trip_data_green"]}[Data],
  SplitColumns = Table.SplitColumn(
    GreenTripData,
    "lpep_pickup_datetime",
    Splitter.SplitTextByDelimiter(" ", QuoteStyle.Csv),
    3,
    "No Data"
  )
in
  SplitColumns
```

Using **`Table.SplitColumn()`**, we have identified the table of data from the previous step, the correct column to split, and used the **`Splitter.SplitTextByDelimiter()`** function to split our column into the spaces found in the row of data. We even added a default value in the event we are missing data so we can easily identify it. But this code block has an error. If you look back at *Figure 9.2*, you will notice that we are performing this transformation on a date/time column. However, the **`Table.SplitColumn()`** function is designed to work on text. As a result, we have two options. The first is to add a preceding step that changes the data type of the column to text so we can perform the transformation. While that is efficient, we can eliminate an additional step by slipping a column transformation in with the **`Table.TransformColumnTypes()`** function with the first parameter. Since we will be revamping this code, we will specify the final column names and add a step to update the data types after the split:

```
let
  Source = Sql.Database("localhost", "NYC_Taxi"),
  GreenTripData = Source{[Schema = "dbo", Item = "trip_data_green"]}[Data],
  SplitColumns = Table.SplitColumn(
    Table.TransformColumnTypes(GreenTripData, {{"lpep_pickup_datetime",
type text}}, "en-US"),
    "lpep_pickup_datetime",
    Splitter.SplitTextByDelimiter(" ", QuoteStyle.Csv),
    {"PickupDate", "PickupTime", "PickupMeridiem"},
    "No Data"
  ),
  ChangeDataType = Table.TransformColumnTypes(
    SplitColumns,
    {{"PickupDate", type date}, {"PickupTime", type time}, {"PickupMeridi-
em", type text}}
  )
in
  ChangeDataType
```

For a simple concept, the advanced editor reveals there are a lot of complicated pieces at work underlying the query. At this point, we have only explored the **Split Column by Delimiter** option. But we have other splitters available to us. Each one has its own purpose and associated function, as explained in the following table:

Splitter functions		
Split type	**Description**	**Function**
By Delimiter	Splits by a specific set of characters as identified in the query.	`Splitter. TextByDelimeter("Delimiter", QuoteStyle)`
By Any Delimiter	Splits column with a series of delimiters identified in the query. Must be added with the advanced editor.	`Splitter.SplitTextByAnyDelimiter( {"Delimiter"}, QuoteStyle)`
By Number of Characters	Splits column based on the number of characters specified and repeats until finished.	`Splitter. SplitTextByRepeatedLengths(N)`
By Positions	Splits column based upon identified positions. Numbers are provided in a list format.	`Splitter.SplitTextByPositions(N1, N2, N3, N4)`
By Lowercase to Uppercase	Splits column when there is a transition from lowercase to uppercase text in a string.	`Splitter. SplitTextByCharacterTranstition( {"a".."z"}, {"A".."Z"})`
By Uppercase to Lowercase	Splits column when there is a transition from uppercase to lowercase text in a string.	`Splitter. SplitTextByCharacterTranstition( {"A".."Z"}, {"a".."z"})`
By Digit to Non-Digit	Splits column when there is a transition from a numeric value to text value in a string.	`Splitter. SplitTextByCharacterTranstition( {"0".."9"}, (string) => not List. Contains( {"0".."9"}, string))`
By Non-Digit to Digit	Splits column when there is a transition from a text value to numeric value in a string.	`Splitter. SplitTextByCharacterTranstition( (string) => not List.Contains( {"0".."9"}, string), {"0".."9"})`

Table 9.3: *List of options for splitting columns and their associated functions*

You will note that the split for digit and non-digit requires the use of a custom function inside of **`Splitter.SplitTextByCharacterTranstion()`**. We have not addressed functions yet, but after you reach *Chapter 14, Functions,* it will become easier to understand.

The last thing we need to address is the process of splitting a column into rows. This is not a common transformation, but there are times when it comes in handy. Often, we need to create a dimension table from a query where a cell contains multiple values, and it must be transformed into rows. We could apply what we learned about splitting columns and then perform a pivot which we learned about in *Chapter 7, Transforming Columns*, but this requires extra steps and requires you to manage the potential for blank rows. Instead, we can simply specify that we want our split to occur into new rows while using the graphical interface, as shown in *Figure 9.3*.

The process of splitting a column into multiple rows can be managed in the advanced editor. However, this process is much simpler to manage in the graphical interface. Ideally, you will split the column into rows using the graphical interface and then perform any updates to the splitter function, as we addressed in *Table 9.3*. Once you have a stronger grasp of functions, it will be easier to understand how this query is structured. However, for those who might be curious anyway, here is a sample of the code we would use to perform that task:

```
let
  Source = Sql.Database("localhost", "NYC_Taxi"),
  GreenTripData = Source{[Schema = "dbo", Item = "trip_data_green"]}[Data],
  SplitColumn = Table.ExpandListColumn(
    Table.TransformColumns(
      Table.TransformColumnTypes(GreenTripData, {{"lpep_dropoff_datetime",
type text}}, "en-US"),
      {
        {
          "lpep_dropoff_datetime",
          Splitter.SplitTextByEachDelimiter({" "}, QuoteStyle.Csv, false),
          let
            itemType = (type nullable text) meta [Serialized.Text = true]
          in
            type {itemType}
        }
      }
    ),
    "lpep_dropoff_datetime"
  ),
```

```
  ChangedDataType = Table.TransformColumnTypes(SplitColumn, {{"lpep_
dropoff_datetime", type text}})
in
  ChangedDataType
```

It is hard to believe that something that seems so simple could become so complicated. But this is the benefit of using Power Query to assist with your transformation. While Excel has helped us split our data in the past, it has never had the level of control and convenience that Power Query provides. You might find yourself needing to practice this skill a few times until you are comfortable making sure you are ready. While it takes time, practice does make perfect, and you will be splitting more columns in no time.

Duplicating columns

Duplicating a column is sometimes an easier process when it comes to managing your transformation. For example, if you need to provide two distinct types of transformations on a single column, you could simply duplicate the column and make your changes. Some might consider this an extra step, but sometimes this provides a little more comfort as it ensures your original column remains untouched as you perform transformations. The process of duplicating a column can be performed in two separate ways in the graphical interface of Power Query. The first option is to right-click on the column header and select **Duplicate Column**. The second option is to select your column, expose the **Add Column** ribbon, and select **Duplicate Column** to activate the function:

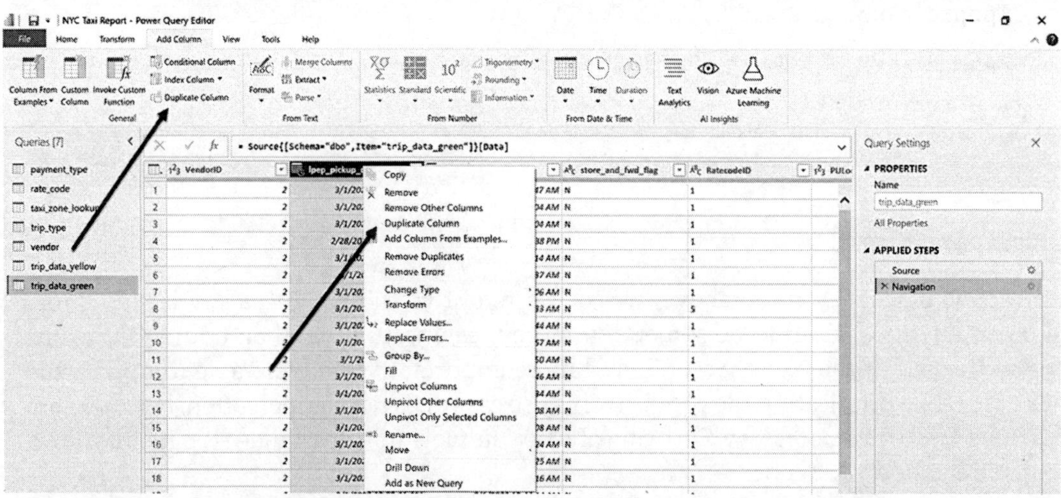

Figure 9.5: Options for duplicating a column in the Power Query editor

There is nothing complicated about this action inside of Power Query. At a minimum, it is worth knowing the code in the advanced editor as you will want to update the column name. However, a hidden use case becomes apparent when using the advanced editor and the **Table.DuplicateColumn()** function:

Table.DuplicateColumn()	
Parameter	Description
Table	A table in Power Query. Usually the preceding step.
ColumnName	Name of the column to be duplicated.
NewColumnName	Name of the new duplicated column.
ColumnType	Optional parameter to set column data type.

Table 9.4: *Table of the Table.DuplicateColumn() parameters*

Depending on your needs, you might need to duplicate a column to use a different data type. Maybe you need to convert a column into text, or maybe you need the precision of a decimal number but want the convenience of a whole number for visualization. Regardless of your scenario, you can extend your use of the **Table.DuplicateColumn()** to transform the data type in addition to the duplication action:

```
let
  Source = Sql.Database("localhost", "NYC_Taxi"),
  GreenTripData = Source{[Schema = "dbo", Item = "trip_data_green"]}[Data],
  DuplicateColumn = Table.DuplicateColumn(
    GreenTripData,
    "lpep_pickup_datetime",
    "lpep_pickup_datetime_text",
    type text
  )
in
  DuplicateColumn
```

In our code block as written above, we took care of two things with a single step. First, we renamed our column to be something more meaningful to us than adding the word copy at the end of the name. Second, and more importantly, we were able to update the data type while duplicating the column. This use case does not happen often, but there are occasions where it is necessary. So, being able to complete this in a single step really allows you to streamline your code.

Ideally, you would want to limit the duplication of columns, as it can cause your model to bloat over time. But like all functions in Power Query, it does have a place in the tool, and when used with the proper scenario, it is quite helpful.

Creating conditional columns

Of all the formulas that you have learned in Excel, conditional statements using the `IF()` function was likely your first. Conditional columns are often an uncomplicated way to aggregate and simplify data analysis. Taking existing data from a column, applying logic, and then determining a result is a fast and actionable way to transform your data. Unlike in Excel, we can construct our conditional statements within the graphical interface by exposing the **Add Column** ribbon and clicking on the **Conditional Column** function:

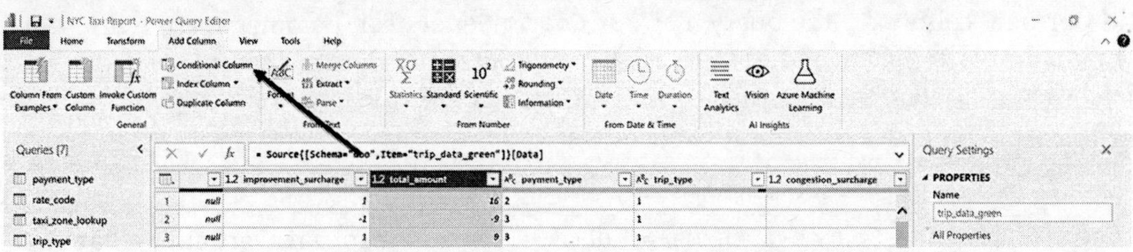

Figure 9.6: *Adding a conditional column in the Power Query editor*

When you click on the **Conditional Column** button, a new prompt appears, asking you to provide the logic for the column. Using the standard operators, you can compare a column in your query to a value and provide an output. You can add clauses to your statement until all scenarios are covered and even have a catch-all with the else bucket at the end. Lastly, make sure you update the column name to something more meaningful than the default **Custom** provided by Power Query:

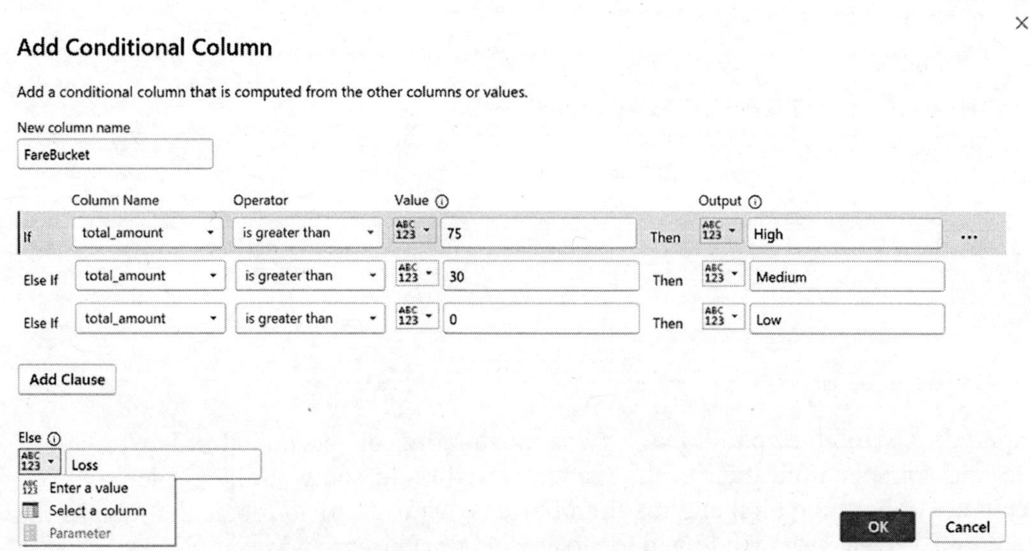

Figure 9.7: *Specifying the clauses for a conditional column*

If you notice in *Figure 9.7*, there is a drop-down exposed for the else statement. Instead of hard coding a value into these buckets, we can reference other columns or even a parameter from Power Query. This allows you the flexibility to not only set static values, but provide contextual values based upon the row of data being evaluated. This makes the conditional column function flexible for all use cases.

At this point you might be concerned about one aspect of the conditional column. We put together three clauses to provide comparisons, but there is only one statement allowed for each clause. What if we wanted to validate two statements at the same time? Or do we want to check for values in two different columns? This is where you will need to leverage the advanced editor to achieve your goal. We will start by using **`Table.AddColumn()`** to add our new column to the query. For our **`ColumnGenerator`** parameter, we will use a combination of **`if`**, **`then`**, and **`else`** to achieve our outcome. Here is a sample of code that matches our inputs from *Figure 9.7*:

```
let
  Source = Sql.Database("localhost", "NYC_Taxi"),
  GreenTripData = Source{[Schema = "dbo", Item = "trip_data_green"]}[Data],
  ConditionalColumn = Table.AddColumn(
    GreenTripData,
    "FareBucket",
    each
      if [total_amount] > 75 then
        "High"
      else if [total_amount] > 30 then
        "Medium"
      else if [total_amount] > 0 then
        "Low"
      else
        "Loss"
  )
in
  ConditionalColumn
```

Compared to Excel, the conditional logic is much more conversational in Power Query. So, to add some complication to the matter, we will add some additional logic to our statement. For both the high and medium buckets, we want to add logic that checks the toll amount as well. We can add **`and`**/**`or`** to any of our clauses to add complexity:

```
let
  Source = Sql.Database("localhost", "NYC_Taxi"),
  GreenTripData = Source{[Schema = "dbo", Item = "trip_data_green"]}[Data],
```

```
  ConditionalColumn = Table.AddColumn(
    GreenTripData,
    "FareBucket",
    each
      if [total_amount] > 75 and [tolls_amount] < 20 then
        "High"
      else if [total_amount] > 30 and [tolls_amount] < 9 then
        "Medium"
      else if [total_amount] > 0 then
        "Low"
      else
        "Loss"
  )
in
  ConditionalColumn
```

It is a small adjustment, but it provides additional logic to simplify your calculations. With the ability to make these adjustments inside of the advanced editor, you can now create an infinite number of conditional statements to meet the needs of your scenario. In addition to multiple clauses, you can apply additional transformations to columns identified such as changing the case of text, extraction portions of a string, applying math functions, or any other transformations we discussed in *Chapter 7, Transforming Columns*. With this knowledge, you will be able to create far more complex conditional statements than you could in Excel with greater ease.

But with all wonderful things, there is always a word of caution. Conditional columns in Power Query are powerful, but they can cause issues as you scale your solutions. A notable example is if you want to change the bucket ranges or even the names of the buckets. To make this change, you would need to update the data model inside of Power Query. While this might not be important for someone working on a model in Excel or Power BI Desktop, this might become a problem when trying to update a query in the Power BI Service. In addition, people use these conditional statements to apply labels for things at a certain point in time. However, over time, the labels might need to be modernized while maintaining historical labels. In short, keep in mind that this solution is an easy one, but it can cause rework in the future. Reserve this function for solutions that do not require long-term maintenance as you might fall into a trap of continually updating a model inside of the Power BI Service.

Creating custom columns

At this point, you have been able to create all the custom columns you need with a few clicks in the graphical interface. This was an intentional design with Power Query. The idea that you could simply apply a transformation and create a column without having to build a formula from scratch reduces the learning curve. It allows you to focus on the analysis of the data instead of the transformation. But even with all the advances that are available from Power Query, there will come a time when you must create a new column using a custom formula that you create using the **Custom Column** function inside the **Add Column** ribbon:

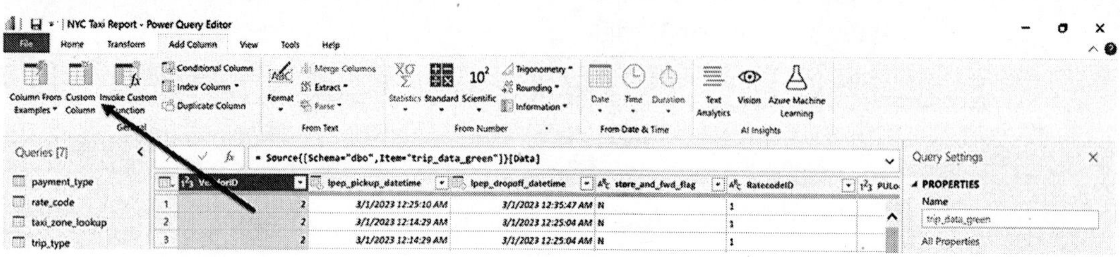

Figure 9.8: Adding a custom column in the Power Query editor

In our scenario, we want to add up the fees, surcharges, and tolls associated with a trip and find out what percentage of the total trip amount makes up those fees. Now, we could simply create one column that totals those amounts and then create another column where we divide it against the trip total to find the percentage. However, we can do it in one single step with our **Custom Column**:

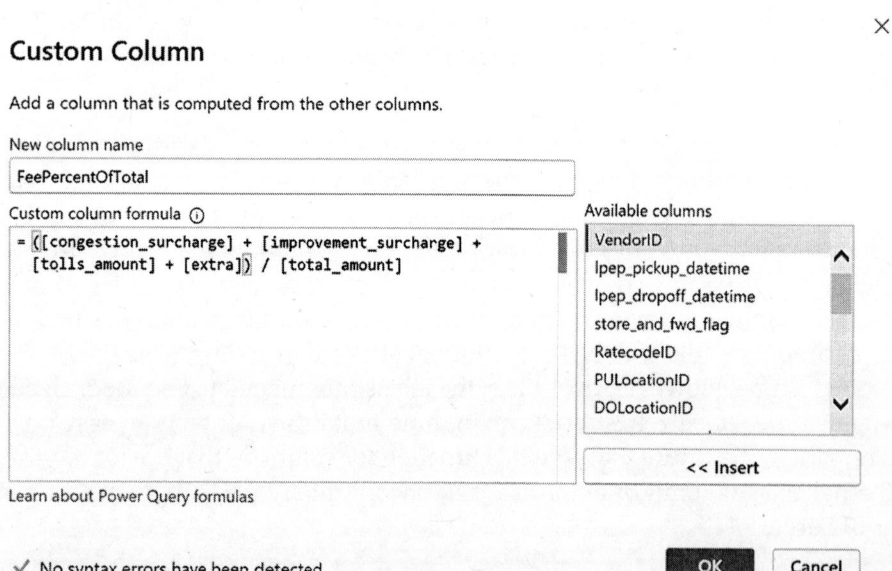

Figure 9.9: Creating a new column in the Custom Column editor window

The **Custom Column** editor window is simple, but it has a lot of notable features. We started crafting our formula by adding the **`congestion_surcharge`**, **`improvement_surcharge`**, **`tolls_amount`**, and **`extra`** columns together and wrapped them in parentheses. To the available columns pane on the right side, select my columns and click **Insert** to add them to the formula. Few people realize this, but you can just double-click on a column in the pane to add it to the formula as well. Just note that this feature inserts columns where your cursor is placed in the **Custom column formula** text box. Once we had our fees totaled together, we used the forward slash symbol so we could divide it against our **`total_amount`** column.

Before we go to click **OK** to add the column to our query, we want to check to see if there are any issues with our query syntax. We can see at the bottom of our window in *Figure 9.9* that we do not have any syntax errors in our calculation. This does not mean that our formula will not have calculation issues. Rather, it checks to make sure there are no errors with your syntax that would prevent you from using your column. If you have any syntax errors, you will receive a warning letting you know what the context of the error is:

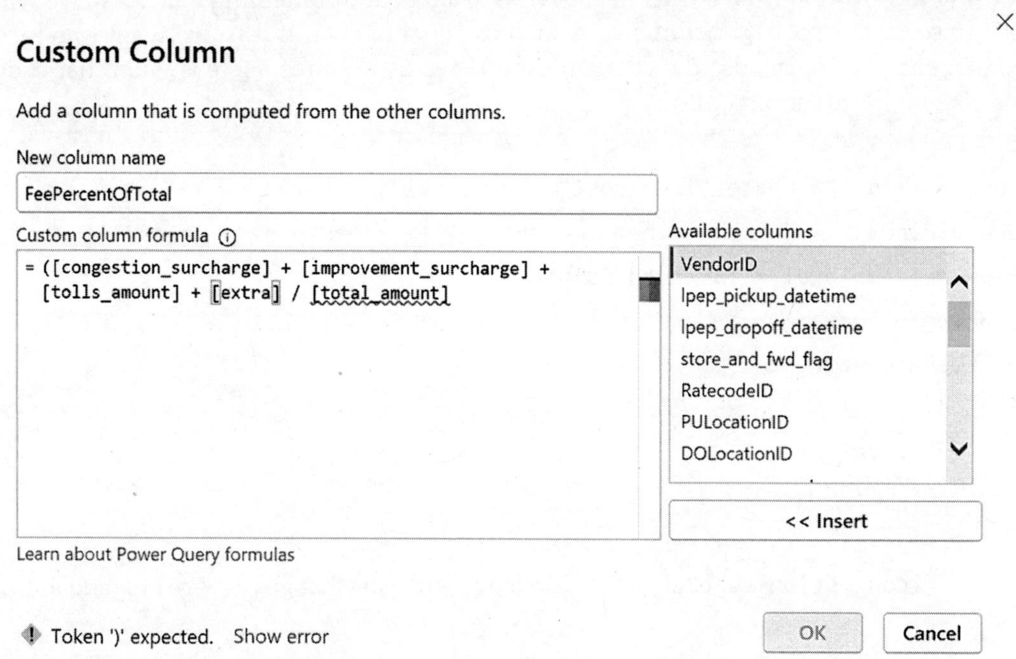

Figure 9.10: *A custom column formula that has a syntax error*

We can tell from the error at the bottom of *Figure 9.10* that we are missing an expected closed parenthesis in our formula. We can see with the red underlines roughly where the error is located inside our formula. While this formula is small, and it is easy to identify the error, we can click on **Show error** to take us to the location of the error so we can resolve it. This is helpful when you are writing complex queries.

It is important to take a moment and remember to **P**lease **E**xcuse **M**y **D**ear **A**unt **S**ally. This is the mnemonic device used in the United States to remember the order of operations when applying math functions. The order of operations goes **P**arenthesis/Brackets, **E**xponents, **M**ultiplication, **D**ivision, **A**ddition, and **S**ubtraction. You might have used this or a similar saying to remember this sequence. However, like other programming languages, Power Query does not really understand how to apply the order of operations the way we know how. As a result, please take care to ensure your formula logic is executing the order of operations correctly. You will notice that our formula was simple, so it was not a big deal. However, you might have a complex formula that requires you to use nested parentheses and deal with exponents. If your formula is not providing a response that you expect, break down your formula step by step to make sure the results are correct at each step of the operation.

To create a custom column with the advanced editor, we will use the **`Table.AddColumn()`** function as we have done throughout this chapter. As we identified in *Table 9.1*, the third parameter, called **`ColumnGenerator`**, is where our custom formula will reside. Instead of just using the formula we were using above, we want to add something to it. First, we will check to see if the **`total_amount`** is less than or equal to zero. If it is, we want to return zero percent. Otherwise, use the custom formula we used above. Here is what that code looks like in the advanced editor:

```
let
  Source = Sql.Database("localhost", "NYC_Taxi"),
  GreenTripData = Source{[Schema = "dbo", Item = "trip_data_green"]}[Data],
  FeePercentOfTotal = Table.AddColumn(
    GreenTripData,
    "FeePercentOfTotal",
    each
      if [total_amount] <= 0 then
        0
      else
        ([congestion_surcharge] + [improvement_surcharge] + [tolls_amount]
+ [extra])
          / [total_amount],
    Percentage.Type
  )
in
  FeePercentOfTotal
```

We added that conditional column code we learned in the last section and used it to augment our existing formula. As a bonus, we also applied **`Percentage.Type`** to the data type of the column in the same step. Individually these are all trivial things, but we just took what could have been a total of five steps and compressed it into a single step. And while this may not seem important, this does go to helping provide efficiencies with your data refreshes as your queries start to grow.

Here is another use case for a custom column. In this scenario, we want to create a custom label for our taxi zones. Each zone is assigned a unique number and name. If you have been driving a taxi in New York City, you probably learned all the zone names and which boroughs they reside in. However, if you are new to the city, you might need some assistance. We are going to create a label that is going to concatenate the zone name, zone id, and borough into a nice package:

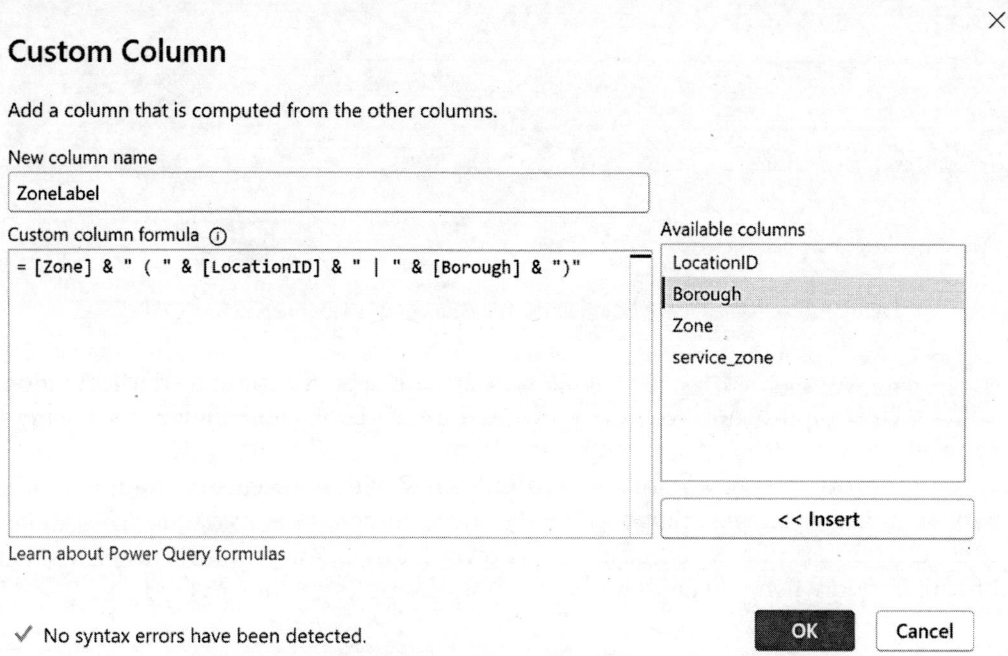

Figure 9.11: *Building a custom label for our taxi zones in New York City*

The formula concept is simple. We will use the ampersand (**&**) symbol to concatenate our three columns together and add a set of parentheses and a vertical bar to make it easier to read. But there is a problem with our formula. The issue is that we are using our **`LocationID`** with other text values to create a text label, but our **`LocationID`** column uses a whole number data type. We could change the data type on our query, but that could cause issues with the relationship to the trip data table and add unnecessary steps to our query. Instead, we will use the **`Number.ToText()`** function to take our zone id and make it a text value, as shown:

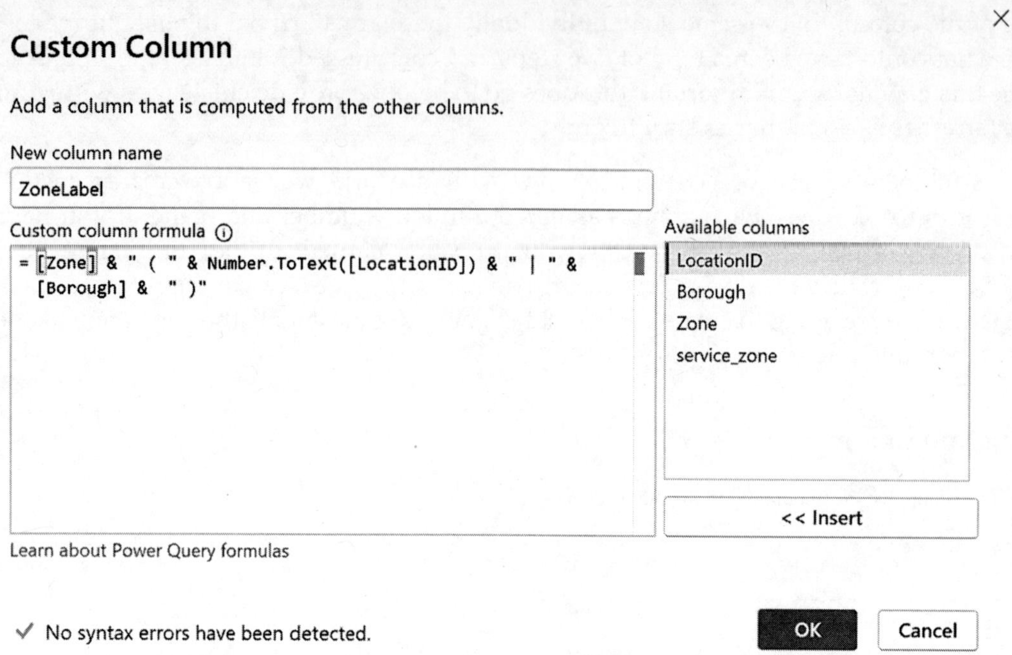

Figure 9.12: *Updated formula for our custom label of taxi zones in New York City*

What that really means is that every data type transformation, column transformation, and column creation function we have addressed in this book can be leveraged inside a custom column. While this might not be something you need to do frequently, you can create complex formulas to achieve desired outcomes with your custom columns. As a recommendation, we suggest that you build your formula a little at a time. This allows you to check your formula as you go along to prevent mathematical and syntax errors that are difficult to find when you are building out your formulas in Power Query.

Creating columns from example

Up to this point, you have learned how to create new columns with a single click, in addition to writing a complex formula. For some of you, it might be intuitive to use the custom column function and create complex formulas. While others might know what the desired outcome is to be, you might not be as comfortable writing your formulas. Power Query has a feature that uses artificial intelligence to assist you with the writing of your column formulas. Instead of hacking your way through it, you can use the **Column From Examples** dropdown inside the **Add Columns** ribbon. To get started, select the columns you wish to use using *Shift + click* or *Ctrl + click* and use the **From Selection** option in the dropdown:

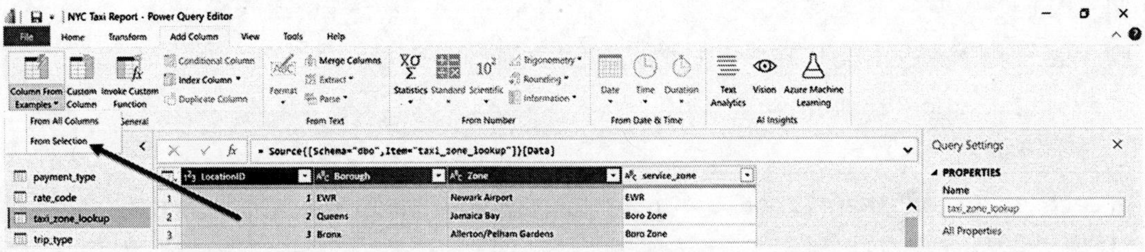

Figure 9.13: Creating a column from an example with selected columns

From there, a new column will appear. You can replace the column header and then start to type in what the desired outcome would be. Using the example of zone labels we used in the last section, we can enter the desired format into the cell, and it will provide a preview of the remaining cells:

Figure 9.14: Creating zone labels from sample columns in our query

Like many things with artificial intelligence, it might not understand what you are trying to do the first time around. As a result, you might need to enter a few rows or even correct others until it understands your expectations. What is neat is that it also shows you the underlying formula to achieve the desired result. Once you are satisfied, you can click OK to apply the formula in the column.

This tool is designed to be part of the graphical interface. It is not something that you can do with the advanced editor. However, you can always look at the underlying code in the advanced editor to see how it is still using **`Table.AddColumn()`** to create the new column:

```
let
  Source = Sql.Database("localhost", "NYC_Taxi"),
  dbo_taxi_zone_lookup = Source{[Schema = "dbo", Item = "taxi_zone_look-
```

```
up"]}[Data],
  #"Inserted Merged Column" = Table.AddColumn(
    dbo_taxi_zone_lookup,
    "ZoneLabel",
    each Text.Combine({[Zone], " ( ", Text.From([LocationID], "en-US"), " |
", [Borough], " )"}),
    type text
  )
in
  #"Inserted Merged Column"
```

While the formula we used in *Figure 9.12* was different than the one created in *Figure 9.14,* the result was the same. Using this tool sometimes allows you to learn about functions that you might not know as well and allows you to see them in action in formulas that you use. It is also a great option if you are in a hurry and need to get a formula in place but do not have time to go back and look up functions in the Power Query M language. Regardless of your use, you will find the **Columns From Example** function extremely helpful in your journey with Power Query.

As a final note, you might realize that we used the **From Selection** option for our new column, but there is an option to use all columns instead. For our purpose, this would not have been an issue with our scenario as the fourth column did not match any other columns. However, for larger tables this can be an issue. We recommend you select the columns that need to be included in the logic to prevent confusion and potential errors with your new formulas.

Introduction to advanced columns

There are five columns that can be created from the **Add Columns** ribbon that we have not addressed in this chapter. This is intentional because we will dive deeper into their use in the *Advanced techniques,* section of this book. Because of how prominent they are placed in the ribbon, we wanted to mention them briefly and what to expect in later chapters.

The first column we want to talk about is the **Index Column**. This column allows us to quickly add an index to our query which helps us identify the row numbers in our query. This is helpful when using formulas that have a row-based context or even to help support a sort order of your data. You can add an Index Column now if you desire, but we will explore using it in *Chapter 12, Indexing*:

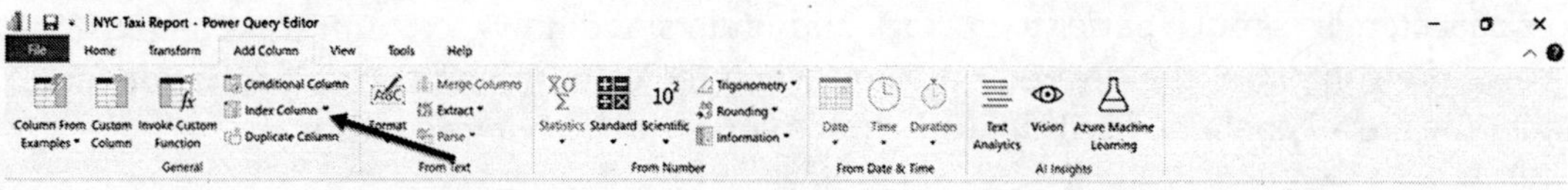

Figure 9.15: Adding an Index Column in the Power Query editor

The second column we can add is a little more complex. The **Invoke Custom Function** column allows us to call a function within Power Query and apply it to a column. We will use this feature to apply functions in our data model and augment our queries with additional data. While you can click the button, you cannot use this feature yet as we have not built any functions inside of Power Query. In *Chapter 14, Functions*, we will learn how to create and apply our functions inside of Power Query:

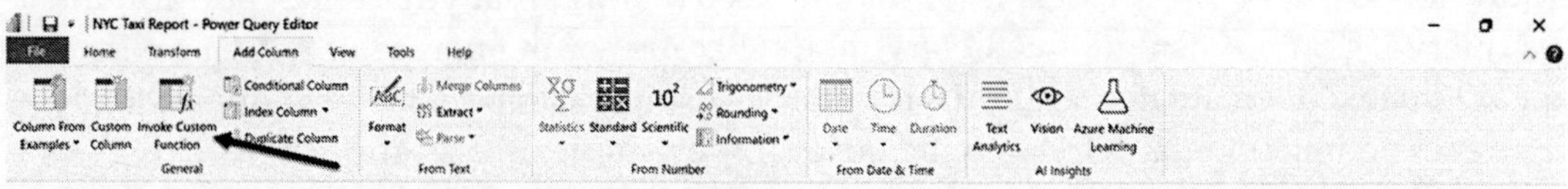

Figure 9.16: Adding a column using a custom function in the Power Query editor

Lastly, there are **AI Insights** columns that are available in Power Query. These columns leverage cognitive services and Azure Machine Learning to provide a deeper analysis of our queries. We have reserved *Chapter 11, Using AI, R, and Python,* to address this topic as there are dependencies required to use them effectively:

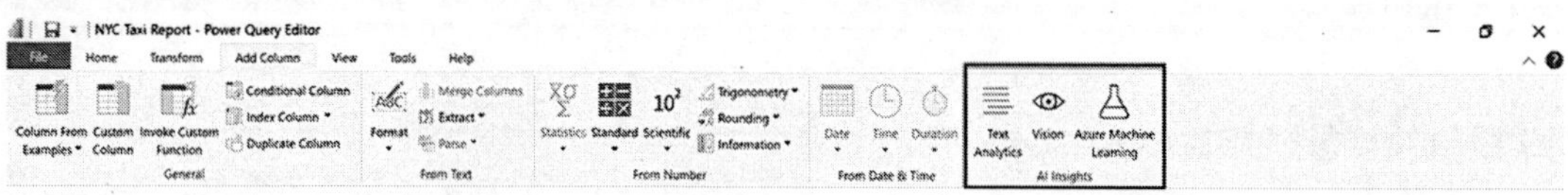

Figure 9.17: Adding AI Insights columns in Power Query

As we stated earlier, we wanted to mention these columns specifically because you might have seen them as we explored this chapter. In fact, some of these features are why you selected Power Query as your tool of choice. We wanted to take a moment to highlight them and share that the complexities found in these columns require a deeper dive into their own respective chapters.

Changing data types

Along every step of the way in this chapter, we have taken the time to highlight that you can update data types as part of the column creation process. While sometimes the data type is not properly assigned, with a little editing, you can update these data types in addition to the column headers. This allows your code to stay compact and simple.

While this is not a requirement and will not really impact your query performance, it allows you to keep all the transformations you have performed on a column inside of a compact step. It is much easier to go back and understand how a column was created and receive the context of the desired outcome when the column name, transformation, and data type are all contained within a single step inside the advanced editor.

Cautions with creating columns

It cannot be stressed enough that creating columns has the potential to impact query folding with your database sources. Just like in past chapters, it always depends on the transformations you are applying to your custom columns. If query folding is in play, you must continually check the status of it as you make transformations to make sure it does not break.

In addition to query folding, it is important to keep in mind that you cannot add columns to a query if you are using DirectQuery mode. Because of the nature of how it operates, you are unable to create new columns for queries using this mode. While it does not have an impact on incremental refresh, which uses Import mode, it does impact hybrid tables, which rely on DirectQuery mode to bring in the most recent data.

If your new columns will have an impact on either query folding or the DirectQuery mode, it is recommended you create these columns in the data layer. This will allow you to maintain your query performance and still achieve the transformations you desire. If you cannot have these transformations performed at the data layer, you will have to either forego these new columns or consider options to provide the best experience for you and your consumers.

Conclusion

In this chapter, we covered how to create new columns within Power Query. We started with an overview of when to create columns in Power Query. Next, we reviewed how to apply our knowledge from *Chapter 7, Transforming Columns* and use it when creating new columns. We then went through the process of splitting columns, duplicating columns, and creating conditional columns. After exhausting the pre-configured options for creating new columns, we learned how to create custom columns using our own formulas. We also explored how to use the columns from the example to simplify that process. Lastly, we reviewed considerations around creating new columns, such as changing data types, query folding, and maintaining DirectQuery mode.

In the next chapter, we will learn how to perform query level manipulations and combine multiple queries into a single table.

CHAPTER 10
Combining and Manipulating Queries

Introduction

In this chapter, we will combine and manipulate queries to simplify their use. We will first explore when and how to aggregate data with our queries to simplify how our data is loaded. From there, we will explore how to join our queries together with a merge. Next, we will learn how to combine queries together by appending them into a single query. We will then explore using data cubes in the Power Query editor. Lastly, we will go over how to suppress queries from loading that might not be required with our data model.

Structure

The chapter covers the following topics:

- Why aggregate data in Power Query?
- Simplify with group by and aggregations
- Use cases for aggregating data
- Understanding join types
- Merging queries
- Understanding Fuzzy matching

- Use cases for merging queries
- Preparing queries for appending
- Appending queries
- Use cases for appending queries
- Suppressing queries

Objectives

By the end of this chapter, you will understand how to use Power Query to combine and manipulate queries for your data model. This will allow you to simplify the queries you load into your data model when upstream transformations are not available.

Why aggregate data in Power Query?

Why should you aggregate your data in a query? This common question is frequently asked by many, but the understanding is often missed. In the early 2000s, it was never an issue to query the transactional detail at the row level. In the last few years, many gripe about how they must specify a range of data they wish to query and do not have the ability to bring it all in at once. Why has this changed?

It cannot be overstated how much the data landscape has changed in the last fifteen years. The proliferation of data has required people to think strategically about what data they are querying. While you may think that you need to bring in all that detail, you might find that you can aggregate that data to reduce the number of rows in your query.

At this point, you might be wondering why it would make sense to perform this aggregation. If you have used Excel or Power BI, you might already know that you can perform this aggregation with DAX or in PivotTables. Why not just bring in all the details and not aggregate the rows that way instead? Does it really make sense to aggregate our data in Power Query? And if we are to aggregate in Power Query, can we not push this transformation to the data source?

We must take a moment to remember that not everyone has access to the same resources to achieve their goals. For some, you might not have access to the data source. The result is this aggregation might be required within Power Query. You can write a native query to achieve this, but what if you do not have a SQL database as a source? Aggregating your data in Power Query allows you to bypass this issue with a few clicks of your mouse.

In addition, another consideration most forget about is the dataset size limit in the Power BI service. If you do not have a premium subscription, you are restricted to a data model of less than one gigabyte. While there are many ways to optimize your dataset size, one option is to reduce the rows through aggregation. This helps reduce the number of rows in your query, which helps reduce the size of your dataset. As a result, it helps keep your licensing costs down as you can manage your model to avoid leveraging premium features.

Lastly, regardless of your experience with data, often we find ourselves looking for data aggregated for display purposes. We have other tools that help us dive into individual rows of data, but we want to create something that is easy to consume. This does not require that level of detail if we just use aggregation to achieve our goals.

Simplify with group by and aggregation

We have already addressed aggregations to some degree in *Chapter 8, Cleansing Data*, when we discussed column profiles. Aggregations are ways we summarize our data into a single value to make it easier to analyze. Power Query allows us to aggregate our data by finding the statistics we found in the column profiles on a more granular level. While we have touched on aggregations already, we have not taken the time to understand the available kinds and how they might be used. In Power Query, we will be able to aggregate our data by providing a sum, average, median, minimum, maximum, count, and distinct count.

At this point, we have only performed aggregations on the entire column. While this serves a purpose for our transformations, it does not necessarily provide the level of detail we need. Often, we want to group our aggregations by a few different fields to help us understand our data better. Power Query allows us to identify columns to group by for each of our aggregations, as shown:

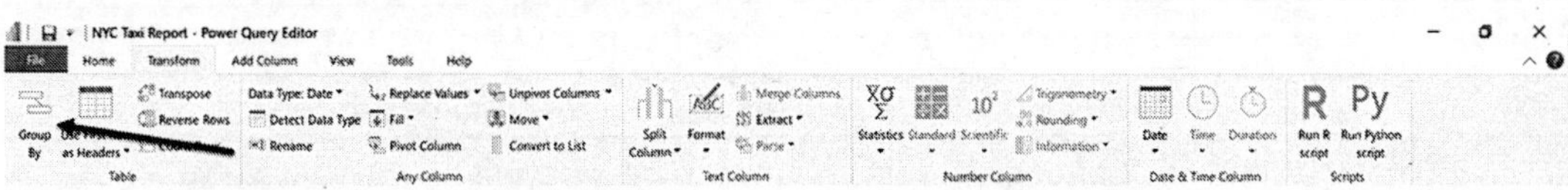

Figure 10.1: *Activating the Group By function in the Power Query editor*

To start aggregating data, go to the Transform ribbon and click on Group By. A new window will appear, prompting for details for your aggregation. For our first scenario, we will aggregate the sum of the total amount of fares by pickup date. The first thing we must do is specify the grouping column. In our scenario, we will use our **`PickupDate`** column for the grouping. Next, we must specify the aggregation details. We will provide a column name, the type of aggregation, and the column that will be aggregated, as demonstrated here:

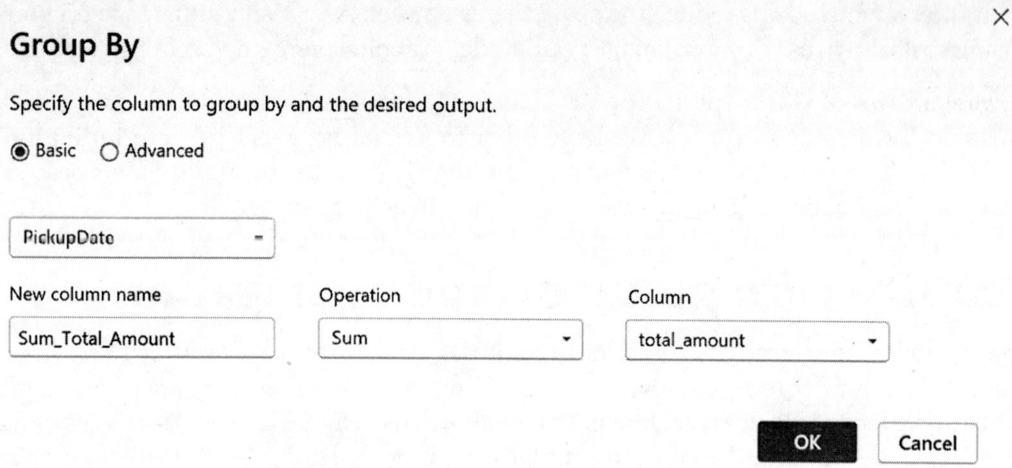

Figure 10.2: *Specifying the aggregation details of a query*

The advanced editor allows us to perform these aggregations with the **`Table.Group()`** function. This function identifies a table, the group by columns, and the aggregation to be performed on the group:

`Table.Group()`	
Parameter	**Description**
`Table`	A table in Power Query. Usually the preceding step.
`Key`	Name of column or list of columns that will be grouped.
`aggregatedColumns`	List of aggregation columns to be grouped by the Key parameter.
`groupKind`	Optional parameter to help with grouping of your query. If rows are already grouped in a consecutive sequence, using `GroupKind.Local` can optimize performance of your query.
`comparer`	Optional parameter that helps test equality and ordering.

Table 10.1: *Table of the Table.Group() parameters*

To achieve the same output as we specified in *Figure 10.2*, we will use this code snippet to achieve the same outcome:

```
let
  Source = Sql.Database("localhost", "NYC_Taxi"),
  TripData = Source{[Schema = "dbo", Item = "trip_data_yellow"]}[Data],
  AggregatedRows = Table.Group(
    TripData,
    "PickupDate",
```

```
    {{"Sum_Total_Amount", each List.Sum([total_amount]), type nullable num-
ber}}
  )
in
  AggregatedRows
```

When you look at the aggregation parameter, you will notice that the formula follows a similar pattern to what we used in *Chapter 9, Creating New Columns*. The difference is that we now use an extension of the **`List`** function to achieve our aggregations. While we are using **`List.Sum`** to total our rows by date, we can use other aggregations as well:

Group by aggregations		
Aggregation	**Description**	**Function**
Sum	Sum of values	**`List.Sum()`**
Average	Sum of values divided by the count of values	**`List.Average()`**
Median	The numeric center of a list of values	**`List.Median()`**
Maximum	Maximum value found in a list of values	**`List.Max()`**
Minimum	Minimum value found in a list of values	**`List.Min()`**
Count	Count of values found in a list of values	**`List.Count()`**
Distinct Count	Count of distinct values found in a list of values	**`List.Count(List.Distinct())`**
Count of Rows	Count of rows in a table	**`Table.RowCount()`**
Distinct Count	Count of distinct rows in a table	**`Table.RowCount(Table.Distinct())`**

Table 10.2: *Table of aggregations in Power Query*

While this outcome is desirable, we might want to get a little more depth from this aggregation. We can easily add our pickup zone to our aggregation by converting our key parameter from a single value into a list. We can also take additional aggregations from *Table 10.2* and add them to our code:

```
let
  Source = Sql.Database("localhost", "NYC_Taxi"),
  TripData = Source{[Schema = "dbo", Item = "trip_data_yellow"]}[Data],
  AggregatedRows = Table.Group(
    TripData,
```

```
    {"PickupDate", "PULocationID"},
    {
      {"Sum_Total_Amount", each List.Sum([total_amount]), type nullable
number},
      {"Max_Total_Amount", each List.Max([total_amount]), type nullable
number},
      {"Min_Total_Amount", each List.Min([total_amount]), type nullable
number},
      {"Average_Total_Amount", each List.Average([total_amount]), type nul-
lable number},
      {"Median_Total_Amount", each List.Median([total_amount]), type nul-
lable number},
      {"Count_Total_Amount", each Table.RowCount(_), Int64.Type}
    }
  )
in
  AggregatedRows
```

With a few small edits, we now know the sum, maximum, minimum, average, and median of the total fare amount for all rides on a date and pickup zone in addition to the count. This will allow us to quickly put together useful visualizations in either Excel or Power Query. If we did not want to write this code, we could still use the graphical interface. If you remember from *Figure 10.2*, we used the basic mode. However, if you switch to the advanced mode, you can achieve the same outcome by using the following configuration:

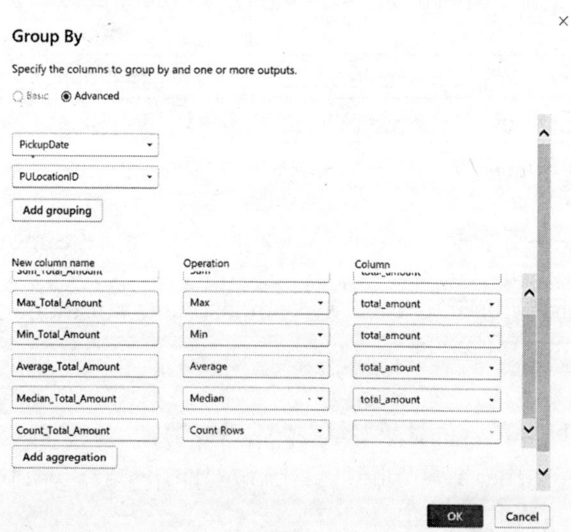

Figure 10.3: *Advanced mode of the Group By function in the Power Query editor*

With a few simple clicks, we can easily provide a series of aggregations that are grouped by a common set of values to simplify our data for analysis.

Use cases for aggregating data

For those who have been working with data for years, the idea of aggregating your queries may seem odd. You might be wondering why you should be performing these aggregations at the query level when it might be better for the analysis to have granular details. Yes, if you are performing a detailed analysis of data, it is best to have each transactional record in your model. However, you likely will be reporting your data at a higher aggregation.

While data professionals like yourself are used to looking at individual rows of data, your target audience likely does not have the time or interest to dig that deep into the data. They are interested in seeing the data aggregated by a particular level, maybe by a date hierarchy, product category, location, or salesperson.

Where this functionality really shines through is when you are new or uncomfortable with the DAX language. Naturally, we encourage you to take the time to learn and understand DAX as you continue your data journey with Excel and Power BI. But if you are new, this might prevent a lot of frustration by sidestepping some measures. You also might be loading this data into a table inside of Excel which will provide easy access to your data in a tabular format.

Regardless of your experience, sometimes speed is the name of the game. While you might be an expert at DAX and know how to build out these measures, the group by function allows you to quickly perform your aggregations with a few clicks of the mouse. The Group By function allows you to rapidly find answers to substantial amounts of data without having to create any special measures or visualizations inside of Excel or Power BI.

While this is not a solution for every project, it is worth considering how to use the group by accelerating your solutions and simplify the queries within your model.

Understanding join types

Our next opportunity to combine queries is to merge two queries together. Before we jump into this portion, it is worth taking a minute to review the various kinds of joins at our disposal. For some of you, this might be a new term for you. If you have experience with writing transactional SQL queries, you probably have a basic understanding. Before we explore the process of merging our queries, we will explore the different joins that are available inside the Power Query editor to make the merge process easier to understand.

Power Query leverages six join types. They are left outer, right outer, full outer, left anti, and right anti. These joins do more than link rows of data together. They provide a level of filtering on your query to eliminate any unnecessary data from being added to your query.

Once you understand the basics of how these joins are leveraged, you will find it easier to manage your data within Power Query.

The first two joins we will address are the left outer and right outer joins. When merging data from two queries, these joins will take one query and find all the matching rows from the other query. To make this easier to understand, we will focus on a left outer join first. We have two queries, one on the left and one on the right. With a left outer join, all rows will be returned from the left query. For the right query, only rows that have a match with the left query will be returned. The principle is the same for the right outer join, except we will return all rows from the right query instead. Here is a Venn diagram that makes it easier to visualize how the outer joins work:

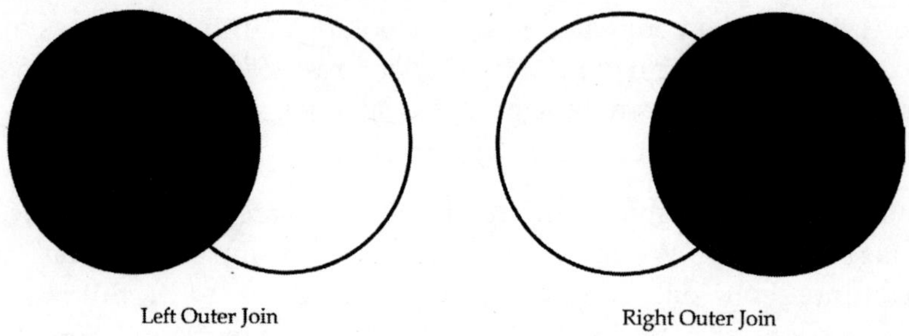

Figure 10.4: *Venn diagram of both left and right outer joins*

As you can see from *Figure 10.4*, we will be combining rows from the other query that overlap with the side of the query we have identified. In a left outer join, any rows of data on the right query that do not match the left will be removed from the query completely and providing additional filtering.

In addition to our left and right outer joins, we have a full outer join and an inner join. Instead of the focus being on one query versus the other, these joins focus on both sides. With an inner join, we only return rows where there is a match on both the left and right query. If a row on either side does not have a pair, it is removed from the query. However, a full outer join brings back all rows on both sides regardless of matches. If there is a match, it is created. However, if there is no match, it will be returned with nulls showing on the other side of the query. Here is a diagram to show how these joins are executed:

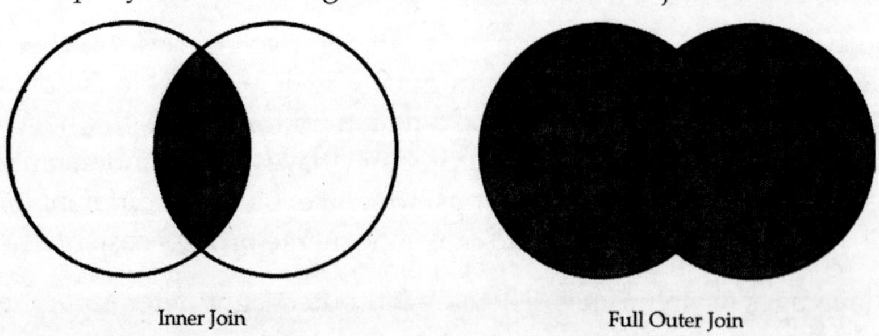

Figure 10.5: *Venn diagram of inner join and full outer join types*

The last set of joins we will review are the left and right anti-joins. These joins are not as common, but they serve a valuable purpose. Keeping in mind that joins help us filter our data, anti joins allow us to filter rows on one side or the other that do not have a match with the other query. This makes it easy to identify any rows that do not have a matching pair. Power Query is focused on bringing data together, so the use case for anti-joins is limited. However, if you are looking to identify issues with your data, this might be a great join type to use to help you quickly identify issues with your data. Here is a diagram to show how the anti-joins are executed:

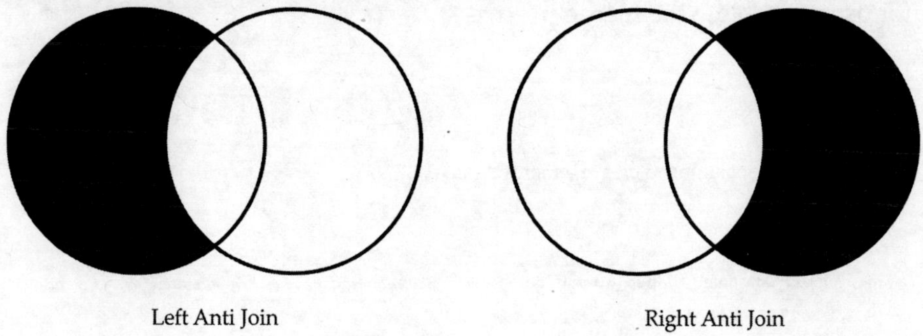

Figure 10.6: *Venn diagram of both left and right anti joins*

It is important to understand which landscape of data we need to leverage when we are looking to perform a merge with Power Query. A common challenge users run into is that they have used the wrong join type which results in dirty data. For example, when you first combined your queries, the left outer join worked perfectly because every row on the left query found a pair. However, over time, you are finding rows that are now missing a match. If this is an undesired experience, then you need to change your join to an inner join instead. In short, it may not seem important in the moment, but the join type you select has an impact on how sustainable your queries are as you continue to refresh them.

Before moving forward with the next section, take a moment to review the different join types one last time. While it may seem inconsequential, decisions like this will have an impact on downstream activities. The better you understand these join types, the easier it will be for you to implement a merge within Power Query.

Merging queries

With a grasp of different join types, it is time to merge our data within the Power Query editor. The purpose of a merge is to bring data from two different queries and combine the rows of data into a single record. Power Query allows us to perform our merge in two ways. The first way is to perform the merge on a query and add the data to your existing rows. The second option is to merge two queries into a new query, leaving the original two in place. Regardless of the option you select, you can pick the option that best meets your scenario on the **Home** ribbon in the Power Query editor, as shown:

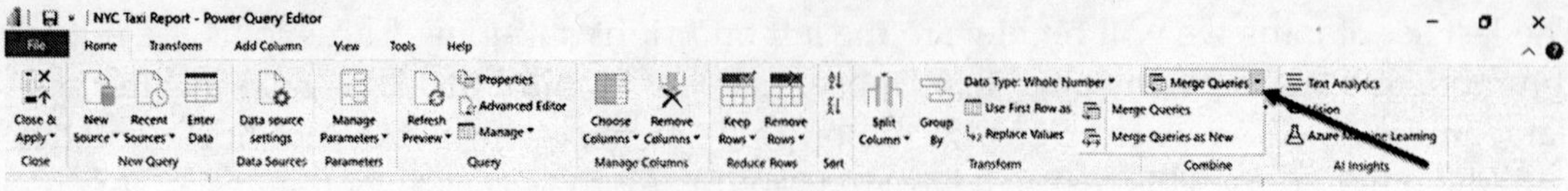

Figure 10.7: Initiating the merge query function in the Power Query editor

For our first scenario, we will simply merge another query with our existing query. To get started, select **Merge queries** from the dropdown to initiate the process. This will open a window for us to complete the merge process:

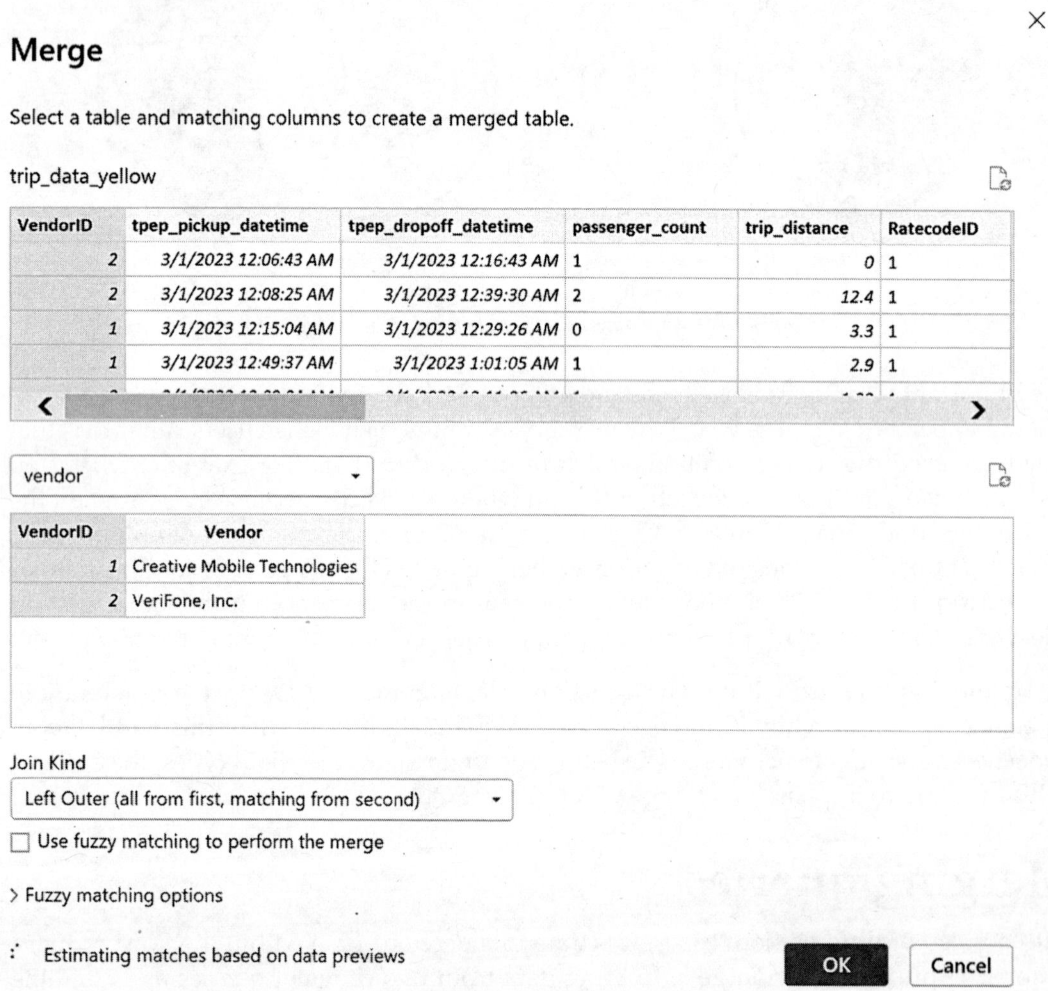

Figure 10.8: Using Power Query to facilitate the merge between two queries

When you initiate the process, you have a sample of the query you have selected for the left side of the merge. This will show all the columns in the current query. From there, you will pick the right side of the query from the dropdown. In this example, we are going to select the vendor table. Once we have our queries selected, we will select the column on each side that will be used for the merge. In our scenario, we will use the **VendorID** column on both sides.

With the queries and join columns selected, it is time to select our join type. For our example in *Figure 10.8*, we selected a left outer join so we can show all trip data even if we are missing our vendor data. Once in place, Power Query will evaluate and return the estimated matches available from the merge.

Now that the join has been facilitated, we need to expand the fields brought in from the other query. A new column has been created using the name of the merged query. We need to expand the records in that column by clicking the expand button on the right-hand side of the column header. From there, a window appears that allows you to select which columns from the merge should be included. When you are merging queries, we will have two columns with the same information. We can deselect that from this dropdown to avoid duplication of data. Lastly, we recommend unchecking the **Use original column as a prefix** option to maintain your original column data:

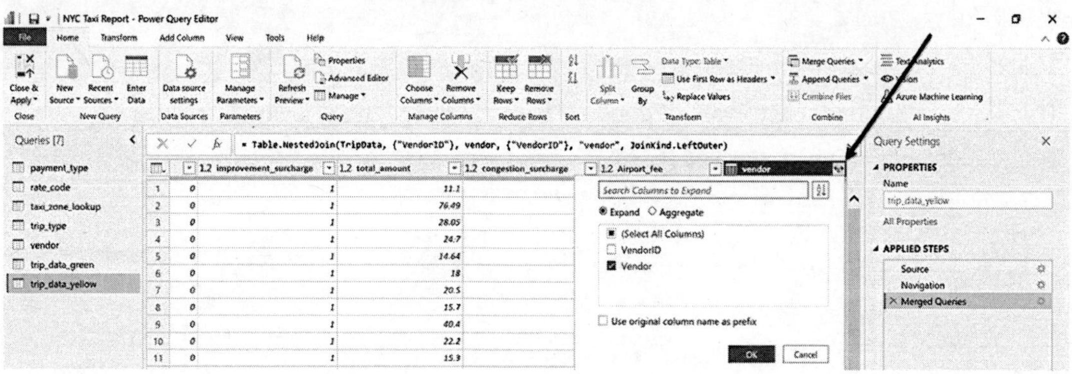

Figure 10.9: Expanding merged data in a query

With this action, we have completed the merge of our two queries. It is important at this moment to note that the merge process takes more than a single step to complete. It will still take two steps, but you can perform the merge of two queries with the advanced editor. We will need to use the **Table.NestedJoin()** function to create the merge:

`Table.NestedJoin()`	
Parameter	**Description**
table1	A table in Power Query. Usually the preceding step.
key1	Name of column or list of columns that will be selected for the merge from the table1 parameter.
table2	Name of another query available in the Power Query editor.
key2	Name of column or list of columns that will be selected for the merge from the table2 parameter.
newColumnName	Name of the new merged column.
joinKind	Optional parameter that helps test equality and ordering.

Table 10.3: *Table of the Table.NestedJoin() parameters*

To initiate the merge, modeled after the one we created in *Figure 10.8*, we will use the **`Table.NestedJoin()`** function to join the **`vendor`** table with our trip data. Take a look at the following code snippet:

```
let
  Source = Sql.Database("localhost", "NYC_Taxi"),
  TripData = Source{[Schema = "dbo", Item = "trip_data_yellow"]}[Data],
  MergeQueries = Table.NestedJoin(
    TripData,
    {"VendorID"},
    vendor,
    {"VendorID"},
    "vendor",
    JoinKind.LeftOuter
  )
in
  MergeQueries
```

Since we were using a left outer join for our merge, we used **`JoinKind.LeftOuter`** to achieve our desired result. We can specify any of our join types just as we did in the graphical interface in *Figure 10.8*. This is an optional parameter that defaults to **`JoinKind.Inner`**, so make sure you specify the right join kind when writing your code.

With our data merged, we need the **`Table.ExpandTableColumn()`** function to expose the merged records:

Table.ExpandTableColumn()	
Parameter	**Description**
`Table`	A table in Power Query. Usually the preceding step.
`Column`	Name of column that contains the merged data that will be expanded.
`columnNames`	List of column names that are selected from the merged record.
`newColumnNames`	Updated column names from the `columnNames` parameter. This is an optional parameter.

Table 10.4: *Table of the Table.ExpandTableColumn() parameters*

We need to add a step in our query that will perform the expansion of the merged data. This sample code uses **`Table.ExpandTableColumn()`** to achieve that outcome:

```
let
  Source = Sql.Database("localhost", "NYC_Taxi"),
  TripData = Source{[Schema = "dbo", Item = "trip_data_yellow"]}[Data],
  MergeQueries = Table.NestedJoin(
    TripData,
    {"VendorID"},
    vendor,
    {"VendorID"},
    "vendor",
    JoinKind.LeftOuter
  ),
  ExpandMerge = Table.ExpandTableColumn(MergeQueries, "vendor", {"Vendor"},
{"Vendor"})
in
  ExpandMerge
```

At this point, we have completed our merge with an existing query. However, we may decide that we need to merge queries into a brand-new query. When using the graphical interface, you will not see much of a difference. The only change with the graphical interface is the ability to select the top query that you see in *Figure 10.8*.

While the graphical interface is simple, we need to manage the merge a little differently with the advanced editor. To start, we will need to create a new **Blank query** from the **New Source** dropdown. We will start by using the **`Table.NestedJoin()`** function we used earlier, but for the table parameters we will use the names from the queries already in Power Query. Once we have the join established, we will still need to use **`Table.`**

ExpandTableColumn() function to expose the merged data from the **table2** parameter. The result is the following code:

```
let
  Source = Table.NestedJoin(
    trip_data_yellow,
    {"VendorID"},
    vendor,
    {"VendorID"},
    "vendor",
    JoinKind.LeftOuter
  ),
  ExpandMerge = Table.ExpandTableColumn(Source, "vendor", {"Vendor"},
{"Vendor"})
in
  ExpandMerge
```

The question that always comes up when it comes to addressing merges is when to use a new query or leverage an existing query. It is recommended that you create a new query if you need to keep your existing queries for another part of your model. For most cases, you will be fine performing the merge on your existing query. Merging with the existing query will also reduce the data model size if that is a concern when working within the Power BI service.

Understanding Fuzzy matching

With the basics covered with merges, most people ask about Fuzzy Matching. Simply put, fuzzy matching is a technique used to match strings of data that are similar but not perfectly alike. As we have expressed throughout this entire book, capitalization counts when it comes to Power Query. If we are performing a comparison on **Data** and **data**, Power Query would return a result of false as these strings are different. However, with fuzzy matching, we can do things like ignore the case of text and return a value of true. To use fuzzy matching with our merges, we can simply check **Use fuzzy matching to perform the merge:**

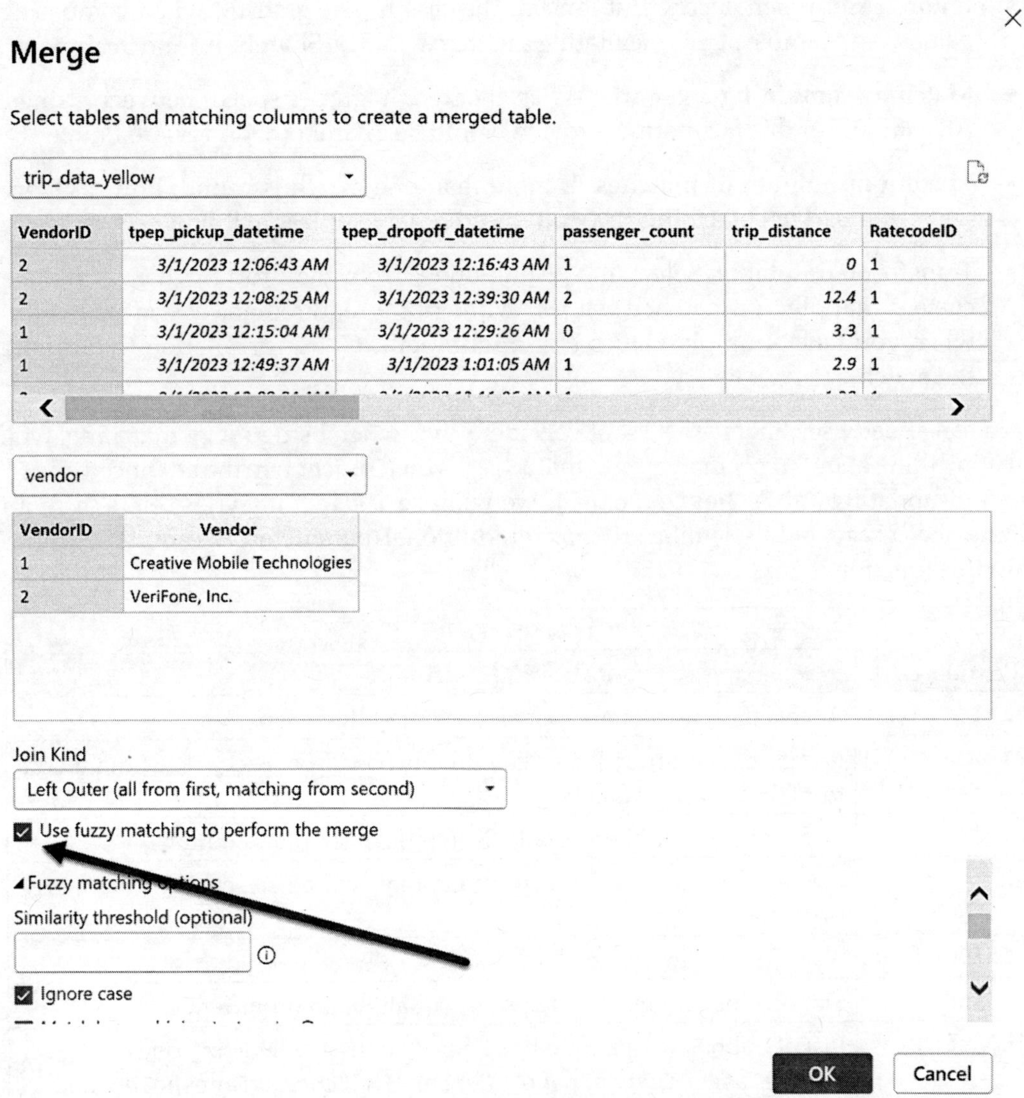

Figure 10.10: *Enabling fuzzy matching when merging queries*

While this seems like a straightforward option, there are some rules and considerations that must be managed before using this feature. It is important to note that this option only works on text-based columns. That means no numeric or date columns can be leveraged with this feature. Once you have determined that you are going to use fuzzy matching, you have a list of options that you can configure:

- **Similarity threshold**: A value between zero and one that represents a percentage of the values that are matched. With fuzzy matching, the default threshold is 0.80, but it can be increased or decreased based upon the challenges of your data model.

- **Ignore case**: When checked; it ignores the case in a text string when comparing values. An example of this facilitating a match would be SharePoint and Sharepoint.
- **Match by combining text parts**: When checked, it ignores spaces between strings. An example of this facilitating a match would be SharePoint and Share Point.
- **Maximum number of matches**: If more than one match is found; Power Query will bring back all matching rows on the other table unless a limit is set.
- **Transformation table**: Select an existing query from the dropdown to provide a custom mapping of matched values. While not a requirement, it can be helpful when you have multiple values that might require a transformation to facilitate the match.

As you can already see, there are a lot of considerations when using fuzzy matching. One interesting thing about fuzzy matching is that it has its own function in the advanced editor. Instead of updating **`Table.NestedJoin()`**, we will use **`Table.FuzzyNestedJoin()`** to facilitate the merge. While similar, there are additional parameters we must consider within this function:

`Table.FuzzyNestedJoin()`	
Parameter	**Description**
`table1`	A table in Power Query. Usually, the preceding step.
`key1`	Name of column or list of columns that will be selected for the merge from the table1 parameter.
`table2`	Name of another query available in the Power Query editor.
`key2`	Name of column or list of columns that will be selected for the merge from the table2 parameter.
`newColumnName`	Name of the new merged column.
`joinKind`	Optional parameter that helps test equality and ordering.
`joinOptions`	List of options wrapped in brackets. Options available include **`IgnoreCase, IgnoreSpace, NumberOfMatches, Threshold, and TransformationTable`**

Table 10.5: *Table of the Table.FuzzyNestedJoin() parameters*

The introduction of **`joinOptions`** provides us the ability to perform the transformations we outlined above. We can leverage **`Table.FuzzyNestedJoin()`** and get the same results as we queried in *Figure 10.10* with the following code:

```
let
  Source = Table.FuzzyNestedJoin(
    trip_data_yellow,
    {"VendorID"},
```

```
    vendor,
    {"VendorID"},
    "vendor",
    JoinKind.LeftOuter,
    [IgnoreCase = true, IgnoreSpace = true, Threshold = 0.75, NumberOf-
Matches = 5]
  ),
  ExpandMerge = Table.ExpandTableColumn(Source, "vendor", {"Vendor"},
{"Vendor"})
in
  ExpandMerge
```

You might be asking why Microsoft did not just add the **joinOptions** parameter to the existing **Table.NestedJoin()** function instead of creating a new one. While there is no definitive proof, speculation would reason that this is to prevent a situation where users might accidentally create matches without having a strong understanding of the implications of their parameters. Each of these options has an accompanying tool tip in the graphical interface, which helps you understand how it will impact your merge. As a result, we have **Table.FuzzyNestedJoin()** to help prevent us from accidentally over-simplifying our model and returning unqualified matches in our query. While this might prove to be annoying, it is an easy update to your query to ensure you do not accidentally match two rows that do not belong together.

Use cases for merging queries

Merging data with Power Query provides a lot of opportunities to simplify and manage your data model. However, we do not want to leverage this function to **flatten out** our queries into a single table. This is a recipe for disaster. We want to use a star schema when building our models as much as possible. So, if a star schema is our goal, why do we use this function at all?

One of the best use cases for merging queries is to simply bring tables that have a one-to-one relationship into a single table. Generally, if you have tables that have a one-to-one relationship, they are likely a dimension table already. You can simplify your model by combining those two tables into a single dimension table. This will simplify the next steps of your report design and help you avoid a snowflake schema.

Another great option with merging is using the anti-joins to find rows of data that do not have pairs. As you continue your journey with data analytics, you will come across scenarios where you will discover there is data missing in your dimensional model. Using the anti joins, you can quickly identify missing data. This can be done while you are transforming your data in Power Query, but also a query for a report view to allow users to quickly identify and remediate issues. While we often use merging to bring data together, we can easily use it to identify any missing data that might cause issues with our models.

Regardless of your use case, make sure that you avoid merging data with your fact table as much as possible. A merge against a fact table will cause your model to bloat. It is best to keep your merges on the dimensional data to prevent any refresh or timing issues.

Preparing queries for appending

Appending is simply bringing two queries together into a single query. However, unlike what we just did with merges, appending adds rows of data to our query. Simply put, we use appends to bring our data together into a single table. Believe it or not, but you have already performed this action without knowing it. Back in *Chapter 2, Connecting to File-Based Sources*, the folder connector took multiple files and appended them together for you into a single query. This saves us some additional work and keeps us from having a messy query window. However, we can use this function with a little bit of prep work.

If you are familiar with SQL, you know this functionality as a **union**. And while useful, you probably know there are some rules when it comes to building out your views. Both select statements must have the same columns identified. If one query is missing the column, you will receive an error. This also means that your column names must match as well. Using SQL, this is what a **union** looks like with our yellow and green taxi queries:

```
SELECT TOP 1000 [VendorID]
      ,[tpep_pickup_datetime] AS pickup_datetime
      ,[tpep_dropoff_datetime] AS dropoff_datetime
      ,[passenger_count]
      ,[trip_distance]
      ,[RatecodeID]
      ,[store_and_fwd_flag]
      ,[PULocationID]
      ,[DOLocationID]
      ,[payment_type]
      ,[fare_amount]
      ,[extra]
      ,[mta_tax]
      ,[tip_amount]
      ,[tolls_amount]
      ,[improvement_surcharge]
```

```
    ,[total_amount]
    ,[congestion_surcharge]
    ,[Airport_fee]
    ,'Yellow' AS taxi_type
    ,null AS ehail_fee
    ,null AS trip_type
FROM [dbo].[trip_data_yellow]
UNION
SELECT [VendorID]
    ,[lpep_pickup_datetime] AS pickup_datetime
    ,[lpep_dropoff_datetime] AS dropoff_datetime
    ,[passenger_count]
    ,[trip_distance]
    ,[RatecodeID]
    ,[store_and_fwd_flag]
    ,[PULocationID]
    ,[DOLocationID]
    ,[payment_type]
    ,[fare_amount]
    ,[extra]
    ,[mta_tax]
    ,[tip_amount]
    ,[tolls_amount]
    ,[improvement_surcharge]
    ,[total_amount]
    ,[congestion_surcharge]
    ,null AS Airport_fee
    ,'Green' AS taxi_type
    ,[ehail_fee]
    ,[trip_type]
```

```
FROM [dbo].[trip_data_green]
```

With Power Query, we do not need to worry about every column name being specified when we append our data. However, our columns must have perfectly matching names to bring them together. This means we must do a little transformation work to prepare our queries before we bring them together in a unified view.

The first step to preparing your queries is making sure that you have the right queries and that the names match. There are a few ways you can do this, but the easiest is to right-click on a query you want to append, click on **Reference** to create a copy of the query, and use the unpivot columns we learned in *Chapter 7, Transforming Columns*, to grab a list of current columns. If you do this to both queries you are looking to append, you can then use the merge function to verify matches. Just make sure fuzzy matching is not used. Using a full outer join, you will see if there are any potential mismatches in your query. If you find any, go back to the original query and make the appropriate changes. Because you are referencing the original query, you will see if the correct changes were made before you move on to the next step. As you can see from our analysis, we will need to resolve an issue with our pickup and drop-off Date/Time columns:

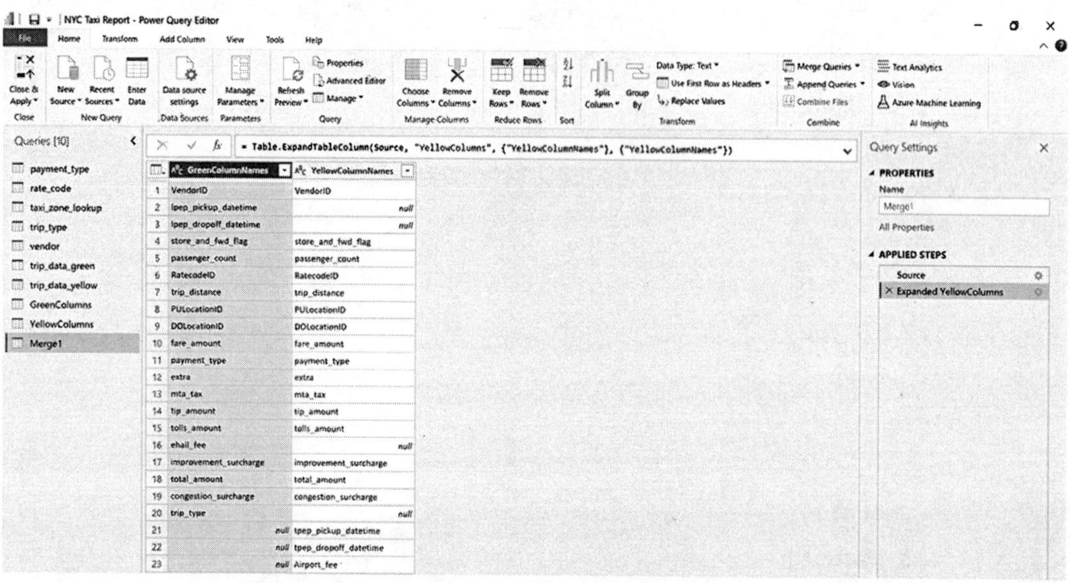

Figure 10.11: *Using Power Query to quickly identify column name mismatches before appending data*

With Power Query, if we are missing a column in one table, we do not need to manufacture it like we did in our SQL code above. Power Query will automatically fill in these cells with a `null` value and save us the extra work of creating the column.

A helpful tip when it comes to appending your queries is to have some way to identify which table or query your data is from. When you use the folder connector, the source file name is included with your query. In our scenario, yellow and green taxis have different columns and rules. As a result, we will add a custom column to each of our trip data queries called **`taxi_type`** which will identify which kind of taxi we are referencing.

One last thing to note is that you can perform your transformation before you append your data, but it is best to wait until you have appended your queries before you apply your transformations. For one, appending your data might undo your data type transformations. But in addition to re-work, you will find that it is easier to maintain your transformations in a single query. This will ensure that your transformations are consistent across the entire query and allow you to perform them once instead of on each individual query. As a best practice, limit any transformations prior to appending your data to what you need to facilitate the appending your queries.

Appending queries

With the groundwork already completed, we can proceed with the appending of our queries. To start the process, we can use the **append queries** dropdown on the home ribbon in the Power Query editor. Just like when merging queries, we can append data to our selected query or append to a new query:

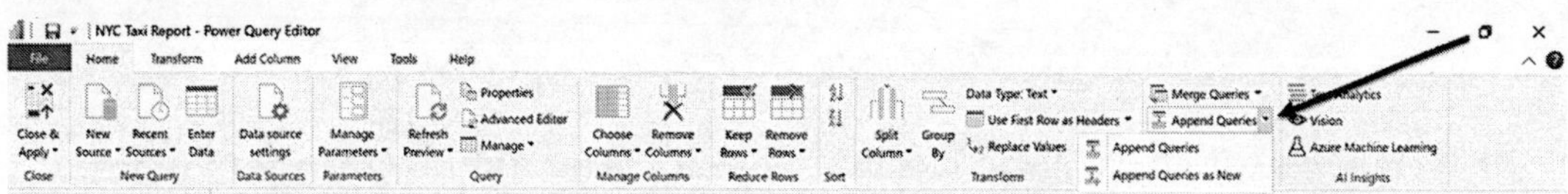

***Figure 10.12:** Initiating the append query function in the Power Query editor*

Once selected, a new window will open to identify the tables that should be appended. By default, Power Query assumes you only want to merge one additional table. If this is true, you can select it in the **table to append** dropdown. If not, select **three or more tables** and add all the tables you wish to append inside the box on the right, as shown here:

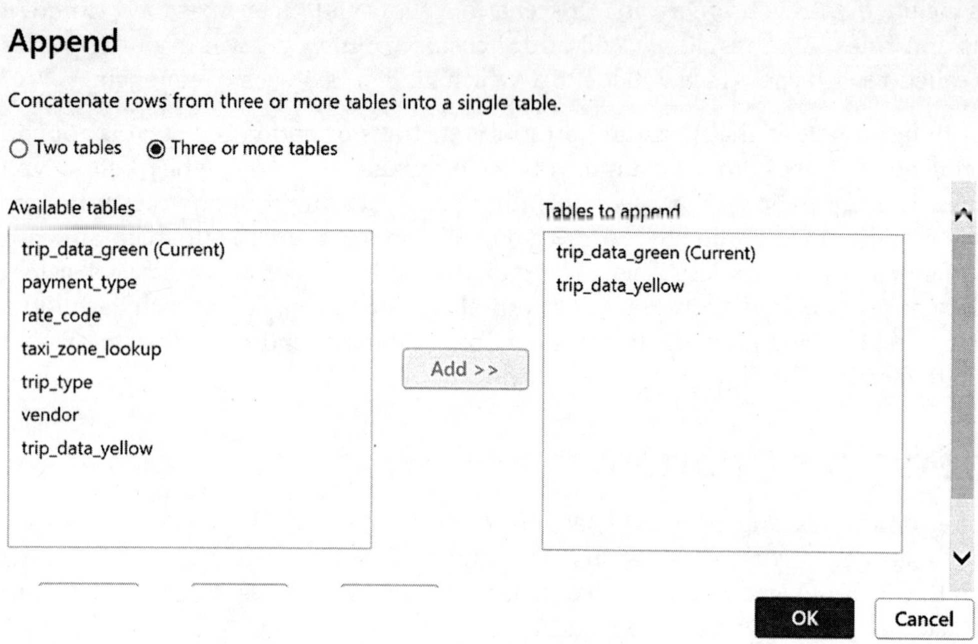

***Figure 10.13:** Selecting multiple tables to append to a query*

To append queries with the advanced editor, we will use the **`Table.Combine()`** function to bring multiple tables into a single query. However, as a bonus, this function allows us to filter the columns we wish to bring together. The parameters for **`Table.Combine()`** are as follows:

`Table.Combine()`	
Parameter	**Description**
`tables`	List of tables wrapped in {}.
`columns`	Optional parameter that can be used to limit columns in the appended view. List column names wrapped in {}.

***Table 10.6:** Table of the Table.Combine() parameters*

To append tables in a new query, we will create a new blank query. For Source, we will use the **`Table.Combine()`** function to bring our yellow and green taxi data into a single query. To simplify things, we will only bring back the pickup and drop-off timestamps and zones with our query:

```
let
  Source = Table.Combine(
    {trip_data_green, trip_data_yellow},
    {"pickup_datetime", "dropoff_datetime", "PULocationID", "DOLocationID"}
```

```
  )
in
  Source
```

The process of appending data into a single query is easy if the groundwork has been properly laid ahead of time. There is not much to the process, and it is often easier than building a union in SQL. That being said, if you are using a SQL-based source, it is ideal for you to push this transformation into the data layer if you are combining substantial amounts of data.

Use cases for appending

As we have already alluded to, if you are combing multiple files, the folder connector is the most ideal option. For one, it is already designed to perform the append action. In addition, it will dynamically expand, and contract based on the files that have already been identified. When using the append queries function, you must explicitly identify the tables you wish to append. This means if you want to append additional tables, you will need to add the data to your model and add it to your **`Table.Combine()`** function. This means you will likely be required to support this model long-term if this is a common occurrence.

The process of appending data in Power Query is ideal when you are trying to bring data from two different data sources together into a single query. As we have already mentioned, it is ideal to combine your queries at the data layer when using a SQL-based source. However, you might be bringing data from multiple sources. For example, you might need to combine customer data from both Salesforce and Dynamics. This might even work for multiple instances of Salesforce or Dynamics for different business units within your organization. Regardless of the source, we can use Power Query to create that unified query.

When you are designing your model, make sure to account for these considerations in these use cases. While some of the decisions you make may seem inconsequential at the moment, you might find yourself creating a solution that is not scalable and sustainable. Take the time to properly filter your data to avoid bloating your model and ensure only the necessary columns are included. This will go a long way to making sure your model will not require your intervention for future refreshes.

Suppressing queries

At this point, we have gone through the process of merging and appending queries. If you choose to perform these actions as new queries, you might find yourself with extra tables in your model when you apply and load. While there might be a use case for loading these extra queries, you might also end up bloating your model with unnecessary data. While this is a common scenario; you might have additional queries that you load that were used for validation but are not required for the final model. Regardless of your requirements, you can suppress your queries.

Inside the Power Query editor, we can stop a query from loading. To perform this action, we can right-click on a query and uncheck the **Enable load** option. When you uncheck this option, the query will not be loaded into the model when you apply your changes. There is no option to enact this feature with the advanced editor, so it must be activated in the graphical interface:

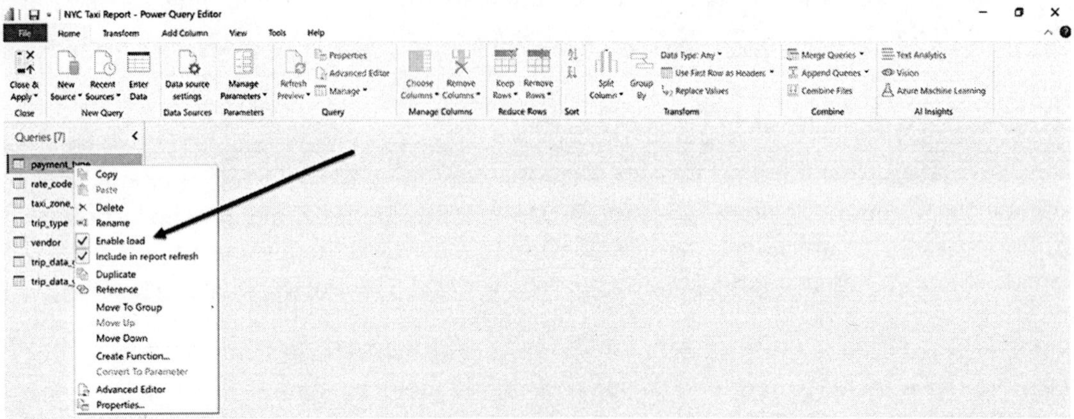

***Figure 10.14:** Disabling a query from loading into the data model*

You will notice that below that option is another one called **Include in report refresh**. This is another feature that can be helpful for queries where you do not have the ability, or requirement, to refresh. If you have a query that will never change or you do not have the ability to refresh from the source in the future, you can disable this feature. When you first apply the query to the model, it will perform the refresh. Once completed, it will not refresh again until you turn this feature off. This can help reduce your refresh time and potentially prevent errors from happening in the future.

As with any change like this, consider the impact it will have on your model. Both features will provide the opportunity to optimize your model in the right scenario. It is a slight change that will have a considerable impact on the overall performance of your model when properly applied.

Conclusion

In this chapter, we covered when and how to aggregate data in Power Query to simplify your tables. We then explored the various kinds of joins that help us bring data from two queries together into a single query. We then applied those joins with the merge query function to combine data into a single table. In addition, we explored how to use fuzzy matching to help manage the merge of data that might not be a perfect match. We then explored how to append multiple queries into a single query and how it is different than doing it with SQL. Lastly, we learned how to suppress queries that are no longer needed after performing a merge or append function.

In the next chapter, we will learn how to leverage advanced analytics tools as we load and transform data inside of Power Query.

CHAPTER 11
Using Python, R, and AI

Introduction

In this chapter, we will use extended techniques with Python, R, and AI to expand our ability to transform our data inside the Power Query editor. Up to this point, you have learned different ways you can transform columns, create columns, and manipulate queries. And while these methods cover most use cases, you might find yourself missing a few items. In addition, you might have AI models that you would like to apply to a query to help with your analysis. This chapter will explore how to leverage these tools to get the most out of your queries within Power Query.

Structure

The chapter covers the following topics:

- Use cases for Python, R, and AI
- What is Python?
- Transforming a column using Python
- What is R?
- Transforming a column using R

- What is AI?
- Leveraging text analytics functions
- Leveraging vision functions
- Leveraging Azure machine learning functions
- Considerations with Python, R, and AI

Objectives

By the end of this chapter, you will understand how to use Python, R, and AI inside the Power Query editor to perform additional transformations that cannot be completed out of the box. This will allow you to take your analysis to the next level with the integration of these tools.

Use cases for Python, R, and AI

For this chapter, we thought it would be good to talk about use cases ahead of time to make sure you get the most value out of this chapter. For this chapter, we will be focusing on some advanced techniques that can be applied with Python, R, and AI. However, this chapter might not be for you right now, and that is okay.

You might have a few blockers that are in your way and keeping you from applying this chapter to your own scenarios. The first one is that these features are only available inside of Microsoft Power BI. While Microsoft Excel has Power Query, it does not contain these features. Maybe that will change, but at the time of writing this book, you cannot use Excel to perform these tasks.

The next blocker might be your experience with writing code with Python or R. If you have never used these languages before, this could prove to be challenging. And if you are just starting your Power Query journey, you might not have the appetite to learn yet another programming language.

Lastly, Azure cognitive services and Azure machine learning require additional cloud services that you might not control or have the funding to enact in your environment. You might have asked why were not allowed to use these tools, which is keeping you from being able to unleash the full power of artificial intelligence in your solutions.

These blockers can be rough, but the goal of this chapter is for you to see the art of the possible. With these tools, you can expand your transformations and even make predictions based on the data you have available to you in Power Query. With Python, you can write scripts that help identify and fill in missing data from your queries. With R, you can write a custom algorithm to make a prediction. With Azure cognitive services, you can perform quick analysis with out-of-the-box models that are ready to be deployed with a few clicks.

With Azure machine learning, you can quickly deploy an AI model endpoint that has been deployed to your organization with minimal configuration.

These tools will not solve all your problems, but they might help you get around some issues that are plaguing your models. This chapter might seem out of your league right now but knowing the art of the possible will allow you to plan for the future. As you read this chapter, do not fret if these concepts seem a little difficult. Instead, take a few minutes to understand how they work so you can use them to transform your queries in the future.

What is Python?

You might have heard of Python before but never thought about it with respect to analytics. Python is considered one of the best first coding languages for beginners to use. It is a functional-based language that is used to build applications, automations, software, and websites. However, most people do not realize that Python is also commonly leveraged for data analytics. With a little knowledge, Python can become a robust tool in your toolbelt when using Power Query.

By default, Python is not ready to use on your device. To get started, you need to head over to **python.org/downloads** to download the latest version of Python for your device. Once, downloaded, install the application on your device. To confirm that everything is properly installed, go to the file tab inside the Power Query editor, go to options and settings and select options. From there, go to the Python scripting section. If installed, the detected Python home directories field should map to a directory like this:

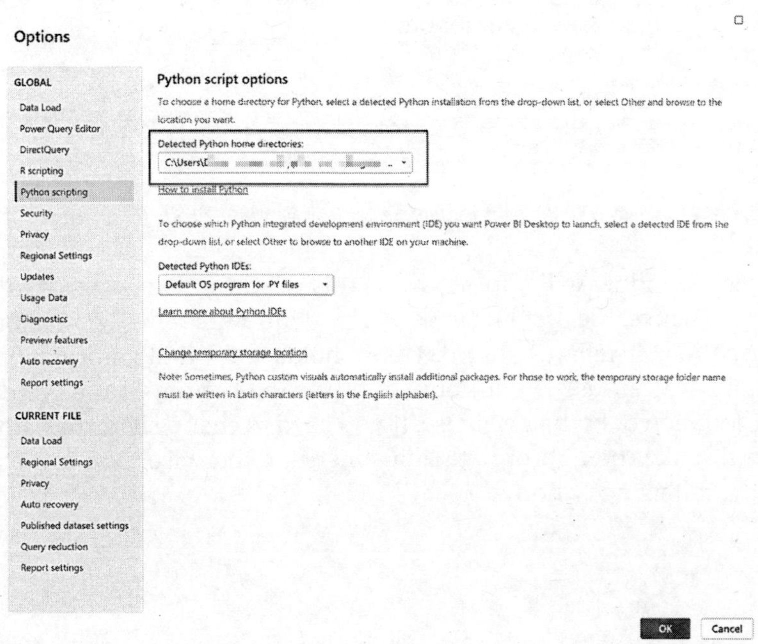

Figure 11.1: *Verifying Python has an available home directory in the Options menu*

As a next step, you will need **pip** to install any modules you will need in your Python code. To perform this task, open a Windows command prompt by going to your start menu and searching for cmd. Once opened, navigate to the directory where your **python.exe** executable is located. Once there, you need to download the Python script to install pip on your device. Type in **curl https://bootstrap.pypa.io/get-pip.py -o get-pip.py** to download the file. Once downloaded, you can run **python get-pip.py** to complete the installation.

With this completed, you can install any additional modules required for your script. In this example, we will use **pandas**, **geopandas**, **geopy**, and **matplotlib**. To install these modules, you will need to run **pip install** with the module name at the end. For example, to install pandas, you will use **pip install pandas**. This will allow you to deploy the code in the next section. Once you have installed the modules you need to use, you are ready to use Python inside of Power Query.

Transforming a column using Python

Power Query allows us to write a Python script to transform out data and potentially provide an output. A common scenario where Python is helpful is when you need to identify the latitude and longitude coordinates of an address for mapping data. While you can perform this action with the mapping visuals in Power BI, it is easier to handle this during the ETL process to avoid any issues with the map visuals. We can write a script that takes the city information and use the script to come back with the points we need. While the result of our script in this situation will create a new column, you will activate the Python script from the **Transform** ribbon:

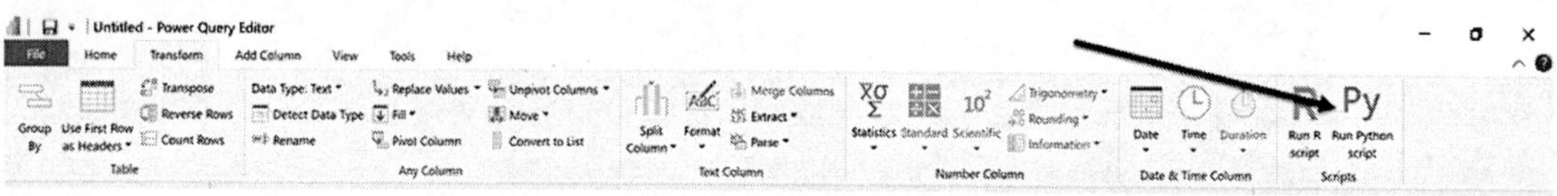

Figure 11.2: *Selecting the Run Python Script function in the transform ribbon*

Once clicked, a new window will appear. Inside this window, you can start to write your Python code. If you notice, the first line in the script window is remarked out but contains important information. It tells us that **dataset** holds the input information from the existing query and we can use it with our script. At the bottom of the window, it also shares which installation of Python is in use. If you need to change it, go back to the screen in *Figure 11.1* and make the appropriate adjustments. Otherwise, you can start adding your code into the following window:

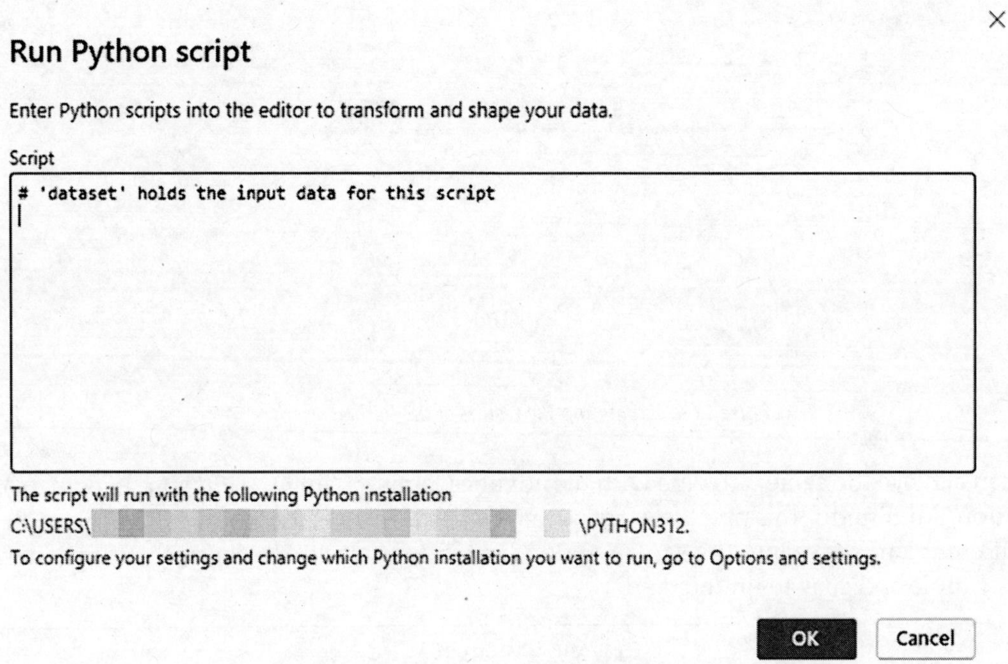

Figure 11.3: *The Python script editor window*

At this point, we are going to take our script and run it on a list of cities we have from our dataset. Using geopandas, we will call the city column and it will return our latitude and longitude in addition to a description of the location where it found a match. Our intent in this chapter is not to teach you how to code in Python, but here is the code we will use to achieve this:

```
# 'dataset' holds the input data for this script
import geopandas


dataset[['LatLong','Description']] = geopandas.tools.geocode(dataset.Name)
```

Our code is simply going to augment our existing dataset and bring back the **`LatLong`** and **`Description`** columns for our use. Once the script has run, we will need to expand the values of the dataset. We can click on the expand button on the right side of the value column, select our columns, and click **OK**:

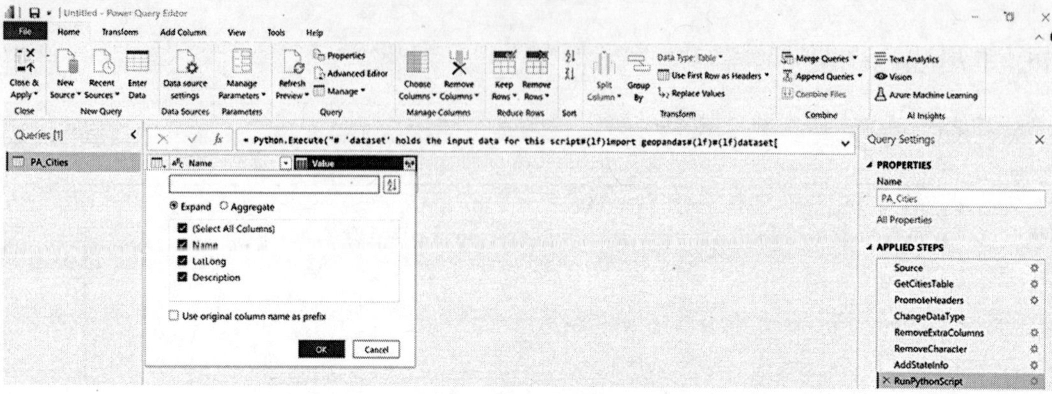

Figure 11.4: Expanding the results of the Python script

We can achieve the same outcome with the advanced editor using the **`Python.Execute()`** function. Admittedly, this process is not as easy to perform as you are now mixing a couple of different languages into the same window, but it does work. However, the function is quite simple and easy to understand:

`Python.Execute()`	
Parameter	**Description**
`Script`	Script written in Python. Make sure to use `#(lf)` to identify new lines of the script.
`Options`	Field is wrapped in `[]` and must be used to specify the `dataset` with a preceding step in the query.

Table 11.1: Table of the Python.Execute() parameters

For this example, we pulled a list of cities in Pennsylvania from Wikipedia. Applying the transformations we have learned in previous chapters, we cleaned up our list, applied **`Python.Execute()`** to run our script to find the coordinates of each city, and expanded our values from the results:

```
let
  Source = Web.BrowserContents("https://en.wikipedia.org/wiki/List_of_cit-
ies_in_Pennsylvania"),
  GetCitiesTable = Html.Table(
    Source,
    {
      {"Column1", "TABLE.wikitable.sortable > * > TR > :nth-child(1)"},
      {"Column2", "TABLE.wikitable.sortable > * > TR > :nth-child(2)"},
      {"Column3", "TABLE.wikitable.sortable > * > TR > :nth-child(3)"},
```

```
      {"Column4", "TABLE.wikitable.sortable > * > TR > :nth-child(4)"},
      {"Column5", "TABLE.wikitable.sortable > * > TR > :nth-child(5)"},
      {"Column6", "TABLE.wikitable.sortable > * > TR > :nth-child(6)"},
      {"Column7", "TABLE.wikitable.sortable > * > TR > :nth-child(7)"}
    },
    [RowSelector = "TABLE.wikitable.sortable > * > TR"]
  ),
  PromoteHeaders = Table.PromoteHeaders(GetCitiesTable, [PromoteAllScalars
= true]),
  ChangeDataType = Table.TransformColumnTypes(
    PromoteHeaders,
    {
      {"Name", type text},
      {"Type", type text},
      {"County[3]", type text},
      {"Class", type text},
      {"Population (2020 Census)", type text},
      {"Incorporationdate (as city)", Int64.Type},
      {"Sq Miles[4]", type number}
    }
  ),
  RemoveExtraColumns = Table.SelectColumns(ChangeDataType, {"Name"}),
  RemoveCharacter = Table.ReplaceValue(RemoveExtraColumns, "†", "", Replac-
er.ReplaceText, {"Name"}),
  AddStateInfo = Table.TransformColumns(RemoveCharacter, {{"Name", each _ &
", PA", type text}}),
  RunPythonScript = Python.Execute(
    "
        # 'dataset' holds the input data for this script
        #(lf)import geopandas
        #(lf)
        #(lf)dataset[['LatLong','Description']] =  geopandas.tools.geo-
code(dataset.Name) ",
    [dataset = AddStateInfo]
```

```
  ),
  ExpandFields = Table.ExpandTableColumn(
    RunPythonScript,
    "Value",
    {"Name", "LatLong", "Description"},
    {"City", "LatLong", "Description"}
  )
in
  ExpandFields
```

It is probably worth taking a moment to realize that while you can write your Python script in the advanced editor, we find it to be much easier to use the graphical interface for this part. This prevents any confusion and does not require you to add the line feed into your code. While that is a small item, it can prove to be a painful experience to resolve if you forgot to add it to your code earlier.

Now that you know the basics, you can apply any Python module to your dataset that is appropriate. Just remember that you will need to install these modules on your device before you leverage them.

What is R?

While Python is a well-known programming language, you might not have heard of R before reading this book. R is an open-source statistical programming language for data analysis, data visualization, and data manipulation. Much like Python, R uses modules known as libraries that extend the usability of the language in your scripts. While primarily used to run queries against algorithms, there are some hidden features that can be leveraged within the Power Query editor with a little effort.

Like Python, you will need to set up your device to use R. Current versions of R can be found at the CRAN repository at **`cran.r-project.org/bin/windows/base`**. Download and install the appropriate version of R for your device. To confirm that everything is properly installed, go to the **File** tab inside the Power Query editor, go to options and settings and select options. From there, go to the R scripting section. If installed, the detected R home directories field should map to a directory like this:

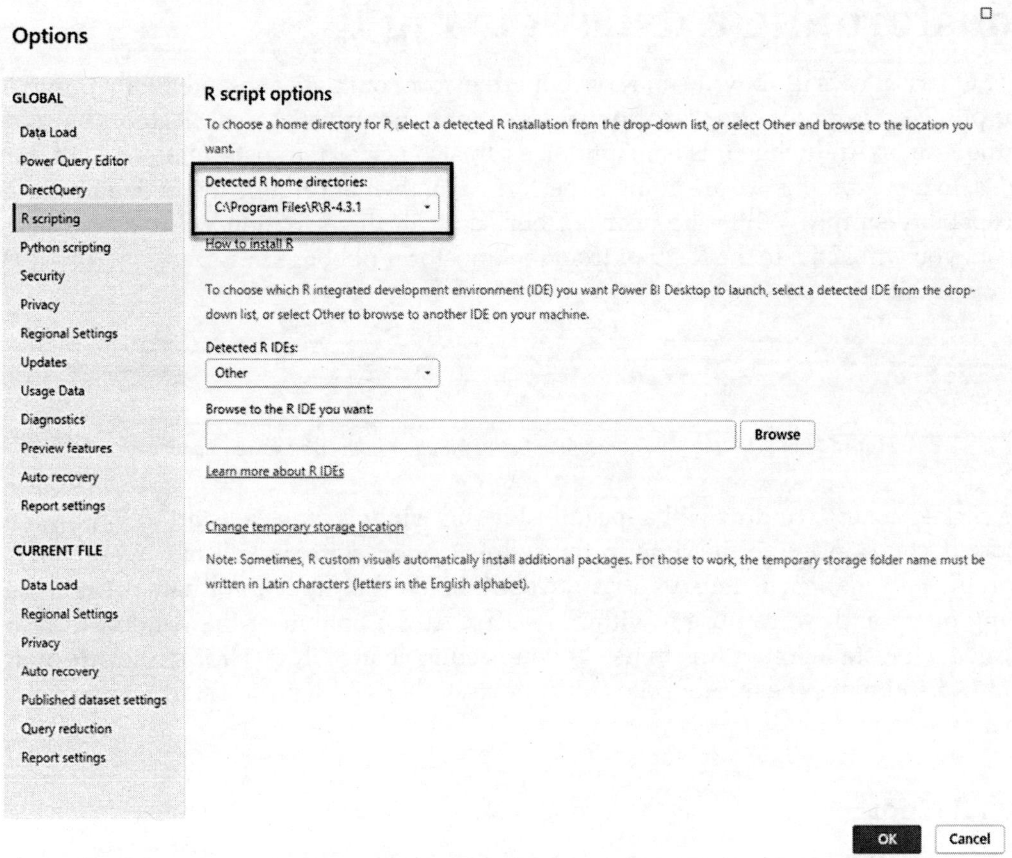

Figure 11.5: *Verifying R has an available home directory in the Options menu*

Next, you will need to set up R to download and install packages. Open the R console, go to the packages menu, select set CRAN mirror, and select your mirror. If you are unsure which one to choose, just use **`0-Cloud [https]`** as your default. Next, to install a package, go to the console and type **`install.packages('readr')`**. This will install the **`readr`** package. You can update this code with different package names that are required for your scripts.

With this completed, you can install any packages you might need for your scripts. In our scenario, we do not need any special packages to complete our script. However, it is important to understand how to install packages in case you need one in the future, or you choose to use some of the R visualizations found inside Power BI's AppSource catalog. Regardless of the reason why you need to install a package, you can easily perform the action with a quick line of code.

Transforming a dataset using R

Power Query allows us to write an R script to transform out data and potentially provide an output. The most common scenarios with R scripts are to run it against an algorithm and find the results. And while this is helpful, we can also perform transformations with our queries. In our example, we are going to perform a mathematical function to demonstrate the capability simply. While the result of our script in this situation will create a new column, you will activate the R script from the transform ribbon:

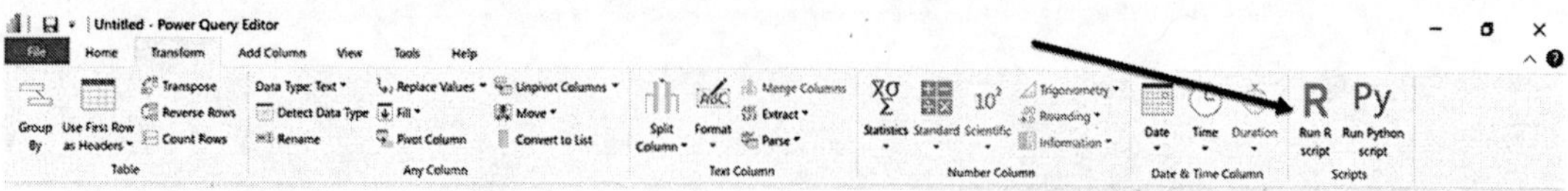

Figure 11.6: Selecting the Run Python Script function in the transform ribbon

Once clicked, a new window will appear. Inside this window, you can start to write your R code. If you notice, the first line in the script window is remarked out but contains important information. It tells us that **dataset** holds the input information from the existing query and we can use it with our script. At the bottom of the window, it also shares which installation of R is in use. If you need to change it, go back to the screen in *Figure 11.5* and make the appropriate adjustments. Otherwise, you can start adding your code into this window:

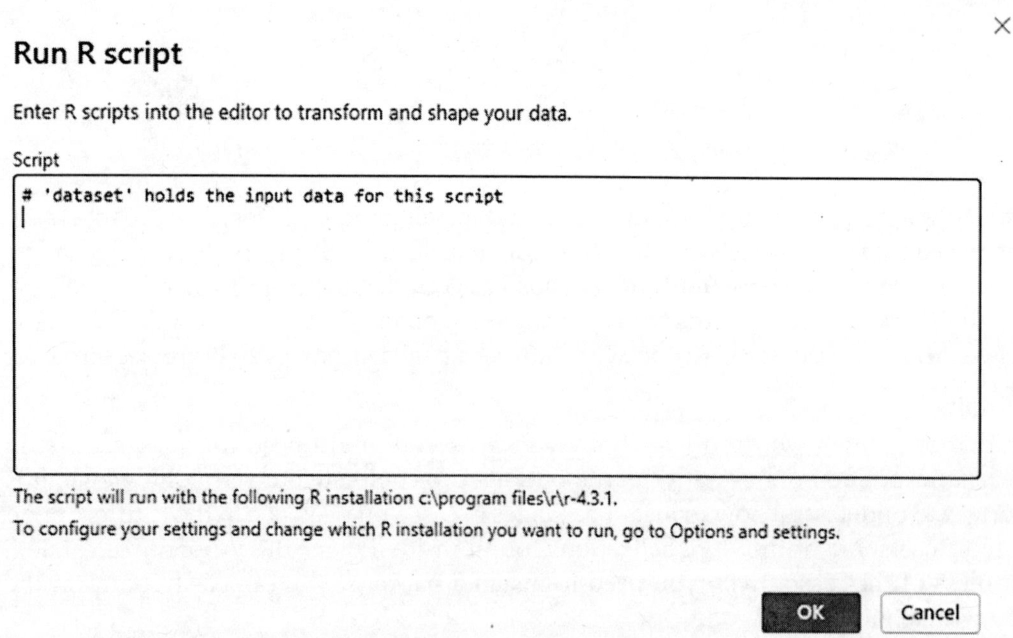

Figure 11.7: The R script editor window

At this point, we are going to write a script to find out the total price per mile for each of our rides. We are going to take our base dataset and save it to a new variable name. Then, we will take the **`total_amount`** column, divide it by the **`trip_distance`** column, and save it to a new column titled **`Price_Per_Mile`**. Our intent in this chapter is not to teach you how to code in R, but here is the code we will use to achieve this:

```
data <- dataset

data$Price_Per_Mile <- data$total_amount / data$trip_distance
```

Our code is simply going to augment our existing dataset and bring back the **`Price_Per_Mile`** column for our use. Once the script has run, we will need to expand the values of the dataset. We can click on the expand button on the right side of the value column, select our columns, and click **OK**:

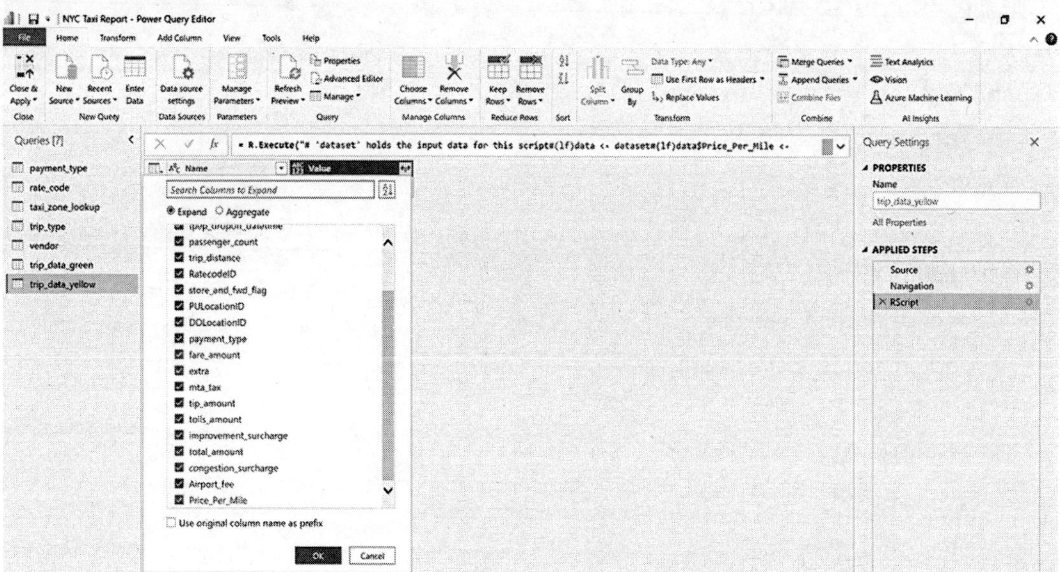

Figure 11.8: *Expanding the results of the R script*

We can achieve the same outcome with the advanced editor using the **`R.Execute()`** function. Admittedly, this process is not as easy to perform as you are now mixing a couple of different languages into the same window, but it does work. However, the function is quite simple and easy to understand:

`R.Execute()`	
Parameter	**Description**
`Script`	Script written in R. Make sure to use `#(lf)` to identify new lines of the script.
`Options`	Field is wrapped in `[]` and must be used to specify the `dataset` with a preceding step in the query.

Table 11.2: *Table of the R.Execute() parameters*

For this example, we are using our yellow cab trip data from our SQL server. Applying the transformations we have learned in previous chapters; we loaded our query and applied **R.Execute()** to find out our price per mile and expanded our values from the results:

```
let
  Source = Sql.Database("localhost", "NYC_Taxi"),
  TripData = Source{[Schema = "dbo", Item = "trip_data_yellow"]}[Data],
  RScript = R.Execute("
    # 'dataset' holds the input data for this script
    #(lf)data <- dataset#(lf)data$Price_Per_Mile <- data$total_amount / 
data$trip_distance",
    [dataset = TripData]
  ),
  ExpandDataset = Table.ExpandTableColumn(
    RScript,
    "Value",
    {
      "VendorID",
      "tpep_pickup_datetime",
      "tpep_dropoff_datetime",
      "passenger_count",
      "trip_distance",
      "RatecodeID",
      "store_and_fwd_flag",
      "PULocationID",
      "DOLocationID",
      "payment_type",
      "fare_amount",
      "extra",
      "mta_tax",
      "tip_amount",
      "tolls_amount",
      "improvement_surcharge",
      "total_amount",
      "congestion_surcharge",
```

```
        "Airport_fee",
        "Price_Per_Mile"
      },
      {
        "VendorID",
        "tpep_pickup_datetime",
        "tpep_dropoff_datetime",
        "passenger_count",
        "trip_distance",
        "RatecodeID",
        "store_and_fwd_flag",
        "PULocationID",
        "DOLocationID",
        "payment_type",
        "fare_amount",
        "extra",
        "mta_tax",
        "tip_amount",
        "tolls_amount",
        "improvement_surcharge",
        "total_amount",
        "congestion_surcharge",
        "Airport_fee",
        "Price_Per_Mile"
      }
    )
in
  ExpandDataset
```

It is probably worth taking a moment to realize that just like Python and the advanced editor, we find it to be much easier to use the graphical interface for this part. This prevents any confusion and does not require you to add the line feed into your code. While that is a small item, it can prove to be a painful experience to resolve if you forgot to add it to your code earlier.

Now that you know the basics, you can apply any R module to your dataset that is appropriate. Just remember that you will need to install these modules on your device before you leverage them.

What is AI?

In the past few years, **Artificial Intelligence (AI)** has become a force in society. It permeates the world we live in and has become an integral part of how things are done. We see examples of it in our lives through things like chatbots, self-driving cars, and even social media. While some may find it intimidating, the reality of AI is that it has the power to make our lives easier.

AI is used to describe technologies that perform tasks that once required human intelligence to complete. When properly deployed, AI models can recognize patterns, solve problems, make decisions, and understand natural language. These models do not organically exist. They are created through extensive training activities to ensure the results you receive are valid. Some of the work you perform with Power Query may result in the creation of a model, while others will leverage one.

Earlier in this chapter, we addressed using Python and R to transform our data inside Power Query. If you are working with these tools already, you might know how to build an algorithm that was created by machine learning that could be applied to your queries. But while that is nice, not everyone who will be creating their own models will understand how to deploy the code to make it a reality. In addition, sometimes you need something quick to do so you can provide quick results. This is where the advantages of a connected platform with Microsoft can make your life easier. In the next three sections, we will walk through deploying AI models leveraging Azure Cognitive Services and Azure Machine Learning.

Before we move forward, it is important to note a few things to make sure you are prepared for these next steps. Unlike Python and R which were deployed locally on your device, these services are based in the Microsoft cloud. If you are using Azure Cognitive Services, you will need a Premium instance of the Power BI Service that has been deployed and has AI services enabled. If you are using Azure Machine Learning, you will need to deploy Azure ML Studio and associated services. In short, these services are not free, and you might not have access to them. Keep that in mind as you follow along, as you might not have the ability to use them without a financial investment and possibly the assistance of your organization's technology department.

Lastly, we will not be addressing how to create models. Our focus is on leveraging them within the context of the Power Query editor. While we will address the components to make AI inside Power Query a reality, we will not cover the process of creating and deploying these models in your environment.

Leveraging text analytics functions

When performing analysis, we want to use stable values in our data sets. When creating surveys, we want to identify questions that either force specific data types like numbers and dates or use option sets to give a list of items to choose from. But no matter how hard we try, someone always creates a comment box at the end of the survey against our wishes. And if you have ever tried to perform analysis on text blocks, you know how challenging this can be. However, you can get around this challenge by leveraging Azure Cognitive Services to perform **Text Analytics** in your comment fields. To get started, go to the **Add column** ribbon and select **Text Analytics**:

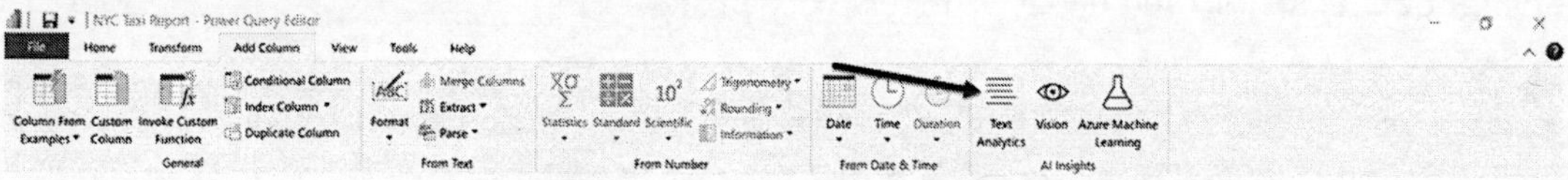

Figure 11.9: *Selecting the Text Analytics function in the add column ribbon*

If this is your first-time leveraging Azure Cognitive Services inside of Power Query, you will be prompted to sign in with your organizational account. From there, you will be able to pick one of three models, as shown:

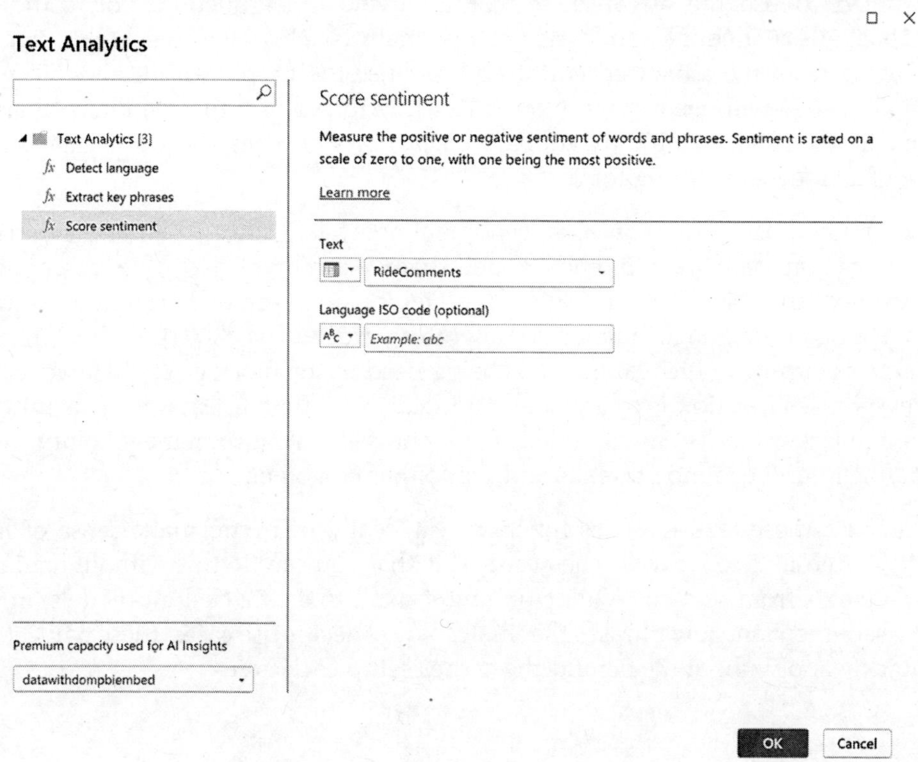

Figure 11.10: *Selecting text analytics model from Azure Cognitive Services*

For our scenario, we want to understand the sentiment of people's comments at the end of their taxi ride. To do this, we will select the **score sentiment** model. We will then identify the column in our query that we want to analyze. We will use the **`RideComments`** column for our analysis. We can also specify the language either by manually typing it in or using a column if that is captured in your query. Lastly, you can choose which premium capacity you wish to use for your insights. In the bottom right-hand corner, you can pick from the capacities you own to perform this action. This is helpful if you are trying to balance the load on your capacities. Once you have everything set, you can click **OK** to enact the model. The result is a column titled **Score Sentiment** that holds a decimal value. The closer to one, the more positive the response. In our example, the comment **`Overall a very great trip!`** scored 0.925, which is very positive:

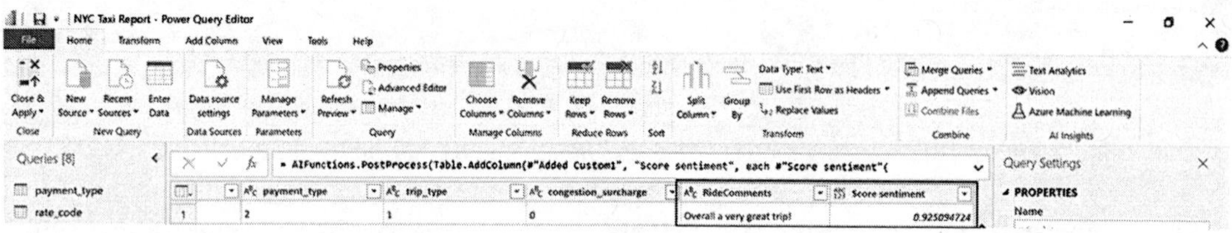

Figure 11.11: Score sentiment model results

If you wanted to use the advanced editor to invoke this function, you could use **`AIFunctions.PostProcess()`** to perform this analysis. However, we highly suggest you stay away from the advanced editor and just use the graphical interface. To write everything out, you will need to write out a function to perform the sentiment analysis. While we will cover how to build functions in *Chapter 14, Functions*, the graphical interface takes care of all the heavy lifting for us.

Now that we have performed the score sentiment analysis, glance again at *Figure 11.10*. You will notice that there are two other models that we can invoke with Azure Cognitive Services for text analysis. You can invoke the **Detect language** or **Extract key phrases** functions. The detect language function is straightforward. You pass a string of text through the model to determine which language is being used in the block of text. However, the extract key phrases function is one you should take some time to explore. This function looks through larger blocks of text and surfaces phrases. This is extremely helpful when you are trying to find common threads and group them together.

As you can see, these text analytics functions can really help you make sense of large text blocks with only a few clicks. The best part is that you can do this without having to create the models from scratch. While you might want to create custom models around things like sentiment and key phrases that match your specific use cases, these will get you started quickly and without the behind-the-scenes setup each time.

Leveraging vision functions

A fun fact about Power Query is that you can import images. When you pull these images in, they are rendered as binary text. However, with proper manipulation, they can be displayed within a Power BI report. This is not a perfect solution, but there might be a situation where you need to perform a quick analysis of some images in a query. Using Azure Cognitive Services inside of Power Query, we can launch the vision function to achieve this goal. You can reference *Figure 11.9* to launch this from the **Add columns** ribbon. However, we can use the **Home** ribbon and select **Vision** to launch this function as well:

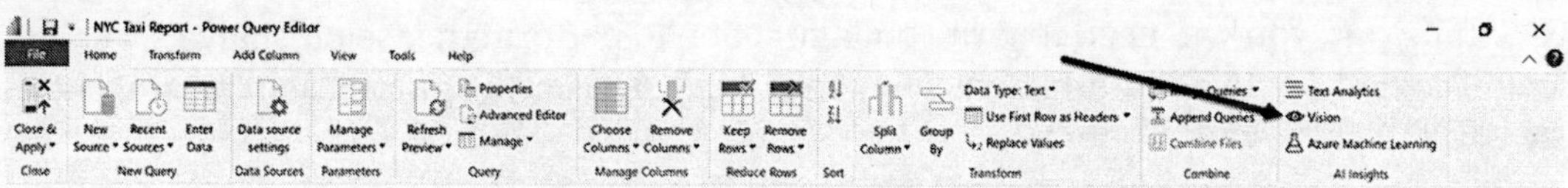

***Figure 11.12:** Selecting the Vision function in the home ribbon*

If this is your first-time leveraging Azure Cognitive Services inside of Power Query, you will be prompted to sign in with your organizational account. From there, you will be able to pick the **tag images** model, as shown:

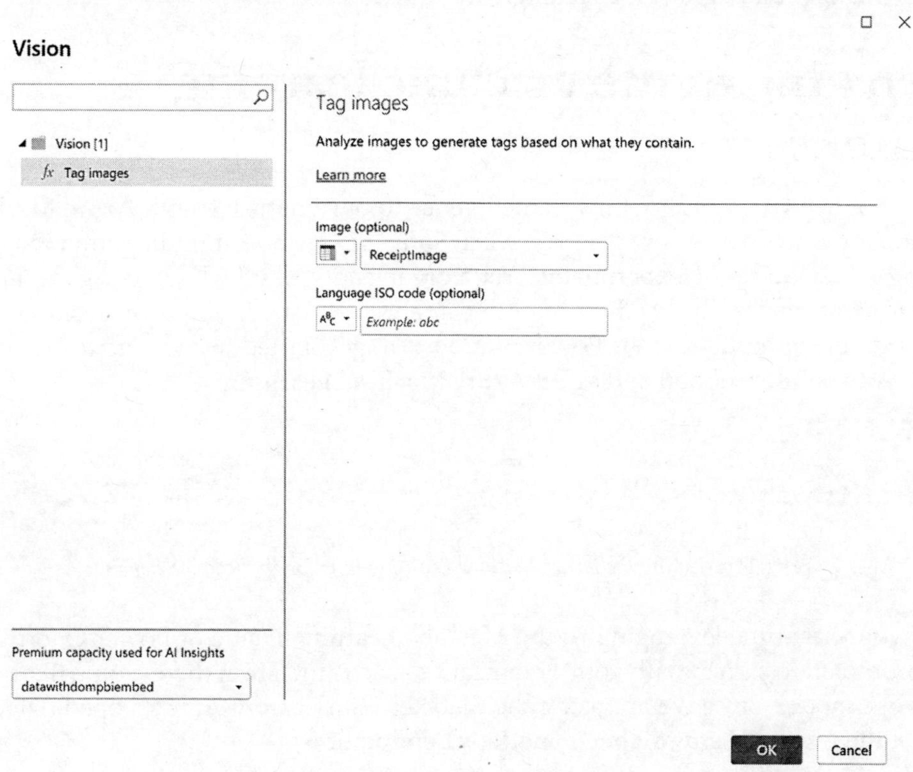

***Figure 11.13:** Selecting tag images model from Azure Cognitive Services*

Unlike text analytics, there is only one model we can select. With tag images, we can pass the column with the image data through, and it will generate tags based on the available image. We will use the **ReceiptImage** column for our analysis. We can also specify the language either by manually typing it in or using a column if that is captured in your query. Lastly, you can choose which premium capacity you wish to use for your insights. In the bottom right-hand corner, you can pick from the capacities you own to perform this action. Once you have everything set, you can click **OK** to enact the model.

If you wanted to use the advanced editor to invoke this function, you could use **AIFunctions.PostProcess()** to perform this analysis. However, we highly suggest you stay away from the advanced editor and just use the graphical interface. To write everything out, you will need to write out a function to perform the vision analysis. While we will cover how to build functions in *Chapter 14, Functions*, the graphical interface takes care of all the heavy lifting for us.

While this functionality is great, it does come with issues. The biggest issue is that there are limits on the amount of data that is found within a cell. This means that not all your images might be passed through to the tag images function. This only works for low-resolution images, which might make it challenging for any meaningful analysis. It might be worth trying it with some smaller images if you are trying to get some quick answers. It is not perfect, but it might just be enough for your solution.

Leveraging Azure machine learning functions

The final way we will apply Artificial Intelligence to our queries is with Azure Machine Learning. Also known as Azure ML, it is Microsoft's platform for building, training, and deploying AI models and experiments. Your organization might have designed an AI model endpoint that can be used for real-time analysis of data. If you have access to that model, you can connect it to your Power BI report. To get started, we will go to either the **Home** or **Add column** ribbon and select **Azure Machine Learning**:

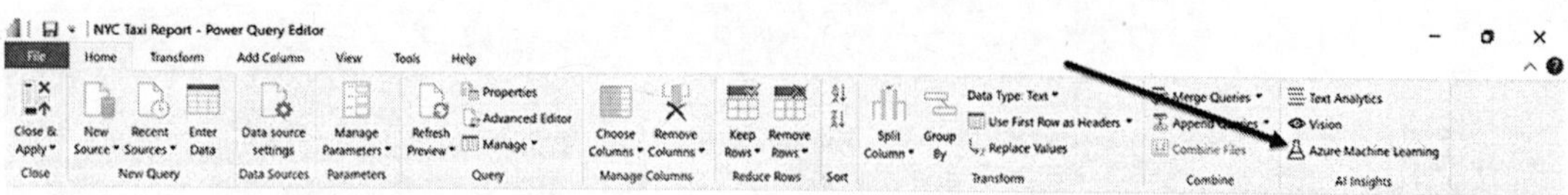

Figure 11.14: Selecting the Azure Machine Learning function in the home ribbon

If this is your first-time leveraging Azure Machine Learning inside of Power Query, you will be prompted to sign in with your organizational account. From there, you will be able to pick your model. Since we are using the diabetes dataset from Azure's open data, we will select the **AzureML.my-diabetes-model-v1** endpoint:

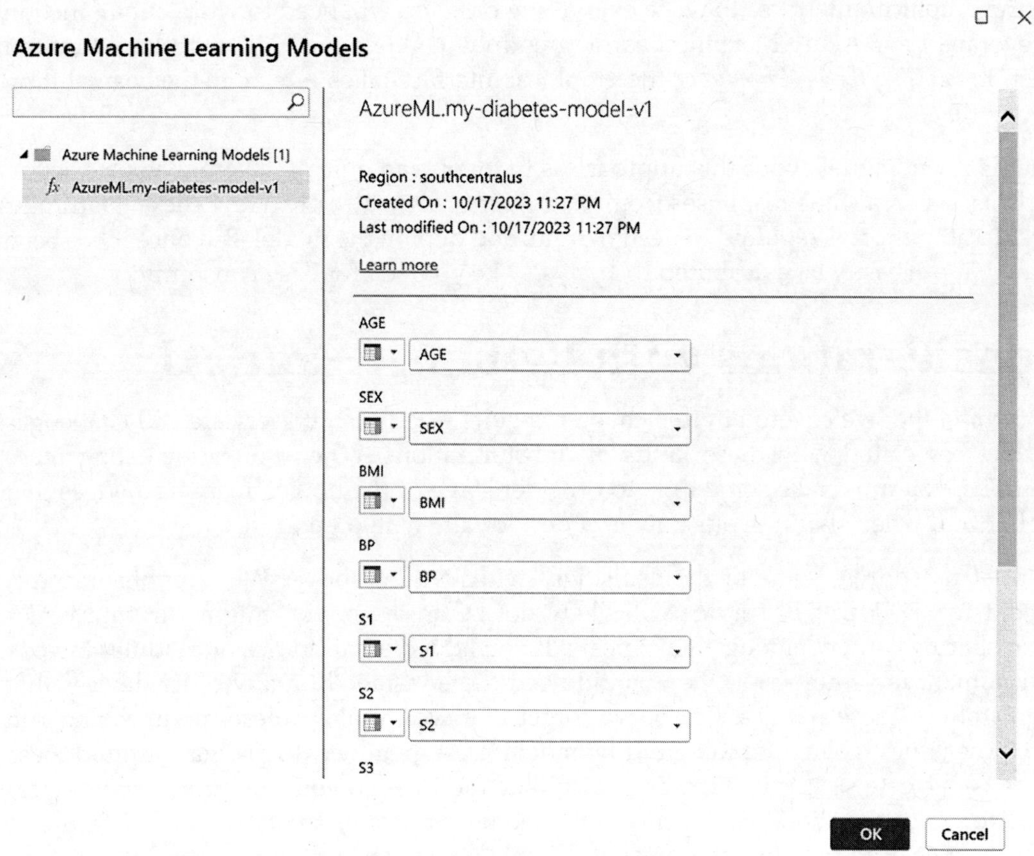

Figure 11.15: Configuring the Azure Machine Learning model in Power Query

For this model, we must specify all ten parameters for this model to function properly. For each one, we can set the associated column to the parameter. When we are finished, we can click **OK**. Once the model has finished running, we can click on the expand button to see our results:

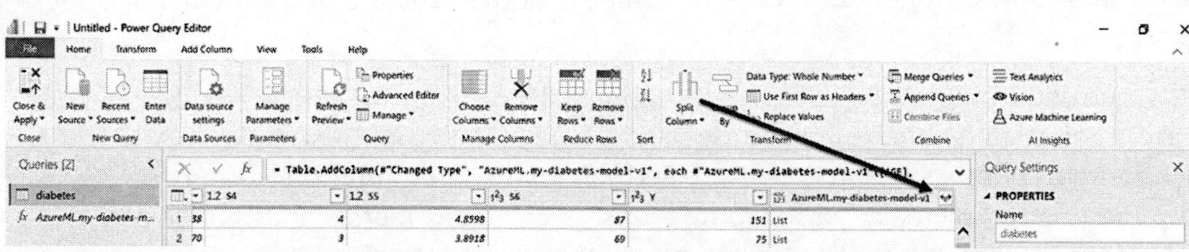

Figure 11.16: Expanding the results from our Azure Machine Learning Model

If you wanted to use the advanced editor to invoke this function, you could use **`Table.AddColumn()`** and call your custom Azure Machine Learning function to perform this analysis. However, we highly suggest you stay away from the advanced editor and just use the graphical interface. To write everything out, you will need to write out a function to leverage your Azure Machine Learning endpoint. While we will cover how to build functions in *Chapter 14, Functions*, the graphical interface takes care of all the heavy lifting for us.

What is phenomenal about this approach is that you can quickly leverage your existing models to get real-time responses from your AI models with only a few clicks. Naturally, considerable effort is required to design, train, and deploy the model. But once it has been created, it can easily be distributed to analysts like yourself for easy consumption.

Considerations with Python, R, and AI

Everything that we covered in this chapter is quite exciting, but there are still challenges that are associated with these kinds of transformations. When you are creating these solutions, you must take some time to consider some of the downstream challenges that might occur when sharing your Power BI desktop file with others.

First, let us address some of the challenges with Python and R. While publishing this content to the Power BI service will likely not be an issue, you might run into issues when sharing content amongst your peers. If you added any libraries or modules to your environment for your script, they would need to be installed on any other devices that might refresh these queries. Often, we forget that we installed these modules and run into these issues when upgrading our own devices. A great way to navigate around these issues is to create scripts that install and update modules so you can quickly get devices ready for these situations. Doing this in the moment prevents frustration in the future as these missing modules always appear at the most inconvenient time.

For Azure Cognitive Services, all text and vision analyses are being performed using premium features within your Power BI tenant. If you are using Power BI capacity, there might be a performance hit on your capacity, which might impact the user experience. This is an important consideration and might require you to perform more intensive refreshes during off-hours to avoid any user impacts. It might also be worth considering acquiring a dedicated capacity or Azure Power BI Embed module for this if the demand is high enough.

Lastly, one of the biggest challenges with Azure machine learning is making sure you have the right resources available for the right situations. First, you must make sure that you have the right permissions to access the endpoint. Next, you might need to consider the computing requirements to perform the refresh. For larger queries, it might be resource-intensive, which could result in higher spend to meet your goals. It may not be the right choice to use these endpoints every time you refresh due to the cost, so consider calling these endpoints when recording the data in your warehouse instead. A little planning could save you a conversation about overspending your Azure budget for the month.

These considerations are not meant to dissuade you from using these features. They are powerful and can provide a lot of value to your solutions. It is just important to understand the potential pitfalls so you can make the right decision to support your organization.

Conclusion

In this chapter, we covered how to transform your queries with Python and R. We learned how to pass data from our existing query into our code and leverage it for transformations. We then explored how Artificial Intelligence could be leveraged within our queries. Starting with Azure Cognitive Services, we used out-of-the-box models to perform text and vision analysis on our data. We then applied a custom Azure machine learning model endpoint to our queries to come back with a response. Lastly, we reviewed some considerations around the use of Python, R, and AI in our queries to ensure the best experience for anyone who might interact with them in the future.

In the next chapter, we will learn how to build indices inside of Power Query to help us build out our own dimension tables with reports.

CHAPTER 12
Indexing

Introduction

In this chapter, we will explore the creation and use of index columns inside the Power Query editor. Seeming simple at first, index columns are a powerful tool when it comes to optimizing your models. If you are attaching to data sources that do not have keys or are not designed in a star schema, you can leverage an index to convert a flattened query into a dimensional model. This chapter will explore how you can leverage indices to simplify your models within Power Query.

Structure

The chapter covers the following topics:

- What is an index column?
- Understanding keys
- Understanding star schemas
- Creating an index
- Creating a dimension from an index
- Optimizing queries to reduce bloat

Objectives

By the end of this chapter, you will understand how to create index columns within the Power Query editor to aid in the manipulation of your model. This will allow you to enact a star schema model for queries that do not fit into a dimensional model.

What is an index column?

If you remember in *Chapter 9, Creating New Columns*, we mentioned that there were two column types we would cover in a later chapter. One was invoking a custom function as a column, a topic we will cover in *Chapter 14, Functions*. The other was creating an **Index column**. If you have created an index column already, you might be wondering why a whole chapter is devoted to this topic. While index columns are basic on the surface, how you might leverage them has a major impact on your data model.

At its most basic, an index column provides a unique identifier for each row. While we can call specific rows within Power Query, the index column would allow us to have the same functionality with DAX in Power BI or Excel. This proves to be helpful when trying to sort, filter, or reference other rows in your query when creating your formulas.

In addition, we can use an index column to create a dimensional model. Power BI and Excel perform best when leveraging a dimensional model. Depending on how your data is structured, you might be bringing in all your data with a single table. With some help using index columns, you can create keys to create a dimension table. This will help set up a star schema to optimize your model.

It may seem excessive, but taking the time to understand how to extend the use of index columns goes a long way when it comes to building out our models.

Understanding star schemas

If you have viewed training materials on Power BI and Excel, you might have already heard about how they like to use a star schema to model data efficiently. Instead of putting repetitive data within your query, we push it to a dimension that allows us to optimize our model. The name star schema comes from the shape it creates. This sample model demonstrates what a star schema looks like in context:

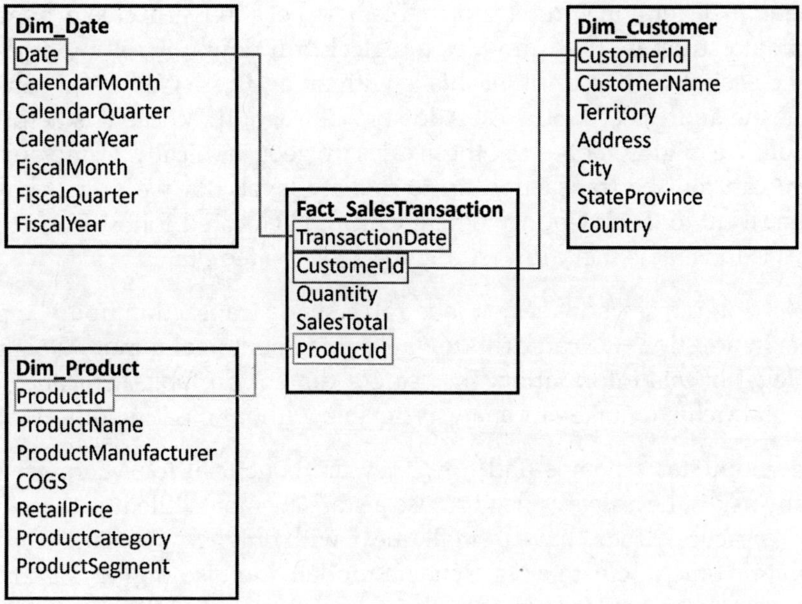

***Figure 12.1:** A sample star schema diagram*

Simply put, a star schema takes a centralized fact table and builds relationships to dimension tables to provide the additional context surrounding the fact table. A fact table is a transaction table that contains granular details of the metrics you are trying to measure. Fact tables are designed to be skinny but are long as they contain millions of rows. If properly designed, they refresh efficiently and take up minimal space. However, if not well designed, the refresh time on your model could double with the addition of only a few columns.

Dimension tables provide context around your fact table. Linked to your fact table with a relationship, they provide dimensional information that helps extract insight around your data. Some common dimension tables you encounter host information such as customer information, address information, product information, employee information, and context around dates. The concept is to provide efficiencies with the modeling and storage of your data to simplify your analysis. Taking repetitive data from your fact table and placing it into your dimension table allows you to reduce the occurrence of repetitive data within the model.

If you remember back in *Chapter 6, Managing Data Types*, we talked about the impact of data types on a model. We learned that the type of column you select could have an impact on the size of your model. Whole numbers, also known as integers, are far more efficient from a data storage perspective than a text value. On top of that, the repetitive nature of text could bloat the size of your model. Using a star schema, we look to limit that repetitive data and push it to a dimension instead.

Another benefit to leveraging dimension tables is the ability to create hierarchies. A hierarchy is a data structure that provides a logical drill down or roll up of data with a dimension. The easiest way to think of this is with an address. We have a customer, Mr. Blues, who has the address of 1060 West Addison, Chicago, IL. While it is helpful to have this information, we might want to roll these sales up geographically. Using our customer dimension, we can roll the transaction up to the city level. But we do not have to stop there. We can roll up to Cook County where Chicago is located followed by the state of Illinois. Illinois is in what is the Midwest region of the United States.

In our example, you can see how easy it is to roll a single transaction up to be part of the bigger picture. In addition, we can drill down on this data to get a more detailed look at the granular level of this information. By using a dimension table, we can provide the context of the hierarchy to make our analysis flexible without bloating our model size.

After reading about star schemas and how they are beneficial for Microsoft Excel and Power BI, many ask if they always need to use a star schema. While it is the ideal model, it is not always practical. If you have a small query with only ten thousand rows, it might not be worth your time to create a star schema model. You also might not have enough data to create a star schema. However, you might need to add a dimension table to help with some analysis. In short, the only hard and fast rule with using a star schema is when you have a model that is connected to a SQL data source with millions of rows of data. It is important for you to take some time and determine what is the right approach for your model as you design it within Power Query.

Understanding keys

If you have worked with databases in the past, you might already be familiar with the term key. A key is used to link different tables together within a database. When creating a relationship in Power BI or Excel, we can link two queries together using key columns. Most people who connect to databases with Power Query rarely need to think about the construction of these keys. However, if we need to create these keys in Power Query, we need to understand how they are structured before we do anything else.

When working with a dimensional model, we need to use a primary key and foreign key. A primary key provides a unique identifier for each row of data within a query. While not always a requirement, we find primary keys on our dimension tables. We will use an index column to create that unique identifier with our existing query which will provide the base for our relationship.

A foreign key is a column that can be referenced against the primary key in another table. Foreign keys are frequently found on our fact tables. We will connect the primary key from our dimension table to our foreign key in our fact table. This will establish a consistent relationship between the two tables allowing us to quickly analyze our data. We can create our foreign key by referencing our primary key. This can be done either by splitting up a single query or by referencing the primary key with a little code.

There are other types of keys that you might encounter such as candidate keys, super keys, or composite keys. While these are leveraged with databases, they will not function as desired within Power BI and Excel. Unfortunately, we can only use a single pair of columns to build our relationships. If this is your situation, you might need to create your own primary and foreign keys to establish your relationships.

Creating an index

Now that we have established some of the use cases for using an index column, we will explore how to create an index. To create an index, we simply must go to the **add column** ribbon and use the **index column** drop down to select the index required for your query:

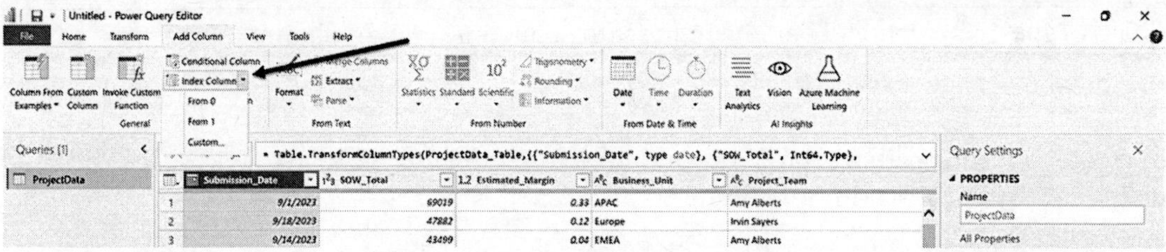

***Figure 12.2** Selecting an index for a query*

This prompts the first decision you must make when it comes to creating an index. We will first focus on the two pre-canned options available within Power Query. We can select an index that starts with zero or with one. You are probably wondering why there are two options available to you. The answer to that has to do with how Power Query is designed. If you want to use an index to identify the row number as assigned in Power Query, you will want to use an index that starts with zero. This is because Power Query assigns row numbers starting with zero. However, for many, it is more comfortable to start your index with one. Regardless of which option you select, it will automatically add a column titled **`index`** into your query, as shown in the following figure:

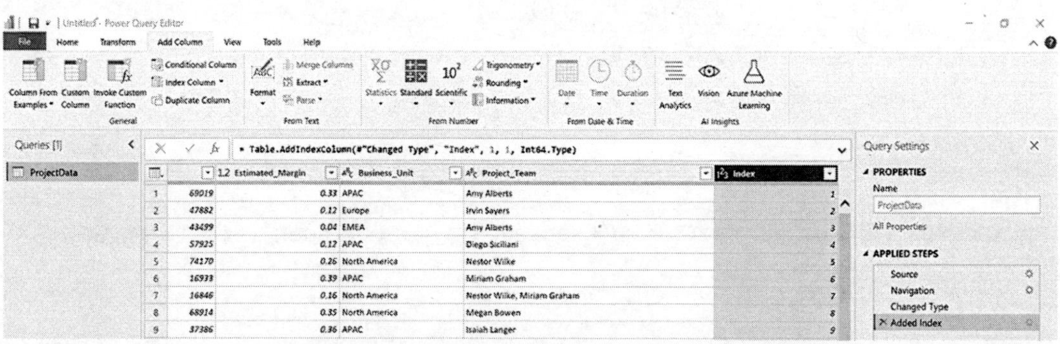

***Figure 12.3:** Index column added to query starting with one*

To create an index with the advanced editor, we must use the **`Table.AddIndexColumn()`** function to add our index. Earlier in the book, we used the **`Table.AddColumn()`** function to create new columns. However, we have a dedicated function for creating an index with its own parameters:

Table.AddIndexColumn()	
Parameter	**Description**
Table	A table in Power Query. Usually the preceding step.
NewColumnName	Name of your index column wrapped in double quotes.
InitialValue	Optional parameter to set the starting number for the index. If left blank, index will start at zero.
Increment	Optional parameter to set the increment of the index. If left blank, increment will be one.
ColumnType	Optional parameter to set the data type on the column.

Table 12.1: *Table of the Table.AddIndexColumn() parameters*

To create an index that starts at one to match *Figure 12.3,* we will use **Table.AddIndexColumn()** to add our column:

```
let
  Source = Excel.Workbook(File.Contents("C:\data\ProjectData.xlsx"), null,
true),
  Data = Source{[Item = "ProjectData", Kind = "Table"]}[Data],
  ChangedDataType = Table.TransformColumnTypes(
    Data,
    {
      {"Submission_Date", type date},
      {"SOW_Total", Int64.Type},
      {"Estimated_Margin", type number},
      {"Business_Unit", type text},
      {"Project_Team", type text}
    }
  ),
  AddIndex = Table.AddIndexColumn(ChangedDataType, "Index", 1, 1, Int64.
Type)
in
  AddIndex
```

At this point, if you are paying attention to the parameters for **Table.AddIndexColumn()** and remember that there was an option to create a custom index in *Figure 12.2,* you are probably wondering how this might work. If you need to create a custom index, you can select custom on the index column drop-down. This will open a window that will allow you to specify your starting index and increment for your query:

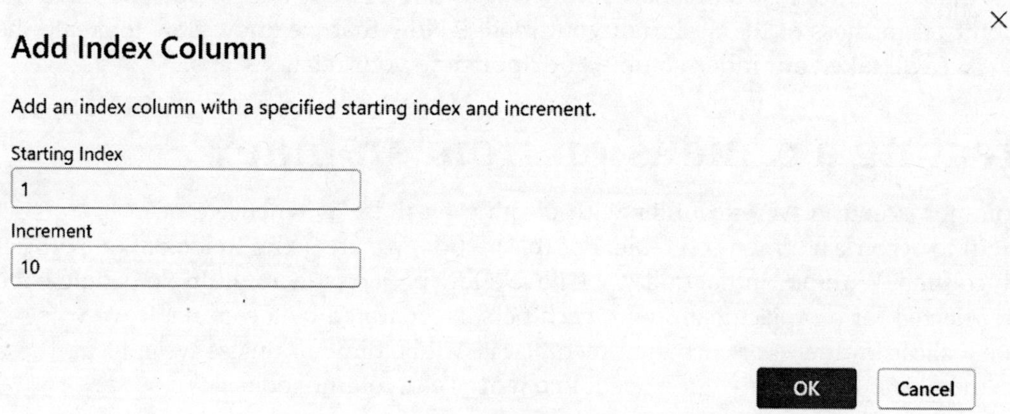

***Figure 12.4:** Creating a custom index in Power Query*

If we wanted to create an index that starts at one and increments in units of ten, we would use the configuration we have in *Figure 12.4*. While the graphical interface takes care of this for us, we will need to update our parameters with the **`Table.AddIndexColumn()`** function to achieve the same outcome:

```
let
   Source = Excel.Workbook(File.Contents("C:\data\ProjectData.xlsx"), null, 
true),
  Data = Source{[Item = "ProjectData", Kind = "Table"]}[Data],
  ChangedDataType = Table.TransformColumnTypes(
    Data,
    {
      {"Submission_Date", type date},
      {"SOW_Total", Int64.Type},
      {"Estimated_Margin", type number},
      {"Business_Unit", type text},
      {"Project_Team", type text}
    }
  ),
   AddIndex = Table.AddIndexColumn(ChangedDataType, "Index", 1, 10, Int64.
Type)
in
  AddIndex
```

Regardless of which option you use for an index, the key is to build it around your use case. With a little planning, you can create an index that meets your needs. A straightforward index that starts from zero or one will often take care of your needs. But you have the flexibility regardless of the design of your model. Now that we know how to create the index, we will take your index column and apply it to your relationships.

Creating a dimension from an index

A common scenario we encounter with creating an index is when we need to parse a column to become a dimension table. For this section, we are going to look at our project team column. With our initial query, we have a few projects where multiple people have been selected for a project team, with each person separated by a comma. If we want to create a slicer to filter a project team member, it will be difficult unless we split up these team members. This is how our current **`Project_Team`** column looks:

		1.2 Estimated_Margin	ABC Business_Unit	ABC Project_Team	123 Index
1	69019	0.33	APAC	Amy Alberts	1
2	47882	0.12	Europe	Irvin Sayers	2
3	43499	0.04	EMEA	Amy Alberts	3
4	57925	0.12	APAC	Diego Siciliani	4
5	74170	0.26	North America	Nestor Wilke	5
6	16933	0.39	APAC	Miriam Graham	6
7	16846	0.16	North America	Nestor Wilke, Miriam Graham	7
8	68914	0.35	North America	Megan Bowen	8
9	37386	0.36	APAC	Isaiah Langer	9
10	14415	0.03	EMEA	Debra Berger, Joni Sherman	10
11	12411	0.36	South America	Joni Sherman, Johanna Lorenz, Lidia Holloway, Lynn Robbins	11
12	51351	0.32	APAC	Grady Archie	12

Figure 12.5: *Note that a few rows have multiple project team members*

To resolve his challenge, we must manufacture a new dimension table that will filter this query. To start, we must add an index column. If you look at *Figure 12.5*, you will see that there is already an index column that starts with one. While this can be achieved with the graphical interface, the code in the advanced editor looks like this:

```
let
  Source = Excel.Workbook(File.Contents("C:\data\ProjectData.xlsx"), null,
true),
  Data = Source{[Item = "ProjectData", Kind = "Table"]}[Data],
  ChangedDataType = Table.TransformColumnTypes(
    Data,
    {
      {"Submission_Date", type date},
      {"SOW_Total", Int64.Type},
      {"Estimated_Margin", type number},
```

```
      {"Business_Unit", type text},
      {"Project_Team", type text}
    }
  ),
  AddIndex = Table.AddIndexColumn(ChangedDataType, "Index", 1, 1, Int64.
Type)
in
  AddIndex
```

This will serve as our key to link our dimension table with our original query. For our next step, we will right-click on our query and select reference. Immediately, it will seem like the query has been duplicated. However, it is referencing your existing query. We will rename this query as **`Project_Team`**.

Once we have our new query set, we will remove all columns except the **`Project_Team`** and **`Index`** columns. Next, we will split our column by our delimiter. We are going to split up our columns with the comma as the delimiter and place them into rows. Go to the **Transform** tab and select **Split column** by delimiter under the **Split column** menu. This menu should feel familiar as we have performed this transformation in *Chapter 9, Creating Columns*. However, this time, we are going to split our data into rows instead of columns:

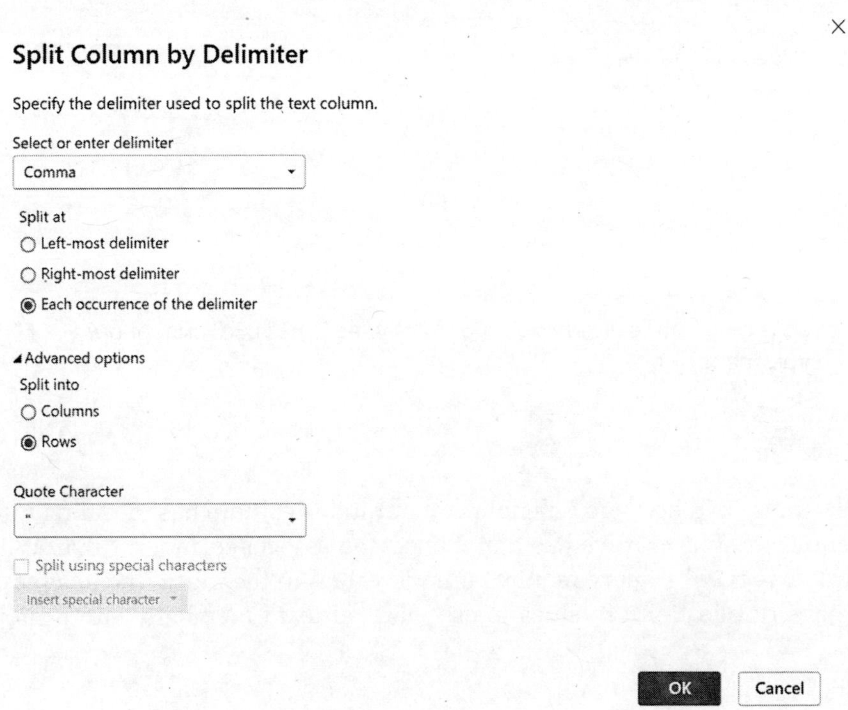

Figure 12.6: *Splitting our project team records into rows*

If you prefer to create the **Project_Team** query with the advanced editor, you will need to reference the **ProjectData** query. From there, you will use **Table.SelectColumns()** to remove the extra columns from the query. Next, you will use **Table.ExpandListColumn()** to split the columns into rows and **Table.TransformColumnTypes()** to update the data type. The result is a block of code that looks like this:

```
let
  Source = ProjectData,
  RemoveColumns = Table.SelectColumns(Source, {"Project_Team", "Index"}),
  SplitColumnToRows = Table.ExpandListColumn(
    Table.TransformColumns(
      RemoveColumns,
      {
        {
          "Project_Team",
          Splitter.SplitTextByDelimiter(",", QuoteStyle.Csv),
          let
            itemType = (type nullable text) meta [Serialized.Text = true]
          in
            type {itemType}
        }
      }
    ),
    "Project_Team"
  ),
  ChangedDataType = Table.TransformColumnTypes(SplitColumnToRows, {{"Proj-
ect_Team", type text}})
in
  ChangedDataType
```

With this new query in place, you will note that our index column has repeating numbers. This is because our split to rows has maintained the associated index value. While the index of our **ProjectData** query requires unique values in the index, the **Project_Team** query will need duplication of values to associate all team members with a project, as shown:

	Project_Team	Index
9	Megan Bowen	8
10	Isaiah Langer	9
11	Debra Berger	10
12	Joni Sherman	10
13	Joni Sherman	11
14	Johanna Lorenz	11
15	Lidia Holloway	11
16	Lynn Robbins	11
17	Grady Archie	12
18	Lynne Robbins	13

***Figure 12.7:** Final transformation of the Project_Team query*

At this point, we have successfully created a dimension table based on the team information. At this point, we have completed the groundwork for building the relationship between these two queries. Unfortunately, the next step is that you will apply these changes so you can assign the relationship. If you are using Microsoft Excel, you will build this relationship in Power Pivot. If you are using Power BI, you will perform this in the relationship view instead.

Optimizing queries to reduce bloat

Another scenario you might consider for an index is to eliminate columns with longer strings of data. Using the same **ProjectData** query in *Figure 12.5,* we are going to replace the **Business_Unit** column with a key from an index column. To start, we will duplicate our **ProjectData** query and rename it as **Business_Unit**. This will replicate the connection to the data source to eliminate any circular reference errors.

Next, we will select the **Business_Unit** column and remove all other columns. Once we have removed these extra columns, we will remove duplicates in that column. With the query transformed, we will now add an index column called **BU_Key** that starts with one that will serve as a key for our business unit dimension:

	Business_Unit	BU_Key
1	APAC	1
2	Europe	2
3	EMEA	3
4	North America	4
5	South America	5

***Figure 12.8:** Business_Unit query as a dimension table*

You can build this query easily with the advanced editor. Just like in the last section, we are performing similar transformations. To achieve the outcome in *Figure 12.8*, we will use the following block of code:

```
let
  Source = Excel.Workbook(File.Contents("C:\data\ProjectData.xlsx"), null,
true),
  Data = Source{[Item = "ProjectData", Kind = "Table"]}[Data],
  ChangedDataType = Table.TransformColumnTypes(
    Data,
    {
      {"Submission_Date", type date},
      {"SOW_Total", Int64.Type},
      {"Estimated_Margin", type number},
      {"Business_Unit", type text},
      {"Project_Team", type text}
    }
  ),
  RemoveColumns = Table.SelectColumns(ChangedDataType, {"Business_Unit"}),
  RemoveDuplicates = Table.Distinct(RemoveColumns),
  BU_Index = Table.AddIndexColumn(RemoveDuplicates, "BU_Key", 1, 1, Int64.
Type)
in
  BU_Index
```

Now that we have built our dimension table for the business unit, we need to go back to our fact table to apply our new key. This is something that must be done within the advanced editor code. To achieve this, the first thing we must do with the advanced editor is reference the **Business_Unit** query and save it to a value in the query.

Once you have the reference established, we will use **Table.AddColumn()** to connect rows to our reference to the **Business_Unit** query. We will call the table, establish the common value between queries, and return the **BU_Key** from the reference. The result is the following block of code to achieve our desired outcome:

```
let
  BU_Data = Business_Unit,
  Source = Excel.Workbook(File.Contents("C:\data\ProjectData.xlsx"), null,
true),
  Data = Source{[Item = "ProjectData", Kind = "Table"]}[Data],
```

```
  ChangedDataType = Table.TransformColumnTypes(
    Data,
    {
      {"Submission_Date", type date},
      {"SOW_Total", Int64.Type},
      {"Estimated_Margin", type number},
      {"Business_Unit", type text},
      {"Project_Team", type text}
    }
  ),
  AddIndex = Table.AddIndexColumn(ChangedDataType, "Index", 1, 1, Int64.
Type),
  AddBU_Key = Table.AddColumn(
    AddIndex,
    "BU_Key",
    each BU_Data{[Business_Unit = [Business_Unit]]}[BU_Key],
    Int64.Type
  )
in
  AddBU_Key
```

Before we remove the **Business_Unit** column, we can validate that our query is working by comparing it to our new **BU_Key** column:

	rgin	Business_Unit	Project_Team	Index	BU_Key
1	0.33	APAC	Amy Alberts	1	1
2	0.12	Europe	Irvin Sayers	2	2
3	0.04	EMEA	Amy Alberts	3	3
4	0.12	APAC	Diego Siciliani	4	1
5	0.26	North America	Nestor Wilke	5	4
6	0.39	APAC	Miriam Graham	6	1
7	0.16	North America	Nestor Wilke, Miriam Graham	7	4

Figure 12.9: Comparing the Business_Unit column with the BU_Key column

With our data validated, we can remove the **Business_Unit** column. We then can apply our queries and build the relationships.

Depending on your comfort level at this point in the book, you might be concerned about writing code from scratch in the advanced editor. While we only wrote two lines of code, it is a little more complicated as you must keep track of curly and square brackets. If you do not write these queries all the time, you might struggle to remember what to do. The good news is that there is an easier way to create this relationship with a little less code. In *Chapter 14, Functions*, we will explore a way to do this using less manual code to make your life a little easier.

Conclusion

In this chapter, we explored index columns and how they are applied for advanced modeling within Microsoft Excel and Power BI. We took time to understand what a star schema is and why it is important for our models. We also touched on keys and how they are leveraged to build out our star schemas. With a command of these modeling principles, we went through the process of creating an index for our queries. Once the index was created, we extended its use by creating new dimension tables in two different scenarios.

In the next chapter, we will learn how to simplify our query writing and management with parameters inside the Power Query editor.

CHAPTER 13
Parameters

Introduction

In this chapter, we will explore the creation and utilization of parameters inside of the Power Query editor. We will first define what parameters are in Power Query and go through the process of creating them. Next, we will apply parameters for incremental refresh for those who are using this feature in Power BI. We will then explore updating parameters without having to open the Power Query editor. Lastly, we will explore some use cases for applying parameters inside of your existing queries.

Structure

The chapter covers the following topics:

- Understanding parameters in Power Query
- Creating parameters in Power Query
- Creating parameter values from existing queries
- Parameters and incremental refresh
- Updating parameters
- Use cases for parameters

Objectives

By the end of this chapter, you will understand how to create parameters within the Power Query editor and how to apply them in your model. This will allow you to simplify the management of your queries and make it easier to update them with minimal rework.

Understanding parameters in Power Query

Depending on what you are doing in Power Query, the term parameter might change based on your context. Parameters are a core element of Power Query. However, they are also a part of custom functions you might create. While the parameters for custom functions are important, we will cover that in *Chapter 14, Functions*. Our focus for this chapter is the core feature built into the Power Query editor.

Parameters in Power Query are designed to allow you to specify values and reference them in your query. When creating your parameter, you can specify a value, create a list of values, or use an existing query for use. In addition to the value, you can set your data type, which helps make your query writing experience easier inside the advanced editor. The creation process only takes a few minutes to create and implement into your query.

Another notable feature of parameters is that they can be identified when you create a template file. Whether you are using Power BI or Microsoft Excel, you can save your file as a template. When you open the template file, you will be asked to specify the parameters. This is a fantastic option when you are creating a solution that will be redeployed multiple times.

Often underutilized, parameters can transform your query writing experience. At their basic level, they can serve as variables. However, properly applied, they can extend the flexibility of your queries. Because of their ability to be customized and implemented, you should consider integrating them into your queries. It may seem trivial now, but it can save you hours of rework in the future.

Creating parameters in Power Query

The process of creating parameters within the Power Query editor is easy. From the **Home** ribbon, we can select **Manage Parameters** to create, modify, or delete our parameters. We also can use the drop-down to create a **New Parameter** to initiate the process for us. We also can select **Edit Parameters** if we want to update the values assigned to our parameters, but more on that later. To make our lives easier, we will use the **Manage Parameters** option to start, as shown:

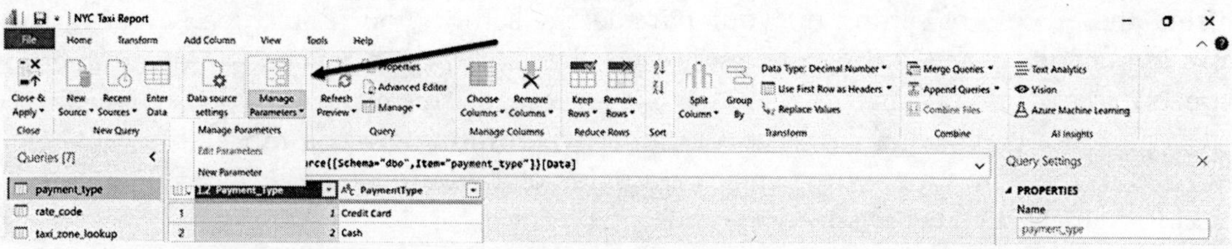

Figure 13.1: Activating the Manage Parameters function in the Power Query editor

Once you have opened the manage parameters window, you can click on **New** to create a parameter. From there, we will assign our parameter a name. To make our lives easier, do not use spaces to make it easier for us to use in the future. Next, we want to give our parameter a description. This is important as it will give the context of how the parameter is used. In addition, it will help those who are updating parameters in the future. After we have provided a name and description, we need to specify the rules for our parameter. First, new parameters are required by default. This means that a value must be present for it to work. Next, you can specify the data type. Since we are looking at taxi zones, we will use a numeric value. Lastly, we must set a value. For now, we will set up our parameter to use any value and specify it in the current value field:

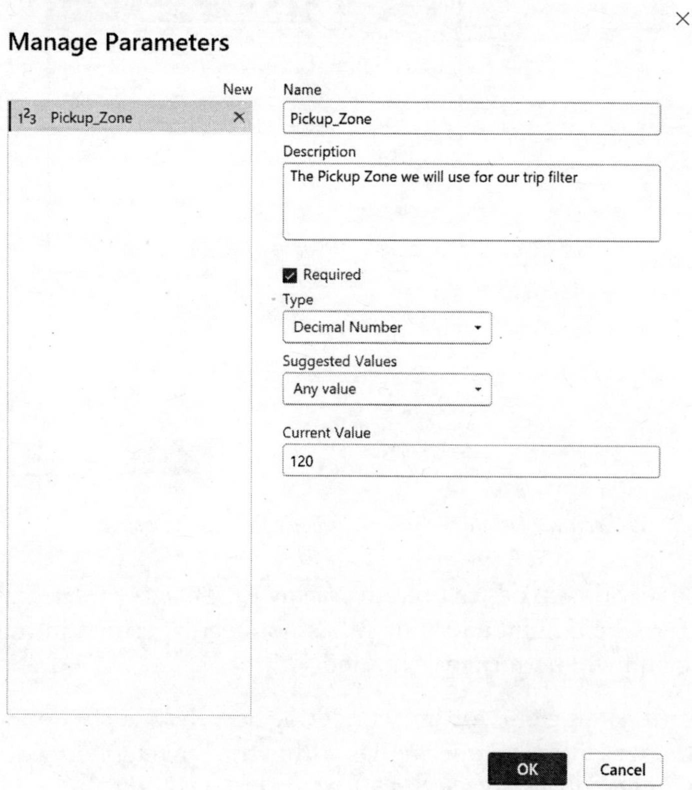

Figure 13.2: Creating a parameter in the manage parameters window

During the process of setting up your parameters, setting your data type is critical to simplifying your query writing process. As you have learned in this book, Power Query expects to see data types match when they are leveraged. This means it expects to see text if it is part of a connection string or a number when filtering a column with a number assigned as the data type. When creating a parameter, you have an array of options to select from that will meet the needs of your query:

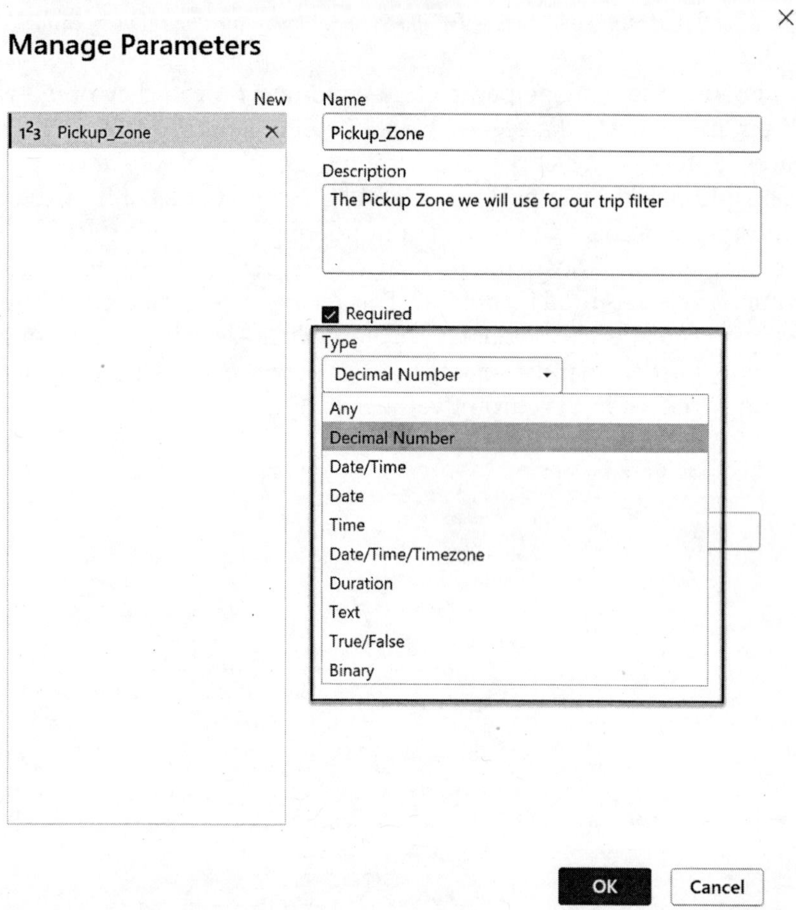

Figure 13.3: *Data type options available for your parameter*

You will note that every data type we used in *Chapter 6, Managing Data Types* is identified in this list except for whole number. While it has not been specified in this list, decimal number works fine and will perform as expected.

Now that we have our parameters, you are wondering how they can be applied. The easiest example is to use them as filters on our queries within the Power Query editor. We will go to our **`trip_data_green`** query, locate the **`PULocationID`** column, and create a numeric filter on the column. Normally, we would manually enter a value into the fields, but we are going to do something different. There is a dropdown next to the equals operator that has 1.2 visible. We are going to change that dropdown to use **Parameter** instead. Once that has been selected, there is a dropdown that allows us to select the parameter we want to use for the filter. Since we are filtering the **`PULocationID`** column, we will use the **`Pickup_Zone`** parameter:

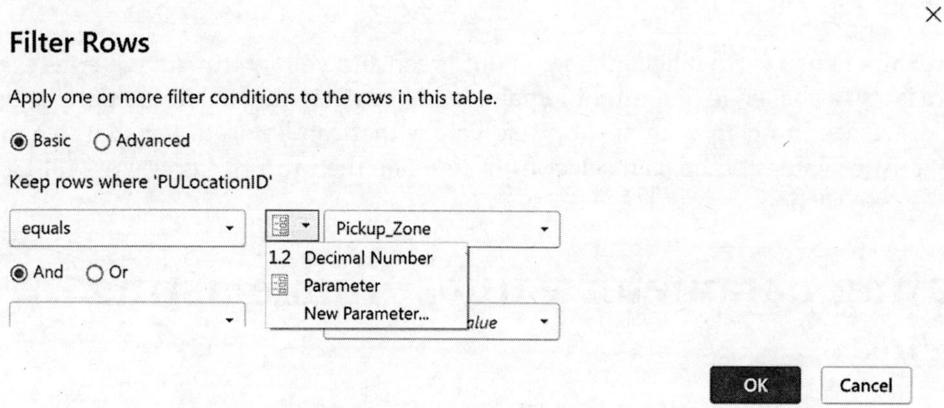

***Figure 13.4:** Creating a filter on a column using a parameter*

What is convenient is that we can create a new parameter in the process to make our lives easier. You might be wondering why we are going to this level of effort to add parameters to enable the filtering process. While this seems excessive, it helps us in the end because we do not have to hunt for the transformation. We have a query that pulls both green and yellow taxi information. Instead of having to update these filters on both tables in the future, we only must update the parameter, and it will adjust the filter context on both tables accordingly.

If you prefer to use the advanced editor to apply these filters, you can do so with the assistance of the **`Table.SelectRows()`** function we learned about in *Chapter 8, Cleansing Columns*. We will simply replace the hard-coded value we used before with the parameter we created. In addition to filtering our pickup zone, we added a filter for our drop-off zone with this block of code:

```
let
  Source = Csv.Document(
    File.Contents("C:\NYC Taxi\trip_data_green.csv"),
    [Delimiter = ",", Columns = 20, Encoding = 1252, QuoteStyle = Quote-
Style.None]
  ),
  PromotedHeaders = Table.PromoteHeaders(Source, [PromoteAllScalars =
true]),
  FilterTrips = Table.SelectRows(
```

```
    PromotedHeaders,
    each [PULocationID] = Pickup_Zone and [DOLocationID] = Dropoff_Zone
  )
in
  FilterTrips
```

These are minor changes to make managing our green and yellow trip data queries easier. Yet, there is still a challenge that might remain. If we are designing a parameter to be used by others, we need to help with appropriate values that can be used. For that, we must provide a list of values others can select from to make the process easier. We will tackle that in our next section.

Creating parameter values from existing queries

As we have addressed throughout this entire book, Power Query expects precision when creating your queries. This means we must be mindful of things such as capitalization, spaces, and data types. For users who are intimately familiar with our queries, it might be fine for us to allow any values in our parameters. However, if we want to share this with others, we can provide some context to make their lives easier. Luckily for us, Power Query already has a solution for this problem. Our first option is to switch our **Suggested Values** field to use a **List of values**, as shown:

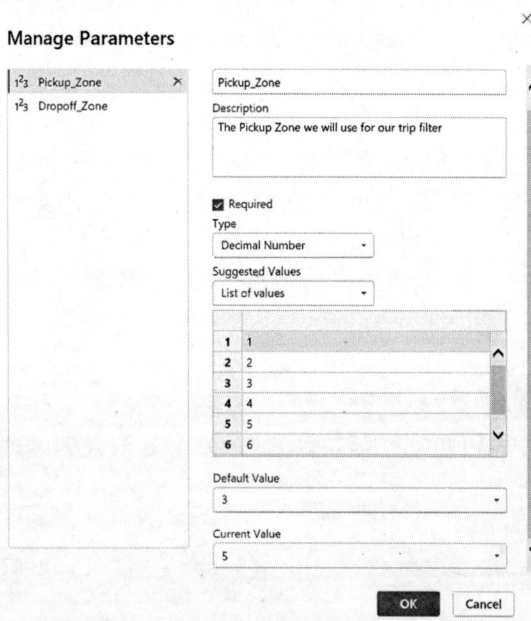

Figure 13.5: Creating a list of values for a parameter

By selecting a list of values, we are now prompted to add values manually into our list. We can add as many as required. Once we have our list set, we can select our default value and update our current value from the list. This is a fantastic solution when you have a small list of values that need to be managed. This also works well if you have a list that will not change. Remember, if you need to add new values to your parameter list, you will need to update it within the Power Query editor. This might not be idea for a list that is constantly being updated.

In a situation where you want to provide dynamic values, we can leverage an existing list of values within Power Query. To achieve, this, we need to do a little preparation to make this a reality. In our scenario, we want to create a list of taxi zones from our **`taxi_zone_lookup`** query. We will simply right click on our **`taxi_zone_lookup`** query and select reference. Once replicated, update the query name to **`zone_list`**. Next, we will select the **`LocationID`** column, go to the **Transform** ribbon, and select **Convert to list**:

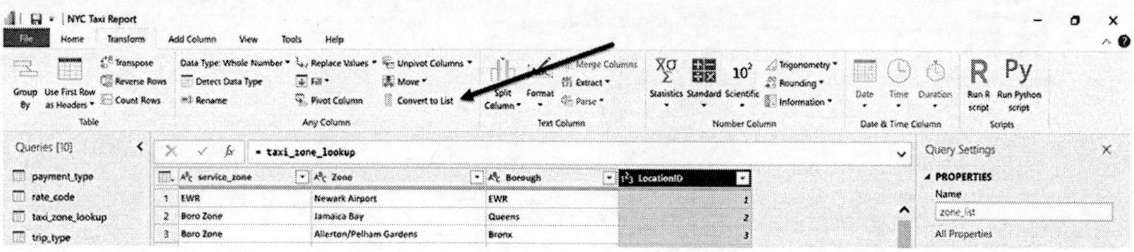

Figure 13.6: *Transforming a column to a list*

This will take the column and convert it into a list of values. It is no longer considered a table but rather just a list of zones. It is just as easy to achieve this outcome in the advanced editor. In fact, it might be the record for the shortest and easiest because we do not need any functions to achieve our desired outcome:

```
let
  Source = taxi_zone_lookup[LocationID]
in
  Source
```

Because we are referencing an existing query, we can just specify the column we want to use wrapped in square brackets. With out list setup, it is time to update our parameter. We will change the **Suggested Values** to use a **Query**. Next, we must specify our query. We will use **`zone_list`** as it is the only query that returns a list of values. Lastly, we will need to enter our current value before we continue, as shown in the following figure:

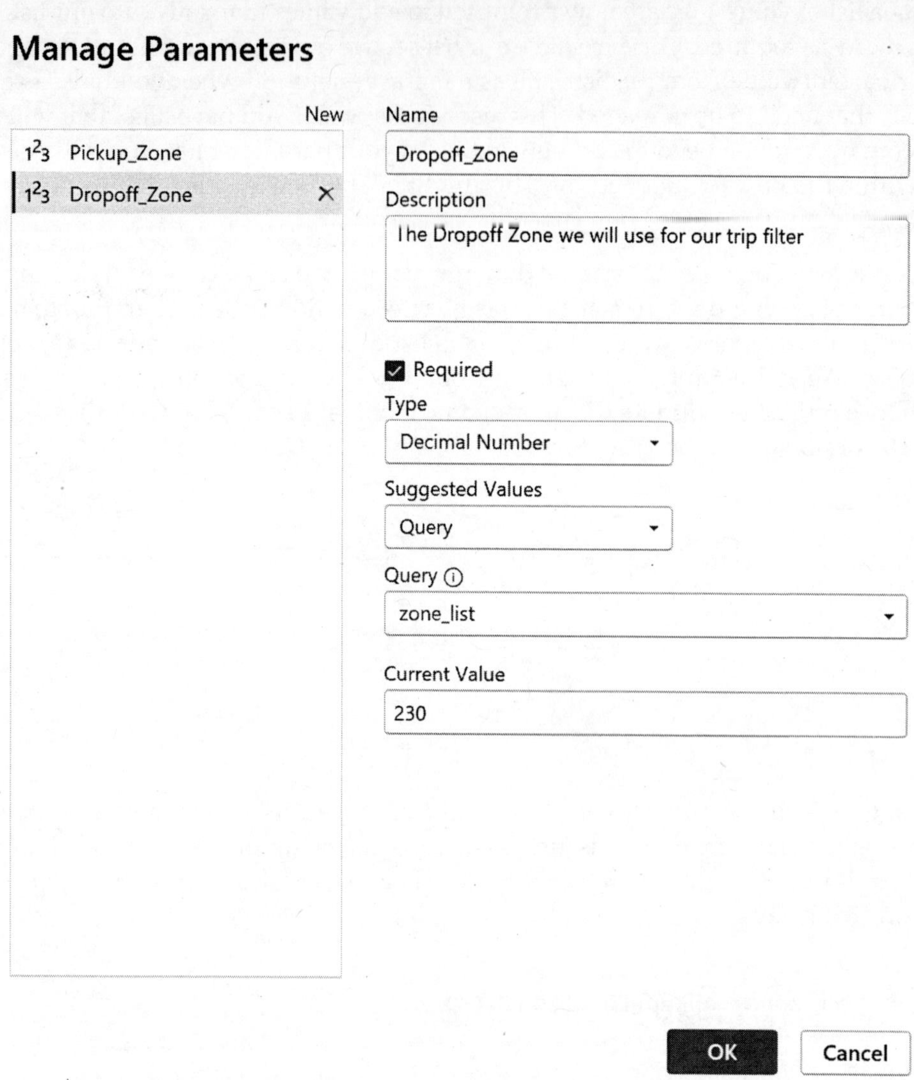

Figure 13.7: Connecting an existing query to a list of values for a parameter

Unlike the list of values, you will note that we cannot set a default value. This is simply because we do not have control over what the query is returning. Because we are providing a dynamic list of values, our default value might disappear. The ability to select a default value is an intentional omission and avoids any conflict of missing values.

Another item to note is that you cannot select your current value from a dropdown list in the manage parameters window. At the time of the writing of this book, the option to select the current value from this view was not available. However, if you select the **Edit Parameters** option from the dropdown in *Figure 13.1*, you can select your current value from the list of query values. It is not clear from Microsoft why this is not available in the manage parameters window, but it is easy to work around it by editing the value in the correct context.

Parameters and incremental refresh

There are several use cases for parameters in Power Query. However, one of the key use cases revolves around incremental refresh and hybrid tables with Power BI. Before digging in, it is important to note that this is a feature that is only available for Power BI when it is paired with the Power BI service. It is a feature that helps reduce the refresh time on large queries using import mode containing transactional data. Simply put, instead of refreshing the last ten years of data, you only refresh a portion of that query that is likely to change. You can set these rules once you load your queries into Power BI. This feature does not work with any queries using DirectQuery mode.

The reason we mention this topic is because it relies heavily on parameters to function properly. There are a few mistakes that can be made along the way that will result in your query not functioning properly. If you have a query that uses an integer date format, this could become increasingly difficult. This section will help you set up your incremental refresh while avoiding some of the common pitfalls along the way.

The first step with incremental refresh is that you need to create two parameters with specific names. You must create a **`RangeStart`** and **`RangeEnd`** parameters for incremental refresh to function properly. Note the use of camel case and lack of spacing in the name. People believe they can use any name for their parameter, but this is not the case. Microsoft's documentation does not always clearly explain that these names are critical, but the names matter.

Next, when you create your parameter, you must use a date/time data type. This plays a role in the filtering of data during the refresh. Power BI requires this data type for the parameter, so you must create it this way. When completed, your parameters should look something like this:

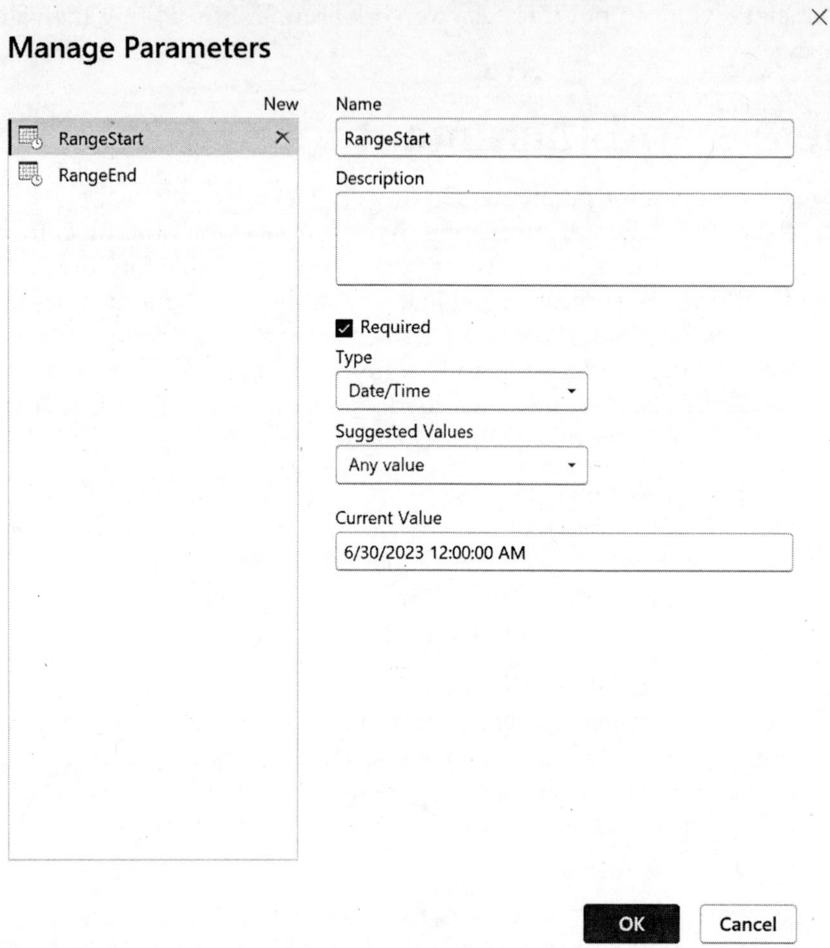

Figure 13.8: *Setting up the RangeStart and RangeEnd parameters for incremental refresh*

One thing that most people forget is that incremental refresh will only take place in the Power BI service. They think they need to set the range to be inclusive of the range they are trying to bring into the model. This is not the case. Instead, bring in the minimal amount of data you need to build out your model when you are creating these parameters. This will prevent you from working with an unwieldy data model within Power BI desktop. This is especially important if you have a machine that does not have the most robust resources to manage this model.

Now that you have your parameters created, you can set your filters. We will apply these parameters to the **`tpep_pickup_datetime`** column for our **`trip_data_yellow`** query. Clicking on the dropdown on the right-hand side of the column header, we will go to **Date/time Filters** and select **Between**. We will change our filters to leverage parameters and specify both our **`RangeStart`** and **`RangeEnd`** parameters:

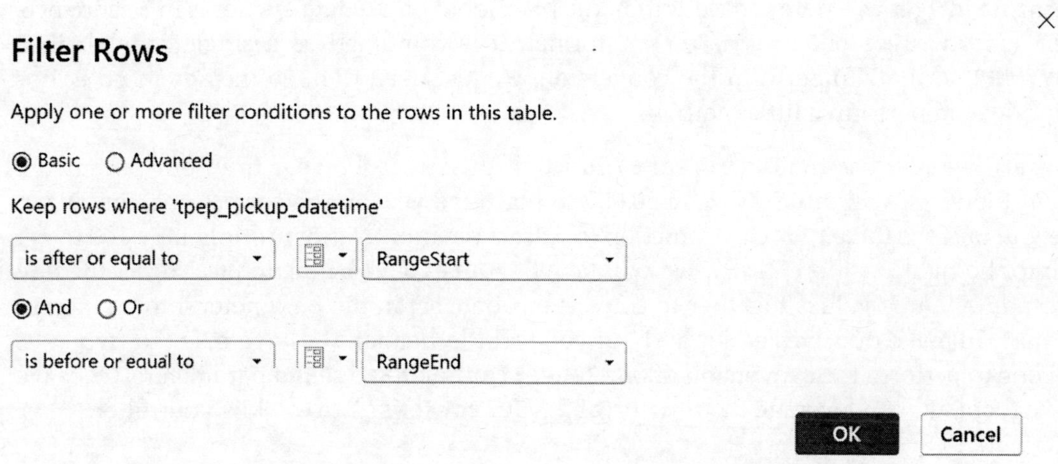

Figure 13.9: Applying our incremental refresh parameters as filters

We can achieve the same output within the advanced editor. Using the **`Table.SelectRows()`** function, we can set our filter on the **`tpep_pickup_datetime`** column so we can finish setting up our incremental refresh:

```
let
  Source = Sql.Database("localhost", "NYC_Taxi"),
  TripData = Source{[Schema = "dbo", Item = "trip_data_yellow"]}[Data],
  IncrementalFilter = Table.SelectRows(TripData,
    each [tpep_pickup_datetime] >= RangeStart and [tpep_pickup_datetime] <=
RangeEnd
  )
in
  IncrementalFilter
```

At this point, you will need to apply the changes to your query and complete the rest of the setup within Power BI by right clicking on the query, selecting incremental refresh, and configuring it to meet your use case.

Now, all of this seems simple until you run into a situation where you need to use incremental refresh, but your query is leveraging dates as integers. If you remember from *Chapter 6, Managing Data Types*, you might encounter queries where the date is specified in an integer format for efficiency purposes. If we must use a date/time parameter, there we will not be able to use it to filter the column due to a data type mismatch. How can incremental refresh be setup with an integer column? We can still setup our incremental refresh, but we must rely upon what we learned in *Chapter 7, Transforming Columns*, to manipulate our parameters.

Using an integer as a date is based upon the placement of the date elements in a sequence. Instead of writing out in a **M/D/YYYY** format, it is combined as a single number in a **YYYYMMDD** format. To perform the conversion, we just need to open the advanced editor window and perform a little math.

To start, we will use the **Date.Year()** function to extract the year from our parameter. From there, we will multiply it by 10,000 to place the year in the correct position. Next, we will take the **Date.Month()** function to extract the month and multiply it by 100 to get it into the right position. Lastly, we will take the **Date.Day()** function to extract the day and add all three values together to convert our date set in the parameter into an integer format. To make our lives easier and our code a little cleaner, we have inserted two lines of code to perform the conversion of our **RangeStart** and **RangeEnd** parameters. Once we have them, we can leverage them with **Table.SelectRows()** to establish our filter:

```
let
  Source = Sql.Database("localhost", "NYC_Taxi"),
  TripData = Source{[Schema = "dbo", Item = "trip_data_yellow"]}[Data],
  FilterStart = (Date.Year(RangeStart) * 10000)
    + (Date.Month(RangeStart) * 100)
    + Date.Day(RangeStart),
  FilterEnd = (Date.Year(RangeEnd) * 10000)
    + (Date.Month(RangeEnd) * 100)
    + Date.Day(RangeEnd),
  IncrementalFilter = Table.SelectRows(TripData,
    each [tpep_pickup_datetime] >= FilterStart
    and [tpep_pickup_datetime] <= FilterEnd
  )
in
  IncrementalFilter
```

Reviewing the preceding code, you can see that we combine standard mathematical functions with our date transformation functions to achieve our desired outcome with an incremental refresh. At this point, you might be wondering why we did not just update the column to become a date/time column instead. Simply put, that would break our query folding, which is a key part of a successful incremental refresh. Even though we are performing transformations within Power Query, we have not adjusted how the native query performs by adding our parameters this way. Besides, we would need to perform just as complicated of a transformation to achieve our outcome when converting our integers into a date/time column. In short, this is the most efficient way to achieve our outcome with integer dates.

As we mentioned at the beginning of this section, this only applies to readers who are using Power BI with the intent to publish their models into the Power BI service. It is not a requirement for every scenario but might make the management of your model long-term easier based on your solution requirements.

Updating parameters

Up to this point, we have focused on the process of creating parameters within the Power Query editor with the hopes of simplifying the management of our queries long term. Now that we have them in place, how do we edit our parameters? We already learned how to edit parameters within the Power Query editor. However, what if we want to share our hard work with someone who needs to update these parameters and is unfamiliar with Power Query? They might not be as technical as you are and be nervous about opening the Power Query editor. While you could suggest they read this book, so they are comfortable with the idea of making changes in the Power Query editor, there is an easier way.

For the Power BI desktop, we can edit our parameters without opening Power Query. In Power BI, we can go to the **Transform Query** dropdown and select **Edit Parameters**:

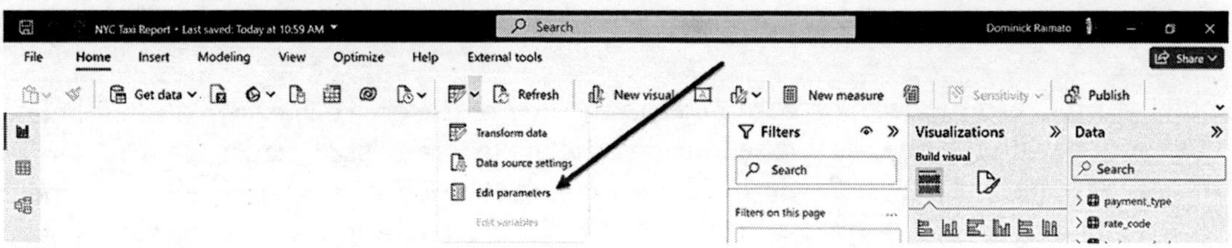

Figure 13.10: Updating parameters inside of Power BI

This will open a window that lists each parameter we have available to us. From there, we can update our parameters or hover over the tool tip to learn more about each parameter:

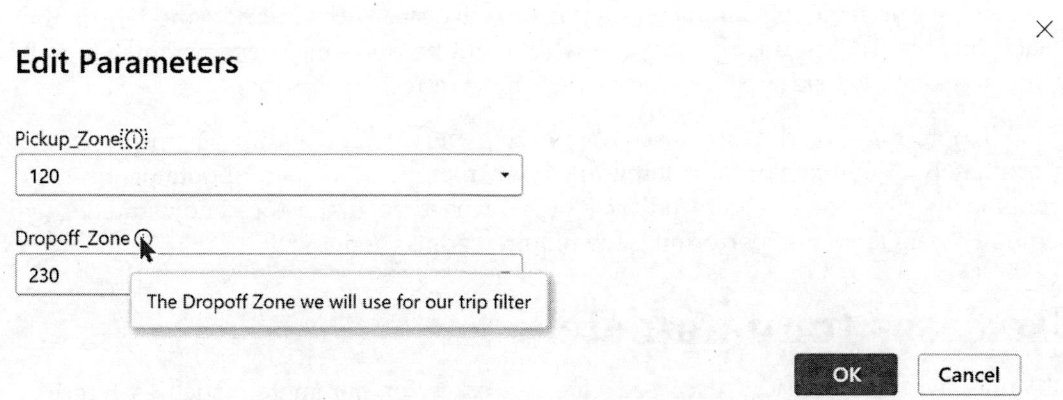

Figure 13.11: Updating our parameters for our queries

We can also update our parameters for our data model within the Power BI service. Go to your workspace, click on the three dots next to your data model and select **Settings**. From there, expand the **Parameters** menu:

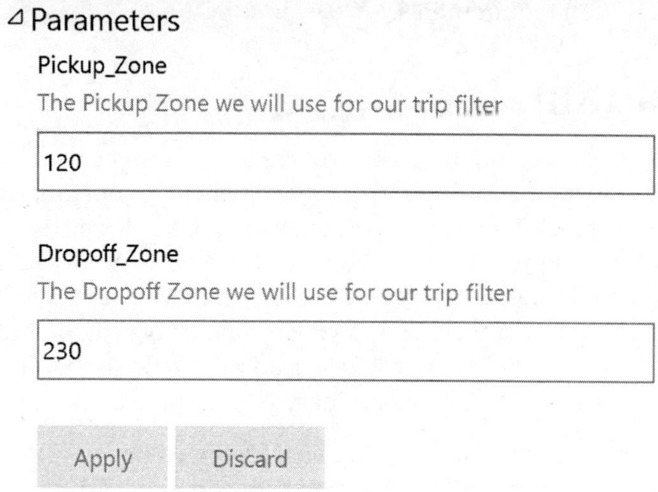

Figure 13.12: *Updating parameters inside the Power BI service*

While the process of updating a parameter in the Power BI service is easy, you will note an inherent flaw in the process. We set our parameters to use a list of values from a query, but that list is not present in *Figure 13.12*. This is huge drawback to the process of using lists with parameters and should be a consideration when creating them. If your end goal is to update your parameters within the Power BI service, it might be more important to provide documentation and context either as part of the parameter description or provide a guide to assist users. This will help avoid confusion with users who might be adjusting these parameters in the future.

Once you have updated the parameters, a refresh will occur with your data model and the affected queries. This means that anyone who might be updating these parameters will require access to the data source so the model can be refreshed.

You will note that we did not discuss updating parameters within Microsoft Excel. Unfortunately, at the time of publishing this book, there is no way to update parameters without using the Power Query editor. You will need to make these adjustments by opening Power Query and performing the required adjustments.

Use cases for parameters

Until now, we have already discussed core use cases for parameters such as filtering queries and enabling incremental refresh. However, our parameters do much more for us than simply filter our data. Properly leveraged, Power Query can transform how we manage our reports and simplify our lives.

The most common challenge people encounter is swapping data sources. This could be because the data source location has changed or simply because they want to switch between a production and a development environment. If you have a data model using several queries, and each one must be updated, you will spend a lot of time making changes when you want to switch between your development and production sources. Instead, it is recommended that you swap out things like your database name with a parameter so it can be easily adjusted. As noted below, we updated the database parameter of the **`Sql.Database()`** function to use a parameter instead:

```
let
  Source = Sql.Database("localhost", Taxi_DB),
  TripData = Source{[Schema = "dbo", Item = "trip_data_yellow"]}[Data],
  ZoneFilter = Table.SelectRows(
    TripData,
    each [PULocationID] = Pickup_Zone
    and [DOLocationID] = Dropoff_Zone
  )
in
  ZoneFilter
```

With this change, we can now swap between my development and production databases with a quick update of our parameters. This means we can quickly test database changes in a production environment and validate that there are no issues before the database administrator pushes them into the production database. It requires a little effort upfront, but it will pay dividends in time savings in the future.

However, you might not be comfortable with writing an entire query from scratch. And the process of updating queries is akin to performing double work. Power Query has this covered for you, but it requires you to turn on a setting. To start, go to the **File** tab, navigate to **Options and settings**, and select **Options**. From there, go to the **Power Query Editor** options under the **Global** section and check **Always allow parameterization in data source and transformation dialogues**:

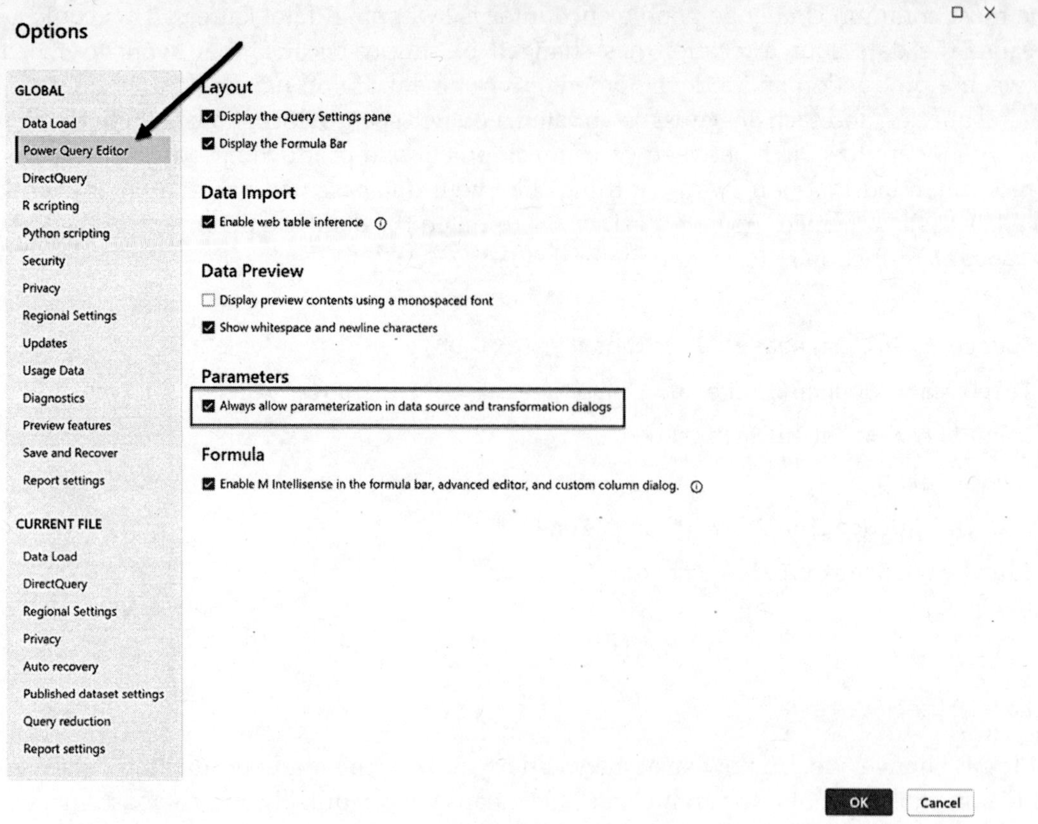

Figure 13.13: Enabling parameterization for data source and transformation dialogues

This feature now allows you to select parameters as you setup your data sources. For example, if we create a new connection to our taxi data, we will select **SQL Server database** and specify our parameter in the database field:

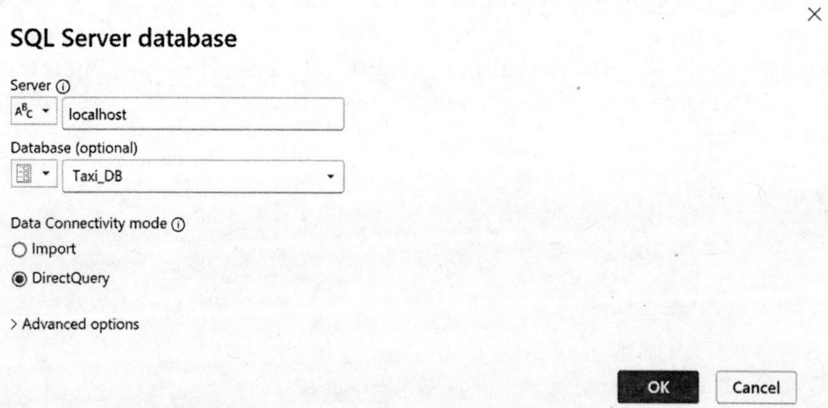

Figure 13.14: Using a parameter for the database field for a new connection

With a little foresight, you can simplify how you connect to all your data sources. Another wonderful use case is if you have an API key that is being used for a web or OData connection. Taking a few moments to create a parameter for your key and base endpoint URL will eliminate the need to repeatedly copy and paste information into your connection window. It is a minor change, but it provides a valuable impact when trying to simplify the management of your queries.

One last consideration for the use of parameters is the ability to leverage it as a variable in your transformations. For example, maybe you have a query that uses paging, or you have a constant value that you want to use in your column transformations. When using a parameter, it helps others who might review your code to understand the purpose of the value and why it is in place. This eliminates confusion and simplifies the code review process. While you can add remarks to the code to provide an explanation, sometimes seeing the parameter in context helps others to quickly understand the purpose of the value without having to look for your remarks.

Conclusion

In this chapter, we explored parameters and how they can be applied to our queries to make life easier. We first took a moment to understand what parameters meant in the context of Power Query. Next, we went through the process of creating parameters that could be updated manually or from an existing list or query. We also went through the process of using parameters to enable incremental refresh within Power BI. Lastly, we went over how to update parameters outside of Power Query and highlighted some use cases where they might serve as a valuable addition to your model.

In the next chapter, we will learn how to take our transformations to the next level by encapsulating them inside a function in Power Query.

CHAPTER 14
Functions

Introduction

In this chapter, we will explore the creation and utilization of functions inside the Power Query editor. We will first define what functions are in Power Query and go through the process of creating them. Next, we will invoke our functions as a custom column in an existing query. After understanding how to create and invoke functions, we will work through three use cases where you can apply them to manage repeatable transformations. Lastly, we will explore some use cases for applying functions with your existing queries.

Structure

The chapter covers the following topics:

- Understanding functions in Power Query
- Creating a function from a query
- Adding parameters to functions
- Creating a custom column from a function
- Convert time zones with a function
- Perform lookups with a function

- Create a date table with a function
- Use cases for functions

Objectives

By the end of this chapter, you will understand how to create functions within the Power Query editor and how to invoke them in your model. This will allow you to quickly redeploy repeatable and complex transformations with only a few clicks.

Understanding functions in Power Query

Functions can be a confusing topic within the Power Query editor. We use functions to complete our transformations. In fact, we have listed out many functions throughout this entire book that you can leverage to achieve your desired outcomes. Functions take a block of code that performs a specific task or transformation as the output that can reused at scale.

A fitting example of a function that simplifies our lives is the **`Date.Year()`** transformation we use in Power Query. This function allows us to pass a date as a parameter, and it returns the year associated with the date. We do not have to use this function as we could use other transformations like return text after delimiter and achieve the same result. However, the **`Date.Year()`** function is far simpler as it requires fewer parameters to achieve the same result. In addition, the name of the function itself tells us what transformation is being applied, which also makes our life easier.

Functions have a way of simplifying complex challenges and removing any barriers. And Power Query allows us to create these functions so we can deploy them within our own queries. In fact, sometimes, we cannot avoid creating our own custom functions to achieve our desired result.

When creating functions in Power Query, there are three key elements that we must consider. The first consideration is what the desired outcome is from our query. This is the base of our function and drives the other two elements. We must determine where we are heading so we can get there in the most efficient route.

The second element we must consider are the parameters we must pass to achieve our desired result. Not every function will require parameters. However, most will require at least one value to be shared in this manner. It is important to consider the parameters you are passing, and the data type required to ensure the proper result is passed back as the output. We only want to pass what is necessary to get the results we need.

The last element is the transformations we will be applying. We want to make sure our transformations are as efficient as possible. Since we will be running the function on each individual row of our queries, the simpler we can make the transformation, the better. We also want to limit the amount of data we need to return as it feeds to the output to prevent any bloat within our queries.

Functions are one of the features within the Power Query editor that require you to use the advanced editor window. While we will use the graphical interface to make some of our transformations easier, we will still require the advanced editor to get the most out of our functions. You will be leaning heavily on previous chapters to ensure transformations are returned as desired, so do not be afraid to reference them if you have questions about some of the code we are writing.

And remember, everyone must start somewhere. Do not get frustrated if your outputs are not as planned. This is a process, but if you follow along with this chapter, you will start to feel more comfortable with the creation of functions.

Creating a function from a query

Creating a function from a query is not a complicated process and can be completed with both the graphical interface and the advanced editor. In fact, it is recommended that you start with an existing query to make your experience with functions easier. This does not always work out for every situation, but sometimes it makes life easier. To get started, we are going to create a basic **Hello World** function we can leverage within Power Query. Go to the **New Source** dropdown, select **Blank Query**, and rename the query to `Hello_World`. Next, open the advanced editor and update the code to match this block of code:

```
let
  Source = "Hello World"
in
  Source
```

Now that we have a query in place, we want to convert it into a function. We can right-click on our `Hello_World` query and select **Create Function** to build a function of our query:

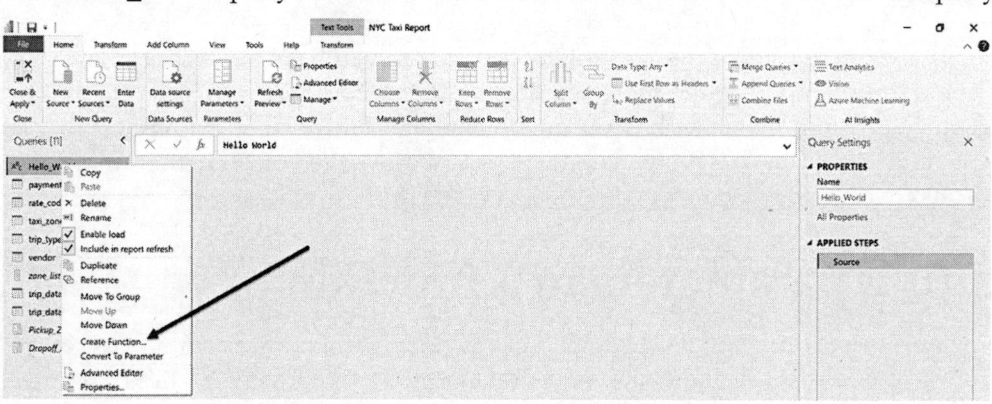

Figure 14.1: Creating a function from a query

You will then be prompted to provide a name for your query. Everyone has options on naming conventions, but the best practice is to keep it consistent. Since we are writing a function, we will simply add **fx_** as a prefix to the current query's name and click **OK**. This will create the function and group it in the queries pane. This will help you keep your functions and their paired queries organized for easy access. You will also note that in place of data, we now have an **Invoke** button that we can click, as shown:

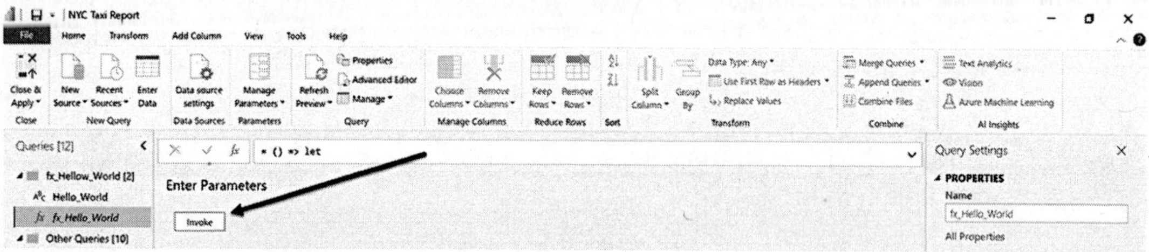

Figure 14.2: Inspecting a custom function inside of Power Query

The invoke button runs the function and returns the output. This often does not provide much value for our model, but it is helpful when you are testing your queries. If you click Invoke, it will create a new query titled **Invoked Function**, which matches **Hello_World** as we have not applied any transformations at this point.

If we want to create our function with the advanced editor, we can do so with a few lines of code. The first thing we want to do is reference our existing query with **Source = Hello_World**. Then, we will insert **() =>** on the first line of our code to signal that his query will become a function. Using a blank query, we can add this code to create **fx_Hello_World**:

```
() =>
  let
    Source = Hello_World
  in
    Source
```

While not as simple as the graphical interface solution, you have more control over your query, and this method is often preferred. It is up to you to consider which option is best based on your comfort level with the M query language. However, it is advisable that you become more comfortable with the language so you can write your functions more easily with your code.

Adding parameters to a function

Parameters are a critical part of functions. Since transformations are a common use case for functions, you need to specify what is to be transformed as a parameter. These parameters are different than the ones we created in *Chapter 13, Parameters*. Instead, we will identify the parameters we need for our function inside the advanced editor. This will allow us to not only prompt for our parameters but also use them as variables within our function.

We will start with a basic function to manage the division. While we can use an existing division function inside of the Power Query editor, we are going to create a function that not only performs division but also returns a numeric value if the denominator is zero. To get started, we will go to New Source, select blank query, and rename our query fx_Division_0. Next, we will open the advanced editor and add **() =>** to convert it into a function. At this point, our code should look like this:

```
() =>
  let
    Source = ""
  in
    Source
```

Next, we will specify our parameters between the parenthesis we added in the first row of our code. We are going to specify a **numerator** and **denominator** parameter. To achieve this, we will add our parameter name, then the word as followed by the data type required. This means we will need to update our code as follows:

```
(numerator as number, denominator as number) =>
  let
    Source = ""
  in
    Source
```

Now that we have established our parameters, we can add our logic. We will use a conditional statement to verify that our denominator is not zero. If it is not zero, we will divide our numerator by the denominator as normal. If the denominator is zero, we will return a zero. This means we will enact the following changes to our code:

```
(numerator as number, denominator as number) =>
  let
    Source = if denominator <> 0 then numerator / denominator else 0
  in
    Source
```

Once we have closed out the advanced editor, we can add values to our parameters and invoke the function to test it. If you enter **10** for the numerator and **5** for the denominator, your output will be **2**. If you enter **10** for the numerator but **0** for the denominator, your output will be **0**.

If we wanted to make this slick, we could add one last parameter to help manage our output. We added a zero as our output for our division because the built-in function brings back a value that might not be as useful. However, we might want to specify the value we want to bring back. This might be the numerator, it might be a zero, or it might be a null. We will add one last parameter called error value, and it will be returned as a number. This will allow us to specify the value we want to return in the event of an error. We will make this function optional by adding that designation with our parameter and update the else statement in the code:

```
(numerator as number, denominator as number, optional ifError as number) =>
  let
    Source = if denominator <> 0 then numerator / denominator else ifError
  in
    Source
```

With this change, we can specify the value if there is a zero in the denominator or leave it blank to return a null. This will come in handy when we go to apply our function as a new column in the next section.

Creating a custom column from a function

Now that we have created our function, it is time to leverage with an existing query. If you remember back in *Chapter 9, Creating New Columns,* we held off on creating two special types of columns. The first was an index column which we addressed in *Chapter 12, Indexing*. The second was adding a column with the invoke custom function feature. The time has come to finally create our column using that function. We have a basic table with two columns in it to serve as our numerator and denominator. We will apply our custom function by going to the **Add Column** ribbon and selecting the **Invoke Custom Function**:

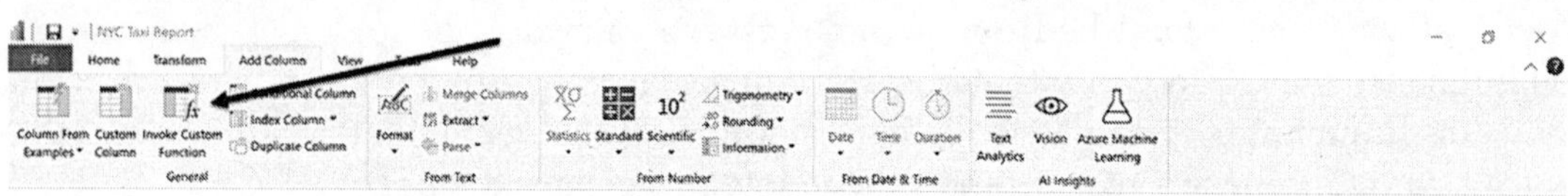

Figure 14.3: Adding a column using the invoke custom function feature

A new window will appear, and you will be prompted to provide information to assist with the next steps. First, the window asks for the **New Column Name**. If you do not specify the name, it will use the function name as the default name. Next, you will be asked to specify the **Function Query** you have created. For our scenario, we will specify **`fx_Division_0`**. Next, the parameters for our function will appear. We have the option to specify either a value or column for each of the parameters. We will use **`Column1`** for the numerator and **`Column2`** for the denominator. For now, we want the value to be blank in the column if the denominator is zero, so we will set the field to a decimal number and leave it blank since it is optional. The result is a window that should look like the following figure when completed:

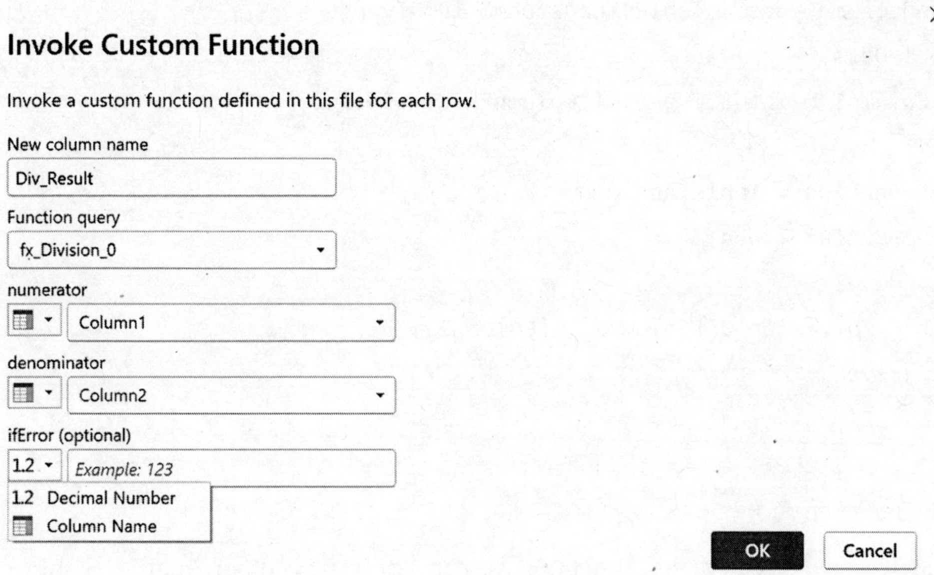

Figure 14.4: *Configuring the parameters for our custom function*

With our function details specified, we can click **OK** to invoke it on each row of our query. The function will go row by row of our query and take the value specified in **`Column2`**, confirming it is not a zero. If it is not zero, it will divide **`Column1`** by **`Column2`**. If it is a zero, it will return **`null`**. This is the result of the **`fx_Division_0`** function:

	1²3 Column1	1²3 Column2	ABC 123 Div_Result
1	10	5	2
2	10	0	null
3	10	2	5
4	25	5	5

Figure 14.5: *Results of our custom function*

If we wanted to invoke this function inside the advanced editor, we can reference it inside of the **`Table.AddColumn()`** function. We will call our custom function just like any other function inside of Power Query. In fact, our parameters will show as tool tips as any other function would. We will simply call the function, specify the parameters, and even identify the data type for the new column. However, this time we will specify zero as the result if we encounter a zero in the denominator, as shown:

```
let
  Source = Excel.Workbook(File.Contents("C:\data\SampleData.xlsx"), null,
true),
  SampleData = Source{[Item = "SampleData", Kind = "Table"]}[Data],
```

```
  ChangedColumnTypes = Table.TransformColumnTypes(
    SampleData,
    {{"Column1", Int64.Type}, {"Column2", Int64.Type}}
  ),
  DivideFunction = Table.AddColumn(
    ChangedColumnTypes,
    "Div_Result",
    each fx_Division_0([Column1], [Column2], 0),
    Int64.Type
  )
in
  DivideFunction
```

Now that we have created this function, we can apply it to other queries within our taxicab data model. We could use this function to calculate total revenue per mile without having to recreate the logic in a custom column. While this function is quite basic, it is the foundation of how we implement them. The next step is to start building out complex transformations within our functions to make our lives easier.

Convert time zones with a function

A common challenge when working with data is the translation of timestamps across time zones. While Power Query has tools to help with managing time zones, it is based on the device's local time zone. There are situations where you might want to load time stamps in multiple time zones into your model, but the translation is complicated. We must consider when daylight savings time is applied. Working off the assumption that our timestamp is set in **Universal Coordinated Time** (**UTC**), we can create a function that will manage any time zone translation we need to apply to our timestamps.

To accomplish this translation, we will need to apply a few new functions for Power Query to achieve our goal. The first function we will need is **`DateTime.AddZone()`** to add the logic affirming our timestamp is set in UTC time zone:

`DateTime.AddZone()`	
Parameter	**Description**
`DateTime`	A properly formatted timestamp value
`TimezoneHours`	Number of hours to adjust for time zone
`TimezoneMinutes`	Optional number of minutes to adjust for time zone

Table 14.1: *Table of the DateTime.AddZone() parameters*

For our timestamp, we will need to set the time zone to zero hours and zero minutes for UTC. Once we have set the origin, we must provide a translation to another time zone. We will use **`DateTimeZone.SwitchZone()`** to translate the time zone. Like **`DateTime.AddZone()`**, we must set the offset between UTC and our desired time zone:

DateTimeZone.SwitchZone()	
Parameter	**Description**
`DateTimeZone`	A properly formatted timestamp value with time zone included
`TimezoneHours`	Number of hours to adjust for time zone
`TimezoneMinutes`	Optional number of minutes to adjust for time zone

Table 14.2: *Table of the DateTimeZone.SwitchZone() parameters*

Lastly, we will need to remove the time zone information. This is so our formatting is clean and represents well on the reporting canvas when we apply our queries. We will remove our time zone information with the **`DateTimeZone.RemoveZone()`** function to clean up our timestamp:

DateTimeZone.RemoveZone()	
Parameter	**Description**
`DateTimeZone`	A properly formatted timestamp value with time zone included

Table 14.3: *Table of the DateTimeZone.RemoveZone() parameters*

Using these functions, we can create a new function that has a timestamp and offset parameter to perform the translation. While we can combine the entire translation into a single step. However, we are going to use multiple steps for the moment to make it easier to understand. The base code for our translation is as follows:

```
(TimeStamp as datetime, TimeZoneOffset as number) =>
  let
    AddUTC = DateTime.AddZone(TimeStamp, 0, 0),
    OffsetZone = DateTimeZone.SwitchZone(AddUTC, TimeZoneOffset, 0),
    CleanUpTimestamp = DateTimeZone.RemoveZone(OffsetZone)
  in
    CleanUpTimestamp
```

While this works, we need to consider how we will navigate daylight savings time. Now, this logic is not the same across the entire world. However, the process for determining the translation is similar. In the United States, we start to observe daylight savings time on the second Sunday in March, and it ends on the first Sunday in November. While we could create a calendar table with this data, we can get to this date with the **`Date.EndOfWeek()`** function to help establish the first Sunday of each month:

Date.EndOfWeek()	
Parameter	**Description**
`DateTime`	A properly formatted date.
`FirstDayOfWeek`	Optional parameter to establish the first day of the week with the `Day` function.

***Table 14.4:** Table of the Date.EndOfWeek() parameters*

Using the first of March and November, we can identify the first Sunday of these months. But to get the second Sunday of March, we will need to use **`Date.AddWeeks()`** to get us there:

Date.AddWeeks()	
Parameter	**Description**
`DateTime`	A properly formatted date.
`NumberOfWeeks`	Number of weeks we want to add to our existing date.

***Table 14.5:** Table of the Date.AddWeeks() parameters*

Now that we have our translation, we need to add one last parameter to manage our translation. Some regions do not observe daylight savings time. Therefore, we want to add a parameter to confirm that it is being observed. With that in mind, we will update our code accordingly:

```
(TimeStamp as datetime, TimeZoneOffset as number, ObserveDST as logical) =>
  let
    TimeStampYear = Date.Year(TimeStamp),
    AddUTC = DateTime.AddZone(TimeStamp, 0, 0),
    OffsetZone =
      if DateTime.Date(TimeStamp)
        >= Date.AddWeeks(Date.EndOfWeek(#date(TimeStampYear, 3, 1), Day.
Monday), 1)
          and DateTime.Date(TimeStamp)
        <= Date.EndOfWeek(#date(TimeStampYear, 11, 1), Day.Monday) and Ob-
serveDST = true
      then
        DateTimeZone.SwitchZone(AddUTC, TimeZoneOffset + 1, 0)
      else
        DateTimeZone.SwitchZone(AddUTC, TimeZoneOffset, 0),
    CleanUpTimestamp = DateTimeZone.RemoveZone(OffsetZone)
```

```
in
    CleanUpTimestamp
```

You will note that if the date falls within daylight savings time and it is observed, we make an adjustment to the time zone offset by adding one hour. In addition to a few small tweaks, you can accommodate time zones that change on a day of the week that is not on a Sunday.

The last thing to note with this solution is what about time zones that are not a perfect hour offset. You will note that we did not create a parameter for a minute offset. If you are looking to create an offset from UTC to India Standard Time, you can use 5.5 as your hour offset and still accomplish the correct translation. This avoids unnecessary additional parameters and keeps your function efficient.

Looking at this code, the process to perform these translations is complicated. By creating the function, we can reuse it for any timestamp we encounter in our model. It is not worth the effort if you only need to represent your timestamp in a single time zone. At that point, you should just use the built-in features with Power Query to accomplish this task. But if you are in a situation where you need to translate into multiple time zones for a single query for display purposes, this function might be the right option to meet that requirement.

Perform lookups with a function

If you are an experienced user of Microsoft Excel, you are likely familiar with **`VLOOKUP()`**. This popular function allows you to look up data in another area of your spreadsheet and return it. With Power Pivot inside of Microsoft Excel and Power BI, we do not need **`VLOOKUP()`** because we can create a star schema model and build relationships between tables. However, we occasionally run into a scenario where we need to perform a lookup.

A scenario that you might encounter is when you want to link a person to an assigned team. Normally, we would just assign the team to a person in a dimension table. While this works, it does not accommodate the movement between teams over time. Luckily, we have recorded team movements in another query. We just need a function that will match up the person and the transaction date with the current team they are on.

At this point, we have already connected to our transaction query and our team assignment query. To prepare for our function, we have already referenced the **`Team_Assignment`** query and renamed it as **`fx_Team_Assignment`**:

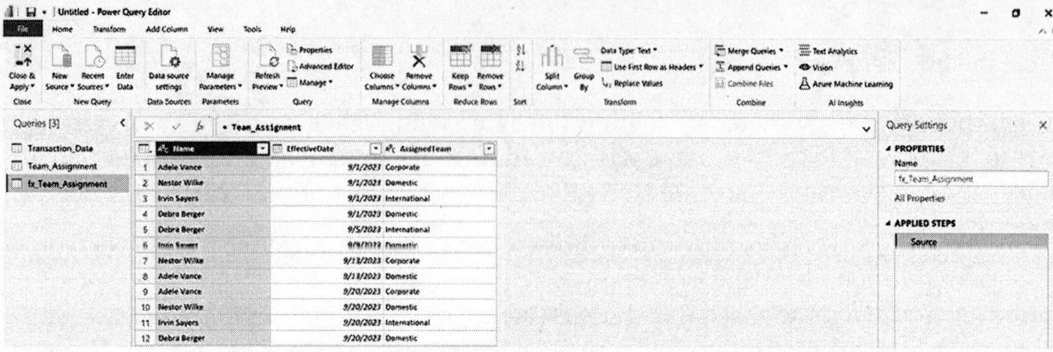

***Figure 14.6:** Team assignment table inside of Power Query*

You will note that every team assignment has a person's name, their assigned team, and an effective date for joining a team. Paired with our existing transaction records, we can easily identify the team by finding the most recent effective date assigned to a person before the transaction date. To start preparing our function, we will use the graphical interface to prepare our transformations. We will start by filtering on an individual followed by a date filter that is on or before a specified date. We will manually select these values for now and update our code later:

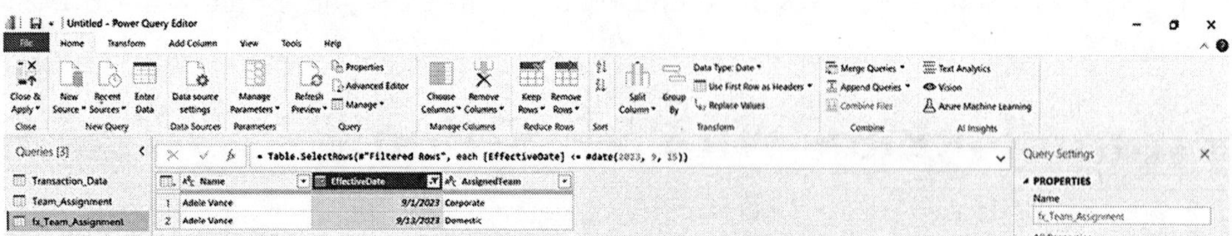

***Figure 14.7:** Filtering team assignments by name and date*

Now that we have our data filtered, we need to sort our effective date from newest to oldest. This will ensure that the most recent date is in the first row. Then we will keep our first row which contains the correct team assignment:

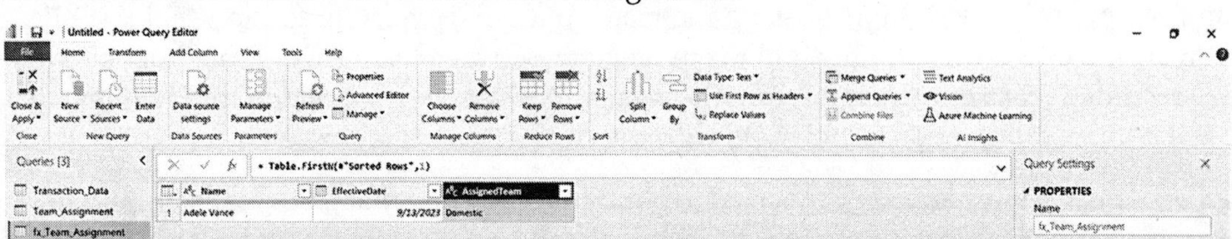

***Figure 14.8:** Sorting rows and keeping the first row for the team assignment*

Now that we have our logic applied, it is time to open the advanced editor. We will need to create two parameters to assist with the filtering. The first parameter, **`PersonName`**, we will use to filter the team member on the **`Team_Assignment`** query. Next, we will create a parameter called **`TransactionDate`** which will filter our query on the date. Once we have our parameters in place, we just need to update our function to use them for filtering. We also will add logic to only return the team assignment, as shown:

```
(PersonName as text, TransactionDate as date) =>
  let
    Source = Team_Assignment,
    FilterPerson = Table.SelectRows(Source, each ([Name] = PersonName)),
    FilterDate = Table.SelectRows(FilterPerson, each [EffectiveDate] <=
TransactionDate),
    SortDates = Table.Sort(FilterDate, {{"EffectiveDate", Order.Descend-
ing}}),
    KeepFirstRow = Table.FirstN(SortDates, 1)
  in
    KeepFirstRow{0}[AssignedTeam]
```

Now that we have our function, it is time to apply it to our transactions. We can create a custom column from our function, and logic will take care of the rest. We will want to validate our data and make sure it is correct, but once verified will scale effectively. As new team assignments are made, the logic of the function will adjust accordingly. You can achieve the same outcome with DAX in Microsoft Excel and Power BI, but transformations like this best work within Power Query if you are not able to apply them in the data layer.

Create a date table with a function

When working with data in Microsoft Excel or Power BI, it is always ideal to have a date table as a dimension. The best practice is to create this dimension in the data layer and leverage it within your model. However, you might not have a date table available from your source. As a result, you must manufacture this table for your use.

While date tables seem to be straight forward, they can become complex depending on some of the rules that might take place. The most common challenge we see is when organizations have a fiscal year that does not align with the calendar year. You might want to augment your dimensional data with things such as holidays or trading versus non-trading days. This logic can add complexity, which could be time-consuming to replicate. However, a well-designed function can allow you to quickly re-deploy a date table repeatedly to simplify this process.

To start this process, we will need to go to **New Source** and create a **Blank Query**. We have renamed the query as **`fx_Generate_DateTable`** so it is easy to identify. Next, we need to generate a list of dates. To accomplish this, we will need to leverage **`List.Dates()`** to establish this list:

`List.Dates()`	
Parameter	**Description**
`Start`	A properly formatted date to start the series.
`Count`	Number of occurrences for the series.
`Step`	Duration of the increments. If daily, use `#duration(1, 0, 0, 0)`

Table 14.6: *Table of the List.Datess() parameters*

To start, we will simply list all the dates in the calendar year 2023 as our base. We will modify this to be dynamic with function parameters later, but we will need a place to start. To list the dates in the calendar year 2023, our code should look like this:

```
let
  Source = List.Dates(#date(2023, 1, 1), 365, #duration(1, 0, 0, 0))
in
  Source
```

With our dates listed, we need to convert our list into a table to start our transformations. A new ribbon titled **List Tools Transform** will appear within the Power Query editor. Inside, we will select **To Table** to convert our list into a table:

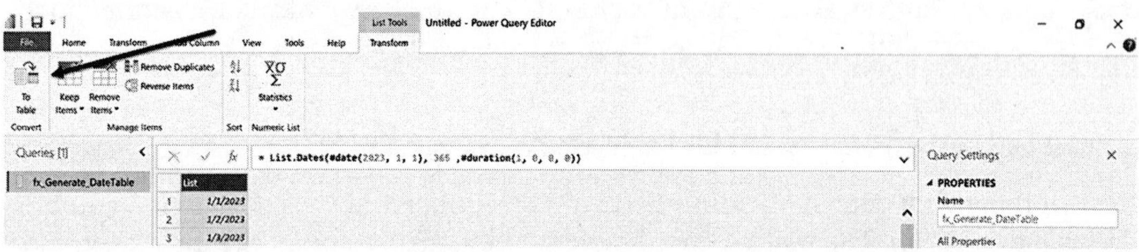

Figure 14.9: *Converting a list into a table under the list tools transform ribbon*

You will be prompted to select a delimiter and how to handle errors. Since we are not splitting our list, we can keep the defaults and click on **OK** to continue. We can convert our list into a table using the **`Table.FromList()`** function in the advanced editor:

`Table.FromList()`	
Parameter	**Description**
`List`	List of values in Power Query.
`Splitter`	Optional parameter to designate a delimiter for items in a list.
`Columns`	Optional names for columns for list values.
`Default`	Optional default values for columns.
`ExtraValues`	Optional function to handle potential errors from extra values.

Table 14.7: *Table of the Table.FromList() parameters*

If we decide to use the advanced editor to convert our list into a table, we can provide a more compact version of our code. As a bonus, we can easily provide a name for our column to avoid using the default name of **Column1**, as shown:

```
let
  Source = Table.FromList(
    List.Dates(#date(2023, 1, 1), 365, #duration(1, 0, 0, 0)),
    Splitter.SplitByNothing(),
    {"Date"},
    null,
    ExtraValues.Error
  )
in
  Source
```

Now that we have our date established, we can add our dimensional data, such as year, month, and day of the week, to our query. You will use *Chapter 7, Transforming Columns* and *Chapter 9, Creating New Columns* to flesh out your date table. The dimensional data your solution requires might be different than this, but it will give you a strong base to work from:

```
let
  Source = Table.FromList(
    List.Dates(#date(2023, 1, 1), 365, #duration(1, 0, 0, 0)),
    Splitter.SplitByNothing(),
    {"Date"},
    null,
    ExtraValues.Error
  ),
  UpdateColumnType = Table.TransformColumnTypes(Source, {{"Date", type
date}}),
  AddCalendarYear = Table.AddColumn(UpdateColumnType, "Year", each Date.
Year([Date]), Int64.Type),
  AddCalendarMonthNo = Table.AddColumn(
    AddCalendarYear,
    "Month",
    each Date.Month([Date]),
    Int64.Type
```

```
  ),
  AddCalendarMonthName = Table.AddColumn(
    AddCalendarMonthNo,
    "Month Name",
    each Date.MonthName([Date]),
    type text
  ),
  AddCalendarDayOfWeek = Table.AddColumn(
    AddCalendarMonthName,
    "Day Name",
    each Date.DayOfWeekName([Date]),
    type text
  ),
  AddDay = Table.AddColumn(AddCalendarDayOfWeek, "Day", each Date.Day([-
Date]), Int64.Type)
in
  AddDay
```

Now that we have our date table built around the calendar year, we want to consider how to add logic to manage a fiscal year. In our scenario, our fiscal year will start on July 1st. This means the fiscal year 2024 will start on July 1st, 2023. We will need to add some calculations to handle this situation.

We will first tackle the fiscal year designation. The logic for this is quite simple. If our fiscal year starts in July, that will be the center of our logic. If the calendar month is greater than or equal to seven (July), then add one to the existing calendar year. Otherwise, just grab the calendar year. Our code for the **`FiscalYear`** column should look like this:

```
if [Month] >= 7 then [Year] + 1 else [Year]
```

Next, we need to reassign month numbers to fiscal period numbers. This means turning calendar month number seven into fiscal period one. We will need to follow a similar logic to achieve this outcome. For periods greater than or equal to seven (July), we will take the month number, subtract the month number that represents the start of the fiscal year, and add one to it. If the month number is less than seven (July), then we will take the month number, add the month number that represents the start of the fiscal year, and subtract one. Our code for the **`FiscalPeriodNo`** column should look like this:

```
if [Month] >= 7 then [Month] - 7 + 1 else [Month] + 7 - 1
```

With our custom columns to manage our fiscal year in place, the code for our date table function should look like this:

```
let
  Source = Table.FromList(
    List.Dates(#date(2023, 1, 1), 365, #duration(1, 0, 0, 0)),
    Splitter.SplitByNothing(),
    {"Date"},
    null,
    ExtraValues.Error
  ),
  UpdateColumnType = Table.TransformColumnTypes(Source, {{"Date", type
date}}),
  AddCalendarYear = Table.AddColumn(UpdateColumnType, "Year", each Date.
Year([Date]), Int64.Type),
  AddCalendarMonthNo = Table.AddColumn(
    AddCalendarYear,
    "Month",
    each Date.Month([Date]),
    Int64.Type
  ),
  AddCalendarMonthName = Table.AddColumn(
    AddCalendarMonthNo,
    "Month Name",
    each Date.MonthName([Date]),
    type text
  ),
  AddCalendarDayOfWeek = Table.AddColumn(
    AddCalendarMonthName,
    "Day Name",
    each Date.DayOfWeekName([Date]),
    type text
  ),
  AddDay = Table.AddColumn(AddCalendarDayOfWeek, "Day", each Date.Day([-
Date]), Int64.Type),
  AddFiscalYear = Table.AddColumn(
    AddDay,
```

```
    "FiscalYear",
    each if [Month] >= 7 then [Year] + 1 else [Year],
    Int64.Type
  ),
  AddFiscalPeriodNo = Table.AddColumn(
    AddFiscalYear,
    "FiscalPeriodNo",
    each if [Month] >= 7 then [Month] - 7 + 1 else [Month] + 7 - 1,
    Int64.Type
  )
in
  AddFiscalPeriodNo
```

With all of this in place, now it is time to add our parameters and convert this into a function. We are going to create two parameters for this function. The first parameter will establish the start date for our date table as a date. The second function will establish the start of the fiscal year as a number.

First, we must update our first line of code to replace the date we entered with our parameter. Next, we need to take **`Duration.Days(DateTime.Date(DateTime.LocalNow()))`** and subtract it against our parameter to establish the number of days to count. This will ensure that there is always data for today's date when the model is refreshed.

Once we have updated the logic to generate the list of dates, we need to replace the hard coded month number for the fiscal year with our parameter. This applies to the fiscal year and fiscal period we created. We will also add an if statement for the last line of our code to ignore the fiscal period and year columns if our fiscal year starts in January. With these final changes in place, the code for our function should look like this:

```
(TableStartDate as date, FiscalYearStartMonth as number) =>
  let
    Source = Table.FromList(
      List.Dates(
        TableStartDate,
        Duration.Days(DateTime.LocalNow() - TableStartDate),
        #duration(1, 0, 0, 0)
      ),
      Splitter.SplitByNothing(),
      {"Date"},
```

```
      null,
      ExtraValues.Error
    ),
     UpdateColumnType = Table.TransformColumnTypes(Source, {{"Date", type
date}}),
     AddCalendarYear = Table.AddColumn(UpdateColumnType, "Year", each Date.
Year([Date]), Int64.Type),
    AddCalendarMonthNo = Table.AddColumn(
      AddCalendarYear,
      "Month",
      each Date.Month([Date]),
      Int64.Type
    ),
    AddCalendarMonthName = Table.AddColumn(
      AddCalendarMonthNo,
      "Month Name",
      each Date.MonthName([Date]),
      type text
    ),
    AddCalendarDayOfWeek = Table.AddColumn(
      AddCalendarMonthName,
      "Day Name",
      each Date.DayOfWeekName([Date]),
      type text
    ),
     AddDay = Table.AddColumn(AddCalendarDayOfWeek, "Day", each Date.Day([-
Date]), Int64.Type),
    AddFiscalYear = Table.AddColumn(
      AddDay,
      "FiscalYear",
      each if [Month] >= FiscalYearStartMonth then [Year] + 1 else [Year],
      Int64.Type
    ),
    AddFiscalPeriodNo = Table.AddColumn(
      AddFiscalYear,
```

```
      "FiscalPeriodNo",
      each
        if [Month] >= FiscalYearStartMonth then
          [Month] - FiscalYearStartMonth + 1
        else
          [Month] + FiscalYearStartMonth   1,
      Int64.Type
    )
  in
    if FiscalYearStartMonth = 1 then AddDay else AddFiscalPeriodNo
```

Date table functions can become quite complex depending on your needs. For some scenarios, you might need to create logic to account for the fiscal week of the year or something that handles a floating first date of a fiscal year. These complications are what make functions work so well for organizations. It requires a lot of setup early on, but once it is in place, you can quickly redeploy it. Some readers who work with multiple organizations might find that they encounter multiple variations in fiscal years. This is why having a function can be critical because it will allow you to quickly redeploy a date table without having to uproot the logic. While this is a great base for your starting point, you are encouraged to expand upon this logic and make it your own. This way, you can get the most out of this function as you redeploy the logic over time.

Use cases for functions

In this chapter, we have already hit on three great examples of use cases for functions within Power Query. First, we looked at a scenario where we performed a complex transformation accounting for time zone changes. Next, we performed a lookup from another query and returned the result into a new column. Then we explored using a date table to deploy a query from scratch.

At this point, it is clear that functions can provide an array of solutions for your models. Your only limitation is your imagination and willingness to create them. Some of the functions we explored early in this chapter could have been handled by existing functions within Power Query. It is not recommended to use functions to replace existing functions, but rather maybe use them to augment them to extend their capabilities.

But what happens when you want to take a function from one instance of Power Query to another? How do you transition it between models? While you could copy the advanced editor code from one instance to another, there is an easier way. If you right-click on a function and click Copy, it will not only copy the function, but any supporting queries behind it. This means that when you go to paste it in the new instance of Power Query, all the connections, data, transformations, and logic will transfer. This eliminates any rework from recreating your functions, allowing you to focus on the rest of your model. It might be recommended to create a file or two with some of your organization's core functions to quickly replicate them into your new instance of Power Query.

In the next chapter, we will use functions to extend the capabilities of the **`Web.Contents()`** connector. This will allow us to create more advanced connections to API endpoints.

Conclusion

In this chapter, we explored functions and how they are applied for advanced transformations within Power Query. The chapter also defined what functions are and how they work within Power Query. Next, we recreated a basic math function from scratch to understand how they are structured. Once we had a grasp of how functions are structured, we applied them as a custom column for existing queries. Then we explored three use cases where we could use functions to augment our models and extend our existing queries.

In the next chapter, we will learn how to create complex connections to API endpoints with Power Query.

CHAPTER 15
Advanced Web Connections

Introduction

In this chapter, we will explore connecting to more advanced web connections within the Power Query editor. We will first review the basics of web connectors and identify the challenges we must overcome to connect to more complicated versions of these endpoints. Next, we will explore how to navigate authenticating to an endpoint using OAuth2 to acquire a token. Lastly, we will explore some use cases for applying functions with your existing queries.

Structure

The chapter covers the following topics:

- Review of web APIs
- Connect to web APIs using POST method
- Connect to web APIs using OAuth2
- Manage paging with skip parameter
- Manage paging with skip token
- Considerations with advanced connections

Objectives

By the end of this chapter, you will understand how to perform advanced connections with your queries within the Power Query editor. This will enable you to create connections to Web APIs that might require complex inputs or requirements.

Review of web APIs

Back in *Chapter 3, Connect to Web-Based Data Sources*, we covered the process of using the web connector to access data with REST APIs. We covered the basic structure of an API and how we can use the `GET` method to retrieve our data. We use the URL endpoint to call our API, parameters to filter or manipulate what we bring back with our call, and headers to help process the request. These were all things we completed as part of that chapter.

However, we mentioned that there was a way to call an API using the `POST` method. When using the `GET` method, we are simply requesting data. However, the `POST` method allows us to send data as a message body to our endpoints. This body sends a message payload for the endpoint, which is then used to process the request.

But what about parameters? Is that not the same thing? No, this is quite different. Parameters are used to help identify and filter data from an endpoint. However, a message body does more for our query. For one, you do not see parameters and a body used in the same query. So, if you need to send details for a `POST` method request, it must be done inside the message body. The second reason is for security. Parameters are exposed in the URL and can be easily viewed. However, the message body is not readily visible in the request providing a layer of security with your request. The use of the `POST` method within Power Query is not a common event. However, it can prove to be a necessary one to accomplish an outcome.

Another challenge that arises from APIs is the need to perform paging. As a method of protection, APIs sometimes limit the number of records that are returned at a time. The use of paging ensures that your query does not exert an undue burden on the request server. This means that you might need to call the same API multiple times to get all records to return. While you could create multiple queries to achieve this goal, there are ways to create your connection, so that it is flexible and scalable without your intervention.

The last challenge you might encounter is the need to create your connection using an Open Authorization flow. **Open Authorization** (**OAuth2**) is a process that manages the authentication flow and returns a token that can be applied for downstream connections. To connect to the API endpoint required for your query, you might need to connect to another endpoint to complete the authentication flow and obtain a token that can be used for your query. This complicates the flow of your query and requires a supporting query to achieve our outcome.

In this chapter, we will tackle all three of these challenges with a single query. The reason we waited until the end of this book to tackle this topic is because you will need to leverage everything you have learned up to this point. We will use functions, parameters, transformations, and the advanced editor to extract our data.

If you choose to follow along, we will be using the Microsoft Graph API and a service principal in Entra ID. This will require some knowledge of how-to setup these elements to ensure they work as expected. Please refer to **https://learn.microsoft.com/en-us/graph/use-the-api** to learn how to set up your Microsoft 365 environment to use these API endpoints.

Connect to web APIs using POST method

The challenge with using the **`POST`** method is that you must use the advanced editor to create your connection. If you are not comfortable with using the advanced editor, this might make the process a little more difficult. However, this section will help you through the entire process. We will be connecting to a service principal inside Entra ID. This will be required for our next section for connecting to an API using OAuth2.

To start, we are going to setup our message body. Our message body requires us to identify four items: **`grant_type`**, **`client_id`**, **`client_secret`**, and **`scope`**. To make our life easier, we will use parameters in Power Query to manage our **`client_id`** and **`client_secret`** values. First, go to **New Source** and select **Blank Query** and rename it as **`AuthToken`**. Using the advanced editor, we will specify the values required for our message body:

```
let
  MessageBody = "grant_type=client_credentials&
        client_id="
    & ApplicationID
    & "&
        client_secret="
    & ClientSecret
    & "&
        scope=https://graph.microsoft.com/.default"
in
  MessageBody
```

Next, we will call our endpoint and retrieve our access token. We will use the **`Web.Contents()`** function paired with our endpoint URL and a parameter for the Tenant ID:

```
let
  MessageBody = "grant_type=client_credentials&
        client_id="
```

```
    & ApplicationID
    & "&
        client_secret="
    & ClientSecret
    & "&
        scope=https://graph.microsoft.com/.default",
  Source = Web.Contents("https://login.microsoftonline.com/" &
    TenantID &
    "/oauth2/v2.0/token")
in
  Source
```

Next, we will need to identify our headers. We have already used the **ContentType** header in *Chapter 3, Connect to Web Based Data Sources*, but we will need to use the **Accept** header as well. Wrapped in square brackets, we will identify the query headers:

```
let
  MessageBody = "grant_type=client_credentials&
        client_id="
    & ApplicationID
    & "&
        client_secret="
    & ClientSecret
    & "&
        scope=https://graph.microsoft.com /.default",
  Source = Web.Contents(
    "https://login.microsoftonline.com/" &
    TenantID & "/oauth2/v2.0/token",
    [Headers = [
      Accept = "application/json",
      ContentType = "application/x-www-form-urlencoded"
      ]
    ]
  )
in
  Source
```

The last step we need to achieve our outcome is to add the message body to our query. We will use the **`Text.ToBinary()`** function to prep our message body for transmission:

`Text.ToBinary()`	
Parameter	**Description**
`Text`	Text value to be converted into binary
`Encoding`	Optional number used to specify encoding if required
`IncludeByteOrderMark`	Optional logical to include the **Byte Order Mark** (**BOM**) for encoding.

Table 15.1: *Table of the Text.ToBinary() parameters*

For our query, we will introduce a content parameter inside of our square brackets. We can call the message body and convert it into binary, all in a single line. Lastly, we will wrap the entire thing with the **`Json.Document()`** function to return and format our query:

```
let
  MessageBody = "grant_type=client_credentials&
        client_id="
    & ApplicationID
    & "&
        client_secret="
    & ClientSecret
    & "&
        scope=https://graph.microsoft.com/.default",
  Source = Json.Document(
    Web.Contents(
      "https://login.microsoftonline.com/" &
    TenantID & "/oauth2/v2.0/token",
      [
        Headers = [Accept = "application/json",
          ContentType = "application/x-www-form-urlencoded"],
        Content = Text.ToBinary(MessageBody)
      ]
    )
  )
in
  Source
```

Next, you will be prompted to enter credentials. Since we are providing our credentials through the message body, we will use an anonymous authentication method for our query. The result of our query is a list of values that includes our access token. It is currently in a list format but can easily be transformed into a table and pivoted. In our situation, we do not want to do manipulate it any further, so we will leave it in the following format:

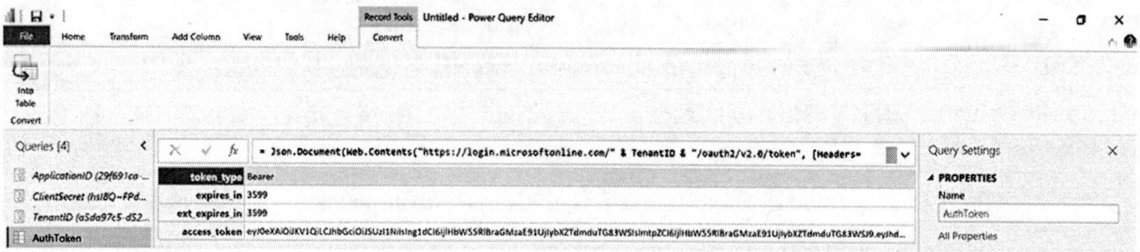

Figure 15.1: Result of our query using the POST method

If you have a similar result to *Figure 15.1*, then you successfully have setup your connection to the OAuth2 endpoint. However, the next step requires you to transform this result so you can use the access token for other endpoints. In the next section, we will extract the token and use it to query the list of groups within the Microsoft 365 ecosystem.

Connect to web APIs using OAuth2

Now that we have connected to our OAuth2 endpoint, we must extract the access token for our use. We will start by taking our **AuthToken** query and converting it into a function. Because we only care about the access token coming back, we can add **[access_token]** to the end of our **source** line in our code in the advanced editor window. This will ensure that we only return our token and no additional noise with our query. Next, we will add **() =>** at the beginning of our query to convert it into a function. We do not require any parameters for our function to operate properly, so we will leave that empty:

```
() =>
  let
    MessageBody = "grant_type=client_credentials&
        client_id="
      & ApplicationID
      & "&
        client_secret="
      & ClientSecret
      & "&
        scope=https://graph.microsoft.com/.default",
    Source = Json.Document(
```

```
    Web.Contents(
      "https://login.microsoftonline.com/" &
      TenantID & "/oauth2/v2.0/token",
      [
        Headers = [Accept = "application/json",
          ContentType = "application/x-www-form-urlencoded"],
        Content = Text.ToBinary(MessageBody)
      ]
    )
  )[access_token]
in
  Source
```

We will rename the query from **AuthToken** to **fx_AuthToken** to keep consistent with our method of identifying functions within Power Query. To test our function, we can invoke it and see the value it returns. It is advisable to test this function, but from experience, if you do not delete the query that is created, it might cause authentication issues while you connect to other queries. Once you have validated that the function works, you should delete it from Power Query.

Now that we have our token identified, we will create a new query to connect to the Microsoft Graph API and query the groups found within the Microsoft 365 environment. We will use the group endpoint paired with the **GraphUrl** parameter to make the connection to the API easier. To get started, go to **New Source** and select **Blank Query**. From there, we will open the advanced editor and start building out our connection string with the **Web.Contents()** function:

```
let
  Source = Web.Contents(GraphUrl & "groups")
in
  Source
```

By using the **GraphUrl** parameter, we are simplifying the process of writing out our queries. Instead of having to reference the details of the endpoint, we just need to update where we are pointing for our query. Thus, making our queries easier to write if using multiple endpoints from the same server.

Now that we have our endpoint identified, we need to add an authorization header and identify our token. We will concatenate the token type, which in this case is a bearer token, with the access token in the header. We will then wrap the entire line with **Json.**

`Document()` to parse the results and return all the groups found in the Microsoft 365 environment:

```
let
  Source = Json.Document(
    Web.Contents(GraphUrl & "groups",
      [Headers = [Authorization = "Bearer " & fx_AuthToken()]]
    )
  )
in
  Source
```

Notice that we can simply call the **`fx_AuthToken()`** function to pull a current access token for our query. Since we might be connecting to multiple endpoints using the same service principal, we can easily duplicate this query and update it as required. While all this work requires additional effort upfront, it has made it easier to redeploy for this model.

Now that we have a result, we must manipulate it to get to the values we desire. Right now, we have returned a list with two values in it. However, we can click on the list value to drill down:

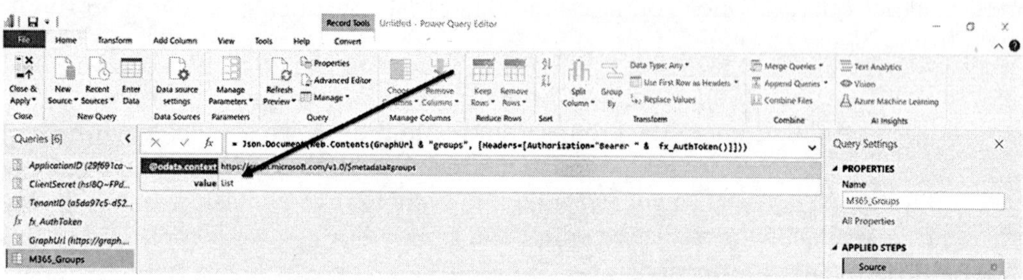

Figure 15.2: Drill down on values returned from our endpoint

Once we have drilled down, we will convert our list to a table and expand the records in the column that was returned. This will return the values provided from the endpoint, as shown:

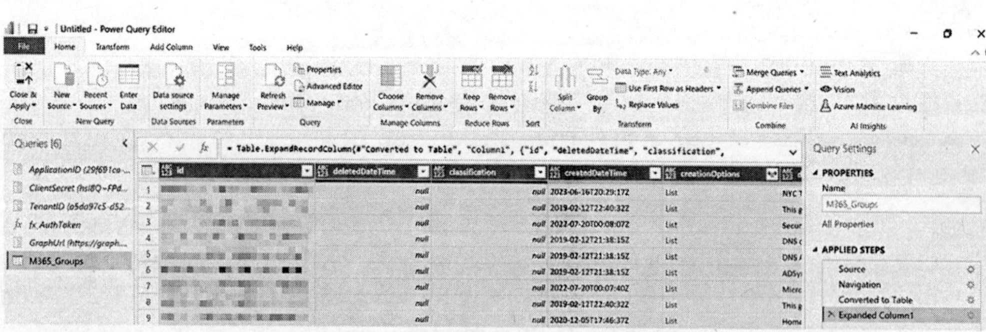

Figure 15.3: Expanded results from our endpoint

We have covered how to convert lists to tables and expand columns in previous chapters in the graphical interface and with the advanced editor. We will use **`Table.FromList()`** and **`Table.ExapndRecordColumn()`** functions as we have before in the advanced editor to achieve the same result. If you prefer using the advanced editor and want to double check your code, it should look something like this:

```
let
  Source = Json.Document(
    Web.Contents(GraphUrl & "groups", [Headers = [Authorization = "Bearer "
& fx_AuthToken()]])
  )[value],
  ConvertList = Table.FromList(Source, Splitter.SplitByNothing(), null,
null, ExtraValues.Error),
  ExpandValues = Table.ExpandRecordColumn(
    ConvertList,
    "Column1",
    {
      "id", "deletedDateTime", "classification", "createdDateTime",
      "creationOptions", "description", "displayName", "expirationDate-
Time",
      "groupTypes", "isAssignableToRole", "mail", "mailEnabled", "mailNick-
name",
      "membershipRule", "membershipRuleProcessingState", "onPremisesDomain-
Name",
      "onPremisesLastSyncDateTime", "onPremisesNetBiosName",
      "onPremisesSamAccountName", "onPremisesSecurityIdentifier",
      "onPremisesSyncEnabled", "preferredDataLocation", "preferredLan-
guage",
      "proxyAddresses", "renewedDateTime", "resourceBehaviorOptions",
      "resourceProvisioningOptions", "securityEnabled", "securityIdentifi-
er",
      "theme", "visibility", "onPremisesProvisioningErrors",
      "serviceProvisioningErrors"
    },
    {
      "id", "deletedDateTime", "classification", "createdDateTime",
      "creationOptions", "description", "displayName", "expirationDate-
Time",
```

```
        "groupTypes", "isAssignableToRole", "mail", "mailEnabled", "mailNick-
name",
        "membershipRule", "membershipRuleProcessingState", "onPremisesDomain-
Name",
        "onPremisesLastSyncDateTime", "onPremisesNetBiosName",
        "onPremisesSamAccountName", "onPremisesSecurityIdentifier",
        "onPremisesSyncEnabled", "preferredDataLocation", "preferredLan-
guage",
        "proxyAddresses", "renewedDateTime", "resourceBehaviorOptions",
        "resourceProvisioningOptions", "securityEnabled", "securityIdentifi-
er",
        "theme", "visibility", "onPremisesProvisioningErrors",
        "serviceProvisioningErrors"
      }
  )
in
  ExpandValues
```

The process of connecting to a query using OAuth2 is complicated but can be executed with Power Query. The key is establishing the proper groundwork to make the process of connecting easier. While it might not be required for every scenario, having this knowledge might assist you in the future.

One last thing to keep in mind is that we are using application-based authentication in this scenario. This is not always feasible and might require password credentials. In addition, depending on how your application flows, password authentication might not work either. Before you go through the process of attempting an OAuth2 authentication process with Power Query, make sure you understand how the flow will work and if it is possible to achieve it. Do not be disheartened if your connection is not working, as it might be an issue with the endpoint than your query. Sometimes no matter how hard you try your queries might not connect due to limitations of the endpoint.

Manage paging with a skip parameter

At this point, we were able to grab a list of our Microsoft 365 groups using the Graph API. However, as we discussed earlier, there is a limitation to the number of groups that can be returned at once. With this endpoint, the limit is one thousand groups. As a result, we must add logic to our query to manage our request. One of the easiest ways to achieve this goal is with a skip parameter.

When reading documentation around APIs, there is often a parameter available to assist you with paging. This could be in the form of a skip parameter that ignores a specified number of records before returning data. It could also be in the form of a page number. Regardless of the method, the concept is the same. It is just how you implement the logic that is different.

To achieve our desired outcome with this query, we will need to identify the number of records being returned from a query. Once we have that count, we will divide it by the limit imposed by our query to determine the number of pages we need to use to pull the complete list. Then, we will generate a series of page numbers and apply a function to pull back the data for each page. It sounds complicated, but the reality is that you have learned how to achieve this outcome at every step of this process within this book. It is just time to pull it all together into a single solution.

The first step in this process is to identify the number of records available with the query. Sometimes we are lucky and receive the information with minimal manipulation. If you look at *Figure 15.2*, some endpoints will bring back a total record count with the query. In that situation, you just need to acquire that count by calling the field by name. Unfortunately, that is not the case with our endpoint. However, we do have the ability to pull a record count by using the **`$count`** parameter with our query. To get started, let us make a copy of our current **`M365_Groups`** query and call it **`fx_M365_Groups`**. That will save us some time as we continue working through this scenario. Inside the **`M365_Groups`** query, remove all the applied steps except for source. In addition, open the advanced editor and remove **`[value]`** at the end of the source line. At this point, your results should look like *Figure 15.2*.

Now that we have our base, we will open the advanced editor for the **`M365_Groups`** query. We are going to add **`/$count`** to the end of our endpoint URL. This will return a numeric count of available groups in the environment. Next, we will add a new header in our options parameter titled **`ConsistencyLevel`**, which is equal to **`eventual`**. With these changes in place, you should see a numeric value return that looks like this:

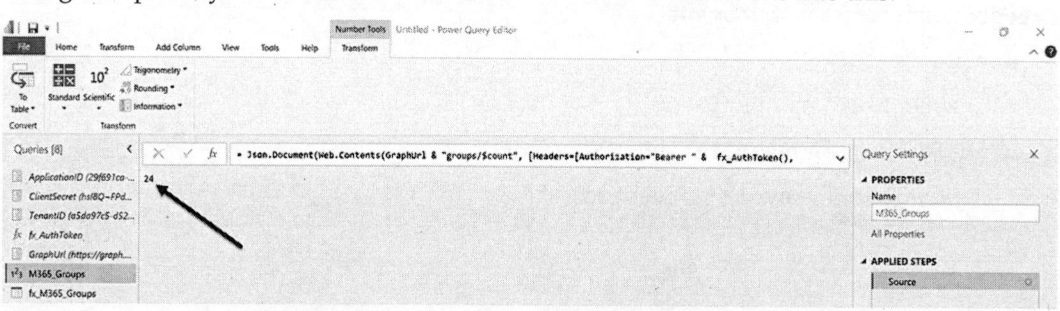

Figure 15.4: *Number of records found from our endpoint*

If you did not receive a result like *Figure 15.4*, you can double check your code to make sure it matches:

```
let
  RecordCount = Json.Document(
    Web.Contents(
      GraphUrl & "groups/$count",
      [Headers = [Authorization = "Bearer " & fx_AuthToken(),
        ConsistencyLevel = "eventual"]]
    )
  )
in
  RecordCount
```

Now that we have our record count returned, we need to determine the number of pages required to achieve our outcome. However, you will note that this environment only has twenty-four groups available, which is well within the one thousand item limit. While it is not required right now, we want to ensure that our solution will scale. To make life easier for ourselves, we will create a new parameter within Power Query called **`RecordLimit`** with a numeric value of five. This way, we can assess the scalability of our query with a smaller dataset and adjust the limit when we are ready to deploy.

With our record count identified and our **`RecordLimit`** parameter in place, it is time to perform some basic math. Inside the advanced editor, we will create a new line called **`PageCount`** and take **`RecordCount`** and divide it by **`RecordLimit`** to determine the number of pages we will need. However, our number will likely return a decimal value. Since we cannot have a fraction of a page, we must wrap our division statement with the **`Number.RoundUp()`** function. This addition will force the rounding logic to always go to the next available whole number:

```
let
  RecordCount = Json.Document(
    Web.Contents(
      GraphUrl & "groups/$count",
      [Headers = [Authorization = "Bearer " & fx_AuthToken(),
        ConsistencyLevel = "eventual"]]
    )
  ),
  PageCount = Number.RoundUp(RecordCount / RecordLimit)
in
  PageCount
```

The last step is to generate a list of values and transform it. If you remember, in *Chapter 14, Functions*, we used **`List.Dates()`** to generate a list of dates. We will use a similar function called **`List.Numbers()`** to generate our page number list:

`List.Numbers()`	
Parameter	**Description**
`Start`	Starting number for the list.
`Count`	Number of items to generate in the list
`Increment`	Optional number that can be used to set an increment that is not one.

Table 15.2: *Table of the List.Numbers() parameters*

For our scenario, we will start with zero and use our **`PageCount`** value as the count. While not required, we will explicitly state our increment as one. Once we have our list, we will convert it into a table using **`Table.FromList()`**. We will also use **`Table.TransformColumnTypes()`** to set the column type to a whole number and rename it using **`Table.RenameColumns()`**, as shown:

```
let
  RecordCount = Json.Document(
    Web.Contents(
      GraphUrl & "groups/$count",
      [Headers = [Authorization = "Bearer " & fx_AuthToken(),
        ConsistencyLevel = "eventual"]]
    )
  ),
  PageCount = Number.RoundUp(RecordCount / RecordLimit),
  PageList = List.Numbers(0, PageCount, 1),
   ListToTable = Table.FromList(PageList, Splitter.SplitByNothing(), null,
null,
    ExtraValues.Error),
   TextToNumber=Table.TransformColumnTypes(ListToTable, {{"Column1", Int64.
Type}}),
  RenamePageNo = Table.RenameColumns(TextToNumber, {{"Column1", "PageNo"}})
in
  RenamePageNo
```

At this point, you have the base of the query set. Next, we will need to iterate through each page with **`fx_M365_Groups`**. However, you might be wondering why we chose to start our page numbers at zero instead of one. That will make more sense once we build out our function. We will start by adding **`(PageNo as number) =>`** at the top of the **`fx_M365_`**

Groups query to convert it to a function. Next, using the **RelativePath** parameter, we will add the skip context with **?$skip**. We then will take our **PageNo** input and multiply it by our **RecordLimit** parameter to get our skip value. Lastly, to prevent any error with our concatenation of these items, we will convert our skip number to text using the **Number.ToText()** function:

```
(PageNo as number) =>
  let
    Source = Json.Document(
      Web.Contents(
        GraphUrl & "groups",
        [
          RelativePath = "?$skip=" & Number.ToText(PageNo * RecordLimit),
          Headers = [Authorization = "Bearer " & fx_AuthToken()]
        ]
      )
    )[value]
  in
    Source
```

As you can see, with the mathematical logic in place to find our skip value, starting our page numbers with zero makes sense because our first query does not require any values to be skipped. Now that we have our function, we can apply it to our **M365_Groups** query by going to **Add Column** and selecting **Invoke Custom Function**.

While not the case in our scenario, some APIs use a parameter identifying the page number instead of a skip value. In that case, it is easier because you do not need to perform any mathematical transformations. The only difference is that you would start your list of page numbers at one to align with the documentation associated with the endpoint. Once you have configured your function and your list of page numbers, you would invoke the function as we outlined already.

Lastly, once you have verified your query functions properly, you can reset your **RecordLimit** parameter to the maximum to provide efficiency when deploying it at scale. This eliminates the need to update all your queries manually while providing context in your code of why it was designed this way.

Manage paging with a skip token

Another scenario you might encounter with endpoints is the use of a skip token. Instead of us having to figure out the number of pages we need to iterate through, a skip token is returned and informs us if we need to continue paging. Once the last page is reached, no skip token is available, which means you can stop the paging process.

To get started, we are going to connect to our group's endpoint. This time, we are going to add a **`$top`** parameter for our endpoint to limit our results. Since our goal is to evaluate with our small sample and allow it to scale, we will use our **`RecordLimit`** parameter in Power Query to set the threshold. While portions of this can be done in the graphical interface, it will be easier to complete using the advanced editor with a new blank query, as shown:

```
let
  Source = Json.Document(
    Web.Contents(
      GraphUrl & "groups",
      [
        RelativePath = "?$top=" & Number.ToText(RecordLimit),
        Headers = [Authorization = "Bearer " & fx_AuthToken()]
      ]
    )
  )
in
  Source
```

With this code in place, you will receive a result like *Figure 15.2*. The difference is that now you will have a value called **`@odata.nextLink`** which serves as your skip token. In short, it brings back a similar endpoint URL to the one we created, but this time it has a **`$skiptoken`** parameter attached to it:

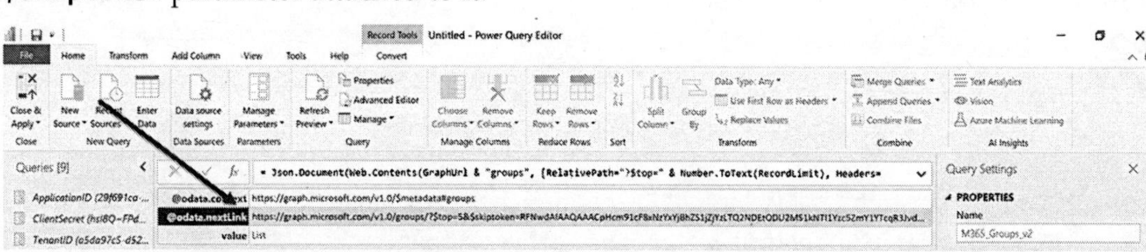

Figure 15.5: *An example of a skip token returned for our endpoint*

With our base query set, we will create a function within a query to achieve our outcome. We will create an internal function named **`GetGroupList`** with a parameter named **`path`**. We will then move the reference to the **`$top`** parameter for the endpoint and call it below:

```
let
  GetGroupList = (Path as text) =>
```

```
    let
      Source = Json.Document(
        Web.Contents(GraphUrl & "groups",
          [RelativePath = "?" & Path,
            Headers = [Authorization = "Bearer " & fx_AuthToken()]]
        )
      )
    in
      Source,
  GroupList = GetGroupList("$top=" & Number.ToText(RecordLimit))
in
  GroupList
```

This change has yielded the same result as found in *Figure 15.5*. All we have here is a more complicated version of our original code. However, with our function inside of the query in place, we can iterate through our pages by extracting the skip token from our results. But what happens if there is no skip token present? We can navigate this with some error handling using the **try** and **otherwise** functions. Operating like a conditional statement, Power Query will **try** and attempt a command. If it is not successful, you will use the command found after the **otherwise** statement.

We are going to modify our internal function a bit. First, we are going to store the results found in the value field in **GroupItems**. Then, we will need to attempt to run our internal function with the skip token. To avoid errors, we will use **Text.AfterDelimiter()** to extract the path we will pass as the input to the function. If this results in an error, we should only return our results in **GroupItems**. This seems complicated, but it is straightforward once you see the code:

```
let
  GetGroupList = (Path as text) =>
    let
      Source = Json.Document(
        Web.Contents(GraphUrl & "groups",
          [RelativePath = "?" & Path,
            Headers = [Authorization = "Bearer " & fx_AuthToken()]]
        )
      ),
      GroupItems = @Source[value],
      Result = try
```

```
        @GroupItems &
          @GetGroupList(Text.AfterDelimiter(@Source[#"@odata.nextLink"],
"?"))
      otherwise
        @GroupItems
    in
      Result,
  GroupList = GetGroupList("$top=" & Number.ToText(RecordLimit))
in
  GroupList
```

From here, we just need to convert our list into a table with the **Table.FromList()** function and expand our columns with the **Table.ExpandRecordColumn()** function. Once finished, this code will allow you to infinitely scale up and down based on the number of records associated with your endpoint:

```
let
  GetGroupList = (Path as text) =>
    let
      Source = Json.Document(Web.Contents(GraphUrl & "groups",
          [RelativePath = "?" & Path,
            Headers = [Authorization = "Bearer " & fx_AuthToken()]]
        )
      ),
      GroupItems = @Source[value],
      Result = try
        @GroupItems &
          @GetGroupList(Text.AfterDelimiter(@Source[#"@odata.nextLink"],
"?"))
      otherwise
        @GroupItems
    in
      Result,
  GroupList = GetGroupList("$top=" & Number.ToText(RecordLimit)),
  ListToTable =
    Table.FromList(GroupList, Splitter.SplitByNothing(), null, null, Ex-
traValues.Error),
```

```
  ExpandRecords = Table.ExpandRecordColumn(
    ListToTable,
    "Column1",
    {
      "id", "deletedDateTime", "classification", "createdDateTime",
      "creationOptions", "description", "displayName", "expirationDate-
Time",
      "groupTypes", "isAssignableToRole", "mail", "mailEnabled", "mailNick-
name",
      "membershipRule", "membershipRuleProcessingState", "onPremisesDomain-
Name",
      "onPremisesLastSyncDateTime", "onPremisesNetBiosName",
      "onPremisesSamAccountName", "onPremisesSecurityIdentifier",
      "onPremisesSyncEnabled", "preferredDataLocation", "preferredLan-
guage",
      "proxyAddresses", "renewedDateTime", "resourceBehaviorOptions",
      "resourceProvisioningOptions", "securityEnabled", "securityIdentifi-
er",
      "theme", "visibility", "onPremisesProvisioningErrors",
      "serviceProvisioningErrors"
    },
    {
      "id", "deletedDateTime", "classification", "createdDateTime",
      "creationOptions", "description", "displayName", "expirationDate-
Time",
      "groupTypes", "isAssignableToRole", "mail", "mailEnabled", "mailNick-
name",
      "membershipRule", "membershipRuleProcessingState", "onPremisesDomain-
Name",
      "onPremisesLastSyncDateTime", "onPremisesNetBiosName",
      "onPremisesSamAccountName", "onPremisesSecurityIdentifier",
      "onPremisesSyncEnabled", "preferredDataLocation", "preferredLan-
guage",
      "proxyAddresses", "renewedDateTime", "resourceBehaviorOptions",
      "resourceProvisioningOptions", "securityEnabled", "securityIdentifi-
er",
```

```
        "theme", "visibility", "onPremisesProvisioningErrors",
        "serviceProvisioningErrors"
      }
    )
in
  ExpandRecords
```

The last thing you will need to do is reset your **RecordLimit** parameter back to the maximum value allowed by your endpoint. This will allow you to scale your query and increase your refresh speed by reducing the number of calls required to your endpoint. It takes time, but building out your query this way allows you to be hands-off after deployment. Any time you can reduce rework within Power Query is a time saver, so do not be afraid to take your time and really dig into the code if you are confronted with a similar scenario.

Considerations with advanced connections

At this point, you are probably realizing that there are a lot of facets when it comes to managing web connections in Power Query. We have covered a lot of ground in this chapter that frames up some of the challenges and concerns that come with these connections. If you do not fully grasp all the concepts in this chapter, that is fine. What is important for you to understand is that while complicated, we can often fit most queries using web APIs into Power Query. The challenge with it is making sure that it is well structured and planned to ensure smooth execution.

One of the biggest concerns when you start creating complex connections is the impact of throttling. For example, we have been using the Microsoft Graph API, which throttles out at various levels based on your endpoint. If things get too hot, you end up receiving a **429 - Too Many Requests** response. This results in receiving what could be junk responses that provide no value. When writing code with other platforms, we can often inject pauses to prevent this throttling from happening. However, with Power Query, we have no way to slow this down. This is a serious design consideration when using an endpoint.

However, not all is lost. Endpoints provided for Google services do a better job of managing throttling. Instead of returning errors, it pauses your connection until the resource is available again. This slows down your refresh but does not require the same level of planning and precision required for the Microsoft Graph API.

It is important to consider these challenges when working with advanced connections of this nature. Because you are relying on multiple calls to your endpoints to achieve your outcome, there is a real risk of hitting the limits of your throttling. In addition, you might be charged for each call you make. Efficiency is key, and the more time you spend planning, the better the result.

It is important to note that you might finish building your model and realize all the lessons learned. The result could be rebuilding it again from scratch to optimize how your queries are structured. This is not only okay but encouraged. While this book goes through some of the ways to manage these endpoints, each endpoint possesses its own challenges. It is not a sign of failure if you need to recreate your model. All of us have done this at some point in our careers, and it is the best way to learn.

Lastly, no matter what you do with advanced web connections, always take the time to read the documentation. So much strife can be prevented by taking a few minutes to read about the endpoint and learn how to best manage it. Not all documentation is created equally, and some of it is not up to par. However, there are always little hints about what you can do with your endpoints if you just take the time to learn about them.

Conclusion

In this chapter, we explored using advanced web connections in Power Query. We did a quick review of APIs and dove into using the **`POST`** method with the **`Web.Contents()`** connector. We then explored how to navigate an OAuth2 flow with endpoints. Next, we went over how to manage paging with APIs using skip parameters and skip tokens. Lastly, we discussed some considerations when using advanced web connections with Power Query.

In the next chapter, we will learn how to update the transformation of files that are ingested with the folder, web, or blob connectors in Power Query.

Join our book's Discord space

CHAPTER 16
Manipulating Supporting Queries

Introduction

In this chapter, we will explore managing and updating supporting queries within the Power Query editor. We will first review how Power Query combines and unifies multiple files into a single query within your model. Next, we will explore how supporting queries are designed to accelerate your transformations. Then, we will address how to make adjustments, such as changing your reference file, managing transformations, and adding new columns to your query. Lastly, we will explore the challenges you might encounter with manipulating your supporting queries.

Structure

This chapter covers the following topics:

- Review unifying files in a single query
- Understanding the transform file query group
- Updating your sample file
- Managing transformations
- Adding new columns to queries
- Common challenges with supporting queries

Objectives

By the end of this chapter, you will understand how to manipulate your supporting queries within the Power Query editor. This will enable you to support long-term changes to your model as your data source continues to evolve.

Review unifying files in a single query

In *Chapter 2, Connect to File Based Data Sources*, we explored some of the challenges that occur when managing multiple files in a single query. Due to size limitations or how data is processed, we can easily end up with multiple files that need to be unified to create a single query. Instead of copying rows of data and pasting them into a single file, we shared how we could use the **folder** connector to unify this data into a single query. This simplified the handling of our data source files and provided a unified query that we could leverage.

Next, in *Chapter 4, Connect to Web Based Data Sources*, we did something similar with files stored within a SharePoint site. We connected to a document library within SharePoint Online, identified a list of files, and combined them all into a single query with a few clicks. Once again, we can scale our query using multiple file data sources without having to manipulate them into a single query for our use.

Then, in *Chapter 5, Connect to Database Sources*, we connected to our Azure Blob storage containers that housed multiple files. Just like with the folder connector, we identified our files, and Power Query ingested them into a single query. This is especially helpful considering how data is often transported into these containers. Most consumers of data stored within a blob container will not understand how to interact with them. This eliminates any complications with accessing your data and streamlines the process.

What is fascinating about all three of these scenarios is how well Power Query was designed to manage these situations. The goal of managing our queries within Power Query is to eliminate the heavy lifting that we repeatedly perform to simplify how we manage our data. It may seem insignificant at the moment, but as you scale your queries, this will be effective. In addition, while these are three unique connectors with their own considerations and challenges, they all behave in a similar fashion once the initial connection is made.

This brings us to the true purpose of this chapter which is to help you simplify how multiple files are processed within Power Query. We have all experienced the challenge when a change is made to a file that has a downstream effect on our data. A column name has changed or how the data is represented. These challenges really can add a wrinkle within our refresh process. While these wrinkles sometimes show up while we are building out our initial queries, they sometimes arise after we have deployed a solution.

The process of updating files before ingesting them into Power Query is cumbersome at best. You must manually intervene in how each file is ingested, which not only takes additional time but is prone to errors. In addition, you have arrived at the concluding chapter of a book that has helped you manipulate your data to eliminate the manual intervention. Once again, if you find yourself encountering this type of scenario, you will be leveraging all the skills you have learned up until this point within the Power Query editor to achieve your desired outcome.

Before we move on with this chapter, it is important to understand that the concepts we will cover in this chapter apply to all the scenarios we have identified in this section. While this chapter will use the folder connector, it applies to any scenario where you combine files into a single query. There might be some nuances around how your data is acquired and the overall connections you are building, but the application of concepts in this chapter are generally universal.

Understanding the transform file query group

If you will recall, every time we combined our files into a single query, we never went through the process of creating this combination within the advanced editor. We mentioned that you could do this, but the process was so complex that it was easier to use the graphical interface to achieve this transformation. And while we still firmly hold that stance, it is time to dig in under the covers of this transformation so we can manipulate these queries. It is still recommended that you use the graphical interface to perform the setup, as it saves a considerable amount of time and frustration. But to achieve our desired outcomes in this chapter, we will need to understand this process a little better.

When we initiate the combination of files in the graphical interface, a new group appears. That group contains the elements we will need to successfully transform our queries. The entire transformation centers around the **`Transform Sample File`** query, which hosts the transformations we will perform. From there, we have three helper queries, **`Sample File`**, **`Parameter1`**, and **`Transform File`**, which are used to support the transformation:

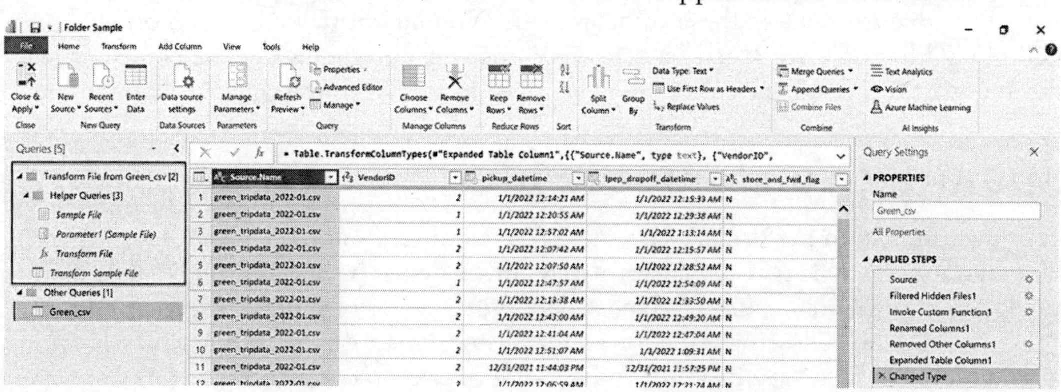

Figure 16.1: Supporting queries contained within the Transform File group

Our goal is to end with a function that will perform the desired transformations on each of our files within the query, but the path to get there starts with the `Sample File` query. This query returns the raw file in a binary format that can be collected. With the folder connector, it brings back the first file in the list. In our scenario, it is bringing back the oldest file as the sort order is from oldest to newest. That is not an issue for us now, but we might want to make a change to that later.

Next, we have a parameter titled `Parameter1` which references our `Sample File` query. Ideally, this would be named better. We can update the name of this parameter under **Manage Parameters**, but we are leaving it as the default for now to avoid any confusion. It seems odd to have a parameter reference a query that already exists. But the purpose of this will make sense shortly.

Next, the `Transform Sample File` query provides a visual reference to the transformations taking place on our sample file. This query references our `Sample File` query via `Parameter1`. The `Transform Sample File` query is where we will perform the transformations that will be applied when our files are combined. While we have a function called `Transform File` that will be called to perform the final transformation, it is linked to the `Transform Sample File` query and is updated every time we make a change. It is important to understand this as it will ensure that your transformations are not only properly tested but updated within your functions.

You might find this process to be excessive. You could just write out your own function from scratch and apply it without all these additional queries. However, you do not want to be short-sighted about your query design. As referenced in the previous section, changes to your file structures are possible. Remember, if we are in control of our source data, then this prevents these issues from occurring. However, if our data is coming from a third-party platform, we might not have the control we desire. This will require us to make changes at some point in the future.

While the ideal scenario would be for us to create a query and never update it again, you might have to make updates because of changes being made. By using this structure, we will be able to manage these updates with minimal effort. Remember, our goal is to eliminate the extra work required for us to deliver our solutions. The better we set ourselves up for success, the easier it will be for us to manage these changes in the future.

Updating your sample file

Every transformation performed with these files requires a sample file to be at the base. Think of it as a template for the transformation. If you do not have a base template in place for your transformation, your function will not properly perform the changes you desire. While the selection of a sample file for your transformation is managed seamlessly with the graphical interface, we must not ignore its importance to the process.

As mentioned in the previous section, our sample file is selected as the first item in the list of files. With the folder connector, our data is ingested and sequenced in a particular order. The prevailing order is usually by the name of the file. This is because some form of date or time is attached to each file that is exported to maintain a unique name. In our scenario, the oldest file in our sample is at the top of the list:

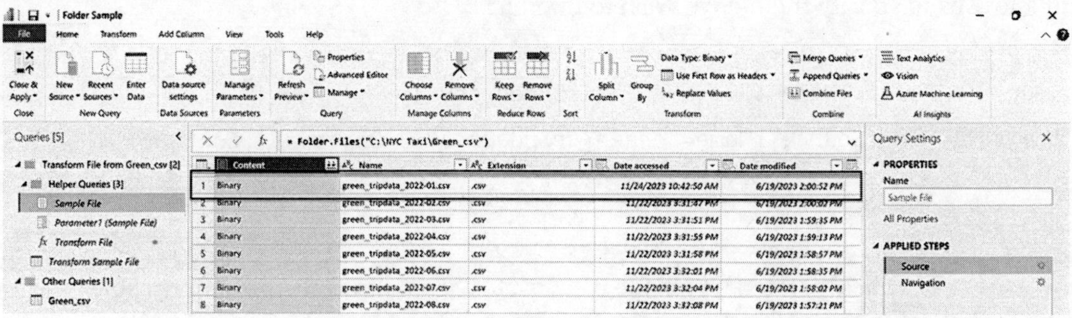

Figure 16.2: *List of files found with the folder connector in Power Query*

When using the graphical interface, Power Query hard codes the first record in the list to be returned. You need to open the advanced editor to see it, but it pulls the first record available to be returned:

```
let
  Source = Folder.Files("C:\NYC Taxi\Green_csv"),
  Navigation1 = Source{0}[Content]
in
  Navigation1
```

If you recall, the curly brackets allow us to specify the row we wish to return. Power Query has designated the first row by using **`{0}`** to pull the first row available. While this is the default, we can update this query to adjust which file is identified for our transformation. The first change we could make is to adjust the sort order of the query. We could simply change the sort order of the name column to bring the newest file to the top. You can select the drop-down on the right-hand side of the column header and change the sort order. In our situation, we would want to change the sort order to descending to bring the newest file in as our sample. If preferred, you can use the **`Table.Sort()`** function inside the advanced editor to achieve the same result:

```
let
  Source       = Folder.Files("C:\NYC Taxi\Green_csv"),
  SortFileName = Table.Sort(Source, {{"Name", Order.Descending}}),
  Navigation1  = SortFileName{0}[Content]
in
  Navigation1
```

This is a viable option and often works well, but it might not be sustainable. As we add new data, we will keep receiving new versions of our files. In addition, what happens when your files are being updated, and you need to test transformations between them? In that case, we need to be a little more prescriptive with our approach. Instead of referencing a row by number, we will provide a conditional statement to achieve our outcome. This will allow us to specify the file we wish to reference:

```
let
  Source = Folder.Files("C:\NYC Taxi\Green_csv"),
  Navigation1 = Source{[Name="green_tripdata_2023-03.csv"]}[Content]
in
  Navigation1
```

Now we have explicitly stated which file we wish to use for our transformations. However, this does not solve our problem if we are looking to provide a unified experience between two different files. Do we have to keep updating the filter context for our **`Sample File`** query every time we want to compare our files?

If you recall, we discussed how we have Parameter1 in place. It seemed odd that we would use a parameter to reference a single query. But if you inspect it, the parameter has a dropdown with currently only one value. This means that if we add additional reference files, we can select different files to check our transformations. If you right-click on Sample File and duplicate it, you can rename and update the query to reference a different file. Our current sample is referencing data from the calendar year 2023, but we can create a new one to use in 2022 instead:

```
let
  Source = Folder.Files("C:\NYC Taxi\Green_csv"),
  Navigation1 = Source{[Name="green_tripdata_2022-01.csv"]}[Content]
in
  Navigation1
```

With this change in place, we can now swap between multiple files and ensure our transformations are consistent. This is a minor change, but it goes a long way to helping you diagnose any errors that might be occurring with your files. Yes, it is easy enough to make updates to the **`Sample File`** query, but the convenience of the dropdown is just not easy to replace:

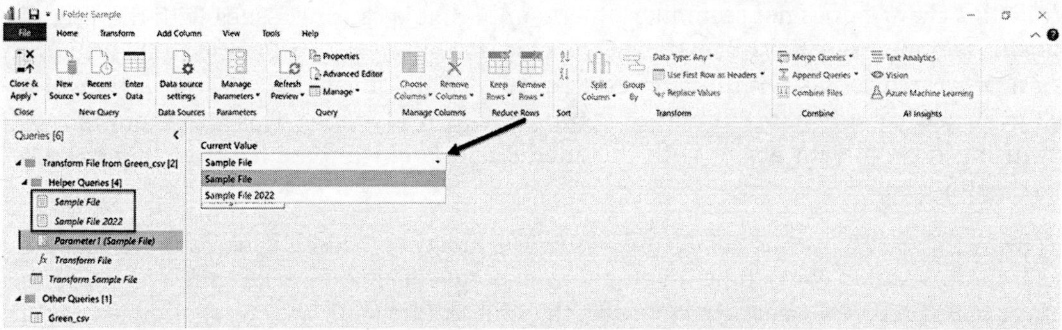

Figure 16.3: Swapping sample files with Parameter1

If your files are in a unified format already, there is no need to go through this effort. However, if you have identified that there has been a change in your source file format, you will want to enact this approach. It simplifies your changes and will help you avoid grief when you create changes to your transformations. This will be helpful as you perform testing with your transformations in the next section.

Managing transformations

Naturally, transformations are often a requirement when connecting to files. Unless we can customize the format of the files exported, you will need to perform transformations within Power Query. One might wonder where do you perform these transformations? Earlier in this chapter, we discussed how the Transform Sample File query can manage transformations for us. However, we normally just perform the transformations on the final query and have left our helper queries alone.

Before we dive into this topic, we want to address where transformations should take place with our queries. When transforming the overall query to prepare it for use, you should use the final query. Things like data types, conditional columns, and other transformations that will be applied to the entire query should take place here. However, if we need to perform transformations on individual files before they are ingested into a single query, we must address them within the **`Transform Sample File`** query. But when is there a scenario where we need to address the transformation of individual files?

In our scenario, we are going to encounter a common challenge that arises with files that are exported from a system. Currently, our files at were exported during calendar year 2022 have two timestamp columns called **`lpep_pickup_datetime`** and **`lpep_dropoff_datetime`**. These two columns represent the pickup and drop-off time for all trips made. In the calendar year 2023, a slight change was made to these columns. They were renamed as **`LPEP_pickup_datetime`** and **`LPEP_dropoff_datetime`**, respectively. The prefix for these two columns is now using uppercase letters instead of lowercase letters.

While this change does not seem like a major impact, it is causing issues with the overall transformation of our files. Remember, the case matters in Power Query, so this change has now caused issues with our refresh. Because of the mismatch, all transactions not using the new column name format are returned with **`null`** values. This means our refresh is causing downstream errors with our model and could impact how our reports are representing data.

There are three ways we can resolve this issue. The first way to resolve the issue is to update the column headers every time a new file is exported. This only takes a few minutes to complete and is an easy change. However, this still requires human intervention. It would be nice to make sure this is managed programmatically so we can automate the ingestion of new export files.

The second way we could resolve this issue is by creating two connections and appending them together. We could create two folders, one for files exported in 2022 and before and the other for 2023 to current. We could also filter down the list of files upstream, allowing us to keep our files in the same folder to achieve the same result. And while this is nice, it could result in more queries being added over time as additional changes are made. It helps us automate the process but might make our models confusing to manage in Power Query in the future.

The third option is to apply the transformation in the **`Transform Sample File`** query. This allows us to create a transformation with our files in a single query and optimizes how data is processed. To start, we will go to our **`Transform Sample File`** query while using a sample file from 2022 and update our column names to **`pickup_datetime`** and **`dropoff_datetime`** respectfully:

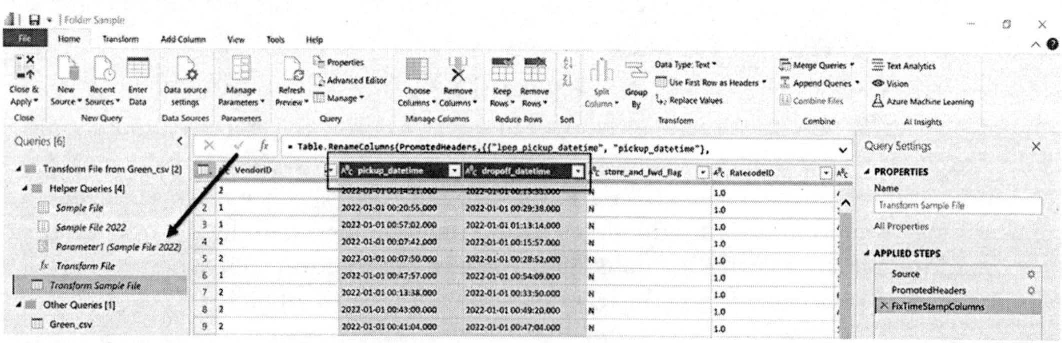

Figure 16.4: Updating column headers for Sample File 2022

Now that we have resolved our column header for our file from 2022, we need to swap to the current file identified with **`Sample File`**. We can update **`Parameter1`** and return to **`Transform Sample File`**, but we will come back to an error message, as shown:

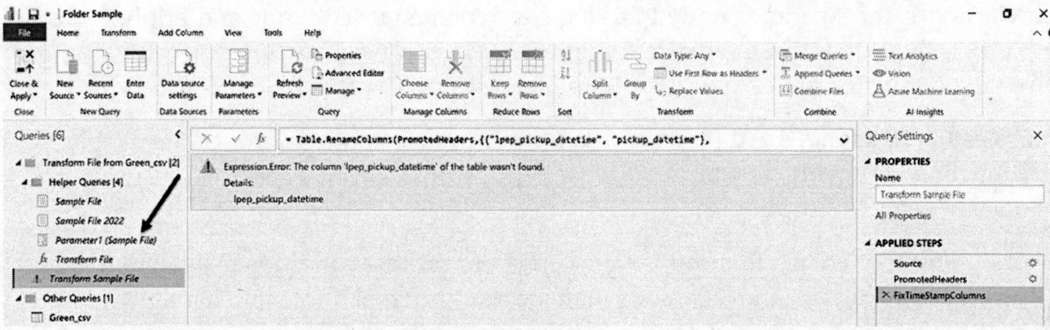

***Figure 16.5:** Error message received with Sample File*

Now, we can go and update our code with the advanced editor to resolve our issue, but we would have the same problem if we went back to **`Sample File 2022`**. But the trick to resolving our issue lies within the advanced editor. If you remember from *Chapter 7, Transforming Columns*, the function **`Table.RenameColumns()`** has a parameter called **`MissingField`**. If we add **`MissingField.Ignore`** to our code, we will remove the error. With that in place, we will now add to our list of columns to be renamed the column names that are associated with our 2023 files:

```
let
  Source = Csv.Document(
    Parameter1,
    [Delimiter = ",", Columns = 20, Encoding = 1252, QuoteStyle = QuoteStyle.None]
  ),
  PromotedHeaders = Table.PromoteHeaders(Source, [PromoteAllScalars = true]),
  FixTimeStampColumns = Table.RenameColumns(
    PromotedHeaders,
    {
      {"lpep_pickup_datetime", "pickup_datetime"},
      {"lpep_dropoff_datetime", "dropoff_datetime"},
      {"LPEP_pickup_datetime", "pickup_datetime"},
      {"LPEP_dropoff_datetime", "dropoff_datetime"}
    },
    MissingField.Ignore
  )
in
  FixTimeStampColumns
```

You will notice that we have added the logic to rename our columns and apply to both sample files. Not only did we create a unified name, but we also performed the change with a single transformation query for both file configurations.

As nice as the **MissingField** parameter is for our transformations, it is not available for every function within Power Query. So, what happens if we need to apply a transformation that does not have this option?

The first thing that comes to mind is that you could write a conditional statement using **if** and **then**. This will allow you to manage the different files, but it might require complex coding if you keep swapping between multiple files. Instead, you can use **try** and **otherwise** to provide error handling in this scenario. We used this in *Chapter 15, Advanced Web Connections,* to allow us to page through multiple queries with an endpoint. However, we could achieve the same here. Taking the code we used before, we can update it to achieve a similar result:

```
let
  Source = Csv.Document(
    Parameter1,
    [Delimiter = ",", Columns = 20, Encoding = 1252, QuoteStyle = Quote-
Style.None]
  ),
  PromotedHeaders = Table.PromoteHeaders(Source, [PromoteAllScalars =
true]),
  Fix_lpep = try
    Table.RenameColumns(
      PromotedHeaders,
      {{"lpep_pickup_datetime", "pickup_datetime"},
      {"lpep_dropoff_datetime", "dropoff_datetime"}}
    )
  otherwise
    PromotedHeaders,
  Fix_LPEP = try
    Table.RenameColumns(
      PromotedHeaders,
      {{"LPEP_pickup_datetime", "pickup_datetime"},
      {"LPEP_dropoff_datetime", "dropoff_datetime"}}
    )
  otherwise
```

```
    Fix_lpep
in
  Fix_LPEP
```

While not as pretty compared to our original code, this would allow you to navigate around functions that do not provide error handling natively in their transformations. With this minor change, you can achieve any transformation you need to your files before they are unified into a single query without errors.

Remember, you only must go to these lengths when you need to standardize the formatting of your files before you append them together. Also, do not think that you are doing yourself a favor by updating data types with the **`Transform Sample File`** query. While you think this is helping you out, this will not provide any value to you. These data types will need to be updated in the appended query anyway, so save yourself the effort and do not agonize over this while you are updating your helper queries.

Adding new columns to queries

Inevitably, at some point your file exports might receive a new column. This is considered a welcome addition to your model. However, this also causes some issues with how your model is managed with Power Query. Since these are individual files and not tables in a database, you will have to add some logic to integrate them into your query. This process builds upon the elements we have applied in the previous section and allows you to integrate this new data into your query.

The first step in the process is to make sure that you have included the new column as part of your **`Transform Sample File`** query. We must first update the source line to bring back an additional column. If you look back in the last section, our query had twenty columns included. However, because of the additional column, we must increase that to twenty-one. This will ensure our new column is included:

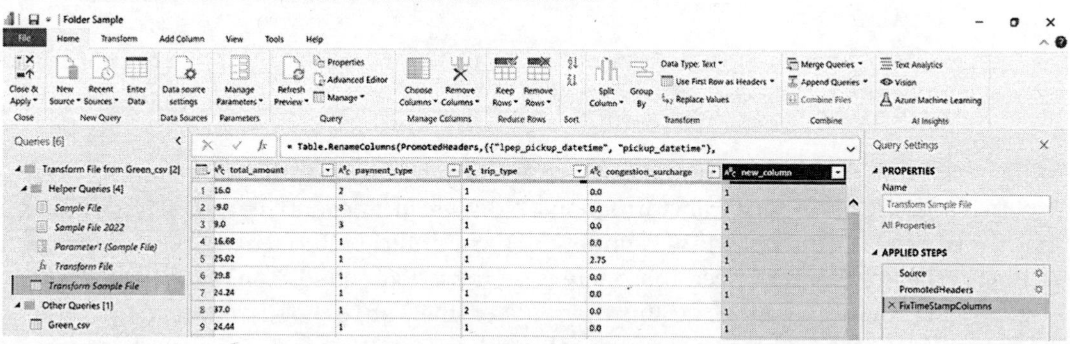

Figure 16.6: *New column from our sample query*

However, there is an issue with this approach. While this might work for our most recent files, our older files are missing this column. If we update **`Parameter1`** to use

Sample File 2022, it will show a blank column in place of **new_column**. Using **Table.RemoveColumns()**. We will identify our blank column with two quote marks as our header value will be empty. We will also use **MissingField.Ignore** to make sure we do not run into any errors with our query, as shown:

```
let
  Source = Csv.Document(
    Parameter1,
    [Delimiter = ",", Columns = 21, Encoding = 1252, QuoteStyle = Quote-
Style.None]
  ),
  PromotedHeaders = Table.PromoteHeaders(Source, [PromoteAllScalars =
true]),
  FixTimeStampColumns = Table.RenameColumns(
    PromotedHeaders,
    {
      {"lpep_pickup_datetime", "pickup_datetime"},
      {"lpep_dropoff_datetime", "dropoff_datetime"},
      {"LPEP_pickup_datetime", "pickup_datetime"},
      {"LPEP_dropoff_datetime", "dropoff_datetime"}
    },
    MissingField.Ignore
  ),
  RemoveEmptyColumn = Table.RemoveColumns(FixTimeStampColumns, {""},
    MissingField.Ignore
  )
in
  RemoveEmptyColumn
```

Just like we did with our transformations, we are adding error handling into our query to simplify it and streamline our transformations. Now, we just need to make one last update. While the **Green_csv** query code was built with the graphical interface, we need to update two items. The first item we need to update is on the **#"Expanded Table Column1"** step in the advanced editor. Inside the third parameter, the **Table.ColumnNames()** function is being used to identify the names of the column headers. We need to make sure that we have updated the query inside of the **Transform Files** function to our sample file query that has the new column. Next, we need to update **#"Changed Type"** to include our new column with the proper data type identified:

```
let
  Source = Folder.Files("C:\NYC Taxi\Green_csv"),
  #"Filtered Hidden Files1" = Table.SelectRows(Source, each [Attri-
butes]?[Hidden]? <> true),
  #"Invoke Custom Function1" = Table.AddColumn(
    #"Filtered Hidden Files1",
    "Transform File",
    each #"Transform File"([Content])
  ),
  #"Renamed Columns1" = Table.RenameColumns(#"Invoke Custom Function1",
{"Name", "Source.Name"}),
  #"Removed Other Columns1" = Table.SelectColumns(
    #"Renamed Columns1",
    {"Source.Name", "Transform File"}
  ),
  #"Expanded Table Column1" = Table.ExpandTableColumn(
    #"Removed Other Columns1",
    "Transform File",
    Table.ColumnNames(#"Transform File"(#"Sample File"))
  ),
  #"Changed Type" = Table.TransformColumnTypes(
    #"Expanded Table Column1",
    {
      {"VendorID", Int64.Type},
      {"pickup_datetime", type datetime},
      {"dropoff_datetime", type datetime},
      {"store_and_fwd_flag", type text},
      {"RatecodeID", Int64.Type},
      {"PULocationID", Int64.Type},
      {"DOLocationID", Int64.Type},
      {"passenger_count", Int64.Type},
      {"trip_distance", type number},
      {"fare_amount", Currency.Type},
      {"extra", Currency.Type},
```

```
      {"mta_tax", Currency.Type},
      {"tip_amount", Currency.Type},
      {"tolls_amount", Currency.Type},
      {"ehail_fee", Currency.Type},
      {"improvement_surcharge", Currency.Type},
      {"total_amount", Currency.Type},
      {"trip_type", Int64.Type},
      {"congestion_surcharge", Currency.Type},
      {"payment_type", Int64.Type},
      {"new_column", Int64.Type}
    }
  )
in
  #"Changed Type"
```

As you are realizing, the process of adding a column might be a little more complex than planned. But consider it in a different light. If you keep getting new columns added to your queries and they are being consumed in a model being used by multiple people, this could cause a lot of confusion. While it is more effort to add columns to your model, it protects you from having to scramble every time a new one is added. While some organizations prefer to have these show up automatically, many have governance around such activities. However, if you wanted to, you could find a way to make this dynamic by managing the sort order of your ingested files ensuring the newest file is always available with column names.

In addition, remember that the new data will not be available for older files already stored in the source. If the data in that column is available for older files, you can export new versions of the file and update your source. However, that is a decision that your organization will need to make. Sometimes the effort is not worth the value of the historical data point. However, if you feel that it is worth the effort, you can still follow these steps to bring in the current data as you work to extract the historical data for that column.

Common challenges with supporting queries

As you can see, there is already a lot happening under the covers with these helper queries. We have addressed some of the shared challenges that arise with these scenarios. But these issues can really be summarized into three buckets.

The first bucket is the lack of context from a sample file. We set up transformations within Power Query using only one sample file, but then are frustrated when downstream errors arise. It is important that we identify **gold standard** files we can use for our samples to make sure we are getting the right data into our model. It also does not hurt to use multiple sample files to make sure your transformations are consistent and free of errors. This will allow you to create a versatile model that can be easily transformed and tested.

The second bucket is the lack of error handling with transformations. When bringing multiple files together into a single query, there are going to be variances. Taking the time to add error handling will not only prevent frustration during future refreshes but will also provide scalability to your model. This really applies to any query but is especially important when you are combining multiple files into a single query.

The last bucket is the management of columns in your query. This will prove to be the most challenging as there are several touch points that must be addressed before a new column appears. If you have set up your helper queries well, this should be easier, but there are multiple areas that must be updated to make your queries work properly. It might be worth adding a few parameters to make things easier, but you will still need to perform some tasks to add your new column to the query.

However, there is one last challenge that comes up that we have not yet addressed in this chapter. That challenge is the consistency of managing your queries. One of the most common errors I hear about is when refreshes break because of the container structure being adjusted. For example, if someone starts exporting data into a new folder, you might update the main query to use the new container. However, if you have not updated your helper queries, this could cause an issue. At some point, someone will come in and clean up these old containers. Because your helper queries rely on existing files to validate their effectiveness and identify the right column headers, we must keep our helper queries coordinated. Even with the best of intentions, people accidentally remove old containers, which results in refresh errors. Yes, it might take extra time, but make sure that your helper queries are always in line with your main query. This is a wonderful use case for parameters inside of Power Query.

Conclusion

In this chapter, we explored the manipulation of supporting queries inside Power Query. We did a quick review of managing multiple files with the folder, web, and Azure Blob connectors. We then explored the helper queries associated with these connectors and how they interact together. Next, we learned how to update our sample file, transform our files, and add columns to our helper queries. Lastly, we discussed some challenges you will encounter when manipulating helper queries inside Power Query.

Index

D

E

F

G

I

J

K

L

M

N

O

P

Q

R

S